Representation

DEMOCRACY, CITIZENSHIP,
AND CONSTITUTIONALISM

Rogers M. Smith and Mary L. Dudziak, Series Editors

REPRESENTATION

Elections and Beyond

Edited by

Jack H. Nagel

and

Rogers M. Smith

PENN

UNIVERSITY OF PENNSYLVANIA PRESS

PHILADELPHIA

Published by
University of Pennsylvania Press
Philadelphia, Pennsylvania 19104-4112
www.upenn.edu/pennpress

Printed in the United States of America
on acid-free paper

10 9 8 7 6 5 4 3 2 1

Library of Congress Cataloging-in-Publication Data

Representation : elections and beyond / edited by Jack H. Nagel and
Rogers M. Smith — 1st ed.
    p.   cm. — (Democracy, citizenship, and constitutionalism)
  Includes bibliographical references and index.
  ISBN 978-0-8122-4514-1 (hardcover : alk. paper)
  1. Political participation—United States—History—21st century.
2. Elections—United States—History—21st century. I. Nagel, Jack H.
II. Smith, Rogers M., 1953— III. Series
JK1764.R455   2013
324.6'3—dc23   2012041496

CONTENTS

Introduction: The Multiplying Challenges of Modern Representation

Rogers M. Smith and Jack H. Nagel

In any democracy, the central problem of governance is how to inform, organize, and represent the opinions of the public so as to promote core values of popular control over leaders, equality among citizens, and competent governance. The authors of the *Federalist Papers* contended that modern republics improved on ancient democracies in part through novel systems of political representation that achieved both popular control and civic equality sufficiently, while also protecting against incompetence (Hamilton, Madison, and Jay 2009: 43, 51–52, 321–22). They also stressed that this third goal was achieved primarily through "*the total exclusion of the people, in their collective capacity*," from any role in directly deciding on laws and government policies (322, italics in original).

They meant that in the new American republics, including the states and the new national constitutional system, the citizenry's elected representatives would do all the governing. The people's role was simply to select the right representatives—and, of course, not all the people even participated in those processes. It is an understatement to say that these views on how early American forms of democratic representation might cure what the *Federalist* authors saw as the evils most incident to popular government have since been heavily contested and in important respects altered, even as many of the conditions affecting modern democratic societies have changed dramatically. Yet it is not true that the representative institutions created for the world's first large-scale democratic republic have been wholly rejected, within or outside the United States. Instead, much is still contested and un-resolved. Complex questions of proper forms of representation remain cen-tral both to modern democratic theory and to modern democratic practices.

This volume explores a wide range of those questions—a wider range than most studies of democratic representation do. Attention, both popular and scholarly, often focuses on voting as the central and essential process in representative democracy. American political science, in particular, has ex-plored in depth the beliefs and behavior of voters. And not inappropriately: voting is indeed essential, and several chapters here show there are serious reasons to be concerned about obstacles to voting that remain, and that in some cases are being added, in the American republics with which the au-thors of the *Federalist* were concerned.

Even so, democratic representation fully understood encompasses a great deal more than just voting behavior, and indeed more than just for-mally competitive elections. As other chapters show, democratic governance at least seems to imply electoral systems that allocate offices in ways that accurately and equally reflect the preferences of citizens, as well as political parties that generate candidates whom citizens desire to have as their repre-sentatives. It requires government bureaucracies that actually deliver the programs and services authorized by the people's elected representatives. It may well demand a civil society in which some citizens are not so much better organized and established within political communications and decision-making systems that they eclipse most others—and perhaps a civil society in which many more private as well as public organizations are in-ternally democratic. It is also hard to escape the conclusion that democratic representation requires active popular decision-making on systems of democratic representation themselves—something that rarely occurs.

Yet in the twenty-first century, innovations are burgeoning in all these areas—in voting laws and practices, in electoral systems, in administrative, political, and civil organizations, in the communication processes that shape public opinion, even in democratic devices for deciding on structures of democratic representation—though change in this last, perhaps most important regard, is coming at a far less dizzying pace than in other areas. The twelve chapters in this volume, written by scholars in political science, history, political theory, and communications whose work spans three con-tinents as well as national, provincial, and municipal governments, collec-tively provide a fascinating overview of these issues and developments. They explore a rich array of the ways in which the beliefs and preferences of citizens are influenced, expressed, and aggregated, and the effects of those methods and practices on political agendas and policy outcomes. Although the chapters sometimes ascend, always accessibly, into rarefied domains of empirical and normative democratic theory, the authors' concerns are ultimately— and in some cases, immediately—practical. They diagnose deficiencies in contemporary democratic practice and point to remedies that can more fully realize democratic values. Several give particular attention to dismaying problems in the American democratic institutions that the authors of the *Federalist Papers* defended, and some draw on comparative democratic practice for inspiration, warnings, or perspective. But others show that difficult challenges to effective democratic representation appear everywhere in the modern democratic world.

In Part I, Elections, the focus is on the traditional core elements of democratic representation: voting, electoral systems, and political parties. The two opening chapters, by Canadian comparativist André Blais and American political philosopher Dennis Thompson, survey American systems of democratic representation from empirical and normative perspectives, and neither analysis would give the *Federalist* authors cause for celebration. Blais bluntly labels American electoral institutions "weird." He reports that most elections experts think poorly of "winner-take-all" or "first-past-the-post" plurality systems, in which only the candidate with the greatest number of votes in each district is elected. Such systems, though still prevalent, are under attack and declining in Britain and its other former colonies—but much less so in the United States. No other contemporary democracy, moreover, uses an electoral college to choose its president. Two that had electoral colleges gave them up as bad ideas. Two-year terms for the House of Representatives are extremely short—or, as Blais puts it, "crazy"—by international standards, since they leave little time for governing as opposed to running for reelection. Foreign observers are also stunned by the extreme decentralization of American electoral law and administration, which leaves ample room for local inconsistencies if not corruption, and by the control of states over eligibility to vote in federal elections. Except for France, other democracies have removed the drawing of constituency boundaries from control by self-interested politicians. The only aspect of elections in which the U.S. might be considered progressive is in giving voters more influence over party nominations through the primary system. Nevertheless, and paradoxically, U.S. elections perform well by two crucial tests—citizens' satisfaction with democracy and losers' acceptance of outcomes. Does Americans' satisfaction mean that their electoral institutions are not so bad after all? Or are Americans not asking enough of their democratic institutions and themselves?

Blais leans toward the latter explanation; and at least one American, Dennis Thompson, does indeed urge his fellow citizens, and all democratic citizens, to ask more of themselves. Fully cognizant of the American framers' fears of direct popular governance, Thompson suggests an answer to at least some of the peculiarities Blais observes. He contends that U.S. electoral institutions have retained much of their elitist heritage even as the political culture has become more democratic. Thompson maintains that, applied to large-scale elections, the core idea of democracy—that the people should rule—implies four things: that citizens should have equal opportunities to vote, compete for office, have their votes count, and influence rules governing elections. He sees reasons to find American institutions and practices deficient in all four regards—and other authors here reinforce and extend those concerns.

Yet Thompson is on balance not quite so dubious about the rationality of American electoral practices as Blais. Although Thompson condemns the bias of American political competition toward plutocracy, incumbency, celebrity, and partisan manipulation, he argues that there can be reasonable disagreement about what it means to achieve greater equality in opportunities to win office, to vote, to have votes counted accurately, and to have votes affect outcomes. In his view, genuinely difficult tradeoffs among competing democratic principles are at the heart of debates over potential reforms in such areas as campaign finance, voting methods, districting arrangements, party systems, the electoral college, and nomination processes. Consequently, Thompson reserves his greatest enthusiasm for the "citizens' assembly," a new democratic means of giving voters opportunities to influence decisions about what electoral rules and systems they prefer, choosing among the inescapable tradeoffs. This enthusiasm is shared, as we shall note, by his fellow political theorist Mark Warren, who has closely studied British Columbia's citizens' assembly on electoral reform. These sorts of innovations are needed in the United States, Thompson contends, because there decisions on electoral systems are usually controlled by political elites who "have a vested interest in protecting their own power."

Thompson does unequivocally see one other urgent task for reformers: ensuring equality of the right to vote itself against such obstacles as defective electoral administration, discriminatory eligibility requirements, and partisan tricks. Alex Keyssar, the historian who has most extensively studied American voting practices, elaborates these concerns in the ensuing chapter. Contrary to popular images of uninterrupted extension of the franchise, Keyssar shows that American voting rights in recent decades have been contracted as well as expanded. Unlike most other democracies, nearly all American states disenfranchise convicted felons, so the steep rise in the use of incarceration since the 1970s effectively denied voting rights to millions of prisoners and former prisoners, a change that disproportionately diluted the voting strength of African-Americans and other minority groups. Growing attention to this problem following the disputed 2000 presidential election led many states to ensure that voting rights are promptly restored to convicted felons who have served their sentences, but nevertheless in 2008 more than 5.3 million Americans were prevented from voting because they had criminal records. And since then, some states have again made it more difficult for felons ever to regain the franchise.

As with felon disenfranchisement, close elections and political polarization have produced intense partisan contestation over several other voting rights issues. Although Democrats appear to have more justification for their complaints of vote suppression by Republican officials and operatives, Republicans have had greater legal success in charging that Democrats promote rampant fraudulent voting. Their major triumph occurred in the Supreme Court's 2007 *Crawford* decision, which upheld an Indiana law requiring voters to present government-issued photo identification at the polls, despite an absence of evidence of any actual vote fraud conducted via voter impersonation. A number of modern democracies around the world do use photo identification systems without controversy, but critics contend that in the U.S., such laws will prevent or inhibit voting by millions of citizens—mostly poor, young, or elderly—who do not have passports or drivers' licenses. Thus, Keyssar concludes, a convergence of partisan interest and popular apprehensions about the poor, African Americans, and immigrants has resulted in a new "narrowing of the portals to the ballot box."

Zoltan Hajnal and Jessica Trounstine next highlight the consequences of an electoral phenomenon to which barriers to voting and elites concerned to protect their own power arguably contribute, but one whose impact is less clear: low voter turnout. Scholars often invoke comparatively lower turnout to explain less redistribution and greater inequality in the U.S. However, Hajnal and Trounstine point out, many empirical studies by political scientists have reported that higher turnout does not have the partisan (pro-Democratic) or policy effects in the U.S. that the conventional wisdom would predict. They conjecture that such results occur because most studies use data from national elections, in which turnout is relatively high and less variable, and minority groups are a small percentage of the population. Hajnal and Trounstine introduce greater variance on both variables by studying turn-out effects in local elections for city councils, and they relate turnout directly to policy outcomes relevant to redistribution—taxing and spending patterns. Their analysis of data from the 1980s, using a nationwide survey of 1066 cities, finds that at the municipal level, higher voter turnout *was* associated with more redistributive spending, higher taxes, and higher government debt. These effects are strongest when electoral competition is higher and when disadvantaged minority groups are a larger share of the electorate. More recent data from California yield similar results. In short, who votes does matter, especially at the local level.

As Blais suggests, the departures from equal representation of the views of all citizens produced by low turnout generally deepen in the sorts of "winner-take-all" electoral systems that predominate in the U.S. That concern is at the heart of formal theorist Anthony McGann's analysis. McGann moves beyond the American context to draw general conclusions about which electoral system best meets the requirements of democracy. In contrast to Thompson's belief that the choice of electoral systems involves a balancing of competing democratic principles, McGann argues that the fundamental democratic goal of equality requires methods of representation that achieve a high degree of proportionality between seats awarded and votes cast. Contrary to U.S. judicial opinions that dismiss proportional representation (PR) as aimed at a balkanizing equal protection of groups, McGann contends that proportionality is required to realize the liberal democratic value of equality among individuals. He contends, however, that existing PR systems with low district magnitude (a small number of representatives per district) fall short of the egalitarian ideal. They are therefore liable to produce biased or manipulable outcomes. In a sharp departure from conventional wisdom in the U.S., McGann advocates the easy entry of new political parties to enable voters to hold accountable the entire political class, not just the governing party. Such entry is also impeded by "winner-take-all" electoral systems in comparison with proportional representation systems, where small new parties can win seats in proportion to their share of the overall vote.

McGann's analysis also highlights the danger of leveraging votes, so that some citizens have far more influence than others, thus increasing incentives for corruption and particularistic policies. This phenomenon is well known in districted systems, such as the U.S. Electoral College or the British House of Commons, where politicians assiduously court swing voters in battleground states or marginal constituencies. McGann shows that leveraging also occurs, though less obviously, in some PR systems which permit votes for individual candidates, rather than parties. If for Thompson the key to improved representation is to develop new devices for representative democratic deliberation, especially on electoral systems themselves, the key for McGann is simply the adoption of electoral processes that enable people with a wide variety of political viewpoints to gain a share of legislative power.

In the final chapter in Part I, Georgia Kernell uses a comparative study of twenty parliamentary democracies to cast doubt on the one element of American electoral processes on which Blais bestows some praise: the democratic selection of candidates through popular primaries. She tests the effect on citizens' political engagement and participation of two practices that are often justified by appealing to democratic norms: decentralized nomination procedures (primaries are the extreme case) and procedures that mandate representation for specific groups via quotas. She finds that although quotas appear to help mobilize voter support, increasing the ability of citizens to select candidates is instead often associated with lower rates of voting and party identification. In some cases this may be because enhanced citizen roles in the selection of candidates come at the price of greater requirements for party membership, but it may also indicate that, as many contend is the case in American primaries, those more partisan voters who mobilize to select candidates often choose ones that do not spur participation by the electorate at large. If so, Thompson's contention that there are often difficult tradeoffs in deciding just how to construct democratic representative processes appears forceful in regard to the internal practices of political parties, as well as representative systems as a whole.

Perhaps we should then be thankful that democratic representation involves much more than voting and elections, central as these are. Yet the chapters in Part II, Beyond Elections, underscore that the challenges of informing, organizing, and representing public opinion in ways that promote popular control, civic equality, and government competence remain daunting when we turn to politically active organizations in civil society, to unelected administrative officials, to communications media, and to other arenas of power in modern life.

Extending the analysis of their influential 2010 book, *Winner-Take-All Politics*, Jacob Hacker and Paul Pierson move beyond electoral systems and voting rights in order to solve what is perhaps the central mystery of American politics over the past forty years. In a period of dramatically widening economic inequality, why has electoral democracy not resulted in countervailing redistribution that would benefit the great majority of voters? Conventional theories that invoke electoral systems, party competition, the composition of the electorate, or the attitudes of voters can help explain why economic inequality has long been greater in the U.S. than in other advanced democracies, but they cannot account for the much greater widening of the income gap in recent decades.

The answer, Hacker and Pierson believe, is to be found by shifting attention to the participants in nonelectoral arenas of political representation. They highlight the surge since the 1970s of lobbying groups, think tanks, PACS and other organizations that represent business interests before legislative committees, executive agencies, and courts and that shape public opinion more broadly, including but not only in electoral campaigns. They contrast that growth with the atrophy during these decades of labor unions and other mass-membership organizations that might otherwise prove countervailing forces. Whatever the formal electoral structures, they contend, in a political climate one-sidedly generated by pro-business organizations, voters are not likely to select or elect candidates, elected representatives are not likely to enact policies, and executive agencies and courts are not likely to interpret or administer laws in ways that give priority to reducing rather than heightening economic equality.

Turning to the world's largest democracy on the other side of the globe, Pradeep Chhibber and Susan Ostermann particularly stress this last element: that true representative democracy requires a well-functioning bureaucracy, one that administers public policies in ways that close the loop among voters, elected representatives, and the state by actually delivering to voters the benefits and services they authorized their representatives to enact. When bureaucracies work well, they maintain, the result is a sympathetic connection between voters and their representatives that is crucial for a representative democracy's ability to fulfill its promise. In contrast, they believe that India's "capricious state" has undermined political representation and sympathetic relationships between voters and their elected officials, even though voters in India still embrace electoral participation as an affirmation of their civic standing. Consistent with Kernell's findings on the consequences of having parties with representational quotas for various social groups, Chhibber and Ostermann also contend that to play their appropriate roles effectively, political parties must represent the interests of social groups, not just those of individual politicians or familial dynasties. On this score, too, they find Indian democracy lacking. They see their two criteria as closely connected, because parties that really represent individuals or dynasties are likely to push bureaucracies to apply policies in biased ways, while parties that represent social groups cannot do so successfully unless there is a bureaucracy that will implement their policies reliably, fairly, and competently.

The next two chapters in this section move still farther away from formal governing institutions to consider impacts of the modern revolution in information technology on the processes of communication and collective action that underpin the effectiveness of democracy. Matthew Hindman explores recent rapid changes in the sources of the political information that a well-functioning democracy requires. He contends that these are reaching a new equilibrium more quickly than many anticipated, but it is not one highly conducive to equal representation of all citizens. The economic impact of the Internet has already greatly diminished the supply of investigative journalism, as traditional newspapers collapse or drastically cut back reporting staffs in a desperate struggle to survive, and this trend seems only likely to continue. Some observers have hoped that proliferating citizen bloggers will serve as a new and more egalitarian substitute for accountability journalism. To the contrary, Hindman argues, the blogosphere has already become highly concentrated and elite-dominated, thus replicating problems of the traditional media, but with a greatly reduced reportorial base, especially at state and local levels.

Hindman believes this structure has already become so deeply entrenched that it cannot easily be altered. Yet he believes some things can be done to foster communication systems more conducive to democracy. He proposes that the leading national blogosphere sites for political news and opinion devote prominent space dedicated to local content, tailored to each reader's city and state. He also suggests that the major parties in each state establish modern Internet versions of the early Republic's partisan newspapers—on-line portals carrying content supplied by the party's legislative staffers, political operatives, and allied outside contributors. These partisan online news sites might inform and engage like-minded citizens more effectively than current media do.

Recognizing with Hacker and Pierson that democratic representation rests on the array of civic associations that exist in a political society, as well as on its electoral institutions, David Karpf's chapter explores the consequences of modern mass media, and particularly the Internet, for the kinds of associations citizens can and do join. Agreeing with Theda Skocpol and other scholars that late nineteenth- and early twentieth-century American mass membership associations gave way in the late twentieth century to elite-dominated, Washington-based advocacy groups with extensive computerized mailing lists of member-donors, Karpf contends that the Internet is enabling a new form of political association, best represented by MoveOn .org. Membership in such groups does not, to be sure, routinely involve the kind of face-to-face meetings and experiences of engaged collective decision-making that, for example, the Sierra Club (in which Karpf has been a nationally elected officer) has long provided its members. But if membership in MoveOn is "thinner" in these regards, the barriers to participation are low; the organization is conducted with assiduous efforts to ascertain the issues and positions favored by its members; and it can sometimes foster off-line collective political actions as well. Without disputing Hindman's portrait of the blogosphere as highly inegalitarian, weighted toward the voices of older, more educated, affluent white males, and unlikely to change in those regards any time soon, Karpf suggests that the Internet may nonetheless be facilitating new forms of political association that can make important contributions to processes of democratic representation.

In a more philosophical chapter with potentially far-ranging implications, political theorist Archon Fung accepts both one of the central messages of Part I—that electoral systems are often not constructed nearly as much in accord with democratic principles and processes as they should be—and one of Part II—that democratic representation is greatly affected by organizations and institutions in civil society as well as by formal governing structures. In light of both these concerns, Fung argues for a new formulation of the "principle of affected interests," long defended by many theorists as a guide to defining the boundaries of political citizenship. Fung contends that, rightly understood, the principle can serve as such a guide—but that it dictates a complex continuing effort to redefine the boundaries of political participants for different governing decisions in light of the varying and shifting populations whose interests are affected by those decisions.

He also contends that, as the contemporary term "governance" connotes, actors and means engaged in achieving common purposes and exercising power over the lives of others now extend well beyond the traditional agencies and tools of government. That shift entails, Fung believes, that "individuals have a claim to influence any organization whose decisions regularly affect their interests," including major corporations and nonprofit organizations in civil society. This principle, he suggests, need not impose impossible demands on individuals' time and capacities, because he interprets "influence" broadly to include indirect and passive channels of impact as well as active and direct forms of participation.

In light of the challenges to adequate democratic representation explored in regard to voting and electoral systems in Part I and in regard to other governmental and civic institutions in Part II, it seems appropriate that in the volume's final chapter, Mark Warren returns to the idea that Dennis Thompson initially endorsed as a partial remedy to the problems of American representative democracy: the temporary assembly of lay citizens chosen on a near-random basis to deliberate on a specific question, and empowered to set the agenda for a subsequent binding decision—such as how democratic representative structures can be improved. Using the 2004 British Columbia Citizens Assembly on electoral reform as his focal example, Warren assesses the strengths and limitations of this novel form of political representation in more detail. He concludes that such bodies have advantages over elected legislatures that make them a valuable supplement—but not a replacement—for certain purposes. In particular, the citizens' assembly is better able to achieve democratic ideals of egalitarian inclusiveness, deliberative internal processes, and discursive accountability to the general public. However, because its members are not accountable to constituencies, such assemblies must be authorized by a legitimating body, such as a legislature. The device may be especially useful on issues where decisions by the legislature itself would be suspect because of a clear conflict of interest, as is the case with electoral reform.

In the aggregate, these chapters show that the tasks of achieving and maintaining democratic institutions that can fulfill the goals of civic representation—popular control of leadership, equality of citizens, and competent governance—involve great difficulties. Some are only being heightened by the interplay of new technologies with old election systems, especially in the United States, and by the transformations in civic and economic associations that are accompanying the growth of a global economy marked by huge inequalities in wealth and resources. Yet the chapters also demonstrate that the modern world displays an impressive variety of institutional alternatives that provide rich resources for reflection on how to improve modern democracies, and they show that promising new ideas are still emerging and being explored in innovative experiments. The limitations of existing democratic processes, and the obstacles to achieving change when power lies with those who benefit from current arrangements, are undeniably daunting, perhaps especially in the United States. Yet the explorations of options for democratic representation collected here suggest it is not only true that, although democracy is a very bad form of government, all the others are so much worse. It is also true that—as the authors of the *Federalist Papers* defending a new Constitution certainly believed—we can see ways this very bad form of government might be made at least somewhat better. And we have good reason to believe that both scholarly and political endeavors to achieve improvements may prove worthwhile.

Reference

Hamilton, Alexander, James Madison, and John Jay. 2009. *The Federalist Papers*. Ed. Ian Shapiro. New Haven, Conn.: Yale University Press.

PART I

Representation Through Elections

CHAPTER 1

Evaluating U.S. Electoral Institutions in Comparative Perspective

André Blais

The purpose of this chapter is to provide an evaluation of U.S. electoral systems and electoral institutions more broadly, in comparative perspective. I will first determine how typical or untypical U.S. institutions are. I will then indicate how comparativists tend to judge these institutions. Finally, I will ascertain how well or poorly these institutions are seen to perform by citizens.

My argument is that the United States has odd institutions, which most comparativists judge negatively (and do not recommend for new democracies), yet American citizens seem to be relatively satisfied. I contend that comparativists are right and people are wrong. Americans should not be satisfied with what they have. So the question becomes: why are Americans satisfied with their institutions (when they should not be)?

A Weird Set of Institutions

I start with the electoral system. Almost all elections in the U.S. are held under first past the post (FPTP), under which the candidate with the most votes is elected in single-member constituencies. The dominant pattern in contemporary democracies is to have proportional representation (PR) or a mixed system with some dose of proportionality. First-past-the-post elections are not exceptional. They prevail in Canada, the Caribbean Islands, India, and the UK, basically in former British colonies. But they do not exist outside former British colonies, and quite a few of these colonies have abandoned them: Ireland for the single transferable vote (STV), Australia for the alternative vote (AV), and New Zealand for a mixed-member-proportional (MMP) system. Even in the UK, FPTP is now used only for national legislative elections. Furthermore, none of the new democracies have adopted it.

Most experts believe that FPTP is not a very good system. Bowler, Farrell, and Pettitt (2005) asked international experts to rank-order nine electoral systems. First past the post came out six out of nine in mean rank, far behind MMP, STV, open-list PR, AV, and even closed-list PR. Expert international opinion is that there should be some dose of proportionality. I should add that expert support for PR has weakened recently, especially among economists who have argued that coalition governments produced by PR systems foster logrolling (see Persson and Tabellini 2003; Bawn and Rosenbluth 2006). The new trend is to argue that the "best" system is one with a weak dose of proportionality, that is, low magnitude district PR (see, most especially, Carey and Hix 2011). Still, the majority view among experts is that first past the post is not a "good" system.

American presidential elections are not held under first past the post. The voting rule is majority, that is, a candidate must obtain more than half of the votes within the Electoral College (though electors are chosen by plurality rule within states). The U.S. is, on this score, unique. No other contemporary nonparliamentary democracy elects its president indirectly (Shugart 2000). The few electoral colleges that existed, such as in Argentina and Taiwan, have been abolished. As Shugart (150) notes, "as long as the representatives who make the selection are themselves democratically elected and accountable through subsequent election, indirect election arguably is no less democratic than direct election, and it may be especially consistent with principles of federalism." Yet the point is that electoral colleges are almost unanimously viewed as "dépassé" and unacceptable in a democracy.

The electoral system literature has come to acknowledge that it is not sufficient to distinguish voting rules on the basis of the electoral formula or district magnitude, but that it is also crucial to take into account how much freedom the voting rule allows citizens to express their views about the candidates (see especially Carey and Shugart 1995; Colomer 2011). From this perspective it is important to consider the system used for the selection of party candidates. In the U.S., the dominant mechanism is the primary. As Jewell (2000: 224) observes, "The United States is the only country in which almost all party nominations are made directly or indirectly by the voters rather than by the leaders or groups of persons who are active in the party." Here again, the United States is exceptional, but contrary to the previous dimension (the Electoral College), the U.S. may be construed as "avant-garde," as something to be emulated. In many countries there has been a clear trend toward selecting party leaders and local candidates by all-member votes rather than by an elite or a convention (Cross and Blais 2012a, b; Rahat and Hazan 2001). Primaries as such remain exceptional, but there is definitely a movement for opening the nomination process to a wider electorate.

I have no data on how international comparative experts evaluate primaries. My impression is that they tend to be viewed positively because they give voters a greater say in the selection of candidates. On this dimension, the U.S. is on the right side of the issue.

In short, in comparative perspective the U.S. has the most untypical electoral system. It is unique in its use of primaries and the presence of an electoral college. Its electoral formula, first past the post, is not exceptional, though it only survives among former British colonies. On two of these three dimensions, U.S. institutions would be considered dépassé and unsatisfactory by most international experts. Only primaries could be construed as something to emulate.

Many other aspects of U.S. electoral institutions appear exceptional in comparative perspective. I will mention three that I find most striking. The first is the frequency of elections. An overwhelming majority of first chambers in the world have four- or five-year terms (Massicotte and Blais 2000: 309). The two-year term for the House of Representatives is extremely short. There is an emerging consensus toward four- or five-year terms: "the thrust of reforms in the twentieth century has been to increase the terms that have been set below four years and to decrease those that exceeded five years (309). I think that most international experts would agree that two-year terms are "crazy."

The second aspect concerns the extreme decentralization of electoral administration. Canadians and Europeans were stunned to learn, during the 2000 presidential election mess, that such fundamental decisions as the right to vote vary from one state to another. This was a most serious problem for Massicotte, Yoshinaka, and myself when we tried to publish our book on election laws, which covers sixty countries but does not include the U.S. Our reasoning was simple and correct: there is no federal electoral law. As far as I can tell, only the U.S. and Switzerland are in such a situation. This is particularly difficult to understand for Canadians. We have a decentralized federation, more decentralized than the American federation. And we do the proper, logical thing. We have two sets of electoral legislation, federal and provincial. Provinces can do what they want, and so does the federal government. This is what separation of power is about. The fact that a state legislature can decide who is allowed to vote in a federal election, in a country that is relatively centralized on most accounts, is absolutely weird. Certainly, we would not recommend this to any emerging democracy.

There is another aspect where U.S. practice appears exceptional: the drawing of constituencies. Constituency boundaries matter only in single-member district systems (or at least low district magnitude). In Canada and Australia (but also the UK and New Zealand), drawing constituency boundaries has been delegated to independent commissions, while this is under politicians' control in the great majority of American states. Clearly politicians are in a conflict of interest situation here, and the American practice is highly questionable. The Americans, on this score, are similar to the French. France has no specified time limit for redistricting, and the process is highly partisan (see Courtney 2000).

It is not only with respect to its electoral system that U.S. institutions appear both exceptional and "incorrect."[1] Obviously, there are too many elections, the country is unable to have national rules for national elections, and politicians are allowed to draw the constituency in which they will run. This should produce a fiasco.

Assessing Performance

Given this odd set of institutions, we would expect American democracy to be a complete failure. Yet American democracy is working pretty well. This judgment depends entirely, of course, on how one evaluates performance. I will be using citizen-based indicators of performance. The first, perhaps the most obvious, is citizens' satisfaction with the way democracy works in their country. I will show that Americans are relatively satisfied, and more so than in most other countries. The second indicator is losers' consent. Democracy succeeds if and only if losers, those who supported losing candidates, accept the outcome of an election that they are displeased with (Nadeau and Blais 1993; Anderson et al. 2005). As I will indicate, Americans appear to be exceptionally gracious losers. The third indicator is turnout. Following Powell (1982), we may construe higher electoral participation as a positive signal of the quality of democracy.

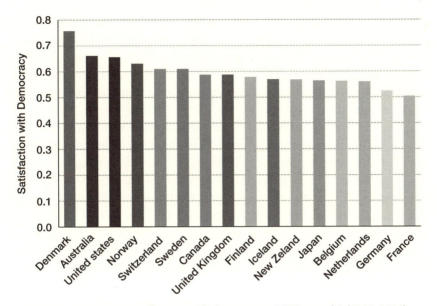

Figure 1.1. Average satisfaction with democracy. CSES round 2 (2001–2006).

The first indicator is satisfaction with democracy. I use data from the second module of the Comparative Study of Electoral Systems (CSES), collected in 2004 for the United States and between 2001 and 2006 for the rest of the countries. The question is "On the whole, are you very satisfied, fairly satisfied, not very satisfied, or not at all satisfied with the way democracy works in (country)?" I use a scale that goes from 0 (not at all satisfied) to 1 (very satisfied). Figure 1.1 presents the mean score obtained in 16 established democracies where CSES data are available. The U.S. scores quite high on this dimension. It comes third of 16, clearly ahead of the UK, France, and Germany, below Denmark but above Sweden and Finland.

The conclusion must be that Americans are quite satisfied with the way democracy works in their country and that they are more satisfied than citizens of most other countries. This is, of course, a disturbing finding, especially when juxtaposed with the previous verdict that U.S. electoral institutions are seriously flawed. To say the least, this is apparently not how ordinary citizens see things.

The second indicator is losers' consent. A democratic election is bound to produce winners and losers (Anderson et al. 2005; Przeworski 1991). The hope is that losers will accept an outcome they dislike, that is, they will recognize that the outcome is legitimate because the process through which the winner was designated was a fair one. There are cases, however, when the outcome of the election is uncertain and/or there are doubts about the fairness of the process. Such cases are bound to happen from time to time, and they test citizens' willingness to abide by the official results of the election.

The 2000 U.S. presidential election certainly fits the bill of a "difficult" election. Gore has more votes, yet he loses. There are serious doubts about how the votes are counted in Florida. The whole issue goes before the courts and takes weeks to be resolved. The final decision is made by the courts, and the judges are divided along partisan lines. All this is awful. Yet in the end the Democrats graciously accept defeat.

The 2000 election shows that there are serious problems in the rules that govern the conduct of American elections. But it also demonstrates the resilience of American democracy. This is truly astonishing.

I kept asking myself at the time how Canadian, or British, or Swedish citizens would have reacted under similar circumstances. It is very tough to tell. My impression is that citizens' reactions would have been more acrimonious, that is, the losers would have not have accepted such a "questionable" defeat so easily. There might not have been serious turmoil, but at the very least the losers would have clung to the view that the outcome was "unacceptable," and there would have been an outcry for electoral reform of some sort. I am not sure that electoral reform would have succeeded, but I think that it would have been high on the political agenda. There have been efforts to improve election administration through the Help America Vote Act (HAVA) and the establishment of the Electoral Assistance Commission, but these efforts appear feeble by international standards.

What this tells us, I think, is that tolerance for malfunctioning institutions is astonishingly high in the United States. My hypothesis is that tolerance is high because patriotism is so strong. People are very proud of their country, more so than Canadians and Europeans. When you feel that you live in a great country, you are more willing to accept "deficiencies." In short, overwhelming patriotism is to be blamed for lack of institutional reform.[2]

Hibbing and Theiss-Morse (2002: 103) provide support for this interpretation. While many Americans are critical about some aspects of the political system (68 percent disagree with the statement that the current system does a good job of representing the interests of all Americans), the great majority (62 percent) subscribe to the view that "our government is the best in the world." When one firmly believes that her country is the "best in the world," there is no need for major institutional reform.

Indeed, Americans are among the most patriotic citizens of the world. In about every country most citizens express national pride, but national pride is particularly high in the U.S. In fact it is the only country where more than 95 percent of respondents said they were proud of their nation in each of the first four waves of the World Value Survey (see Dalton 2004: Table 2.7).

The third indicator is turnout. The prevailing view is that American performance on this dimension is dismal (Powell 1986). That view needs to be updated and qualified.

As in the case of satisfaction with democracy, I will compare turnout in the U.S. with that in established democracies. I will confine myself to countries where voting is not compulsory. I examine mean turnout from 2000 to 2012.

Comparative analyses use two different indicators of turnout, which differ with respect to the denominator. Turnout can be measured as a percent of registered electors (REG) or as a percent of voting-age population (VAP). There exists a third possible indicator, proposed by Michael McDonald, where the denominator is the voting-eligible population (VEP). Note that the latter is not available outside the U.S. The measures I have used here are those provided by IDEA (http://www.idea.int/vt/index.cfm), except for the U.S., which come from McDonald (http://elections.gmu.edu/voter_turn out.htm).

If, as is the case in most established democracies, only those who are registered have the right to vote and it is up to the state to register electors, turnout as a percent of registered electors is the most meaningful measure. As can be seen in Figure 1.2, turnout measured this way is clearly above average in the U.S.

This is not fair, however, since in the U.S. many of those who do not want to vote simply do not register. In other countries, these people would be registered by the state and would be counted in the denominator. Thus the idea that we should use voting-age population as the denominator appears to be more appropriate. One problem, of course, is that in the U.S. at least, many people over eighteen do not have the right to vote, as McDonald and Popkin (2001) have shown, because they have not acquired citizenship or because they are felons or ex-felons. This is why the denominator should be those who are eligible to vote. This is not the only problem, however. The use

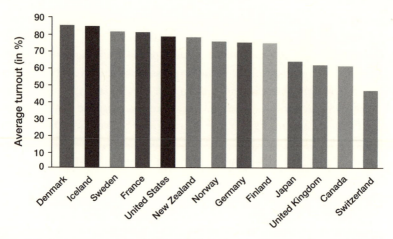

Figure 1.2. Average turnout in 2000–2012 based on registration for presidential elections in France, Finland, and USA, and parliamentary elections elsewhere. IDEA (www.idea.int).

of VAP or VEP measures forces researchers to depend on census figures which may be more or less reliable and outdated, depending on the country.

Mean VEP turnout in U.S. presidential elections thus far in the twenty-first century has been 59 percent, similar to VAP turnout in Japan, the UK, and Canada. It is lower than that observed in many small democracies, but not atypical for a large democracy. If we take into account that registration is more difficult than in most other countries, people are more mobile, and there are far too many elections (as in Switzerland), then the conclusion that turnout is low in the U.S. must be revisited.

In short, turnout is not exceptionally low in the U.S. I would argue that it is relatively high, given the extra hurdles imposed by the registration process and the exceptional mobility of its citizens.

Conclusion

American electoral institutions are in many ways exceptional. The most original features are the Electoral College and the primaries. Except for primaries, these institutions are construed to be "bad" by electoral engineers around the world. The U.S. is definitely not perceived as a model to be emulated.

Yet Americans are pretty satisfied with the way democracy works in their country, they are gracious losers even when the election outcome is

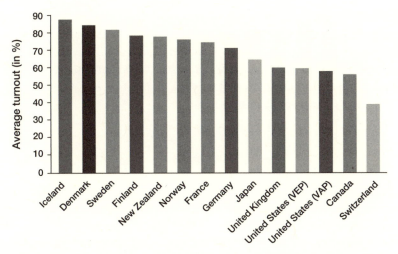

Figure 1.3. Average turnout in 2000–2012 based on voting-age population for presidential elections in France, Finland, and USA. parliamentary elections elsewhere. IDEA (www.idea.int). Source for USA VEP data, Michael McDonald's United States Election Project, http://elections.gmu.edu/index.html.

extremely close and highly contentious, and turnout is "good" given the presence of registration barriers, high frequency of elections, and high citizen mobility.

So why are Americans so satisfied if their institutions are so "bad"? One possibility is that these institutions are not so bad, after all. Perhaps electoral engineers and experts are wrong. I do not find such an interpretation plausible. It does not make sense to let an electoral college choose the president or to have elections every two years.

The most plausible interpretation is that American democracy is so strong, sociologically and normatively, that it can thrive while keeping perverse institutions. Tocqueville, it seems, had it right.

Many of these institutions maintain themselves because of the presence of veto points in the system. Still, electoral reform is possible in the U.S., the most obvious illustration being the adoption of term limits. I am particularly intrigued by the absence of reform in the domain of electoral administration. Electoral administration is highly partisan in the U.S. A strong case can be made that parties and politicians are in a conflict of interest and that the drawing of constituencies and the counting of the votes should be left with independent commissions. This is very much in line with popular resentment with partisan politics. Furthermore, the 2000 election has high-lighted the perverse effects of partisan electoral administration. I am thus intrigued to see how weak the movement for nonpartisan redistricting appears to be in the U.S. The culprit, I suggest, is blind patriotism. Americans are so proud to be Americans that they are unable to see that their electoral institutions are in a very bad shape.

References

Anderson, Christopher J., André Blais, Shaun Bowler, and Ola Listhaug. 2005. *Losers' Consent: Elections and Democratic Legitimacy.* New York: Oxford University Press.

Bawn, Kathleen, and Frances Rosenbluth. 2006. "Short Versus Long Coalitions: Electoral Accountability and the Size of the Public Sector." *American Journal of Political Science* 50: 251–65.

Bowler, Shaun, David M. Farrell, and Robin T. Pettitt. 2005. "Expert Opinion on Electoral Systems: So Which Electoral System Is 'Best'?" *Journal of Elections, Public Opinion and Parties* 15 (1): 3–19.

Carey, John M. and Simon Hix. 2011. "The Electoral Sweet Spot: Low Magnitude Proportional Electoral Systems." *American Journal of Political Science* 55: 323–39.

Carey, John M,. and Matthew Soberg Shugart. 1995. "Incentives to Cultivate a Personal Vote: A Rank Ordering of Electoral Formulas." *Electoral Studies* 14: 417–39.

Colomer, Josep, ed. 2011. *Personal Representation: The Neglected Dimension of Electoral Systems.* Essex: ECPR Press.

Courtney, John. 2000. "Reapportionment and Redistricting." In *International Encyclopedia of Elections*, ed. Richard Rose. Washington, D.C.: Congressional Quarterly.

Cross, William, and André Blais. 2012a. *Politics at the Centre: The Selection and Removal of Party Leaders in the Anglo Parliamentary Democracies.* Oxford: Oxford University Press.

———. 2012b. "Who Selects Party Leaders?" *Party Politics* 18: 127–50.

Dalton, Russell J. 2004. *Democratic Challenges, Democratic Choices: The Erosion of Political Support in Advanced Industrial Democracies.* Oxford: Oxford University Press.

Hibbing, John R., and Elisabeth Theiss-Morse. 2002. *Stealth Democracy: Americans' Beliefs About How Government Should Work.* Cambridge: Cambridge University Press.

Jewell, Malcom E. 2000. "Primary Elections." In *International Encyclopedia of Elections*, ed. Richard Rose. Washington, D.C.: Congressional Quarterly. 224–27.

Linz, Juan J. 1990. "The Perils of Presidentialism." *Journal of Democracy* 1: 51–69.

Massicotte, Louis, and André Blais. 2000. "Term of Office, Length of." In *International Encyclopedia of Elections,* ed. Richard Rose. Washington, D.C.: Congressional Quarterly.

Massicotte, Louis, André Blais, and Antoin Yoshinaka. 2004. *Establishing the Rules of the Game: Election Laws in Democracies.* Toronto: University of Toronto Press.

McDonald, Michael P., and Samuel Popkin. 2001. "The Myth of the Vanishing Voter." *American Political Science Review* 95: 963–74.

Nadeau, Richard, and André Blais. 1993. "Accepting the Election Outcome: The Effect of Participation on Losers' Consent." *British Journal of Political Science* 23: 553–63.

Persson, Torsten, and Guido Tabellini. 2003. *Economic Effects of Constitutions.* Cambridge, Mass.: MIT Press.

Powell, G. Bingham, Jr. 1982. *Contemporary Democracies: Participation, Stability, and Violence.* Cambridge, Mass.: Harvard University Press.

———. 1986. "American Voter Turnout in Comparative Perspective." *American Political Science Review* 80: 17–43.

Przeworski, Adam. 1991. *Democracy and the Market: Political and Economic Reforms in Eastern Europe and Latin America.* New York: Cambridge University Press.

Rahat, Gideon and Reuven Y. Hazan. 2001. "Candidate Selection Methods: An Analytical Framework." *Party Politics* 7: 297–322.

Shugart, Matthew Soberg. 2000. "Indirect Elections." In *International Encyclopedia of Elections*, ed. Richard Rose. Washington, D.C.: Congressional Quarterly.

Shugart, Matthew S., and Martin P. Wattenberg, eds. 2000. *Mixed-Member Electoral Systems: The Best of Both Worlds?* Oxford: Oxford University Press.

CHAPTER 2

Are American Elections Sufficiently Democratic?

Dennis F. Thompson

The question posed in the title would have astonished the framers of our constitution, but not because they believed that they were proposing a republic rather than a democracy.[1] Contrary to Madison's often-quoted comment in the *Federalist*, that distinction was not commonly accepted (Dahl 2003: 179–83; Adams 1980: 106ff). The terms "republic" and "democracy" were mostly used interchangeably, and Madison did not himself respect the distinction when he defined a republic as deriving its powers "directly or *indirectly* from the great body of the people" (Hamilton et al. 1961: 39).

The question would have been surprising not because of some general view about the republican character of the constitution, but because of a more specific assumption about the undemocratic nature of elections as a political institution. An election, the framers believed, is not a democratic device at all. Every reputable political theorist they could have consulted would have agreed (Manin 1997: 102–31). Elections are the way aristocracies or oligarchies choose leaders. Appointing by lot is the way a proper democracy does it. Aristotle, Montesquieu, and Rousseau all explicitly saw elections as a distinguishing characteristic of an aristocratic form of government, and regarded lotteries as characteristic of the democratic form.

One reason elections were considered aristocratic—or we could say elitist—is that they were assumed to result inevitably in rule by the few. The framers hoped that the few would be the best and the brightest, though they took precautions in case enlightened statesmen were not always at the helm. Although there was no property qualification for holding office, that seems to have been only because the framers could not agree on a workable criterion, not because they took a stand on egalitarian principle (Manin 1997: 107). Elections were elitist in another even more obvious way: only some citizens could vote. Women and African Americans were constitutionally excluded. In some states the franchise was also limited to property holders or taxpayers.

Elections were deliberately elitist in yet another way: citizens voted only indirectly for senators and the president, and their decisions were filtered through a system that ensured that votes were not counted equally. Finally, the rules governing elections were elitist in the way they were adopted. They were made and approved by a select few. The constitution was ratified, not by the people directly, not even by the state legislatures, but by specially elected conventions, which included many of the delegates to the constitutional convention. These delegates were ratifying a document that they themselves had helped write. In some states, notably Massachusetts, the anti- Federalists were systematically pushed aside in a process that some historians regard as undemocratic and unethical (Main 2006: 202).

So we have come a long way—or have we? With respect to three of these four elitist tendencies, our system today is no more democratic—and to some extent less democratic—than the framers left it. Most of the framers would not be disappointed. They did not want too much democracy, which is why they designed the system to temper the growing democratic spirit in some of the states. Over time, our political culture has become more democratic, but our institutions have not always followed. The electoral process to a remarkable degree retains more of its elitist heritage than is commonly recognized. If we wish to make elections more democratic (as many believe we should), we face some formidable obstacles, not the least of which is to be found in the nature of the electoral institutions themselves.

In its simplest form, the core idea of democracy is that the people should rule. Or, practically speaking in a large society, the people should choose the people who rule. Applied to elections, this idea implies at least four principles, which mirror the four elitist tendencies just described. Citizens should have equal opportunities to vote, compete for office, have their votes counted equally, and make the rules that govern elections. Each is important but in different ways that are not always adequately distinguished. (For analysis of democratic principles for assessing the electoral process, see Thompson 2002.)

Voting

With the principle that citizens should have an equal opportunity to cast a ballot, we can claim to have done better than the framers, now that all adult citizens except felons have at least the right to vote. But many obstacles remain, some of which are deliberate, and targeted against the very groups that were once denied that right. Registration remains more difficult than it should be, and voting itself has become more difficult in some states. The voter ID requirement upheld by the Supreme Court is a case in point (Crawford et al. 2008). Other sources of discrimination are new and burdensome requirements on registration drives, inadequate staffing at the polls, and shortages of reliable voting machines. Many of these problems affect already disadvantaged groups more than others. The Help America Vote Act (2002) was intended to address some of these problems but so far has made only limited progress (GAO 2005). Some partisans still use money, technology, and old-fashioned dirty tricks to try to prevent people from voting, again targeting the less informed and more vulnerable. The struggle for equal voting rights continues, and some of the historical resistance persists in new forms (Issacharoff et al. 2001: 216–40; Keyssar 2001). Making the right to vote more effective for all citizens may still be the most urgent practical goal in electoral reform.

But the principle supporting it is well understood, if not well implemented, and does not itself create any obstacles to making elections more democratic. There is nothing inherent in the idea of an election that should limit those who can participate. The limits in the past were all based on other external values or principles that we now mostly recognize as prejudice: property, race, and gender. Absent these prejudices, the principle presses naturally toward a more inclusive electorate.

Competing for Office

The opposite is true of the second principle, that citizens should have equal opportunities to compete for office. It refers to the electable rather than the electorate. Elections by their nature— even in theory—are intended to be selective. The point is not just that not everyone can rule (because ruling and being ruled in turn is not feasible in large polities). It is that only those with certain characteristics or qualities have an effective opportunity to rule. Successful candidates must have some quality that distinguishes them from others. It is in that sense necessarily exclusionary. This was the logical basis for the classification that designated elections as aristocratic or oligarchic (Manin 1997: 132–92). The anti-Federalists tried to mitigate this tendency by insisting that representatives be just like ordinary people. We see echoes of this impulse today. Is Obama too different from us? Is Bush the kind of guy you would like to have a beer with—though perhaps we should have asked if he is the kind of guy you would want to start a war with? But the point of an election is to select some candidates over others, and to do that the elected must have some distinguishing qualities. Some voters may choose on the basis of competence, others on character, or charisma, or simply prejudice. There may be no one set of qualities, but the choice is not random.

Why is this problematic from a democratic perspective? As long as everyone has an equal chance to choose, voters themselves in effect decide what qualities their representatives should have. If each citizen has an equal opportunity to vote, then each has an equal opportunity to decide what qualities should count. The vote expresses that choice. Is not that democratic enough?

The problem is that by the time to vote arrives, voters do not really have much scope for a choice about what qualities should count. American elections today are biased in favor of certain types of candidates: those who have or can raise money; those who already hold office; and those who are media-adept. Elections do not favor the best and the brightest, except by accident. Some of the more discerning framers might well have said that we have created a plutocracy rather than an aristocracy. We have a long way to go if we wish to make elections more democratic on this principle (equal opportunity to rule). Campaign finance reform, despite its many problems, may be a step in the right direction (Corrado et al. 2005). But its progress has been thwarted by recent court decisions such as *Citizens United* and various agency rulings. Even its proponents have focused more on preventing corruption than on democratizing candidate selection. Furthermore, many voters have no real choice because the elections in their districts or states are not competitive at all. In addition, the opportunities to influence the process that determines who becomes candidates (the party primaries) are nearly as unequal as the opportunities to become a candidate. It is not just that the pool of candidates has been narrowed (that is necessary and desirable), but that it has been narrowed in a process over which most voters have little or no control.

Counting Votes

The current system does not come close to satisfying the principle that votes should count equally, but, unlike the principle demanding an equal opportunity to vote, there is reason to think we should not try to satisfy it fully. Other principles—which also express democratic values—come into play, and justify putting limits on equal weighting. These other principles provide reasons to oppose, or at least restrain, many of the reforms that have been proposed to further equality in this sense. Several examples can illustrate how democratic principles conflict in evaluating reforms.

Voting methods. Proportional representation would give more voters a chance to elect their preferred candidate and in that sense would give each vote a more nearly equal weight (Farrell 2001). But majoritarian systems have other advantages. They tend to produce more unified governments, which voters can more readily hold accountable. Because accountability is a democratic value too, the question is not which system is more democratic but which achieves the right balance between these competing values.

Single-member districts. If you are a Democrat in a district that always send a Republican to Congress, your vote does not count equally in any real sense. You might prefer multi-member districts or at-large elections (which until 1842 some states used to elect members of Congress) (Zagarri 1987). But as a small "d" democrat you would want to remember that the larger districts that these reforms would require tend to give citizens less control over, and less access to, their representatives between elections as well as at election time.

The two-party system. If third parties were more viable, more voters would have more choice, and in that respect a greater chance to have their votes count equally (Rosenstone et al. 1996). But our electoral laws and campaign practices systematically discourage third parties: the methods include fusion bans and other ballot restrictions, closed primaries, majoritarian rules, restricted debate participation, and biased media access, among others. Yet these restrictions may be defended by appealing to the value of the two-party system. It presents a clearer choice for the general direction of government, discourages coalition governments, forces coalition-building into the open, and thereby provides greater accountability. Still, we might reasonably believe that the balance between equality and accountability has in this part of the process tilted too far toward accountability, and that we could give third parties more scope without completely undermining the two-party system. The parties have an interest in preserving not only the two-party system but the existing two parties. This common interest leads to what have been called "partisan lockups," in which dominant factions within a party or the dominant parties erect entry barriers against nonmembers or third-party challengers (Issacharoff and Pildes 1998). In addition to imposing fusion bans, parties may implicitly conspire to discourage challengers by ensuring that party leaders hold safe seats and by preserving campaign finance regulations that benefit incumbents.

The electoral college. Eliminate the electoral college—no electoral reform is more often proposed around election time, and then more quickly ignored (Edwards 2005; Ross 2004). From the perspective of democratic equality (counting all votes equally), it is hard to defend this institution. Why should votes of citizens in Wyoming count more than 2.6 times more than votes of citizens in Pennsylvania? But the college has its defenders, and they are not without democratic arguments. Unequal representation forces candidates to pay more attention to local interests (in office as well as during the campaign). A constitutional amendment to elect the president by the plurality of the popular vote "would redirect the candidates' attention to national audiences. National issues would drive out any attention to local concerns or personalities. National television would play a larger role than it does now . . . . Economic interests—large business groups, unions and special interest groups whose focus was national, not local—would play a still larger role in presidential politics" (Fried 2000). In this respect the electoral college protects democratic representation. Also, its replacement with a national popular vote, according to some analysts, would favor medium-sized one-party states (which are mostly in the South) against large urban states and small two-party states (Polsby and Wildavsky 2000). This alternative could produce as many deadlocks as the current system, undermining democratic legitimacy.

Presidential primaries. Sequential primaries give voters in some states more power than those in other states, though it may not always be easy to predict in advance which states (Mayer 2008). A national primary—or several regional primaries in rotating order among the states—would mitigate the inequality in the current system. But it would do so at a cost to other democratic values: the importance of giving voters more information about their choice (how the candidates perform in face-to-face settings and how they handle the pressures of a longer campaign) and the benefit of giving voters a greater range of choices (by increasing the chances of dark horse candidates). The democratic purposes of primaries may be better served by a drawn-out process that takes place in many different states (Thompson 2010).

Deciding about these and other proposals to make elections more democratic by giving votes more equal weights involves a choice among competing democratic values. Many of the reforms could be justified as reasonable choices, but so could some of the practices in the current system. Democratic principles do not require that votes should count equally. There is reasonable disagreement about what the right balance is. Even if a reform is more democratic in the sense that it more nearly fulfills this principle of equality, that does not mean the reform is more democratic all things considered (that is to say, all democratic values considered). The constitution of a robust democracy is a principled compromise: a balance of competing principles.

So does this mean that the equal-weight reformers are misguided—that they should stop complaining about unequal votes and accept the current system as a reasonable compromise? There is reason to doubt that the current system is the best possible compromise. One reason to question the particular compromise that now prevails is that public opinion polls suggest that many Americans are strongly dissatisfied with the current system and favor many of these reforms. Polls generally find substantial majorities in favor of eliminating the electoral college, holding national presidential primaries, empowering third parties, and imposing more restrictions on campaign contributions and expenditures (Panagopoulos 2004; Shaw and Ragland 2000). Alternative voting methods are gaining support: voters in four different jurisdictions in 2006 overwhelmingly approved ballot measures for instant runoff voting (IRV): in California, voters in Oakland approved the idea with a landslide 69 percent of the vote, as did 56 percent in Davis. In Minneapolis, a landslide 65 percent of voters passed an IRV ballot measure, as did 53 percent in Pierce County, Washington (Instant Runoff Voting Project 2008).

We should not, of course, take polls as decisive on these questions. Some aspects of electoral reform are quite complex, the consequences often counter-intuitive. Voters are generally not well informed about these reforms, and are more easily swayed by partisan appeals than by disinterested consideration of their democratic merits. Nevertheless, the polls serve as an unmistakable reminder that the people have not chosen the rules that govern elections. The people might well favor a different balance of values if they had the chance to choose.

Governing Elections

The recognition that the people have not really chosen this balance of values brings us to the fourth principle—that citizens should have an equal opportunity to make the rules that govern elections (Thompson 2002: 119–84). With respect to this principle we are no better than the framers (and perhaps worse because they at least let elected conventions decide the constitutional rules for elections). Major electoral reform has been rare not only in the U.S. but in most democracies, and when it has occurred has almost always been carried out by elites, usually party leaders, legislative commissions, or constitutional courts. These elites have a vested interest in protecting their own power. The least democratic part of the electoral process is arguably the control of the process itself. This is in principle fundamentally wrong: if the people have the right to choose their representatives, surely they have the right to choose the method by which they choose. The method after all affects and often determines the results.

How could the people gain more control over the process? The only way the U.S. Constitution now offers to change some of the less democratic procedures in our electoral system is by the even less democratic process of amendment. It is less democratic in the sense that by requiring super-majorities in both Congress and the states it gives substantially extra weight to the votes of those who are against any change. Some reformers eager to abolish the electoral college have found a way that they believe circumvents the need for a constitutional amendment. The National Popular Vote Plan provides that the states enter into a binding agreement to award the electoral votes to the national popular vote winner. Although it has become law in nine states, some observers doubt that it will gain the 49 percent of the electoral votes it needs to be activated, and if it does, whether it will pass constitutional muster (Koza et al. 2006; National Popular Vote 2012). Some of the other less democratic procedures, such as plurality voting or district-based representation, could be changed by state legislatures or Congress. But legislators cannot be relied on to make major changes to a system that elected them.

The devices of direct democracy—the initiative and referendum—avoid these problems. They were part of the means by which major electoral reform was accomplished in New Zealand in the early 1990s and more recently in the Canadian provinces of Prince Edward Island and New Brunswick—though only after expert commissions framed the alternatives. But direct popular votes on electoral reform are problematic. Because the issues are complex and raise questions to which most voters have not previously given much thought, the well-known defects of direct democracy—low information, low turnout, capture by special interests—are magnified.

A new kind of institution that combines direct democracy with a representative assembly holds more promise. It is called the citizens' assembly. In British Columbia in 2004–5, 160 randomly chosen ordinary citizens gathered to decide whether to change the province's electoral system and, if so, how to change it (Warren and Pearse 2008; see also Warren in this volume). This was the first time in the history of democracy that a body of ordinary citizens has been authorized to recommend a major change in the electoral system of a state. Since then this institutional innovation has been adopted by other Canadian provinces and also in the Netherlands. It offers the potential for returning control of the electoral process to the people.

The B.C. Citizens' Assembly was charged with deciding whether to keep the province's first-past-the-post majoritarian system, or to replace it with some form of proportional representation. The group spent nine months—mostly long weekends—learning and arguing about electoral systems (Citizens' Assembly 2004a, b). They concluded that the current system should be changed, and that the two best alternatives were a mixed-member system (similar to Germany's) and proportional representation (similar to Ireland's). In the end they opted for proportional representation, specifically a system of the single transferable vote. Their proposal did not win the required super majority when submitted to the people in two separate referenda.

Despite the outcome of the referenda and regardless of the merits of the system proposed, we should be encouraged by the quality of the discussion in the Assembly (Thompson 2008). Everyone who observed and studied the

Assembly was impressed by how well informed and public-spirited the members became during this process. The discussion in the Assembly focused on how each alternative system promotes or fails to promote three goals—effective local representation, greater voter choice, and fair electoral results (by which they chiefly meant proportionality between votes and seats in the legislature). Typically, members would try to show that their preferred system is optimal: though it might not promote one goal as well as the rival systems, it does not fall fatally short, and it performs significantly better on other goals. Without making their method explicit, they found ways to compare incommensurable values; they made tradeoffs among values, and reached thoughtful all-things-considered judgments.

Generally, the spirit was deliberative in ways that should warm the hearts of not only deliberative democrats but any democrat who hopes for greater control by citizens. The members did not come across as partisans or zealous advocates. They typically said that they saw the virtues of the other systems and appreciated the arguments of their opponents. Many changed their minds. In a speech on the last day that many later praised, Ray Spaxman, a member representing Vancouver, captured this spirit quite well. He said he had listened to the speeches, read the web pages, and had tried to remain open-minded, and believed that others had also done so. He had gone "back and forth" about his conclusion, and could still "waver," but was inclined to vote for STV.

The Assembly came about as a result of political events and principled leadership that cannot be counted on to occur regularly. And it required an investment of time and money that cannot be expected to be allocated routinely. The Assembly itself was not without flaws: members did not have complete control over the agenda, some participated more than others, and some groups were not adequately represented.

The most serious obstacle to citizens' gaining control over their electoral process is not the difficulty of establishing an effective assembly, but the challenge of overcoming the inevitable gap between any such assembly and the general public. The members of these assemblies engage, on relatively equal terms, in a process of deliberation that the electorate can never hope to match. Members enjoy an opportunity that their fellow citizens cannot share. They are changed by the experience in ways that sets them apart from the electorate. They reach conclusions for reasons that most ordinary voters are not likely to appreciate fully. The members begin as ordinary citizens but end as nascent experts. Designed to reduce the gap between citizens and experts, the process itself reproduces the problem that it was intended to overcome.

But this gap is not as objectionable as it might seem, at least not if we do not insist that equality means only equal participation in every part of the process. The assembly process institutionalizes a division of labor—the members propose, the voters decide—which properly implemented expresses a form of equality, a mutual respect among moral equals. If assembly members take seriously their obligation to explain the process to voters, and voters are prepared to trust the judgment of members, the moral gap disappears, even if a competence gap remains. A voter can say to an assembly member not only, "I trust you because you engaged in a process that seems fair and reasonable" (that might be said to any representative), but also "I trust you because you are a person not so different from me, and you decided as I can imagine that I might have done in similar circumstances." There is some evidence that the B.C. voters thought in exactly these terms as they decided how to vote in the first referendum, in which the Assembly's proposal won substantial majorities (Cutler et al. 2008). Had more thought in these terms, the proposal might have carried. Unlike members of expert commissions, even some legislators and other elites, assembly members not only are ordinary citizens before they serve but also resume that role after they serve. Their service exemplifies a pure form of rotation in office: Ruling and being ruled in turn—in effect recapturing the classical idea of democracy.

The process in which the B.C. citizens engaged stands as an exemplar that can guide future efforts to give citizens greater control over their electoral systems. As a result of the Assembly's achievement, no democracy can now responsibly undertake electoral reform without seriously considering an assembly of citizens as part of the process. We cannot be confident that American elections are sufficiently democratic until citizens have a chance to decide whether they are.

References

Adams, Willi Paul. 1980. *The First American Constitutions: Republican Ideology and the Making of State Constitutions in the Revolutionary Era.* Chapel Hill: University of North Carolina Press.

Citizens' Assembly. 2004a. *Making Every Vote Count: Final Report.* Vancouver,

———. 2004b. *Making Every Vote Count: Technical Report.* Vancouver.

———. 2004c. "The Learning Phase" (13 Disks); and "Citizens' Assembly Plenary Meetings," ("Decision Weekend" of the Deliberation Phase, October 23–24, 2004) (3 disks). DVD disks.

Corrado, Anthony, Daniel R. Ortiz, Thomas E. Mann and Trevor Potter. 2005. *The New Campaign Finance Sourcebook* Washington, D.C.: Brookings Institution Press.

Crawford et al. v. Marion County Election Board et al. 2008 553 U.S. 181.

Cutler, Fred, Richard Johnston, R. Kenneth Carty, André Blais, and Patrick Fournier. 2008. "Deliberation, Information, and Trust: The British Columbia Citizens' Assembly as Agenda Setter." In *Designing Deliberative Democracy: The British Columbia Citizens' Assembly*, ed. Mark Warren and Hillary Pearse. Cambridge: Cambridge University Press, 166–91.

Dahl, Robert A. 1998. *On Democracy.* New Haven, Conn.: Yale University Press.

———. 2003. *How Democratic Is the American Constitution?* 2nd ed. New Haven, Conn.: Yale University Press.

Edwards, George C., III. 2005. *Why the Electoral College Is Bad for America.* New Haven, Conn.: Yale University Press.

Farrell, David M. 2001. *Electoral Systems: A Comparative Introduction.* New York: Palgrave.

Fried, Charles. 2000. "How to Make the President Talk to the Local Pol." *New York Times*, November 11.

General Accounting Office. 2007. "Federal Efforts to Improve Security and Reliability of Electronic Voting Systems Are Under Way, But Key Activities Need to Be Completed." http://www.gao.gov/highlights/d05956high.pdf.

Hamilton, Alexander, James Madison, and John Jay. 1961. *The Federalist Papers.* Ed. Clinton Rossiter. New York: New American Library.

Help America Vote Act. 2002. Pub. Law 107-252, 107th Congress.

Instant Runoff Voting Project. 2008. "The Road to Better Elections." http://instantrun off.com/.

Issacharoff, Samuel, Pamela S. Karlan, and Richard H. Pildes. 2001. *The Law of Democracy: Legal Structure of the Political Process.* 2nd ed. New York: Foundation Press.

Issacharoff, Samuel, and Richard Pildes. 1998. "Politics as Markets: Partisan Lockups of the Democratic Process." *Stanford Law Review* 50: 643–717.

Keyssar, Alexander. 2001. *The Right to Vote: The Contested History of Democracy in the United States.* New York: Basic Books.

Koza, John R., Barry Fadem, Mark Grueskin, Michael S. Mandell, Robert Richie, and Joseph F. Zimmerman. 2006. *Every Vote Equal: A State-Based Plan for Electing the President by National Popular Vote.* National Popular Vote Press.

Main, Jackson Turner. 2006. *The Anti-Federalists: Critics of the Constitution, 1781–1788.* Chapel Hill: University of North Carolina Press.

Manin, Bernard. 1997. *The Principles of Representative Government.* New York: Cambridge University Press.

Mayer, William G., ed. 2008. *The Making of Presidential Candidates 2008*. Lanham, Md.: Rowman and Littlefield.

National Popular Vote. "The National Popular Vote Plan Is Now at Half-Way Point." http://nationalpopularvote.com/index.php. Accessed September 2, 2012.

Panagopoulos, Costas. 2004. "The Polls—Trends." *Public Opinion Quarterly* 68: 623–40.

Polsby, Nelson W., and Aaron Wildavsky. 2000. *Presidential Elections: Strategies and Structures of American Politics*. 10th ed. New York: Chatham House.

Rosenstone, Steven J., Roy L. Behr, and Edward H. Lazarus. 1996. *Third Parties in America*. Princeton, N.J.: Princeton University Press.

Ross, Tara. 2004. *Enlightened Democracy: The Case for the Electoral College*. Dallas: Colonial Press.

Shaw, Greg M. and Amy S. Ragland. 2000. "The Polls—Trends: Political Reform." *Public Opinion Quarterly* 64: 206–26.

Thompson, Dennis F. 2002. *Just Elections: Creating a Fair Electoral Process in the United States*. Chicago: University of Chicago Press.

———. 2008. "Who Should Govern Who Governs? The Role of Citizens in Reforming the Electoral System." In *Designing Deliberative Democracy: The British Columbia Citizens' Assembly*, ed. Mark Warren and Hillary Pearse. Cambridge: Cambridge University Press, 20–49.

———. 2010. "The Primary Purpose of Presidential Primaries." *Political Science Quarterly* 125: 205–32.

Warren, Mark, and Hilary Pearse, eds. 2008. *Designing Deliberative Democracy: The British Columbia Citizens' Assembly*. Cambridge: Cambridge University Press.

Zagarri, Rosemarie. 1987. *The Politics of Size: Representation in the United States, 1776–1850*. Philadelphia: Temple University Press.

CHAPTER 3

Barriers to Voting
in the Twenty-First Century

Alexander Keyssar

Crime and Punishment

In the summer of 1997, a small group of inmates at Norfolk State Prison in Massachusetts formed a political action committee to influence public debate about criminal justice and social welfare issues. As had been true of inmates in the commonwealth since the American Revolution, the men in Norfolk were legal voters. An underlying goal of the political action group, according to one of its founders, Joe Labriola (a decorated Vietnam veteran serving a life sentence for murder), was "to make prisoners understand that we can make changes by using the vote."[1]

Within days of its founding, the prisoners' PAC drew fire from politicians as well as victims' rights groups. Acting governor (and Republican gubernatorial candidate) Paul Cellucci led the charge, declaring: "the idea of prisoners organizing politically is to me repugnant." Cellucci and his allies in the state legislature then filed an amendment to the state constitution that would prohibit prisoners from voting. As required by law, the proposed amendment was submitted to two successive sessions of the state legislature (in 1998 and 2000), both of which endorsed it by large majorities. The final step in the amendment process was taken on November 7, 2000, when the state's electorate voted on the measure. Despite opposition from leading newspapers and liberal organizations, it passed easily, winning almost two-thirds of the votes cast. "The hammer sure came down in a way we didn't

expect," concluded one of the original members of the PAC. For the first
time in the state's history, Massachusetts had amended its constitution to
narrow the breadth of the franchise. Once the amendment took effect,
Maine and Vermont became the only states in the nation that permitted inmates to cast ballots.[2]

This local episode—largely unnoticed by the national press—was a vivid
demonstration of the nonlinear evolution of the right to vote: contrary to
traditional accounts of unrelenting democratic progress, the franchise could
contract as well as expand, even at the dawn of the twenty-first century.
Nonetheless, the Massachusetts rollback in the rights of prisoners—similar
to a step taken by Utah in 1998—ran counter to the predominant trend in
felon disfranchisement law. During the final decades of the twentieth century, numerous states were loosening, rather than tightening, their restrictions, ending the automatic lifetime disfranchisement of convicted felons or
adopting more flexible policies towards those on probation or parole. The
impulse to press farther in this direction was strengthened by the attention
brought to the issue in Florida in 2000. The Sunshine State, which disfranchised convicted felons for life, contained by far the largest number of persons (approximately 800,000) barred from voting because of their criminal
records. (That number would grow in ensuing years.[3]) Partisan concerns
aside, the figure was shocking to many Americans, particularly since it included hundreds of thousands of individuals who had completed serving
their sentences (Manza and Uggen 2006: 192, 286).

The issue of felon disfranchisement was also gaining visibility because of
the extraordinary growth in the size of the nation's prison population. Between 1972 and 2003, the number of persons in prison or jail increased tenfold,
from 200,000 to more than two million; the number of parolees and probationers rose almost as fast. Although crime rates did not rise significantly
during this period, arrest and conviction rates did, and those convicted
tended to serve longer sentences—giving the United States by far the highest
incarceration rate in the world. What this meant, of course, was that the
number of persons potentially subject to felon disfranchisement laws was
soaring: in 2000, according to the most widely credited estimate, the nation
contained 4.7 million persons who were disfranchised because of their
criminal records. The figures for African Americans (and especially African
American males) were even more dramatic and disturbing. Almost half the
prison and parole populations were African American; more than 20 percent of African American men born between 1965 and 1969 had prison rec-

ords. In some states more than 15 percent of adult African American men were disfranchised (Manza and Uggen 2006: 69–76, 95–102, 251–53).

Campaigns to promote reform were vigorously pushed forward in different states by voting rights, civil rights, and prisoners' rights organizations, including the American Civil Liberties Union and the small but effective Washington-based Sentencing Project. The thrust of their efforts was not to enfranchise incarcerated prisoners—although prisoners did vote in many countries around the globe—but to ensure the rapid restoration of political rights once a convicted felon had served his or her term. Doing so meant persuading state legislatures and governors to modify permanent disfranchisement provisions (which were still in force in a handful of states), to permit probationers and parolees to vote (they were barred in most states), and to streamline the procedures through which ex-felons could regain their voting rights. In some states, eliminating waiting periods and financial obstacles to enfranchisement (such as the payment of fines) were key issues.[4] With strong support in the African American community and among progressive Democrats (for whom principle and partisan interests coincided), advocacy groups argued both that it was unfair for political penalties to persist after felons had "served their time" and that re-enfranchisement would strengthen the integration of offenders back into the community (Manza and Uggen 2006: 113–64, 223–25, 247).

These efforts bore considerable fruit: between 2000 and 2008, more than a dozen states liberalized their felon exclusion laws, although some of these changes were reversed after Republican electoral successes in 2010. Delaware, Maryland, Nebraska, and New Mexico repealed lifetime disenfranchisement provisions, while in Iowa governor Tom Vilsack obviated the need for a constitutional amendment by issuing an executive order creating an automatic restoration process for those who had completed their sentences. (In 2011, his Republican successor Terry Branstad rescinded that order.) In Florida in 2007, governor Charlie Crist fulfilled a campaign promise (and broke with his predecessor, Jeb Bush) by pushing through the Clemency Board a rules change authorizing almost automatic restoration of the franchise to felons who had served their time for nonviolent crimes. The change potentially affected more than 400,000 men and women, 115,000 of whom had regained their rights by late spring 2008. When "someone has paid their debt to society, it is paid in full," Crist declared. (In 2011, after Crist left office, Florida reinstated a five-year waiting period before felons could apply to have their voting rights restored.[5]) Pennsylvania and Nevada eliminated post-prison waiting periods for restoration of rights, while Connecticut and Rhode Island voted to eliminate disfranchisement of probationers (in Rhode Island, parolees as well). In numerous states, the processes through which ex-felons applied to have their rights restored were simplified and expedited.[6]

Still, resistance to liberalization of the laws had not disappeared even prior to the conservative electoral swing of 2010. Kansas tightened its restriction in 2002 (disfranchising probationers), while Mississippi in 2008 considered adding drug-related offenses to the constitutional list of offenses that led to disfranchisement (the original list was written in 1890). In numerous states, proposals for liberalization lacked sufficient support to win passage through legislatures, while in others—including Alabama and New York—the rules governing the restoration of rights remained so complex and confusing that many ex-felons were deterred from even attempting to regain the franchise. Evidence abounded, in fact, that ex-felons in many states lacked a sure grasp of their legal rights.[7]

The issue, moreover, was frequently—and perhaps inescapably— embedded in partisan politics. Both Democrats and Republicans assumed, probably correctly, that most ex-felons—coming from working-class backgrounds and being disproportionately African American or Hispanic— would vote Democratic. Many Republicans were consequently reluctant to support legislation that could hurt their own electoral fortunes, and they regarded Democratic support for liberalization as transparently partisan. A Republican legislator in Tennessee, for example, claimed that Democrats "are desperate to find new voters, and they'll get them from the prisons if that's what it takes." According to news reports, partisan concerns had also been crucial to Governor Jeb Bush's opposition to reform in Florida, despite the unwelcome attention that the state had garnered for having such a huge number of disfranchised citizens.[8]

Resistance to liberalization was also apparent in Congress, in part because of an enduring conviction (or at least an enduring rhetorical stance) that felon disfranchisement laws were state, rather than federal, matters. In 2002, a proposal that would have prevented states from limiting voting rights of ex-felons was overwhelmingly defeated in the Senate. Three years later, Senator Hillary Clinton (among others) sponsored a bill that would have guaranteed the voting rights of ex-felons in national elections, but it never came close to passage. For the most part, attempts to challenge the exclusion of ex-felons in state and federal courts were also unsuccessful (Manza and Uggen 2006: 223; Fund 2005).[9]

By summer 2008, advocates of reform could point to a mixed record of successes and failures. Without doubt, the most significant change was the dismantling of many lifetime exclusions still in force during the final years of the twentieth century: seven of the nine states that had had such laws either repealed them or instituted restoration procedures that were far more accommodating to (at least some) ex-felons. (In 2011, after the pendulum had moved in a more conservative direction, four states had lifetime disenfranchisement for all felons, and eight disenfranchised some ex-offenders, or imposed waiting periods before ex-offenders could apply for restoration of their political rights; Sentencing Project 2011). This shift reflected an increasing consensus that a convicted felon should not be deprived of political rights for a period longer than his or her sentence. There was, however, far less agreement about precisely when a felon's sentence should be considered to have ended. Only in fourteen states (all in the north or west) was the franchise regained automatically when a person was released from prison. Elsewhere, ex-felons had to wait until they were no longer on parole or probation. Inmates themselves remained vote-less except in Maine and Vermont.[10]

Despite the liberalization of many state laws, moreover, the number of persons subject to disfranchisement continued to climb. By 2008, one of every hundred adults in the United States (and one of every fifteen adult African American men) was behind bars; a total of more than 7 million people were in prison, on probation, or on parole. These historically high figures meant that more than 5.3 million Americans were barred from the polls because of their criminal records. Men and women with felony convictions remained, thus, the most sizable group of American citizens who lacked the right to vote. That this group consisted so disproportionately of African Americans and other minorities led the UN Committee on the Elimination of Racial Discrimination to call on the United States to automatically restore the franchise to those who had completed their criminal sentences.[11]

Suppression, Fraud, and Photo ID

Partisan tension over voting rights was not limited to issues involving ex-felons. Indeed, in ways profoundly reminiscent of the late nineteenth and early twentieth centuries, the years between 2000 and 2008 were marked by frequent political disputes and incessant skirmishing over the exercise of the right to vote. Neither the passage of HAVA nor the 2006 reauthorization of the Voting Rights Act tempered the acrid distrust between the two major political parties that had become so visible in 2000. Bitter debates over voting and election issues were commonplace in state legislatures, while lawsuits abounded both before and after elections. Business was brisk for attorneys who specialized in election law.

In the eyes of many Democrats, voting rights activists, and African Americans, the primary source of conflict was the ongoing Republican strategy—or at least proclivity—to suppress voters, to keep legitimate, lawabiding citizens from registering and casting ballots. Poor and minority communities seemed to be particular targets of suppression efforts since their members (especially African Americans) were regarded as overwhelmingly likely to vote Democratic. The accusation of "voter suppression" was a contentious, even incendiary one both because it rubbed the wounds of historical patterns of exclusion and because it implied that Republicans were unwilling to respect a basic tenet of democratic practice.

Yet incendiary or not, evidence kept accumulating that at least some Republicans were, in fact, engaged in actions designed to keep citizens from voting. In Florida in 2004, for example, Republican officials again developed a list of felons whose names were to be purged from the voter rolls—despite the problems that had arisen with such lists in 2000. Remarkably the 2004 list also proved to be severely flawed, containing the names of thousands of persons whose rights had already been restored. Even more disturbing, the purge list was racially skewed in a manner difficult to explain: it included the names of more than 22,000 African Americans yet only 61 Hispanics. (Many Hispanics in Florida, particularly Cuban Americans, voted Republican.) After journalists exposed these problems in summer 2004, the lists were withdrawn from use.[12] During the same election season, Republicans in cities around the country sent poll watchers into predominantly black neighborhoods to challenge prospective voters, leading to complaints about intimidation, while in South Dakota there were well-documented instances of Native American voters being barred from the polls because they failed to present identification papers (which the law did not require them to do). In July 2004, a Republican legislator in Michigan told the *Detroit Free Press* that "if we do not suppress the Detroit vote, we're going to have a tough time in this election cycle." Meanwhile, Colorado's secretary of state announced that provisional ballots cast at the wrong polling place would not be counted in a Senate race that was expected to be close.[13]

Republican officials, both state and federal, also attempted to block voter registration drives aimed at new voters. In New Mexico in 2004, rules were adopted prohibiting the registration of new voters at hospitals and clinics run by the federally run Indian Health Service—although registration activities were permitted at local army bases. In 2008, the Department of Veterans Affairs took a similar step, banning registration drives among veterans at nursing homes, shelters, and rehabilitation facilities across the country. That same year (as well as in 2006), Florida's state government effectively shut down registration drives by the League of Women Voters when it decided to enforce new laws that imposed heavy fines on groups that lost registration forms or turned them in late. Throughout these years, moreover, the Department of Justice seemed little interested in safeguarding the political rights of minorities: Joseph Rich, former chief of the voting section of the Civil Rights Division, reported that "from 2001 to 2006, no voting discrimination cases were brought on behalf of African American or Native American voters."[14]

For many Democrats and activists, any doubts about the existence of a Republican suppression strategy were dispelled by what transpired in Ohio before and during the 2004 presidential election. Ohio, of course, was a critical swing state, and, as many analysts had predicted, President Bush's narrow victory in the state proved to be essential to his reelection. Beginning months before the election, Republican officials in Ohio, led by secretary of state J. Kenneth Blackwell, were taking steps tailored to encourage that outcome—steps that went beyond the normal rough-and-tumble of partisan politics. Faced with a major registration drive that was signing up large numbers of Democratic voters, for example, Blackwell issued a highly unusual directive to county election boards instructing them to reject all registration forms not "printed on white, uncoated paper of not less than 80 lb. text weight." After weeks of protest and ridicule (it turned out that the forms from Blackwell's own office were on 60 lb. paper), he withdrew the directive. The secretary had more impact with a set of directives regarding provisional ballots: he (illegally) ordered election officials not to offer provisional ballots to individuals they did not personally recognize or to people who claimed not to have received absentee ballots. In addition, he instructed county boards not to count provisional ballots cast by voters who had reported to the wrong polling place—a policy technically permitted by HAVA but clearly violating its intent. On election day itself, urban residents—particularly those in poor and minority neighborhoods—found themselves further disadvantaged by county-level decisions regarding allocation of voting machines. Suburban, Republican areas received proportionally more machines than did urban, Democratic ones, leading to extremely long lines at the polls in cities like Columbus and Cleveland. In addition, the state Republican Party engaged in the unusual tactic of sending registered letters to new voters in urban neighborhoods and challenging the registrations of those for whom they did not receive return receipts. Several investigations in the wake of the election concluded that this assembly of steps likely cost the Democrats tens of thousands of votes.[15]

Nonetheless, Republicans emphatically denied they had any strategy of "voter suppression," and on occasion they even turned the tables, pointing to instances where Democrats had allegedly tried to prevent Republicans from voting (by, for example, slashing tires of Republican get-out-the-vote vans in Milwaukee). More commonly, Republican analysts, like the *Wall Street Journal*'s John Fund, acknowledged that some "dirty tricks" had occasionally been played, yet they insisted that, since the 1980s, there had been no programs aimed at preventing "minorities from voting." Any steps Republican activists or strategists had taken were straightforward measures designed to prevent fraud, to insure that only legal voters were able to cast ballots (Fund 2008: 20–21).[16]

Indeed, many Republicans remained convinced that election fraud was a widespread and systemic problem, rooted largely in Democratic efforts to enroll new voters (qualified or not), get them to the polls (sometimes with cash inducements), and remove legal safeguards (like the presentation of identification documents) that could protect the sanctity of the ballot box. Among the most frequently cited instances of such fraud were the Miami mayoral election of 1997, the close Missouri elections of 2000 and 2004, and the high-stakes senatorial election in South Dakota in 2002, where Native American votes were critical to the outcome. One Republican activist, attorney Mark F. (Thor) Hearne, testified to Congress that there had also been "massive registration fraud" in Ohio in 2004, including the submission of phony registration forms for Dick Tracy, Mary Poppins, and Michael Jackson.[17]

Whether such examples—even if accurately depicted and however colorful the details—amounted to a systemic problem was the question at the heart of an increasingly rancorous partisan debate. Books, reports, and testimony piled up on both sides of the issue, sometimes recycling disputed allegations, sometimes offering point-by-point refutations of opposing claims.[18] In 2006, not inappropriately, the Election Assistance Commission stepped into the fray–only to get burned for doing so. The EAC commissioned a study of voter fraud, to be carried out by two consultants with different partisan inclinations, Tova Wang from the Century Foundation and Job Serebrov, a Republican election lawyer from Arkansas. A draft report of their study was submitted to the EAC in August 2006. It concluded that apprehensions about voter fraud were often overstated and based on anecdotes rather than systematic evidence. Among experts, they concluded, "there is widespread but not unanimous agreement that there is little polling place fraud." The EAC declined to release the draft report, and four months later issued a revised document with the far more equivocal conclusion that "there is a great deal of debate on the pervasiveness of fraud." In 2007, congressional Democrats demanded the release of the original draft report and excoriated the EAC for having succumbed to Republican pressure by altering the report's conclusion. EAC members responded that the draft report's research was not adequate to support its conclusions.[19]

Whether the EAC was, in fact, pressured by Republican officials remains unclear (despite a formal investigation by the commission's inspector general).[20] But there can be little doubt that a wing or faction of the national Republican Party was intent on establishing that fraud had become so pervasive that it threatened the fabric of American democracy. In a speech to Republican lawyers in 2006, Karl Rove, President Bush's top political adviser, warned that there was "an enormous and growing problem with elections in certain parts of America today." It was, he maintained, "beginning to look like we have elections like those run in countries where the guys in charge are colonels in mirrored sunglasses." A year earlier, the Senate Republican Policy Committee had insisted that "voter fraud continues to plague our nation's federal elections, diluting and cancelling out the lawful votes of the vast majority of Americans."[21]

Making the public case about fraud appears to have been the impetus behind the creation, in 2005, of the American Center for Voting Rights, a formally nonpartisan, nonprofit organization led by Mark Hearne, a lawyer who had worked for the Bush/Cheney campaign and maintained close ties to Rove. Within days of the organization's founding, Hearne testified to a House committee about the "unprecedented number of fraudulent voter registrations" in Ohio in 2004. Several months later, the ACVR issued a detailed

report on "Voter Fraud, Intimidation and Suppression in the 2004 Presidential Election." The report listed numerous allegations of fraud in sixteen
states (almost all involving Democrats) while asserting that "paid Democrat
operatives were far more involved in voter intimidation and suppression
activities than were their Republican counterparts."[22]

Hearne's testimony and the ACVR reports were forceful productions,
and they succeeded in getting the ACVR a seat at the table in debates about
election reform—which was remarkable for a new organization that had no
office, undisclosed financial support, and an address that turned out to be a
mailbox in Dallas. Hearne made frequent media appearances, transmitted
reports to Congress and the Justice Department, and was named as an "aca-
demic adviser" to a commission headed by former president Jimmy Carter
and former Secretary of State James Baker. The ACVR, in effect, became the
conservative counterweight to the voting rights think tanks and advocacy
organizations that had been in operation for years and had generally concluded that fraud was not one of the pressing problems facing American
democracy. The meteoric rise of the ACVR, however, drew criticism as well
as attention, first in the blogosphere and then in the mainstream press.
Many of its allegations of fraud were sharply disputed, and its claim to be
nonpartisan (and thus tax-exempt) seemed to strain credulity. The *Pittsburgh Tribune-Review* called the ACVR itself a "fraud," while other critics
lambasted it as a front for the Republican Party rather than a nonprofit center for research. In spring 2007, as Hearne and some of his allies began to
come under scrutiny for their roles in the controversial firing of eight U.S.
attorneys, the ACVR suddenly and without explanation disappeared: its
website was abandoned, its reports vanished, and references to it were removed from the biographies of its principal actors.[23]

The firing of the U.S. attorneys in late 2006—a highly unusual step by an
administration in the middle of its second term—also had roots in the preoccupation with voter fraud. At least three of the eight federal prosecutors
fired (and five of the twelve originally targeted) had antagonized high-ranking
Republican officials, including Karl Rove, because of their failure to zeal-
ously prosecute alleged instances of fraud by Democrats. John L. McKay of
Washington, for example, was criticized for taking no action in response to
Republican fraud claims in the 2004 gubernatorial election, which the
Democrats had won by a razor-thin margin. "They wanted me to go out and
start arresting people," he later told an interviewer. But there was "no evi-
dence." Todd Graves of Missouri (a swing state in presidential elections) had

refused to support a Justice Department lawsuit against the Missouri secretary of state for not purging the state's registration lists. In addition, he had brought only four misdemeanor voting fraud indictments in his five years in office, despite recurrent claims of widespread irregularities. In New Mexico, another swing state, David Iglesias, a highly rated conservative, was pressured by Bush campaign lawyers in 2004 to pursue charges stemming from faulty registration cards turned in during a registration drive conducted by a liberal activist group. Iglesias investigated more than 100 allegations, found few that had any merit, and concluded that none warranted indictment. His decision led to complaints to the Justice Department from Rove and President Bush as well as from Patrick Rogers, a local attorney who had been active in the ACVR.[24]

The forced resignations of these three officials (coupled with evidence that voting issues had played a role in targeting others for possible firing) demonstrated not only that the Justice Department had become highly politicized but that voter fraud had acquired an outsized partisan urgency for some influential Republicans. Iglesias himself commented that both Rogers and Rove were "obsessed" with the matter, and that obsession may have clouded the strategic judgment of Rove and his colleagues. Firing federal prosecutors with good job performance ratings was risky (particularly with the Democrats regaining control of Congress), and it soon backfired, leading to the resignations of several top Justice Department officials and contributing to the fall of attorney general Alberto Gonzales. Ironically, the episode—and its gradual public unveiling in spring 2007—also made plain that not all Republicans shared the preoccupation with fraud or believed it to be a compelling problem. Iglesias and McKay, among others, were willing to investigate allegations put before them, but they concluded that there had been few significant violations of the law in the states in which they lived and worked.[25]

Indeed, despite Rove's sunglass-wearing colonels and Hearne's heated rhetoric, very little evidence was developed during these years to support the claim that voter fraud was widespread. In 2002, attorney general John Ashcroft had announced that "election fraud and corruption offenses" were a top priority of the Justice Department, yet over the next five years only 120 indictments were filed, yielding 86 convictions in jurisdictions scattered around the nation. Most of the charges that were brought, moreover, involved individuals who were mistaken about their eligibility (including both immigrants and ex-felons) or participants in small-scale vote-buying schemes for relatively obscure local offices. In Florida, a legal immigrant (but non-citizen) from Pakistan was convicted of a misdemeanor and deported because he had filled out a voter registration form while renewing his driver's license. A Milwaukee woman went to jail for a year because she voted while on probation (and then tried to rescind her vote when she learned that she had been ineligible).[26]

Yet no evidence materialized of any large-scale, organized efforts to affect the outcomes of either federal or state elections through fraudulent voting. Thor Hearne's bill of particulars regarding registration fraud in Ohio did not lead to the filing of any criminal charges: Dick Tracy may have been registered to vote, but neither he nor Mary Poppins actually voted. To be sure, the paucity of criminal charges could not *prove* that crimes themselves were rare. But given the intensity of the spotlight focused on the issue, the scantiness of state or federal charges was difficult to reconcile with the conviction that fraud was systematic. Moreover, as political scientist Lorraine Minnite pointed out in one of the few careful studies of the subject, many of the widely mentioned instances of alleged fraud turned out, on investigation, to have other explanations: mistaken news reports, sloppy record keeping, methodologically inadequate efforts to match names on different lists, grossly mismanaged registration systems, clerical errors by election officials, voter error, unhappy losing candidates, and disgruntled ex-employees. To cite just one example, the frequently repeated news report that 132 dead people had voted in Detroit proved to have nothing to do with corruption. As Michigan's Republican secretary of state eventually reported, absentee ballots had been mailed to 132 people who then died in the weeks before election day. The vast majority had not filled out their ballots.[27]

Identify Yourself

The problem of fraud may have been miniscule, even inconsequential, but the Republicans' preferred solution to it was nonetheless gaining ground. Beginning soon after the 2000 election and accelerating after 2004, Republicans around the nation pressed state legislatures (and Congress) to pass legislation that would require all prospective voters to present government-issued photo identification documents when they showed up at the polls. These proposals were justified in the name of fraud protection and advocated, by Republican politicians as well as operatives like Mark Hearne, as essential weapons in the fight to restore the "integrity" of American elections.

Not surprisingly, existing identification requirements varied considerably from state to state. Many states already insisted that voters present some form of identification at the polls, but a wide array of documents (with and without photographs) could satisfy the requirement: utility bills, paychecks, bank statements, and driver's licenses commonly did the trick. In a few states, such as Louisiana, a photo ID was requested, but a voter who lacked such a document could sign an affidavit instead. In nearly half of all states, no identification was demanded except of those persons who fell under the HAVA rule, that is, they were first-time voters who had registered by mail and had not provided identification when they registered (*Electionline.org.* 2008).

Republicans maintained that this state of affairs was an invitation to election fraud. An imposter could turn up at a polling place, pretend he was someone else, and cast a ballot—unless he, unluckily, pretended to be someone who was personally known to a precinct worker. Even more devious imposters could generate phony utility bills on their home computers. A government-issued photo ID requirement could prevent such crimes—or at least make them more difficult to execute. The core argument for tightening things up was straightforward, and, according to opinion polls, not lacking in public support. In an era when photo ID was needed to board an airplane or enter an office building, it was surely not unreasonable to impose similar safeguards on the ballot box. An added benefit—and a later twist to the argument—was that photo ID requirements would restore confidence in elections among "legitimate" voters who worried about the possibility of fraud (whether or not such fraud existed). The campaign to institute these safeguards received a major boost in 2005 when the concept was endorsed by a majority of the bipartisan Carter-Baker election reform commission.[28]

The proposals for photo ID were met with sharp resistance and partisan opposition. Critics were quick to point out that the rationale for such reforms was flawed, if not spurious: not only was election fraud, in general, rare, but the type of fraud ID requirements could deter—in-person impersonation of a voter—was almost nonexistent. Georgia's secretary of state indicated in 2005 that she could not recall a single documented instance of such fraud during her ten years in office. The Democratic leader of the Kansas state senate insisted that a proposed ID law was "a solution in search of a problem." Kansas governor Kathleen Sebelius vetoed the measure in 2008, concluding that it sought "to solve a problem of voter fraud which does not exist in our state."[29]

Of equal if not greater importance, opponents maintained that photo ID requirements would effectively disfranchise large numbers of voters. Men and women who had driver's licenses or passports could easily meet the requirements, but in every state there were thousands of eligible voters who did not possess those documents. According to the 2001 Carter-Ford Commission, as many as 19 million potential voters nationwide did not possess either a driver's license or a state-issued photo ID. Even if a state created procedures for those individuals to obtain photo IDs (as was proposed in all the pending bills), the procedures themselves were inherently burdensome and potentially costly. Moreover, the people most likely to be adversely affected (those without driver's licenses) were not a random cross-section of the population: they were disproportionately young, elderly, poor, or African American—which meant, of course, that they were significantly more likely to vote Democratic than Republican. To Democratic legislators across the country, photo ID requirements were simply a new, legal, form of voter suppression designed to serve partisan, Republican interests.[30]

Nonetheless, identification requirements were tightened in a variety of states, and, after the 2004 elections, Republicans succeeded in passing relatively strict photo ID rules in several, including Georgia, Arizona, Missouri, and Indiana.[31] (Measures were vetoed in a few places, including Pennsylvania and Michigan.) All these laws were challenged in the courts, as violations of state and federal constitutional principles as well as the Voting Rights Act. The most common arguments were that they imposed an undue burden on the right to vote, that they had disparate impacts on different classes of citizens, and that they amounted to extra-constitutional franchise requirements that could not be put in place by legislatures alone. The responses of the courts, both state and federal, were mixed. In October 2006, the Missouri State Supreme Court struck down its law, but several days later the U.S. Supreme Court, overruling a circuit court decision, permitted Arizona's measure to remain in effect for the November election. Georgia's law, which in its original form compelled citizens to buy a new card from the state if they did not already possess a government-issued photo ID, was (surprisingly to many) pre-cleared by the Justice Department; but it was struck down in federal court as an unconstitutional tax on voting. The state then revised the law, making the new IDs free of charge. The revised version passed muster with the same federal judge who had tossed out the original bill.[32]

The uncertainties in the lower courts led the Supreme Court to intervene. In fall 2007, it agreed to hear the case of *Crawford v. Marion County Election Board*, a challenge to the constitutionality of Indiana's ID law. The Indiana law, approved by the state legislature in a sharply partisan vote—no Republicans voted against it, while no Democrats voted for it—was the strictest in the nation. It required voters to present an unexpired government-issued photo ID. Those who showed up at the polls without such documents could cast provisional ballots that would be counted only if the voter reported to a county clerk's office to present the requisite ID within ten days of the election. An appeals court panel of three judges had approved the law by a 2-1 vote that also followed party lines. Although the state of Indiana acknowledged that there had been no recent instances of the kind of voter impersonation fraud the measure would prevent, the panel's majority concluded that the law would burden few prospective voters and that "voting fraud impairs the right of legitimate voters to vote by diluting their votes." Judge Terence T. Evans, the Democrat who dissented, took a more cynical view. "Let's not beat around the bush," he wrote. "The Indiana voter photo ID law is a not-so-thinly veiled attempt to discourage Election Day turnout by certain folks believed to skew Democratic."[33]

The Supreme Court upheld the Indiana law by a vote of 6-3, announcing its verdict in April 2008. In the lead opinion, Justice John Paul Stevens maintained that the "risk of voter fraud" was "real" (citing as one example New York's infamous election of 1868) and that there was "no question about the legitimacy or importance of the state's interest in counting only the votes of eligible voters." He also concluded that for voters who lacked ID, the "inconvenience" of gathering documents (such as birth certificates) and traveling to a motor vehicle bureau office did not amount to an "excessively burdensome" requirement. Justice David Souter, in one of two dissents, disagreed sharply, insisting that the burden imposed would be "nontrivial" for some voters (particularly the poor and the elderly) and that, in the absence of known cases of voter impersonation, there was no demonstrable need for the law. The "onus" of the law, Souter concluded, "correlates with no state interest so well as it does with the object of deterring poorer residents from exercising the franchise." All the justices who voted to uphold the law had been appointed by Republican presidents (as was Souter).[34]

"This is over," declared Mark Hearne, after the decision was announced. "The whole debate over voter ID is over." Hearne may have exaggerated, but the political conflict over voter ID had surely entered a new phase. In several states, legal challenges to photo ID laws were expected to recede in the wake of the Supreme Court decision. With key constitutional issues settled, more-over, Republicans across the nation began to press for the passage of new photo ID laws, often modeled on Indiana's.[35] In nineteen states, they fol-lowed Arizona's example and went a step further, sponsoring legislation or constitutional amendments that would require all prospective voters to also provide proof that they were U.S. citizens. (In some locales where immigra-tion was a heated issue, such proposals had significant public support.) Democrats meanwhile stuck to their strategic guns in state legislatures, re-sisting both photo ID and citizenship requirements, blocking their passage wherever they held legislative majorities. In Indiana, a new lawsuit was filed, claiming that the state's photo ID law violated the Indiana State Constitu-tion.[36] The ACLU and other liberal organizations filed suits challenging voter ID laws in other states.[37]

How many people would be prevented from voting by the new ID laws remained unclear. The first scholarly studies, as well as common sense, sug-gested that the laws would definitely have an impact; and, sure enough, within weeks of the Supreme Court decision, several elderly nuns were prevented from casting ballots in the Indiana primary elections because they lacked photo identification. Yet just how large that impact would be was uncertain. Nor was it clear whether Democrats and voting rights groups would be able to narrow the bite of the laws by devising methods of helping the poor and the elderly to obtain their photo IDs (much as the urban machines had helped immigrants satisfy registration requirements in the late nineteenth century). How many states would end up adopting photo ID laws was an-other large, lingering question, the answer to which likely hinged less on the virtues of the measures themselves than on the shifting partisan currents of the post-Bush era.[38]

What was clear by summer 2008—and dramatically underscored by developments after the 2010 elections—was that parts of the nation were once again experiencing a narrowing of the portals to the ballot box. A sig-nificant segment of the American populace favored tilting election law in the direction of "security" rather than "access." As had been true during ear-lier episodes of effective franchise contraction, in particular the years be-tween 1870 and 1915, this narrowing was brought about by a convergence of

partisan interest and class apprehensions, by the intermingling of a calculated desire to win close elections and a more inchoate fear that poor people,
African Americans, and immigrants were particularly prone to corruption
and fraud. It did not seem coincidental that this most recent spasm, this
willingness to disfranchise in the name of the "purity of the ballot box," occurred, yet again, at a moment when African Americans were gaining some
political power and immigration levels were at historic highs.

References

ACLU. 2007. "State Legislative and Policy Reform to Advance the Voting Rights of
    Formerly Incarcerated Persons." August 22. http://www.aclu.org/votingrights
    /exoffenders/statelegispolicy2007.html.
Alvarez, R. Michael, Delia Bailey, and Jonathan N. Katz. 2008. "The Effect of Voter
    Identification Laws on Turnout." California Institute of Technology: Social Sci-
    ence Working Paper 1267R, January.
Alvarez, R. Michael, Henry E. Brady, Guy-Uriel Charles, et al. 2005. "Challenges Fac-
    ing the American Electoral System: Research Priorities for the Social Sciences."
    Social Science Research Council, March 1. http://www.vote.caltech.edu/media/
    documents/FinalReport030105.pdf.
American Center for Voting Rights Legislative Fund (ACRV). 2005. "Vote Fraud, In-
    timidation and Suppression in the 2004 Presidential Election." August 2. http://
    www.foxnews.com/projects/pdf/Vote_Fraud_Intimidation_Suppression_2004_
    Pres_Election_v2.pdf.
———. 2006. "Supplemental Comment Letter to John Tanner, Chief, Voting Rights Sec-
    tion, Department of Justice." April 20. http://web.archive.org/web/20061019072835
    /http://www.ac4vr.com/app/content.asp?ContentId=783.
Brady, Henry E., Guy-Uriel Charles, Benjamin Highton, Martha Kropf, Walter R.
    Mebane, and Michael Traugott. 2004. "Interim Report on Alleged Irregularities
    in the United States Presidential Election of 2 November 2004." Social Science
    Research Council, December 22. http://www.vote.caltech.edu/media/documents
    /InterimReport122204-1.pdf.
Carter-Baker Commission on Federal Election Reform. 2005. "Building Confidence
    in U.S. Elections." September. http://www.american.edu/ia/cfer/report/full_report
    .pdf.
Conyers. John. 2005. *What Went Wrong in Ohio: The Conyers Report on the 2004
    Presidential Election*, intro. Gore Vidal, ed. Anita Miller. Chicago: Academy Chi-
    cago.
Electionline.org. 2008. "Voter ID Laws," January. http://www.pewcenteronthestates
    .org/uploadedFiles/voterID.laws.6.08.pdf.

Epps, Garrett. 2007. "Karl Rove's Big Election-Fraud Hoax." *Salon.com*, May 10.

———. 2008. "The Voter ID Fraud." *The Nation*, January 28.

Fitrakis, Bob. 2007. "Ohio, the DOJ Scandal and 'Thor'—the God of Voter Suppression." *Independent News Media*, June 18.

Fund, John H. 2005. "My Felon Americans." *New York Sun*, March 8.

———. 2008. *Stealing Elections: How Voter Fraud Threatens Our Democracy*. New York: Encounter Books.

Gordon, Greg. 2007a. "2006 Missouri's Election Was Ground Zero for GOP." McClatchy Newspapers, May 3.

———. 2007b. "Was Campaigning Against Voter Fraud a Republican Ploy?" McClatchy Newspapers Washington Bureau, July 1.

Haines, Errin. 2007. "Federal Judge Tosses Suit." *Associated Press*, September 7.

Hasen, Richard L. 2007. "The Fraudulent Fraud Squad: The Incredible, Disappearing American Center for Voting Rights." *Slate*, May 18.

Hearne, Mark Thor, II. 2005. Testimony, House Committee on Administration, April 21. 109th Cong., 1st Sess.

———2008. "Make Cheating Tough." *USA Today*, January 1.

Hitchens, Christopher. 2005. "Ohio's Odd Numbers." *Vanity Fair*, March.

Hebert, J. Geraldt. 2038. "'He Said, She Said' at the EAC." *Campaign Center Legal Blog*, March. http://www.clcblog.org/blog_item-216.html.

Isikoff, Michael. 2007. "Fuel to the Firings." *Newsweek*, August 21.

Keyssar, Alex. 2009. "The Story Unfinished." In *The Right to Vote: The Contested History of Democracy in the United States*, rev. ed. New York: Basic Books. 258–94.

Kennedy, Robert F., Jr., 2006. "Was the 2004 Election Stolen?" *Rolling Stone*, June 15, 46–114.

King, Ryan S. 2006. "A Decade of Reform: Felony Disenfranchisement Policy in the United States, 1997–2006." Sentencing Project, October 3–21.

Lee, Tanya. 2007. "Ex-Justice Official: Native American Vote May Be Issue in U.S. Attorney Firings." *Targeted News Service*, July 11.

Leopold, Jason. 2008a. "Bush Operative Pushes Voter-ID Law." *Public Record*, May 14. http://www.pubrecord.org/index.php?view=article&id=41%3Abushoperative pushesvoter-idlaw&option=com_content&Itemid=9.

———. 2008b. "'Myth' of Voter Fraud Focus of Senate Hearing," *Baltimore Chronicle and Sentinel*, March 10.

Lester, Will. 2006. "Report: Voter Fraud May Be Overstated." *Associated Press Online*, October 11.

Logan, John and Jennifer Darrah. 2008. "The Suppressive Effects of Voter ID Requirements on Naturalization and Political Participation." Brown University: Report of the American Communities Project, January 2. http://www.s4.brown.edu/voterid/.

Manza, Jeff and Christopher Uggen. 2006. *Locked Out: Felon Disenfranchisement and American Democracy*. New York: Oxford University Press.

McCaffrey, Shannon. 2007. "State Begins Education Effort for Voter ID Law." *Associated Press*, August 10.

McCool, Daniel, Susan M. Olson, and Jennifer L. Robinson. 2007. *Native Vote: American Indians, the Voting Rights Act, and the Right to Vote*. New York: Cambridge University Press.

McDonald, Laughlin. 2003. "The New Poll Tax." *American Prospect*, December 30.

Miller, Mark C. 2008. Testimony to U.S. House Committee on the Judiciary, May 15. http://judiciary.house.gov/oversight.aspx?ID=442.

Minnite, Lorraine C. 2007a. "The Politics of Voter Fraud." Project Vote, March 6. http://www.projectvote.org/images/publications/Policy%20Reports%20and %20Guides/Politics_of_Voter_Fraud_Final.pdf.

———. 2007b. "An Analysis of Voter Fraud in the U.S." *Demos*, December 19. http:// www.demos.org/publication/analysis-voter-fraud-united-states-adapted-2003 -report-securing-vote.

Minnite, Lori and David Callahan. 2003. *Securing the Vote: An Analysis of Election Fraud*. New York: Demos, 2003.

Mulhausen, David B. and Keri W. Sikich. 2007. "New Analysis Shows Voter Identification Laws Do Not Reduce Turnout." Heritage Foundation Center for Data Analysis, September 11. http://www.heritage.org/research/LegalIssues/cda07-04.cfm.

Murray, Matthew. 2007a. "EAC Blasted Again for Burying Study," *Roll Call*, April 9.

———. 2007b. "Durbin, Feinstein Slam EAC over Voting Studies." *Roll Call*, April 16.

National Commission on the Voting Rights Act. 2006. *Highlights of Hearings of the National Commission on the Voting Rights Act 2005*, February. Washington, D.C.: Lawyers' Committee for Civil Rights Under Law.

National Conference of State Legislatures. 2007, 2008, 2012. "Voter Identification Requirements." http://www.ncsl.org/programs/legismgt/elect/taskfc/voteridreq .htm.

Neas, Ralph G. 2006. "Whitewashing the Facts: EAC Report Ignores Key Data." People for the American Way Foundation, December.

Overton, Spencer. 2006. *Stealing Democracy: The New Politics of Voter Suppression*. New York: Norton.

Palazzolo, Joe. 2007. "From Fired U.S. Attorneys, Blame for Gonzales, Not Bush." *Legal Intelligencer*, November 26.

Pew Center on the States. 2008. *One in 100: Behind Bars in America 2008*. Washington, D.C.: Pew Center, February.

Rich, Joseph. 2007. "Playing Politics with Justice." *Los Angeles Times*, March 29.

Sentencing Project. 2008. "Felony Disenfranchisement Laws in the United States," March. http://www.sentencingproject.org/PublicationDetails.aspx?Publication ID=335.

Sentencing Project. 2008. "Disenfranchisement News."

———. 2011. "Felony Disenfranchisement Laws in the United States." December.

Suillinger, Jim. 2008. "Sebelius Vetoes Bill Requiring Voters to Show Photo ID." *Kansas City.com*, May 19.

Toobin, Jeffrey. 2004. "Poll Position." *New Yorker*, September 20.

———. 2008. "Fraud Alert." *New Yorker*, January 14.

Tumulty, Karen and Massimo Calabresi. 2007. "Inside the Scandal at Justice," *Time*, May 21, 44–49.

U.S. EAC. 2006. "Election Crimes: An Initial Review and Recommendations for Future Study." December.

U.S. EAC, Office of Inspector General. 2008. "Report of Investigation: Preparation of the Voter Fraud and Voter Intimidation Report." March.

Wang, Tova Andrea. 2005. "Carter-Baker's Risky Scheme." *PR Newswire*, 22 September.

———. 2006. "Fraud, Reform, and Political Power: Controlling the Vote, from Nineteenth-Century America to Present-Day Georgia." Century Foundation Issue Brief. http://www.tcf.org/Publications/electionreform/wang_historyvoterfraud .pdf.

———. 2007. "A Rigged Report on U.S. Voting." *Washington Post*, 30 August.

Wood, Erica. 2009. "Restoring the Right to Vote." Brennan Center for Justice, New York University School of Law, May 5.

CHAPTER 4

Uneven Democracy: Turnout, Minority Interests, and Local Government Spending

Zoltan Hajnal and Jessica Trounstine

We know that the majority of Americans usually do not vote. At best roughly half of adults vote in national contests. At worst, fewer than 10 percent of adults vote in local elections (Bridges 1997; Hajnal and Lewis 2003). We also know that those who do turn out to vote look very different from those who do not. Study after study of American elections has found that individuals with limited resources—the poor, racial and ethnic minorities, the less educated—vote much less consistently than those with ample resources (Verba et al. 1995, Rosenstone and Hansen 1993).

The skewed nature of the vote raises real concerns about how well the interests of different groups are served in democracy. As V. O. Key noted decades ago, "The blunt truth is that politicians and officials are under no compulsion to pay much heed to classes and groups of citizens that do not vote" (1984: 99). The fear is that individuals and groups who do not participate in the voting process will be overlooked and their concerns ignored (Piven and Cloward 1988). Policies will be biased, outcomes unfair, and in the end American democracy will represent the interests of the privileged few over the broader concerns of the masses (Schattschneider 1970).

But are these fears founded? Conventional wisdom suggests that they are. In almost any political campaign actors on all sides repeatedly cite turnout as one of the most critical factors in determining the outcome of the election. After any close contest, candidates and commentators are likely to agree that "turnout emerged as a decisive factor in [the] elections" (Bumiller

and Nagourney 2002). The notion that the electorate will tilt to the left if the electorate expands has, in fact, been one of the core principles behind Democratic Party efforts to make the vote more accessible and Republican efforts to oppose any such changes.

However universal this view may be among political practitioners, empirical evidence usually suggests that fears of a skewed electorate leading to biased outcomes are largely unfounded. Research on recent American elections has usually found that in the end turnout is not a problem for American democracy (but see Hill and Leighley 1992).[1] First, empirical studies have tended to show that the preferences of nonvoters do not differ markedly from the preferences of voters (e.g., Wolfinger and Rosenstone 1980). Even Verba, Schlozman, and Brady, who lament the distortion created by the unrepresentativeness of nonvoting forms of political participation, nevertheless conclude that "Voters are relatively representative of the public" (1995: 512). Indeed, according to Ellcessor and Leighley, "one of the least contested conclusions in the study of political behavior is that voters' political attitudes and policy positions are fairly representative of non-voters" (2001: 127). In other words, voters and nonvoters may look very different but they do not think all that differently.

More importantly, there is little evidence to suggest that increasing or decreasing turnout would change who wins and loses. Although some studies have found that increasing turnout might alter the margin of victory slightly in some contests, the findings are often highly variable and the effects are usually not large (Citrin et al. 2003; DeNardo 1980; Nagel and McNulty 1996). There is even a prolonged debate over whether marginal benefits would always accrue to Democrats rather than Republicans if turnout expanded (DeNardo 1980; Tucker and Vedlitz 1986). Most important, few of the elections examined would have ended with a different victor. "Simply put," say Highton and Wolfinger, "outcomes would not change if everyone voted" (2001: 179). It follows that we need not be all that troubled by America's low turnout and its skewed electorate.

Why Turnout Might Still Matter

In this paper, we challenge this conclusion. We argue that the non-impact of a skewed electorate stems in part from the narrow focus of much of the existing empirical research. Nearly every study that looks at the effect of voter

turnout on democratic outcomes focuses on the national electorate in Presidential and congressional elections.[2]

This narrow focus reduces the possibility of finding bias for two reasons. First, simple logic dictates that the *possible* extent of any skew produced by uneven turnout decreases as overall turnout levels increase. As detailed in Tingsten's (1937) "law of dispersion," the chances of skew are inversely proportional to overall electoral participation. If almost everybody turns out, there can be very little skew. If, however, only a small fraction of the population turns out, skew can be severe. Thus, if we are interested in revealing just how much turnout matters, we should not confine our research to national elections, where turnout is relatively high. Bias could certainly exist at the national level where only about half of all eligible voters turn out, but it could be that much worse at the local level where turnout averages half or less than half that of national elections (Karnig and Walter 1983; Hajnal et al. 2002).

Second, by looking at the national electorate as a whole one ignores substantial variation in group size across geographic boundaries and almost necessarily diminishes the role that small minority groups can play. In national contests, only a few very large groups can have a significant effect on the outcome of the vote. Asian Americans, for example, are the third largest racial and ethnic minority group, but they make up less than 5 percent of the total national population. Whether they vote is almost immaterial to the outcomes of national contests.

The same is not true for smaller geographic localities. Because people are distributed unevenly across geographic boundaries, groups that are small minorities and largely insignificant at the national level can be major players within many states, districts, or cities. This is especially true for race and ethnicity, but segregation by income, education, and other measures of well-being also occurs. African Americans, for example, make up half or more of the population in Philadelphia, New Orleans, Atlanta, and Washington. In fact, segregation by race and ethnicity is the rule rather than the exception. Although the national population is only 13 percent African American, 16 percent Latino, and 5 percent Asian American, data from a nationwide survey (the American Citizen Participation Study, Verba et al. 1995) indicate that the average Latino lives in a city that is 39 percent Hispanic, the average African American in a city that is 35 percent black, and the average Asian American in a city that is 7 percent Asian American.

Thus, if we are concerned about the effects of a skew in the electorate we need to look not just at the national electorate as a whole but at a series of

smaller political units where the effect of different groups could begin to weigh in.[3] Only by examining each of these smaller units separately will we begin to get a second, perhaps more revealing look at the effects of uneven turnout on voting outcomes.

We are by no means the first to consider the implications of turnout for subnational politics. There have been, in fact, a number of studies that consider the relationship between turnout and state policymaking. Three landmark studies have demonstrated a clear link between how well different economic classes of voters are represented among a state's voters and welfare policy in that state (Hill and Leighley 1992; Hill et al. 1995; Peterson and Rom 1989), and one other study has demonstrated a relationship between state level turnout and tax progressiveness (Martinez 1997).[2] These studies are encouraging of the turnout hypothesis and suggest that shifting to an examination of lower levels may be informative. But they still focus on elections with relatively high turnout and geographic areas with relatively low concentrations of minorities. If we want to understand just how much turnout can matter, we need to focus on the local level.

Unfortunately, although there are strong reasons to suspect that turnout is critical at the local level, there is, to date, little empirical evidence addressing this question. Scholars of urban politics have long suspected that skewed turnout affects outcomes (Dahl 1961; Browning et al. 1984; Bridges 1997), but systematic tests are rare. Leighley (2001) and Verba et al. (1995) briefly report on participation rates for different racial, ethnic, and demographic groups in local elections, but there is little research that looks systematically across cities at the *consequences* of a skewed electorate at the local level.[3] Thus the question of whether or not turnout matters remains largely unanswered.

In this paper we show that a narrow focus on national contests has produced misleading or at least incomplete conclusions about the consequences of an unrepresentative electorate. By shifting the focus of attention to local contests, we find that turnout matters. Changes in the percentage of voters who turn out can and do alter the core priorities of local government.

Turnout and Local Government Spending

To gauge the importance of voter turnout in local democracy, we focus on arguably the most critical feature of local government policy making—where governments spend (and raise) their money. Governments serve a

variety of purposes, but one of their most vital functions is the distribution of resources. Where those resources are distributed and who receives them are among the most fundamental questions facing a democracy. The local political arena is no exception. Nationwide, local governments spend over a trillion dollars annually (Bureau of the Census 2003). Local politics, at its core, is often a battle over who is going to get those dollars. If voter turnout can help determine who wins and who loses this battle, then there can be little doubt that turnout matters.

In our analysis, we break down government spending and fiscal policy into different areas that are more or less popular among different segments of the city population. We especially want to isolate spending on the priorities of groups like racial and ethnic minorities and other disadvantaged populations who vote less regularly and contrast this with spending on the priorities of more advantaged interests who vote more consistently. To map onto these divergent priorities as closely as possible, we focus on three standard spending areas: (1) redistributive spending, (2) developmental spending, and (3) allocational spending (Peterson 1981). Redistributive policies are those that target and benefit less advantaged residents. They include functions like welfare, public housing, health care, and education. Development policy, by contrast, is focused on programs which seek to encourage economic growth and the ongoing economic vitality of a city. Developmental spending includes outlays for highways, streets, transportation, and airports. Finally, allocational policy is spending on a range of basic city services that can be considered housekeeping. This includes services like parks, police and fire protection, and sanitation. In addition, to see whether turnout affects more fundamental decisions about overall fiscal capacity, we look at two further measures: (4) per capita taxation, and (5) per capita debt.

Although it is clear that no racial/ethnic group or other demographic group unanimously prefers one spending area overall, there is ample evidence indicating that spending priorities diverge across groups in the urban context. Surveys of urban residents and evidence from national polls show divergent priorities between poor, minority respondents who vote less regularly and more advantaged, white respondents who vote more regularly. Employing a range of surveys of the urban population, Alozie and McNamara (2008), Welch et al. (2001), Lovrich (1974), and Deleon (1991) all find that poor, minority voters are especially concerned about redistribution and social services, while whites and the middle class are especially concerned about attracting businesses and other aspects of development, reducing

taxes, and improving their quality of life through better parks and recreation and easier transportation.[4] The differences between advantaged and disadvantaged interests on distributional and developmental policy are the starkest, but there are also clear differences on allocational spending. Lovrich (1974), in particular, finds that whites ranked police protection and environmental issues like garbage collection, pollution, and parks and recreation as top urban priorities, while blacks and Hispanics did not. Whites, who generally did not favor greater spending, were nevertheless willing to support increased funding for these kinds of allocational services. National and state-level polls also regularly reveal sharp differences in preferences both on overall spending and taxation and on more specific spending areas. Verba et al. (1995), and Kinder and Sanders (1996) both report that redistributive policies garner more support among racial and ethnic minorities and other less advantaged groups than among whites and other more privileged interests. As Lovrich puts it, there is "a degree of consensus among minority voters as to priorities which cluster very differently from those of Anglo voters" (1974: 707). If local governments respond to who actually turns out to vote, then increases in voter turnout that add more disadvantaged, minority voters into the electorate should lead to significant changes in local government spending. As turnout increases, we should see a greater concentration of resources on redistributive programs and a lower proportion of spending on allocational and developmental policies.

Other Controls

Turnout is certainly not the only factor that could affect local government spending priorities. The urban politics literature offers a range of different accounts of government decision-making that we also need to incorporate. According to the economic imperatives model developed by Peterson (1981) and others, competition between cities for mobile capital and labor severely constrains local governments. Cities must seriously consider reducing taxes and providing a mix of services that is most likely to attract and/or retain more privileged economic interests. This often leads to a pro-growth focus and a range of spending policies that encourage economic development (Logan and Molotch 1987). If this theory is accurate, we would expect to see very little redistributive spending.

The main alternative to this economic imperatives model is a pluralist account of urban policy making. Rather than seeing local government decisions as driven by economic constraints, pluralists see local policy as fundamentally driven by political considerations (Dahl 1961). The key to understanding local decision-making, according to pluralists, is to recognize that elected officials need public support in order to govern and to win reelection. If most residents in a given locality favor greater redistribution of public resources, we should expect political actors in that locality to enact measures to increase redistribution.[5]

According to a third group of observers, local policy is less a function of economic competition or political preferences and is instead more a function of local needs (Mladenka 1980). From this bureaucratic perspective, city governments operate in a technically efficient manner and simply distribute resources and services to those who need them. If this is true, one might expect governments in cities with large poor populations or severely disadvantaged neighborhoods to expend substantial resources on redistributive functions.

Institutional structure is a fourth factor that, according to many, helps constrain local government decisions (Sharp 2002; Pelissero and Krebs 1997). Institutionalists tend not to deny the existence of any of the other factors that have already been mentioned.[6] They do, however, contend that governing structures can also change the nature of the local political game and shape the incentives that local political actors face. This institutionalist perspective comes in two variants: one that focuses on local institutions and another that sees the federal institutional structure as more critical.

Although almost any institutional lever at the local level could conceivably help determine government behavior, institutionalist scholars have focused on a handful of key structures. In particular, nonpartisan elections, the city manager form of government (as opposed to the mayor/council form), weaker mayoral powers, and the absence of term limits are all viewed by at least some urban scholars as reducing the responsiveness of local government to minority or lower-class interests (Bridges 1997). Although evidence for many of these relationships is still limited, there is a widespread belief that reform institutions have been instrumental in maintaining middle-class white control in a number of urban centers.

Other institutionalists point to the placement of local governments at the bottom of the hierarchy of the federal system as a critical factor in local policy-making (Orfield 1974; Salzstein 1986). Since a quarter of local government

revenues are dispensed by state and federal governments, and since much of this federal and state funding is earmarked toward specific functions, local governments often have little power to control the direction of their own spending. Thus, rather than reflecting the preferences of local actors, local government spending may be more likely to reflect the priorities of state and national governments. In the remainder of this paper, we assess the effects of turnout, controlling for these other accounts of local government finance.

Data and Methods

To see whether turnout matters in the local context, we focus on the relationship between voter turnout in city council elections and government spending priorities. We focus on turnout in city council elections because they are arguably the most central election in most cities. Most U.S. cities have a council/city manager form of government, and even in cities with mayors, the mayor seldom has veto power or unilateral control over the budget (Hajnal and Lewis 2003). Thus, council elections are almost always central to local policy-making (Pelissero and Krebs 2003). The only survey with local turnout figures for a large, nationally representative sample of localities is the 1986 International City/County Managers Association (ICMA), which surveyed all municipalities with over 2,500 residents. It thus becomes the core data set for this study.

We use aggregate voter turnout in each contest, since data on the class or racial skew of the local electorate in different cities are simply not available. We expect that as turnout in city council elections expands, the vote will be less skewed by class or race and less advantaged interests will have more say in determining outcomes.

There is an important assumption behind this test—namely, that turnout will be more uneven across groups as turnout declines. Fortunately, there is ample available evidence indicating that this assumption is accurate. Hill and Leighley (1992), Citrin et al. (2003), and Jackson et al. (1998) have all shown that turnout is more uneven at the state level as turnout declines.[7] To supplement these findings, which are admittedly not directly focused on local voter turnout, we collected exit poll data for as many local mayoral elections as we could find. Across these cases, higher registered voter turnout in mayoral elections is associated with a sharp decrease in the overrepresentation of white voters and sharp increases in the representation

of black, Asian American, and Latino voters. Across these mayoral elections, registered-voter turnout was correlated with the representation of white, black, Latino, and Asian voters at -.47, .69, .47, and .68 respectively.[8] The number of cases in our data set of exit polls is relatively small—20 elections across 5 cities—but all the available evidence clearly indicates that higher-turnout elections tend to be much more representative of the city population.

Although we now know that higher turnout at the local level means less skew, it is still clear that aggregate turnout will only be an imprecise proxy for class or racial/bias. Given the noise in our measure, our results should, if anything, underestimate the magnitude of the effects of class or racial/bias on government spending patterns. If this noise is too severe or if we are wrong and there is no underlying relationship between local voter turnout and the skew of the electorate, our tests should reveal no relationship between turnout and government spending.

The ICMA survey was mailed to city clerks in every city in the United States with over 2,500 residents and has a response rate of 66 percent.[9] The survey reports figures for registration and turnout in the most recent city council election. Clerks were asked to provide the percentage of eligible voters who are registered to vote and the percentage of registered voters who voted in the most recent city-wide election.[10] In subsequent analysis we focus primarily on turnout of registered voters, but in alternate tests we repeat the analysis with turnout of eligible voters.[11]

For spending data we utilize data from the Census of Governments and focus on the 1987 Census because it has data on local spending for the year *after* the turnout data. In line with Peterson (1981), Stein (1990), and other research on local government spending, the specific local government functions that fit into each spending area are as follows: redistributive (welfare, public housing, health services, and education), developmental (highways, streets, transportation, and airports), and allocational (fire protection, police and correctional services, sewerage, and solid waste). For each of the three spending areas, we measure the proportion of *total* government expenditures that goes to programs in that area.[12]

In each spending area, we only include those specific spending categories that fit clearly. We drop from the analysis categories of spending (like government administration, judicial functions, or insurance) that are harder to categorize. Nevertheless, even among the categories we do include, there are some specific spending areas that fit less well into the three larger categories. Some could argue, for example, that educational spending is not

clearly redistributive as it serves both advantaged and disadvantaged interests. To address this issue, we repeated the subsequent analysis two different
ways. First, we dropped specific categories of spending like education that
arguably fit less clearly into one of the three larger spending areas. Second,
we broke down the larger spending areas into their constituent components
and re-ran the regressions focusing on each single spending category. This
secondary analysis generally confirmed the primary analysis.[13]

In the analysis, we include the range of other factors that have been
linked by past research to local government spending. First, to see whether
local governments are responding to political considerations and in particular to public preferences, we include a measure of the Democratic presidential vote share at the county level (Bureau of the Census 1986).[14] Specifically,
we average the 1984 and 1988 Democratic vote share.[15] Second, to account
for economic competition and the belief that governments will only expend
substantial resources on redistributive functions when they have considerable financial resources and excess spending capacity, we include a range of
measures of overall spending capacity. These include total general revenue,
recent changes in government revenue, per capita debt, the existing tax rate,
and local bond ratings. Revenue data as well as all tax and debt figures are
from the 1987 Census of Governments. Bond ratings are compiled in the
City and County Data Book (1986). Third, to see whether local governments
are more technocratic and are simply providing services to those who need
them, we include several measures of need. Specifically, the analysis incorporates the poverty rate in the city, the proportion of the population that is
African American or Hispanic, and the citywide crime rate. Demographic
data are from the Census (1990). Crime figures are derived from the City
and County Data Book. Fourth, since urban theorists have cited electoral
institutions as a central influence on government spending decisions and
have pointed to reform structures as being particularly unsupportive of minority, disadvantaged interests, we assess the roles of nonpartisan elections,
the city manager form of government (as opposed to the mayor/council
form), weaker mayoral powers, and term limits. The other institutional
structure that could affect American cities is federalism. Specifically, each
city is subject to different constraints and opportunities related to its status
in a federal system (Stein 2003; Schneider 1989). We test for three different
aspects of that system. To address the possibility that local government
spending may be affected by fiscal constraints placed on city government by
state law, we control for the existence of a constitutional or statutory limita-

tion on the amount of debt a city may incur and the presence of constitutional or statutory law mandating a balanced budget for the city (U.S. Advisory Commission on Inter-Governmental Relations 1993). Also, since local governments that are more successful at tapping into federal or state funds may have more leeway in spending and may thus be able to increase redistributive spending, we included the proportion of all revenue from state and federal governments as a measure of intergovernmental revenue (Schneider 1989). As well, to control for the fact that different localities have different spending mandates imposed on them from above, in alternate tests we included a count of the number of specific spending categories (within each of the three broader spending areas) in which the locality spent no money. Data on local institutional structure are derived from the 1986 ICMA survey. Intergovernmental revenue is from the Census of Governments (Bureau of the Census 1987).

Finally, we also take into account a range of smaller features of the local environment that have been shown to be relevant to at least some aspect of fiscal policy. Since the nature of cities differs substantially by region, city type, and city size, we add dummy variables for each region (West, Midwest, Northeast, and South) and city type (suburb and central city) and measures for city size (total population and population growth). Another potentially important characteristic of the urban environment is the number of cities that are nearby. Schneider (1989), in particular, argues that the more local governments a city has to compete with the more constrained its own spending will be. To control for this possibility, we include a measure of the number of incorporated places in the county (Source: Census of Governments 1987). Finally, we control for basic demographics (percent Asian American, percent college educated, percent homeowner, percent noncitizen) that could be viewed as potential influences on government spending decisions. Each of these measures is derived from the Census (1990).

Turnout and Government Spending Priorities

Does turnout affect government spending priorities? In Table 4.1 we begin to answer this question by assessing the effects of voter turnout on three broad categories of government spending. Specifically, the table reports the results of three OLS regressions with the proportion of city expenditures going to redistributive, developmental, and allocational spending as the

Table 4.1. Effects of Turnout on Government Spending Priorities

	Proportion of government expenditures to		
	Redistributive spending	Developmental spending	Allocational spending
VOTER MOBILIZATION			
Registered voter turnout	.043 (.020)**	−.003 (.012)	−.054 (.022)**
MASS PREFERENCES			
Democratic vote for president	.082 (.041)**	−.067 (.024)***	.042 (.046)
SPENDING CAPACITY			
Government revenue	.381 (.130)***	−.159 (.077)**	−.353 (.144)**
Change in revenue	.730 (.221)***	−.275 (.132)**	−.869 (.250)***
Median household income	−.009 (.005)*	.002 (.003)	.016 (.005)***
NEEDS			
Percent poor	.016 (.087)	.085 (.052)*	.098 (.096)
Percent black	−.089 (.039)**	−.037 (.023)	−.036 (.043)
Percent Latino	−.082 (.065)	−.026 (.039)	.086 (.072)
LOCAL INSTITUTIONS			
Mayor vs. city manager	−.045 (.010)***	.011 (.006)*	.026 (.011)**
Mayoral veto	.027 (.010)***	−.011 (.006)*	−.009 (.011)
Term limits	.009 (.016)	.006 (.010)	−.009 (.018)
Nonpartisan	.062 (.011)***	−.001 (.006)	−.038 (.012)***
FEDERALISM			
Legal limits on debt	−.061 (.019)**	−.002 (.011)	−.011 (.022)
Balanced budget provision	−.010 (.014)	−.002 (.008)	−.011 (.015)
Total state/federal govt. revenue	.317 (.036)***	−.025 (.022)	−.084 (.041)**

CITY TYPE			
Suburb	−.023 (.013)*	.013 (.079)	.063 (.015)***
Central city	.024 (.014)*	−.001 (.008)	−.003 (.015)
Population	−.051 (.017)***	.018 (.007)**	.048 (.013)***
Population growth	.004 (.011)	−.002 (.006)	−.052 (.011)***
Number of places in county	.079 (.023)***	.001 (.014)	−.071 (.026)***
REGION			
West	−.023 (.018)	.065 (.011)***	−.043 (.020)**
Midwest	−.013 (.015)	.045 (.009)***	−.059 (.016)***
Northeast	.124 (.018)***	.007 (.011)	−.110 (.019)***
DEMOGRAPHICS			
Percent Asian	−.096 (.103)	−.076 (.061)	−.052 (.114)
Percent college educated	−.028 (.049)	.057 (.029)*	.129 (.054)**
Percent homeowner	.045 (.041)	.043 (.024)*	−.139 (.046)***
Percent non-citizen	.232 (.117)**	−.031 (.070)	−.195 (.130)
Constant	−.055 (.040)	.069 (.024)***	.435 (.045)***
Adj. R-squared	.39	.17	.14
N	1067	1066	1066

Source: Census of Governments 1987; ICMA Survey 1986; Census 1990, 2000. Figures are coefficients and standard errors. ***$p<.01$, **$p<.05$, *$p<.10$.

dependent variables.[16] The key independent variable is the percent of registered voters that turned out in the city's most recent election. As turnout increases across cities, we expect that racial and ethnic minorities and other disadvantaged groups are more likely to vote and more likely to have their preferences translated into public policy.

The results indicate that turnout does matter. As can be seen in the first row of Table 4.1, higher turnout in local elections leads to significant increases in the proportion of spending on redistributive functions and significant declines in the proportion of spending on allocational programs.[17] Even after controlling for public preferences, spending capacity, and needs, the more people who turn out to vote, the more likely local governments are to spend their money on welfare, public housing, and other redistributive programs and the less likely they are to spend it on waste management and other forms of allocational spending.[18] This implies that if more racial and ethnic minorities and members of other disadvantaged groups do turn out to vote, they may be able to pressure governments into spending on policies that are more in line with their preferences.

Figure 4.1 also indicates that the effects of turnout are meaningful. The figure shows the substantive effects of turnout on redistributive and allocational spending, as derived from the regression in Table 4.1. The black lines show expected spending at different levels of turnout—all else equal.[19] The gray lines represent 95 percent confidence intervals around the predicted values.

Increasing the proportion of registered voters who turn out from 19 percent (one standard deviation below mean turnout) to 59 percent (one standard deviation above the mean) would increase the proportion of city government spending on redistributive programs by 1.8 percentage points.

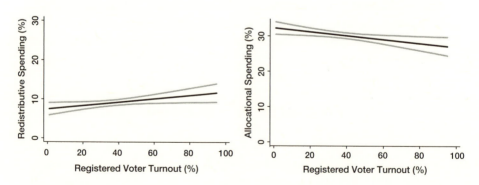

Figure 4.1. Effects of turnout on government spending.

This may not seem like a substantial shift. However, given that the average city spends only 7.8 percent of its budget on these programs, this increase in turnout could potentially increase the amount of redistributive spending by one quarter. As Figure 4.1 shows, the effect of a large boost in turnout on allocational spending is equally large. Moreover, it is not unreasonable to expect large changes in turnout in some cities. Simply changing the timing of local elections to coincide with national elections increases registered voter turnout by 36 percentage points (Hajnal 2010).

Turnout is not a panacea. Many cities already have fairly high voter turnout, and even the highest-turnout cities do not redistribute more than a small fraction of their revenue. Nevertheless, the results here suggest that attainable changes in voter turnout could have a significant impact on how many local governments spend their money and at least partially affect who wins and who loses in local democracy.

The results in Table 4.1 do, however, reveal one area where turnout has no obvious effects. There is no clear link between turnout and developmental spending. This is, at least at first glance, somewhat counterintuitive. Since developmental spending tends most directly and most immediately to benefit privileged interests in society, it might be the first thing that poor, minority residents would want to cut when they turn out to vote. The fact that developmental spending does not go down when turnout expands may indicate that cities feel they cannot cut developmental spending if they want to remain competitive and continue to attract businesses, or it may mean that cities expand overall spending by increasing taxes or debt—a subject we address below. Consistently high spending on developmental programs may also be a sign that cities, almost irrespective of who is involved in the electoral arena, tend to be dominated by business interests. Turnout and politics may play a role in some areas of local spending, but the imperatives of the economic market and competition between cities appear to be dominant in other areas.[20]

The Fiscal Effects of Voter Turnout

There are many ways local governments can affect local policy. They can, as we have shown, affect policy by deciding how to split up the existing revenue pie. But local governments can also affect policy through more fundamental fiscal decisions like raising money via higher taxes or incurring greater debt.

In other words, they can change the size of the existing revenue stream. Especially in today's fiscally challenged urban environment, these kinds of fiscal decisions may represent one of the few avenues through which local governments can initiate major policies that affect the well-being of different groups.

To see if voter turnout impacts this broader range of government behavior, in Table 4.2, we assess the link between voter turnout and tax and debt policy. Since the existing survey evidence indicates that racial and ethnic minorities and other disadvantaged groups not only favor greater government spending but also are more willing than privileged groups to increase taxes to pay for that spending, one should expect that as the size of the electorate expands and the number of relatively needy or disadvantaged voters grows, local governments will choose to increase the local tax rate and the size of the existing debt (Alozie and McNamara 2008; Lovrich 1974; Deleon 1991; Welch et al. 2001). Put another way, to try to satisfy the increasing demand from less advantaged voters for more services, local governments should raise more money by raising taxes or incurring greater debt.

Table 4.2 suggests that voter turnout also matters for these more fundamental government policy decisions. Greater turnout translates into substantially higher per capita debt. All else equal, moving from a city one standard deviation below mean turnout to a city at one standard deviation above mean turnout leads almost to a doubling of per capita debt. Greater turnout also appears to lead to increased per capita taxes. The relationship between turnout and taxes in the second column of Table 4.2 is positive but not quite significant. However, an alternate regression using turnout of eligible voters instead of turnout of registered voters shows a substantial, significant, and positive relationship between turnout and local tax policy (analysis not shown). In short, when a larger and more diverse set of residents turns out to vote, governments appear to comply with this increased demand by raising taxes and increasing local debt. The poor and other disadvantaged groups want more government services. If they vote more regularly, they often get funds for those services. This is yet another sign that who votes matters.[21]

The Contingent Effects of Turnout

Turnout should not always matter for these spending decisions. If elections are not competitive and incumbents know that they have very little chance of losing the next election, there is little incentive to respond to the pressures

Table 4.2. Local Voter Turnout: Fiscal Effects

	Per capita debt	Per capita taxes
VOTER MOBILIZATION		
Registered voter turnout	1.39 (.554)**	.055 (.034)
MASS PREFERENCES		
Democratic vote for president	−3.09 (1.16)***	.178 (.072)**
SPENDING CAPACITY		
Government revenue	12.8 (3.72)***	1.14 (.229)***
Change in revenue	26.2 (6.36)***	1.25 (.392)***
Median household income	.065 (.139)	.011 (.008)
NEEDS		
Percent poor	−4.48 (2.46)*	−.089(.152)
Percent black	.955 (1.11)	.006 (.068)
Percent Latino	−.495 (1.85)	−.267 (.114)**
LOCAL INSTITUTIONS		
Mayor vs. city manager	−.174 (.282)	−.054 (.017)***
Mayoral veto	−.106 (.288)	.032 (.018)*
Term limits	−.440 (.462)	.018 (.029)
Nonpartisan	.300 (.310)	.073 (.019)***
FEDERALISM		
Legal limits on debt	−.996 (.551)*	.019 (.034)
Balanced budget provision	.084 (.396)	.033 (.024)
Total state/federal govt. revenue	−1.70 (1.03)*	.048 (.064)
CITY TYPE		
Suburb	1.47 (.374)***	−.014 (.023)
Central city	−.520 (.396)	.047 (.024)*
Population	−.016 (.003)***	−.012 (.002)***
Population growth	.619 (.303)**	−.041 (.019)**
Number of places in county	.031 (.066)	.096 (.041)**
REGION		
West	.385 (.508)	.052 (.032)
Midwest	.376 (.414)	−.026 (.026)
Northeast	−.142 (.503)	.195 (.031)***
DEMOGRAPHICS		
Percent Asian	−.483 (2.94)	−.553 (.182)***
Percent college educated	−.270 (1.38)	.204 (.085)**
Percent homeowner	−.124 (1.16)	−.034 (.072)
Percent non-citizen	1.31 (3.35)	.435 (.207)**
Constant	2.88 (1.14)**	.013 (.017)
Adj. R-squared	.06	.25
N	1070	1070

Source: Census of Governments 1987; ICMA Survey 1986; Census 1990. Figures are coefficients and standard errors. ***$p<.01$, **$p<.05$, *$p<.10$.

of newly mobilized voters. If however, elections are competitive and an incumbent stands a good chance of losing his or her next election, there is a much greater incentive to be aware of the preferences of new voters and to respond to these preferences. Similarly, if elections are competitive and a challenger wins over an incumbent, there is a real incentive for the new leader to follow the policy preferences of the new voting bloc. In short, the higher the turnover and the greater the competition, the more that voter turnout should affect government policy.

To see if the local electoral context helped shape the relationship between turnout and government spending patterns, we added a measure of turnover or competition—the percentage of incumbents who won reelection in the most recent city council election—and an interaction term for turnout and turnover to the regression model in Table 4.3.[22] If, as we suspect is the case, turnout matters more in competitive, high turnover cities, the interaction term should be negative and significant.

As the first column of Table 4.3 illustrates, competition is an important intervening variable. The interaction term is negative and significant, indicating that the effects of turnout on representation are significantly lower in cities with less competitive local elections. We suspect that two processes are at work. In one scenario, expanded turnout is leading to the election of a new and different set of leaders who then institute policies that are more in line with preferences of their core constituency. In a second scenario, in order to try to stave off electoral defeat, incumbents increase redistributive spending to respond to the preferences of an expanded and more diverse electorate. In either case, the fewer incumbents who lose, the less turnout matters. Moreover, this interaction effect is substantial. All else equal, in a highly competitive city where half of incumbents lose their reelection bids, moving from low to high turnout leads to a 43 percent increase in redistributive spending (8.2 to 11.7 percent of the budget). In contrast, in an uncompetitive city where all incumbents win, moving from low to high turnout only leads to a 14 percent increase in redistributive spending (8.4 to 9.6 percent of the budget).

To assess further how the local electoral context affects the impact of turnout, we looked at the link between voter turnout and racial and ethnic minority representation on the local city council. Presumably, if turnout affects spending by increasing the number of local leaders who represent less advantaged segments of the population, increases in turnout may matter even more when they are accompanied by a shift in racial and ethnic leadership

Table 4.3. Contingent Effects of Turnout on Redistributive Spending

	Model 1	Model 2
VOTER MOBILIZATION		
Registered voter turnout	.156 (.057)***	.051 (.021)**
LOCAL COMPETITION		
Percent incumbents winning	−.031 (.026)	—
Percent incumbents winning × Voter turnout	−.126 (.063)**	—
RACIAL REPRESENTATION ON COUNCIL		
Percent black on council	—	.113 (.095)
Percent Latino on council	—	.005 (.110)
Percent Asian American on council	—	−.007 (.322)
Percent black on council × voter turnout	—	−.224 (.209)
Percent Latino on council × voter turnout	—	−.044 (.242)
Percent Asian on council × voter turnout	—	.094 (.628)
MASS PREFERENCES		
Democratic vote for president	.091 (.042)**	.084 (.041)**
SPENDING CAPACITY		
Government revenue	.379 (.132)***	.392 (.132)***
Change in revenue	.711 (.226)***	.702 (.228)***
Median household income	−.009 (.005)*	−.009 (.005)*
NEEDS		
Percent poor	.019 (.089)	.012 (.088)
Percent black	−.097 (.039)**	−.110 (.051)**
Percent Latino	−.064 (.067)	−.074 (.082)
LOCAL INSTITUTIONS		
Mayor vs. city manager	−.047 (.010)***	−.045 (.010)***
Mayoral veto	.028 (.010)***	.027 (.010)***
Term limits	.009 (.017)	.009 (.016)
Nonpartisan	.063 (.011)***	.062 (.011)***
FEDERALISM		
Legal limits on debt	−.062 (.019)**	−.063 (.019)**
Balanced budget provision	−.009 (.014)	−.008 (.014)
Total state/federal govt. revenue	.308 (.037)***	.316 (.036)***

Table 4.3. (continued)

	Model 1	Model 2
CITY TYPE		
Suburb	−.023 (.013)*	−.025 (.013)*
Central city	.022 (.014)	.023 (.013)*
Population	−.050 (.012)***	−.051 (.012)***
Population growth	.004 (.011)	.004 (.011)
Number of governments in county	.077 (.025)***	.079 (.024)***
REGION		
West	−.027 (.018)	−.026 (.018)
Midwest	−.013 (.015)	−.015 (.015)
Northeast	.128 (.018)***	.122 (.018)***
DEMOGRAPHICS		
Percent Asian	−.082 (.110)	−.096 (.113)
Percent college educated	−.029 (.050)	−.024 (.049)
Percent homeowner	.030 (.044)	.040 (.041)
Percent non-citizen	.218 (.120)**	.222 (.126)*
Constant	−.076 (.048)	−.053 (.040)
Adj R-squared	.39	.39
N	1034	1066

Source: Census of Governments 1987; ICMA Survey 1986; Census 1990. Figures are coefficients and standard errors. ***p<.01, **p<.05, *p<.10.

on city councils. Leadership turnover may be important, but it may be even more important when racial and ethnic minority leaders enter office. We test this possibility by adding measures of the proportion of African Americans, Latinos, and Asian Americans on the city council and interaction terms for turnout and the racial makeup of the council.[23]

The results, as reported in the second column of Table 4.3, suggest that racial or ethnic minority representation on the city council is not necessary for turnout to affect local government spending priorities. The interaction terms are insignificant and the key independent variable, registered voter turnout, remains significant, indicating that turnout matters regardless of the racial and ethnic makeup of the city council.[24] This implies that both white and nonwhite elected officials are recognizing and responding to changes in who turns out to vote.

Table 4.3 also indicates that the number of black, Latino, and Asian American council members has no direct effect on government spending.

Net all the other factors, having more minorities on the council does not lead to significant shifts in spending. This is probably not surprising, given that the model controls for the size of each racial group in the city, voter turnout, and public opinion in each city.

One issue we have not yet raised in the analysis in this chapter is the direction of causality. Governments could spend more money on certain policy areas in order to encourage certain groups to turn out at higher levels in the future. For our purposes, it does not actually matter whether turnout increases affect spending priorities or whether spending changes increase turnout. In either case, the interests of more voters (and presumably more diverse voters) are more closely reflected in policy decisions when turnout is higher.

Nevertheless, there is some evidence to suggest that turnout causes spending changes rather than the reverse. One piece of evidence is temporal. The turnout data are generally from a year or more preceding the spending data. It seems unlikely that spending that occurs after an election is causally related to changes in turnout in the preceding election. Also, it is difficult to explain how the pattern of spending and taxing we see in the data could lead to increases in turnout. Logically, one would not expect increases in taxes to trigger greater turnout among less advantaged groups. More generally, it is not at all clear that increases in spending in one area should lead policy winners to turn out more than policy losers. Changes in spending could increase the turnout of policy losers as much or more than policy winners (but see Griffin and Flavin 2009). In short, there is no obvious story that can readily explain expanded turnout as a function of increased spending on redistributive functions, decreased spending on allocational programs, and higher taxes and debt. As well, anecdotal evidence from many of these cities indicates that major policy changes tend to occur after new a set of candidates is elected rather than before. Finally, as the last set of analyses showed, the effect of turnout depends greatly on having incumbents lose—a pattern that fits better with a causal story that views turnout as a cause of policy change rather than as the result of policy change.

Turnout Effects in More Recent Elections

One concern with the results that have been presented up to this point is that they may be outdated. The data, in fact, are derived from elections that occurred almost three decades ago. Given the recent devolution of policy responsibilities from the federal government to local municipalities, the increasingly difficult fiscal situation faced by many cities, and dramatic shifts in the racial and ethnic makeup of the urban population, there is at least some reason to suspect that cities may be functioning differently today from the way they have in the past. In particular, turnout might matter less today than it has in the past. To assess this possibility, we obtained data on turnout in recent elections in California. With support from the Public Policy Institute of California, in 2000 we polled city clerks in every incorporated city in the state to acquire data on voter turnout in the most recent city council election and on the institutional structure in each city.[25] We then merged this with spending data from the 2001 Census of Governments and 2000 Census data on the racial makeup and demographics of each city. With all these measures, we can repeat our earlier analysis to see whether turnout effects continue to shape local democracy.

California is just one state and is obviously not representative of the nation as a whole, but California provides an excellent setting for studying the impact of voter turnout on minority representation for several reasons.[26] The biggest advantage of using California is its size and diversity. California's large size means that our survey contains enough cities to allow for rigorous empirical analysis. Also, our almost 400 city observations vary enormously across measures of racial diversity, population size, socioeconomic status, industrial base, urbanization, and most other relevant characteristics. There are cities in California that are comparable to most American cities on most important dimensions. Second, although there are clear differences between the racial makeup of the state and the nation as a whole, California's present racial makeup presages the projected makeup of the whole country in the mid-twenty-first century. Finally, examining local voter participation within a single state avoids some problems of unmeasured heterogeneity due to state-level differences such as registration rules and Motor Voter Law implementation.[27]

Table 4.4 shows the effect of registered voter turnout on the same three categories of spending we looked at earlier—redistributive, allocational, and developmental spending. Each regression also incorporates an almost identical set of economic, political, bureaucratic, institutional, and demographic controls. Once again, turnout is an important determinant of policy outcomes. The results for California do not perfectly mirror the results from the nation as a whole, but it is clear that in California as in the broader nation higher turnout is coupled with policies that are more in line with the

Table 4.4. Effects of Turnout on Government Spending Priorities—California

	Proportion of government expenditures to . . .			
	Redistributive spending	Redistributive spending (larger cities)	Developmental spending	Allocational spending
VOTER MOBILIZATION				
Registered voter turnout	−.005 (.004)	.133 (.053)**	−.088 (.031)***	−.087 (.039)**
MASS PREFERENCES				
Democratic vote for president	.131 (.071)*	.181 (.087)**	−.061 (.056)	−.048 (.073)
SPENDING CAPACITY				
Government revenue	−.028 (.161)	−.028 (.197)	.074 (.127)	−.092 (.160)
Median household income	−.007 (.005)	−.004 (.126)	.008 (.036)	.035 (.046)
NEEDS				
Percent poor	.077 (.132)	.315 (.248)	.179 (.104)*	−.287 (.136)**
Percent black	−.062 (.115)	−.181 (.125)	−.181 (.092)**	−.011 (.011)
Percent Latino	.026 (.060)	−.186 (.086)**	−.133 (.047)***	.219 (.068)***
LOCAL INSTITUTIONS				
Mayor vs. city manager	.051 (.034)	−.013 (.071)	−.015 (.027)	−.004 (.034)
Mayoral veto	−.009 (.041)	.002 (.041)	−.037 (.032)	−.014 (.041)
Term limits	−.022 (.016)	−.004 (.017)	−.048 (.120)	.029 (.156)
Concurrent election	.014 (.015)	−.046 (.022)**	.025 (.012)*	.012 (.016)
FEDERALISM				
Total state/federal govt. revenue	.018 (.014)	.160 (.044)***	.009 (.012)	−.019 (.015)

Table 4.4. (continued)

	Proportion of government expenditures to . . .			
	Redistributive spending	Redistributive spending (larger cities)	Developmental spending	Allocational spending
CITY TYPE				
Suburb	.043 (.018)**	—	-.018 (.014)	-.057 (.018)***
Central city	-.005 (.022)	-.043 (.020)**	-.025 (.017)	.012 (.022)
Population	.005 (.006)	.026 (.019)	-.004 (.005)	.004 (.006)
Population growth	.037 (.022)*	-.084 (.051)*	.017 (.017)	-.037 (.022)
Number of places in county	-.037 (.289)	.035 (.040)	.049 (.234)	-.123 (.030)***
DEMOGRAPHICS				
Percent Asian	.197 (.071)***	.118 (.080)	-.098 (.055)*	.014 (.072)
Percent college educated	-.027 (.064)	-.200 (.096)**	.055 (.050)	.015 (.006)**
Percent homeowner	.033 (.065)	.198 (.117)*	.147 (.050)***	-.048 (.067)
Percent citizen	-.037 (.141)	-.314 (.208)	-.144 (.111)	.336 (.145)**
Constant	.000 (.168)	-.056 (.355)	.239 (.132)*	.022 (.168)
Adj. R-squared	.15	.26	.15	.19
N	412	125	412	412

Source: Census of Governments 2001; PPIC Survey 2001; Census 2000. Figures are coefficients and standard errors. ***$p<.01$, **$p<.05$, * $p<.10$.

preferences of most minorities and the poor. Cities in California with higher turnout spend significantly less on allocational spending and significantly less on developmental spending—two areas that polls show are less important to minorities and the poor. The finding regarding development policy is noteworthy in that it suggests that at least under certain circumstances, political considerations can impact this arena of government policy—a finding that runs at least somewhat counter to Peterson's (1981) contentions and earlier results from the national data. The other important difference between the state and the nation is that, at least at first glance, there appears to be no clear relationship between aggregate turnout and redistributive spending in the state. However, when we investigated this relationship more fully, we did find a link between turnout and redistributive spending for at least a subset of California cities. We suspected that the lack of a connection between turnout and redistributive policy was due to the fact most California cities—and especially most smaller cities—do not have any responsibility for a range of social welfare functions. To test this possibility, we re-ran the analysis looking at only the largest half of California cities. In these larger cities, most of whom do provide a range of redistributive functions, there is a significant link between voter participation and policy. As we found with the rest of the country, higher turnout means more redistributive spending.

The magnitude of the effects that we see in California is not quite as large as in the rest of the nation but it is still substantial. For the larger cities, a move from a city with turnout that is one standard deviation below the mean (29 percent) to a city that is one standard deviation above the mean (58 percent) is associated with a 33 percent increase in redistributive spending (from 11.8 percent to 15.7 percent of total spending). A similar increase in turnout for a typical city is associated with a 17 percent decrease in development spending and an 11 percent drop in allocational spending. This is not a massive transformation of spending priorities, but it is enough to have a real impact on many members of the poor population and many racial and ethnic minorities.

In addition to focusing on these three spending categories, we also looked at how turnout affected more fundamental fiscal decisions like tax and debt policy. Using the same empirical model, we found that as with the nation as a whole, increased turnout in California was associated with higher per capita taxes. When a larger and more diverse set of residents turns out to vote, cities in the state appear to respond by expanding costly

redistributive policies and by raising taxes to pay for those increased programs (analysis not shown).[28] There was, however, no clear link between
participation and per capita debt in California.

Finally, to see whether turnout effects in California depended to the
same extent on competitive elections as they do in the larger nation, we
added a measure of competition—the percentage of incumbents losing
reelection—and an interaction for turnout and turnover to the basic regression model.[29] As one would predict, the results suggest that turnout mat-
tered much more when competition was high. All else equal, when elections
are highly competitive and half of the incumbents lose, an increase in turnout from 29 to 58 percent of registered voters is associated with a doubling
of redistributive spending (from 9 to 19 percent of the budget). By contrast,
the same gain in turnout meant only a 17 percent increase in redistributive
spending in cities where all the council incumbents won reelection (analysis
not shown).

All told, voter turnout appears to play a strikingly similar role in California's cities in recent years to that it did across the nation two decades ago. In
both cases, higher voter turnout means policies that are more in line with the
preferences of minorities and the poor. There is every reason to believe that
if the poor and other disadvantaged groups voted more regularly, outcomes
would change and governments would serve their interests more closely.

Conclusion

The story presented here is fairly clear. Who votes seems substantially to affect how governments raise and spend their money. When fewer people vote
and turnout is more skewed by race, income, and other factors, governments appear to behave differently from the way they do when turnout is
higher and less skewed. Fewer voters mean less redistributive spending,
more allocational spending, lower taxes, and smaller government debt. This
suggests that when disadvantaged groups fail to vote, local officials are likely
to be unresponsive to their concerns. In an era of policy devolution, as more
and more policies are both initiated and implemented at the local level, this
is no small matter.

These findings represent an important addition to the existing body of
work on American democracy for three reasons. First, and most obviously,
they further corroborate the importance of turnout in American elections.

This kind of evidence is critical in light of the strong assertions of many scholars who continue to claim that "outcomes would not change if everyone voted" (Highton and Wolfinger 2001: 179). Second, they highlight differences between local and national politics and suggest that broad conclusions about the merits or shortcomings of American democracy based exclusively on assessments of either national politics or local politics are likely to be misleading. Third, these findings should help us to understand better where turnout matters. Turnout matters more when turnout is exceptionally low (more in local than in national elections), where disadvantaged, minority groups represent large shares of the electorate (more in local than in national elections), and where electoral competition is higher (more in some cities than in others). Turnout does not always matter, but if the right combination of circumstances is present, large segments of society can lose out when they don't vote.

What can we do to help increase the participation and influence of traditionally disadvantaged groups in urban elections? A range of potentially fruitful policy prescriptions already exists. For example, research has already shown that moving the dates of local elections to coincide with the dates of national elections can almost double local voter turnout (Hajnal and Lewis 2003; Hajnal 2010). Since many cities around the United States are already moving to concurrent elections as a cost saving measure, this is a solution that has the potential to be broadly enacted. Research has also revealed that personal contact with racial and ethnic minority residents can greatly increase turnout (Lee et al. 2008). And if the contact is by canvassers of the same race/ethnicity as the residents, it can have an even greater effect. Other solutions are more controversial. Advocates of greater voter participation among less advantaged segments of the population have also pushed for a streamlined citizenship process, proportional representation, cumulative voting, and universal registration (Shaw et al. 2000; Guinier 1992). Just how much of an impact each of these solutions can have remains an open question, but given the existing imbalances in American democracy, it is clear that some sort of reform is needed.

The second story that emerges out of this research relates to the question of who governs. Urbanists have long debated who or what it is that controls local government decision-making. The results presented here suggest that the decisions local governments make are more complex than at least some previous accounts have suggested. What local governments do is a function of a complex interplay of politics, economics, and institutions. Municipal decision-makers are businessmen reacting to economic constraints. They are politicians who listen to the views of the entire public. They are office seekers who respond to the preferences of active voters. And finally, they are rational actors constrained by the particular features of their local institutional structure. If we want to improve local policy outcomes or even if we just understand how certain outcomes are reached in our cities, we need to consider the interplay of all these factors.

References

Aghion, Phillippe, Alberto Alesina, and Francesco Trebbi. 2005. "Choosing Electoral Rules: Theory and Evidence from U.S. Cities." NBER Working Paper 1143. http://www.nber.org/papers/w11236.

Alozie, Nicholas O., and Catherine McNamara. 2008. "Anglo and Latino Differences in Willingness to Pay for Urban Public Services." *Social Science Quarterly* 89 (2): 406–27.

Bridges, Amy. 1997. *Morning Glories: Municipal Reform in the Southwest.* Princeton, N.J.: Princeton University Press.

Browning, Rufus R., Dale Rogers Marshall, and David H. Tabb. 1984. *Protest Is Not Enough.* Berkeley: University of California Press.

Bumiller, Elisabeth, and Adam Nagourney. 2002. "The 2002 Campaign: The Republicans: In Homestretch, Bush Makes Push for G.O.P. Gains." *New York Times*, October 23, A1.

Census Bureau. 1964–2003. *City Government Finances.* Washington, D.C.: Bureau of the Census.

———. 1994, 1990, 1986, 1978. *City and County Data Book.* Washington, D.C.: Bureau of the Census.

Citrin, Jack, Eric Schickler, and John Sides. 2003. "More Democracy or More Democrats? The Impact of Increased Turnout on Senate Elections." *American Journal of Political Science* 47 (1): 75–90.

Dahl, Robert A. 1961. *Who Governs? Democracy and Power in the American City.* New Haven, Conn.: Yale University Press.

Deleon, Richard. 1991. "The Progressive Urban Regime: Ethnic Coalitions in San Francisco." In *Racial and Ethnic Politics in California*, ed. Byron O. Jackson and Michael B. Peeston. Berkeley, Calif.: Institute for Governmental Studies. 157–91.

DeNardo, James. 1980. "Turnout and the Vote: The Joke's on the Democrats." *American Political Science Review* 74, 2: 406–20.

Ellcessor, Patrick, and Jan E. Leighley. 2001. "Voters, Non-Voters and Minority Representation." In *Representation of Minority Groups in the U.S.: Implications for the*

Twenty-First Century, ed. Charles E. Menifield. Lanham, Md.: Austin and Winfield.

Griffin, John, and Patrick Flavin. 2009. "Policy, Preferences, and Participation: Government's Impact on Democratic Citizenship." *Journal of Politics* 71 (2): 544–59.

Guinier, Lani. 1992. "Voting Rights and Democratic Theory: Where Do We Go From Here?" In *Controversies in Minority Voting: The Voting Rights Act in Perspective*, ed. Bernard Grofman and Chandler Davidson. Washington, D.C.: Brookings Institution. 283–91.

Hajnal, Zoltan L. 2010. *Uneven Democracy: Turnout, Race, and Representation in Local Politics*. Cambridge: Cambridge University Press.

Hajnal, Zoltan L., and Paul G. Lewis. 2003. "Municipal Institutions and Voter Turnout in Local Elections." *Urban Affairs Review* 38, 5: 645–68.

Hajnal, Zoltan L., Paul G. Lewis, and Hugh Louch. 2002. *Municipal Elections in California: Turnout, Timing, and Competition*. San Francisco: Public Policy Institute of California.

Highton, Ben, and R. E. Wolfinger. 2001. "The Political Implications of Higher Turnout." *British Journal of Political Science* 31 (1): 179–92.

Hill, Kim Quaile, and Jan E. Leighley. 1992. "The Policy Consequences of Class Bias in State Electorates." *American Journal of Political Science* 36 (2): 351–65.

Hill, Kim Quaile, Jan E. Leighley, and Angela Hinton-Anderson. 1995. "Lower-Class Mobilization and Policy Linkage in the U.S. States." *American Journal of Political Science* 39 (1): 75–86.

Jackson, Robert A., Robert D. Brown, and Gerald C. Wright. 1998. "Registration, Turnout, and the Electoral Representativeness of U.S. State Electorates." *American Politics Quarterly* 26 (3): 259–82.

Karnig, Albert K., and B. Oliver Walter. 1983. "Decline in Municipal Voter Turnout: A Function of Changing Structure." *American Politics Quarterly* 11 (4): 491–505.

Key, V. O. 1984. *Southern Politics in State and Nation*. Knoxville: University of Tennessee Press.

Kinder, Donald R., and Lynn Sanders. 1996. *Divided by Color: Racial Politics and Democratic Ideals*. Chicago: University of Chicago Press.

Lee, Taeku, Ricardo Ramirez, and Karthrik Ramakrishnan, eds. 2008. *Transforming Politics, Transforming America: The Political and Civic Incorporation of Immigrants in the United States*. Charlottesville: University of Virginia Press.

Leighley, Jan E. 2001. *Strength in Numbers? The Political Mobilization of Racial and Ethnic Minorities*. Princeton, N.J.: Princeton University Press.

Logan, John R., and Harvey L. Molotch. 1987. *Urban Fortunes: The Political Economy of Place*. Berkeley: University of California Press.

Lovrich, Nicholas. 1974. "Differing Priorities in an Urban Electorate: Service Priorities Among Anglo, Black, and Mexican-American Voters." *Social Science Quarterly* 55 (2): 704–17.

Martinez, Michael D. 1997. "Don't Tax You, Don't Tax Me, Tax the Fella Behind the Tree: Partisan and Turnout Effects on Tax Policy." *Social Science Quarterly* 78 (4): 895–906.

McDonald, Michael. 2008. *Voter Turnout 2008.* http://elections.gmu.edu/voter_turnout .htm.

Mladenka, Kenneth R. 1980. "The Urban Bureaucracy and the Chicago Political Machine: Who Gets What and the Limits of Political Control." *American Political Science Review* 74 (2): 991–98.

Nagel, Jack H., and John E. McNulty. 1996. "Partisan Effects of Voter Turnout in Senatorial and Gubernatorial Elections." *American Political Science Review* 90 (4): 780–93.

Orfield, Gary. 1974. "Federal Policy, Local Power, and Metropolitan Segregation." *Political Science Quarterly* 89 (2): 777–802.

Pacek, Alexander, and Benjamin Radcliff. 1995. "Turnout and the Vote for Left-of-Centre Parties: A Cross-National Analysis." *British Journal of Political Science* 25 (1) (January): 137–43.

Parker, Frank R. 1990. *Black Votes Count: Political Empowerment in Mississippi After 1965.* Chapel Hill: University of North Carolina Press.

Pelissero, John P. and Timothy B. Krebs. 2003. "City Councils." In *Cities, Politics, and Policy,* ed. John P. Pelissero. Washington, D.C.: Congressional Quarterly Press. 169–95.

———. 1997. "City Council Legislative Committees and Policy-Making in Large United States Cities." *American Journal of Political Science* 41: 499–518.

Peterson, Paul E. 1981. *City Limits.* Chicago: University of Chicago Press.

Peterson, Paul E., and Mark Rom. 1989. "American Federalism, Welfare Policy, and Residential Choices." *American Political Science Review* 83 (3): 711–28.

Piven, Frances Fox, and Richard A. Cloward. 1988. *Why Americans Don't Vote.* New York: Pantheon.

Radcliff, Benjamin, and Martin Saiz. 1995. "Race, Turnout, and Public Policy in the American States." *Political Research Quarterly* 48 (3): 775–94.

Rosenstone, Steven J., and John Mark Hansen. 1993. *Mobilization, Participation, and Democracy in America.* New York: Macmillan.

Saltzstein, Alan L. 1986. "Federal Grants and the City of Los Angeles." *Research in Urban Policy* 2 (A): 55–76.

Schattschneider, E. E. 1970. *The Semisovereign People: A Realist's View of Democracy in America.* New York: Harcourt Brace.

Schneider, Mark. 1989. "Intermunicipal Competition, Budget-Maximizing Bureaucrats, and the Level of Suburban Competition." *American Journal of Political Science* 33 (3): 612–28.

Sharp, Elaine B. 2002. "Culture, Institutions, and Urban Officials' Responses to Morality Issues." *Political Research Quarterly.* 861–83.

Shaw, Daron, Rodolfo O. de la Garza, and Jongho Lee. 2000. "Examining Latino Turnout in 1996: A Three-State, Validated Survey Approach." *American Journal of Political Science* 44, 2: 332–40.

Stein, Robert M. 1990. *Urban Alternatives: Public and Private Markets in the Provision of Local Services*. Pittsburgh: University of Pittsburgh Press.

Tingsten, Herbert. 1937. *Political Behavior: Studies in Election Statistics*. London: P.S. King.

Trounstine, Jessica L. 2008. *Political Monopolies in American Cities: The Rise and Fall of Bosses and Reformers*. Chicago: University of Chicago Press.

Tucker, Harvey, and Arnold Vedlitz. 1986. "Does Heavy Turnout Help Democrats in Presidential Elections?" *American Political Science Review* 80 (4): 1291–1304.

U.S. Advisory Commission on Intergovernmental Relations. 1993. "State Laws Governing Local Government Structure and Administration." Washington, D.C.

Verba, Sidney, Kay Lehman Schlozman, and Henry E. Brady. 1995. *Voice and Equality: Civic Voluntarism in American Politics*. Cambridge, Mass.: Harvard University Press.

Welch, Susan, Lee Sigelman, Timothy Bledsoe, and Michael Combs. 2001. *Race and Place: Race Relations in an American City*. Cambridge: Cambridge University Press.

Wolfinger, Raymond E., and Steven J. Rosenstone. 1980. *Who Votes?* New Haven, Conn.: Yale University Press.

CHAPTER 5

Fairness and Bias in Electoral Systems

Anthony McGann

As scientists and citizens, we would like to evaluate objectively the fairness and bias of electoral systems. However, this is claimed to be impossible by many political scientists, as well as by various practicing politicians and the U.S. Supreme Court. The argument commonly made is that there are multiple, competing conceptions of fairness; and that once you exclude the most egregious and obvious violations, you cannot talk about one electoral system being fairer or less biased than another, but only lay out the choices or tradeoffs between competing goals. The claim that there are many definitions of fairness then slides very easily into the conclusion that they are all equally deserving of consideration. I wish to reject this relativism. I wish to do this not because it is normatively enfeebling, but because it is logically flawed. It is, in fact, possible to evaluate fairness and bias in electoral systems objectively, at least if you define fairness in terms of *liberal equality*, that is, treating *each voter* equally. And once we do this, the existing empirical literature tells us all we need to know to draw conclusions.

In order to evaluate the fairness and bias of electoral systems, we need two things: a way of classifying electoral systems in terms of their mechanics, and a benchmark for evaluating fairness/bias. In terms of the first requirement, there is a well-developed literature classifying electoral systems that we can draw upon (see among others Rae 1967; Taagepera and Shugart 1989; Lijphart 1994; Katz 1997; Farrell 2001; Taagepera 2009). As Taagepera and Shugart (1989) argue, district magnitude (number of seats per electoral district) provides a first approximation for such a classification. This, of course, captures the distinction between single-member-district plurality election (district magnitude of one) and proportional representation (multi-member districts). Furthermore, many of the other relevant characteristics can be expressed in terms of the equivalent district magnitude required to produce the same outcome. For example, Taagepera and Shugart (1989) introduce the concept of effective district magnitude, which combines the effect of district magnitude and electoral thresholds. Likewise, Taagepera (2009) shows that mixed electoral systems and differences in electoral formulas can be accommodated by the same measure. Of course, all characteristics of electoral systems cannot be reduced to a single unidimensional measure, so I will make use of other features (such as whether the system is open or closed list, for example) as necessary.

The second thing we need is a benchmark against which to measure the bias of electoral systems. The principle of proportionality—seats awarded are proportional to votes—provides such a baseline. Not only is it mathematically simple, but it is logically implied by liberal political equality, as demonstrated formally by Hout and McGann (2009a, b). If seats are not allocated proportionally, then it *must* be the case that everyone is not being treated equally. This then poses the question of who is benefiting from this bias and who is losing. The main task of this paper is to classify and understand these various biases.

An obvious objection is that I have just *assumed* a normative preference for proportional representation. This is actually not the case. The principle of proportionality can be shown to be logically necessary if all individual voters are to be treated equally—that is, if the electoral system is to be unbiased. Therefore, deviations from proportionality imply bias, which it is then our task to explain. Furthermore, it is important to note that proportionality is a principle, not an election system—proportional representation (PR) electoral systems are designed to produce proportionality, but vary considerably in how far they achieve this goal, especially when they have low district magnitude. Likewise, single-member-district plurality systems may sometimes approximate proportionality. Indeed, if we have a single-member-district system, we are likely to be interested in what biases result from the way this system is implemented (for example, how the districts are drawn). Using proportionality as a benchmark for comparisons does not limit us to simplistic statement of the type "PR good, SMDP bad," but actually allows us to build a framework in which we can make nuanced comparisons of small differences in electoral institutions.

It is notable that the standard of treating all voters fairly is more demanding than that of treating all parties fairly. If we were only interested in treating parties equally, the quality of symmetry would suffice. Symmetry means that if two parties get the same number of votes, they get the same number of seats. If there are only two parties, this means that the one that get the most votes, gets the most seats. However, it does not violate symmetry if we give 80 percent of the seats to a party that wins 55 percent of the vote, provided we would give 80 percent of the seats to the other party if it won 55 percent of the votes. The concept of symmetry has proved useful in evaluating the fairness of electoral systems with regard to districting and gerrymandering (see Grofman and King 2007). Clearly, if a system violates symmetry, it is seriously biased. However, even if symmetry is satisfied, an electoral system can still treat different voters quite unequally. If we wish to guarantee that all voters are treated equally, we require proportionality.

There are many forms of electoral system bias, resulting from many different institutional mechanisms. The most obvious is the bias in favor of large parties (and in particular, the largest party) as opposed to small parties. This divides single-member-district plurality and PR systems, and thus has received a great deal of attention. However, other forms of bias are also important. For example, we can consider the degree to which there is a bias in favor of established parties against new competitors. It is notable that low-district-magnitude PR systems impose considerable barriers to entry, so this kind of bias is only eliminated by high-district-magnitude PR systems. There are a variety of ways in which particular types of voters are advantaged over others, even in systems where there is no explicit malapportionment (although this is surprisingly common). We will also consider a form of bias ("leveraging") that encourages fraud and vote buying. First, however, I will justify the use of proportionality as a baseline.

The Norm of Proportionality

In order to compare the behavior of electoral systems, we need a benchmark to compare them against. Following Taagepera (2009), we use proportionality as such a benchmark. There are two reasons for doing this. First, proportionality is mathematically the simplest way of translating votes into seats. Second, and more important, proportionality is logically related to political equality—that is to say, unbiasedness. If we treat all voters equally (that is, the electoral system is unbiased), then the electoral system must be proportional (McGann 2006; Hout and McGann 2009a, b). Therefore proportionality is a natural "zero point"—it indicates a lack of bias. When we observe a deviation from proportionality, this is evidence of bias, and we need to ask who benefits from it. As noted before, proportionality is a property of an electoral system (seats are proportional to votes), not an electoral system itself—PR electoral systems may satisfy proportionality to a greater or lesser degree.

The simplicity of the norm of proportionality can be seen from the following graphs derived from Taagepera and Shugart (1989). Proportionality just translates the number of votes a party or list of candidates receives into seats in a straightforward linear manner. (It should be noted that proportionality does not require that the alternatives are necessarily political parties. Some systems, such as that in the Netherlands, give parties very few privileges not accorded to nonparty citizen lists.) Of course, no electoral system satisfies pure proportionality, in that seats are not infinitely divisible. Thus there are always some threshold of representations and lists that receive too few votes to win any seats. However, once this threshold has been passed, the allocation can be proportional (second graph in Figure 5.1). With nonproportional systems, the effect of winning extra votes varies depending on the size of the party. For example, with the single-member-district plurality (first-past-the-post) system, winning extra votes has little effect until the party reaches the point where it becomes the largest single party, but then the seats-votes response becomes extremely strong. Once a party has a considerable majority of seats, the response flattens again. Imperfectly proportional systems (such as PR with low district magnitude) typically work in a similar but less pronounced way.

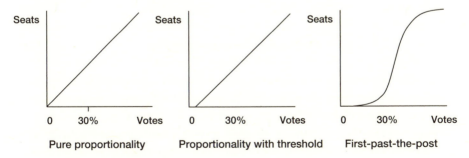

Figure 5.1. Votes-seats profiles.

A completely proportional system is also simple in that every vote, no matter where it is cast, has the same effect. However, with a district-based system, where votes are cast matters. As a result, the votes-seats profile does not completely capture the subtlety of these systems. A party whose support is regionally concentrated will often receive more seats than a party whose support is evenly distributed throughout the country. There may well be other biases, for example, features (discussed below) that favor certain regions over others.

With respect to the logical connection between unbiasedness and proportionality, Hout and McGann (2009a, b) show that if we treat all voters equally, then the electoral system must produce a result essentially identical to that produced by proportionality. The details of the argument are beyond the scope of this chapter, but it is possible to give the intuition. If we treat all voters equally, then the names of the voters should not matter. This implies the quality of *anonymity*—rearranging the voters' identities should not change the result. Neither should the names of the candidates (or parties or lists or slates) matter. This implies the quality of *neutrality*—swapping the names of the candidates or parties does not change the result. Finally we need the quality of non-negative responsiveness—if a party or list wins extra votes it does not lose votes as a result. This is a commonsense technical desideratum. If we combine these three axioms, then the resulting electoral system must produce a coalition structure identical to that produced under pure proportionality. That is to say, the result of the election must produce exactly the same possible governing coalitions as proportionality.

There is, of course, considerable literature arguing about the justice and fairness of various electoral systems. Nearly all these arguments (including those in favor of PR) are based on fairness to groups, be it political parties, their supporters, or geographical constituencies. Given that society can be divided into groups in many different ways, it is not surprising that we can generate many different arguments in favor of the fairness of this or that electoral system. However, if we insist on a liberal conception of equality, based on the equal treatment of individual voters, this relativism disappears. Although it has often been assumed that PR requires justification in terms of fairness to groups, or that it is a separate value in itself, it turns out to be a logical requirement of a liberal conception of equality.[1]

Of course, it can be asked why we should prefer liberal or individual equality over some group-based conception. There are two reasons. First, we may value *liberal* political equality for philosophical reasons. That is, we may view society as being made up of individuals, and consider that equality among these individuals is what matters. However, even if we do not accept this doctrinal liberalism, there is another reason to accept liberal political equality: it provides a standard to adjudicate between different group-based conceptions of equality. One can certainly argue for the fair treatment of group identities. The problem is that someone else may divide society into groups in a different way. Who gets to decide which group identities are salient? If we argue that the voters should decide (and what else can we do that would democratically acceptable?), we are back to liberal political equality—we have to treat individual voters equally so that they can decide which group identities *they* consider relevant (see Hout and McGann 2009b for an extended version of this argument).

One notable recent example of the argument that the case for proportionality rests on group rights occurs in the U.S. Supreme Court case *Vieth v. Jubelirer*.[2] Justice Scalia, joined by Chief Justice Rehnquist and Justices O'Connor and Thomas, argued that claims of partisan gerrymandering cannot be judicially determined because there is no manageable standard for judging such gerrymandering.[3] They rejected the standard that a majority of voters should be able to elect a majority of representatives on the ground that this assumes a right to proportional representation, which the Constitution does not provide. It is argued that the Constitution only guarantees equal protection to individuals, not to social groups. The assumption here is that a right to proportional representation cannot be derived from equal protection of individuals, but requires an argument in terms of group rights. As explained above, this assumption is incorrect (see McGann 2012 for a extended discussion of *Vieth v. Jubelirer* in terms of social choice theory).

Thus we have a benchmark against which to evaluate the bias of electoral systems. If the results deviate from proportionality, then there is some bias. The task then is to identify who benefits from it and to understand the mechanism that produced it. The implicit use of the norm of proportionality by the plaintiffs in *Vieth v. Jubelirer* in their attempts to convince the Supreme Court that there is a viable standard for fair electoral districting in fact illustrates the usefulness of this approach applied even to non-PR systems, notwithstanding the plaintiffs' failure to convince the Court that their standard could be grounded in individual rights. In the next section we turn to the task of classifying and explaining the most common forms of bias found in electoral systems.

Comparing the Performance of Electoral Systems

We now turn to the various form of bias produced by electoral systems. Essentially this amounts to analyzing deviations from proportionality and whom they benefit. First we will consider how electoral systems discriminate between parties of differing sizes. Next we will deal with the barriers to entry they impose on new parties. Then we will consider how they discriminate between different voters. Finally, we will consider the concept of *leveraging*, or how electoral systems may create pivotal groups of voters who have a disproportionate impact on the outcome. The latter concept is important in understanding how vulnerable a system is to corruption, fraud, and vote-buying.

Bias in Favor of Large Parties

We start with bias towards large parties, because this to a considerable degree determines the character of electoral politics. If there is a bias towards large parties, it is more likely that politics will be dominated by a small number of large parties for purely mechanical reasons (Duverger 1954). Furthermore, the parties and voters may react to this, causing second-order "psychological" effects. Voters may choose not to vote for the disadvantaged small parties, and these parties may even choose not to compete. This in turn increases that probability that one party will have a legislative majority as opposed to having to build a governing coalition. Even if there is no legislative majority, a bias toward large parties may produce a situation where one party is in a dominant position, requiring only a small, junior coalition partner, as opposed to having to engage in coalition bargaining among equals.

It is widely believed that single-member-district elections discriminate strongly in favor of the largest party and against smaller parties (often giving them no representation at all), while PR treats all parties proportionally. However, PR systems vary considerably in their proportionality, and many existing PR systems are not that proportional at all. PR systems only produce approximately proportional results as district magnitude becomes large. A PR system with a low district magnitude will still discriminate strongly in favor of larger parties, albeit less so than a single-member-district system. Of course other factors affect this relationship. Second-tier compensation seats can produce proportionality in spite of low district magnitude in the lower tier. Entry thresholds have the opposite effect, producing a step-shaped vote-seats function, where a party wins no seat until it has a certain required share of the vote. Taagepera and Shugart (1989) propose the concept of *effective district magnitude*, which takes into account the combined effect of district magnitude, second-tier compensation seats, and entry thresholds—simplifying, Effective DM = min (DM, 50/Threshold).

Low-district-magnitude PR systems favor the larger parties. However, exactly which party benefits most depends on whether the district magnitude is odd or even. If the district magnitude is odd, then the main beneficiary will be the largest party. Thus in Greece, where district magnitude is 3, the system gives disproportionate representation to the largest party and often produces a legislative majority from a mere plurality of the vote. Thus the system behaves in a manner very similar to a SMD system. However, if the district magnitude is small and even (DM = 2 or 4), then the bias will be in favor of the second-largest party. This is because the two main parties will draw in most districts even though one party may have a considerable advantage. A notable case of this is Chile, where district magnitude is two. This effectively guarantees the opposition (the post-Pinochet right) almost 50 percent of the seats provided it wins 33 percent of the vote. There are also many countries where district magnitude varies among districts. Low district magnitude provides an opportunity for gerrymandering, where a party seeks to have odd numbered districts where it is strong, and even-numbered districts where it is weak (see Farrell 2001 for an example of this in the Republic of Ireland).

All this can be illustrated graphically with the votes-seats functions in Figure 5.2. The 45-degree dotted line represents proportionality. Under PR with medium district magnitude (between 5 and 15 with no second-tier compensation), we see the pattern in the first panel. Very small parties receive nothing, and small parties are underrepresented until they reach a certain threshold. The higher the district magnitude, the lower the threshold. After that the system behaves proportionally. With a district magnitude of 3, responsiveness varies considerably, depending on the size of the party. This is due to the fact that within any district a party is guaranteed to win a

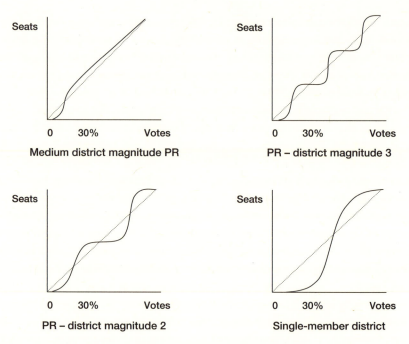

Figure 5.2. Votes-seats functions for various electoral systems.

seat with 25 percent of the district vote, but is not guaranteed another seat until it wins 50 percent. For example, in Greece the largest single party usually wins a majority even though it wins only a little over 40 percent of the vote. In this respect the system functions like a single-member-district system, in that a small vote change around 40 percent can have very large consequences in terms of seats. However, landslide victories that often occur in SMDP countries like the UK are unlikely in Greece. This is because it is extremely difficult to win two seats a district over the entire country. A similar effect occurs in two-member-district PR, but with very different consequences. If a party or coalition can win 33 percent of the vote in a district it is guaranteed one of the seats; but to be guaranteed two it would need 66 percent. Thus in Chile, the two coalitions receive almost equal representation, even though they are quite different in vote share.

Different PR formulae also have effects on the bias towards large parties. The Sainte-Laguë divisor and Hare quota come closest to proportionality, while the D'Hondt divisor and the Droop and Imperiali quotas advantage larger parties. These effects can be considerable when district magnitude is small, but become modest as district magnitude becomes large (all the commonly used formulas approach proportionality as district magnitude becomes large and the remainders become comparatively small). Taagepera (2009) provides a method to combine district magnitude and the effect of the distribution formula.

Mixed electoral systems (where some seats are allocated by PR and some by single-member-district plurality elections) can be accommodated in this framework. If the system is compensatory (if a party wins many district seats, it receives fewer PR seats to restore proportionality), then its effective district magnitude is determined by the PR part of the election. Thus Germany's effective district magnitude is 10, as a result of the 5 percent electoral threshold. However, if the system is noncompensatory (the PR and plurality parts of the election are separate), then the effective district magnitude is simply the average district magnitude. Thus the effective district magnitude of the current Italian election system is about 1.3 (600 seats/475 districts). Thus there is a large-party bias, as we would expect with a small effective district magnitude. However, there are more parties than we would expect. This has been explained by the fact that small parties can win some seats in the PR elections, and then negotiate alliances with larger parties to field joint candidates in district elections (see Sartori 1997).

Now let us consider the effect of district magnitude and large party bias on the party system. Taagepera (2009) produces some remarkably simple theoretical relationships for the effect of district magnitude and assembly size on party system characteristics. These estimates are derived by simply taking the geometric mean or the highest and lowest theoretically possible value of each variable, but fit the empirical data remarkably well. The main results are

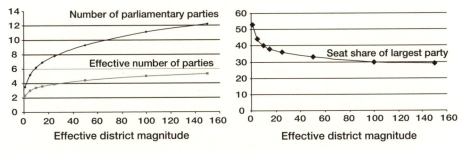

Figure 5.3. Effective district magnitude and the party system.

Number of parties in legislature $= (ms)^{1/4}$,

Effective number of parties[4] $= (ms)^{1/6}$,

Seat share of largest party $= (ms)^{-1/8}$,

where m is district magnitude and s is the size of the assembly.

The implications of these results become apparent when we graph them against district magnitude (Figure 5.3). It is clear that the relationships are nonlinear, and that there are "diminishing returns" to district magnitude. That is, increasing district magnitude increases the number of parties in parliament and the effective number of parliamentary parties, and decreases the seat share of the largest party; however, going from a medium district magnitude to a high district magnitude does not change these values very much. For example, Germany, with an effective district magnitude of 10, has 5 parliamentary parties, while the Netherlands, with an effective district magnitude of 150, still has only 9.

We can draw two complementary conclusions from this. We can get many of the distinctive characteristics of PR without going beyond moderate district magnitude. For example, if district magnitude is above 5, it is extremely unlikely that one party will win a majority of the seats, and coalition government will be the norm. Furthermore, those parties that do win seats will do so almost proportionally to their vote, barring other distortions (see below). By the same token, going from moderate-district magnitude PR to large-district or national PR will not produce drastic changes in the party system. We would not expect to see (and indeed do not see empirically) the instability predicted by critics of "extreme" PR. As district magnitude becomes very large, the number of parties increases slowly and the effective number of parties even more slowly. Even as we move toward national PR, we would still expect the largest party to win around 30 percent of the vote, which is indeed what we see in the Netherlands, the country with the highest effective magnitude in the world.

Carey and Hix (2011) note the nonlinear relationship between district magnitude and party system characteristics, but draw conclusions from it that I do not think can be sustained. They argue that a low-district-magnitude PR is optimal because it offers the best tradeoff between representation (which is improved by high district magnitudes) and accountability (which is best at lower district magnitudes). There are several problems with this. First, they do not show that there is in fact a tradeoff between representation and accountability. Rather they simply assert this, and equate party-system fragmentation (the effective number of parties) with reduced accountability.

Second, even if we accept that party system fragmentation can be interpreted as lack of accountability, going from low-district-magnitude to high-district-magnitude PR does not increase this fragmentation very quickly. In fact, the effective number of parties seems to reach an asymptote beyond which it does not go, no matter how high the district magnitude. Of course, Carey and Hix argue that the "benefits" of PR—such as more accurate representation—display the same asymptotic behavior, and thus they argue there is little to gain from high district magnitudes. However, they ignore one vital characteristic that is related to district magnitude in an (inverse) linear manner—the ease with which new parties can enter. Large district magnitudes make it far easier for new parties to challenge existing parties than low district magnitudes do. If we take this into account, the electoral "sweet spot" may well be a corner solution—high-district magnitude-PR. We turn to bias in favor of established parties in the next section.

Bias in Favor of Established Versus New Parties

While many characteristics of party competition do not change much when we go from moderate district magnitude to national PR, this is not the case for the entry threshold for new parties to win representation. Whereas the number of parliamentary parties, the effective number of parties, and the size of the largest party are all functions of a fractional power of district magnitude, the entry threshold depends on district magnitude directly. According to Taagepera and Shugart (1989), the effective entry threshold will equals 50 percent/(district magnitude), or the legal entry threshold (whichever is higher). Thus there is a linear relationship between district magnitude and entry threshold. Thus we would not expect going from moderate to national PR to make all that much difference in the number of parliamentary parties; however, it will make a dramatic difference in how easy it is for a new challenger party to enter the legislature.

Consider the cases of Germany and the Netherlands. Germany has an effective district magnitude of 10, while for the Netherlands it is 150. As expected, the Netherlands has more parliamentary parties, but not dramatically more (currently 9 parties as opposed to 5). However, the effective entry threshold is far lower in the Netherlands—0.66 percent as opposed to 5 percent in Germany. As a result it is very easy to form a new insurgent party in the Netherlands, but very difficult in Germany. Indeed, since the introduction of the 5 percent threshold in 1953, only two new parties have entered the Bundestag—the Greens in the 1980s and the post-communist PDS after re-unification (the PDS has sometimes failed to make the 5 percent threshold but has been granted representation on grounds of regional strength). In the Netherlands, however, entry by new parties is a regular occurrence. For ex-ample, at the end of the 1960s there were a large number of new radical par-ties, in 1994 there were two pensioners' lists that won representation, and in 2002 the Lijst Pim Fortuyn and Socialist Parties emerged. Many of the new entries do not last very long before their issues are taken up by mainstream parties, or they consolidate into larger groupings, which explains why all this entry does not lead to a very large number of parliamentary parties.

Nevertheless, the ease of entry is important for a number of reasons. First, there is a fundamental matter of democratic choice. As stated above, liberal political equality implies proportionality, in that the only way to treat all vot-ers equally is to distribute seats proportionally. However, this equality is sub-stantively empty if the choice of options given to voters is limited. All voters may be treated equally, but if they are forced to choose between candidates they find equally undesirable, who cares? Higher district magnitude will tend to increase the number of viable parties and thus may increase voter choice. However, the only way to guarantee that this choice is substantively meaningful is to make it realistically possible for dissatisfied voters to create their own parties or electoral lists. Large district magnitude and the very low entry threshold it produces make it possible for a roomful of dissatisfied people to create their own electoral list and have a realistic chance of win-ning parliamentary representation. This has often happened in the Nether-lands, and it is worth noting that many of the new entrants have been ad hoc citizen lists without (at least to begin with) any organized political party.

The ability of new parties to enter the legislature is also extremely im-portant in terms of accountability. If it is very difficult for new competitors to enter the legislature, then the existing parties form a cartel with monop-oly power, and it will be very difficult to hold them accountable collectively, especially on issues where they take similar positions. For example, if you were a British voter in 2005 trying to hold the Labour government to ac-count for its part in the Iraq war, you had a problem. The only viable alterna-tive governing party was the Conservative Party, which was, if anything, more even more pro-war than Labour. Some voters did switch to the Liberal Democrats (who opposed the war), but, given the first-past-the-post elec-toral system, this resulted in electoral gains for the Conservatives (the most pro-war party) not the Liberal Democrats! A PR system makes this effect less likely, in that there are likely to be more parties (for example, in 2003 in Germany SPD voters switched to the Greens, which sent a clear message to the SPD Chancellor about public opinion concerning the Iraq war). However, the only way to make completely sure that the entire political class cannot keep an issue off the political agenda is to make it possible for people who care about that issue to form a viable party and enter the legislature.

There are also times when it is important to be able to hold the entire political class to account collectively. This requires that the established parties be subject to competition from the outside, and not just from each other. For example, the standard justification given for the Westminster political system is that it is possible to hold the governing party accountable by replacing it with the opposition. However, this does not help in cases where the entire political establishment—both government and opposition—are guilty of serious abuses. For example, in 2009 widespread abuse of legislative expense accounts by both government and opposition legislators in the UK came to light. Unfortunately the only way voters could sanction the (apparently corrupt) governing party was to vote for the (apparently equally corrupt) opposition. More floridly, to sanction the party that uses public money to speculate in London property, you have to vote for the party that uses government money to clean the moats on their country estates! With a low entry threshold, however, it is possible for voters to hold all established parties to account. For example, in the Netherlands in 1994 and in 2002, all the established parties lost votes, as new parties entered the legislature. The established parties do not have monopoly power and are held in check by the possibility of competition from new parties and citizen lists.

Finally, a high threshold of entry may freeze in old conflicts or division in politics, while a low threshold may allow for the entry of new parties and allow the emergence of new political dimensions. This point is particularly relevant for new democracies, and especially those with a history of ethnic division. Suppose that we have a country where the main parties all have an ethnic identity. An electoral system that makes entry by new parties difficult will preserve this status quo and make it difficult for new cross-ethnic parties to emerge. This may be desirable for the leader of the existing (ethnic-based) parties, but is unlikely to be desirable for society as a whole.

There are a couple of arguments other than accountability made for having a high threshold of entry. It has sometimes been argued that a high threshold is justified by the need to prevent extremist parties from getting representation.

This argument is, of course, illiberal, in that it seeks to exclude people from being represented based on their opinions. It is also antidemocratic, in that it argues that electoral engineers, and not voters, should decide what kind of opinions get to be represented. Finally, even if the goal is reduce the influence of extremists, denying them representation may well be counterproductive. When extremist voters are not represented, they do not simply go away. In France, for example, the Front National has had considerable influence on policy, even though the electoral system largely denies them national representation (see Mayer 1998). Because these voters cannot elect extremist representatives, the mainstream parties end up crafting policies to appeal to them. Right-wing extremist parties in Europe seem to have had far more influence through these indirect effects than through direct representation (see Minkenberg 2001). It is also sometimes claimed that a low threshold of entry leads to there being many small parties that have disproportionate influence. This argument has been debunked. Where entry is easy, small parties will not have much influence, because there will be many of them, and it will be easy for large parties to play them off against one another (McGann, Ensch, and Moran 2009; Nagel 2012). This applies particularly to Israel, frequently claimed to be a case where small parties are disproportionately powerful.

Thus, I would reject Carey and Hix's (2011) assertion that high-district-magnitude PR reduces accountability. Low district magnitude makes it difficult for new parties and citizen lists to win representation. It thus protects existing parties and gives then an oligopolistic position. To describe protecting the oligopolistic position of existing parties as increasing accountability seems to me a curious use of the English language. Of course, low-district-magnitude PR is very convenient for medium-sized parties that manage to cross the threshold of representation—they get the representation that plurality elections would deny them, without having to worry about new competitors. For them it may indeed be a "sweet spot." However, it is large-district-magnitude PR systems that allow equal treatment of new and established parties and thus allow voters to hold *all* parties to account by creating their own alternatives.

Bias in Favor of Some Voters over Others

There are a variety of ways in which electoral systems can favor some voters and regions over others. First, there is malapportionment, where districts are not equally sized and the number of representatives per voter varies. As

Samuels and Snyder (2001) report, severe malapportionment is present in many systems, particularly in Latin America and Africa. It is most pronounced in second chambers. For example, the U.S. Senate is the fifth most malapportioned chamber in the world, after the second chambers of Argentina, Brazil, Bolivia, and the Dominican Republic. This is often due to the fact that the second chamber is elected on the basis of subnational units of government. Unfortunately, the principles of equal representation for individuals and equal representation for territories are logically incompatible—give a sparsely populated territory equal representation with a populous one, and you have given some individuals more representation than others (see McLean 1991: 193–94). The usual justification that one chamber represents the interests of individual citizens and the other represents the interests of subnational territories fails, because legislatures do not just "represent" interests, but also have to reach binding decisions. Individuals are not equally represented unless they are equally represented in the whole process, not just in one chamber.

Second, there is gerrymandering, or the deliberate drawing of boundaries to engineer particular results. This can be done either to maximize the seat share of one party, in which case the boundary drawer will try to draw the boundaries to give that party many close victories in order to use their votes most efficiently; or it can be done to ensure that incumbents in all parties have safe margins of victory, in which case boundaries are drawn to make all seats safe. There is a tradeoff between these two goals—maximizing a party's seat share can produce many close races that will leave incumbents exposed if the party loses support. Gerrymandering is most notable in single-member district systems. The United States is particularly notable, in that state legislatures, rather than independent commissions, typically draw national legislative boundaries, and this has produced some incredibly shaped districts. However, gerrymandering is possible in any system with districts. For example, Farrell (2001) reports that in the Republic of Ireland governments have attempted to use the differing size of districts to engineer results, as explained in the previous section.

Even without malapportionment or deliberate gerrymandering, differences in district magnitude within a country can create a powerful bias (Monroe and Rose 2002). Typically this bias favors rural voters (where district magnitude is small) over urban voters. For example, in Spain Madrid has a magnitude of 44, while some rural districts are of magnitude 3. In such a district a party that wins 50 percent of the vote is guaranteed to win two seats out of three, while in Madrid there is proportionality. Monroe and Rose find that this effect is very powerful in many countries, including Spain, Argentina, Switzerland, Portugal, Ireland, and Belgium.

Districts (and especially districts with small magnitude) discriminate in favor of some voters over others in another way. Unless public opinion is evenly distributed throughout a country, there will be a tendency for some districts to be safe and other districts to be competitive. In the competitive districts, a small number of voters can change the result, whereas in the safe districts they cannot. In technical language, districts violate anonymity— voters are not treated equally, because if you swapped a group of voters in one place with a group of voters in another, it would change the result. This would be less of a problem if all districts had a roughly equal chance of being competitive in any given election. This, however, is clearly not the case—in the next U.S. presidential election we have a very good idea which states will be close, just as in the next British general election we have a good idea which seats will be safe. Furthermore, politicians know this and adjust their strategies accordingly. Thus campaign resources (and perhaps even government resources) are directed to the jurisdictions that matter, and away from those that do not.

District-based systems also tend to discriminate in favor of voters that are optimally concentrated against those that are dispersed. This is because a group that is a small minority nationally may, if it is concentrated, be a local majority or at least a large local minority. Thus it may be able to elect a representative in a single-member district or low-magnitude PR system. A small group that is dispersed evenly across the country will nowhere be a local majority or large minority, and thus will not do as well under a small-district-magnitude system. Of course, in a national PR system whether a group is geographically concentrated or not does not matter. It is not obvious whether two-tier systems with low-district-magnitude lower tiers and national compensation seats behave like district systems or national PR systems in this regard.[5]

Leveraging

Finally, we will consider the concept of *leveraging*. In a high-district-magnitude PR system, any vote has the same effect as any other vote. In a single-member-district system, however, some votes are more important than others. A large number of votes in a safe seat has no effect on the out-come, while a few votes in a marginal district may be extremely valuable. Similarly, in an open-list PR system (Italian-style, simultaneous primary) a small number of preference votes may be enough to leverage all the votes cast for the party for one candidate.

Leveraging is important in that it presents a vulnerability to corruption, fraud, and vote-buying. Generally speaking, these activities are expensive, and it is not profitable to try to buy the entire electorate. This is why parties compete in terms of public goods and public policy. However, if a party or candidate is able to pinpoint certain voters who are pivotal, the calculus changes, and buying their votes may be very worthwhile. This explains Carey and Shugart's (1995) finding that higher district magnitude reduces corruption and particularism in closed-list systems, but increases it in open-list systems. In a closed-list system with high district magnitude, no voters are particularly pivotal from the point of view of the parties, and there is no intraparty competition on Election Day. However, with open-list PR, the higher the district magnitude, the more intraparty competition. Larger dis-trict magnitude means that the number of preference votes a candidate needs is reduced, and the greater the incentive (and possibility) to buy these votes.

The concept of leveraging distinguishes between different PR systems that allow voters to indicate preferences for candidates. Normally a distinc-tion is made between closed-list PR systems, where voters vote for the party and the party list determines which candidates are elected, and open-list systems, where the voter is able to indicate a preference for a specific candi-date as well as a party. However, finer distinctions are required. It is neces-sary to distinguish between Dutch-style open list (sometimes unfortunately referred to as semi-open list) and Italian-style open list. In Dutch-style open list, voters vote for candidates. If the candidate the voter chooses does not get elected, that candidate's votes are redistributed to the party list. In the Italian-style open list (in use until 1994), voters vote for a party and a candi-date. The party's share of the vote determines the number of seats allocated to the party. However, who fill these seats is determined by which of the party's candidates receive the most votes. This amounts to a simultaneous primary by plurality voting (actually single-non-transferable vote, as there are multiple positions to be filled), with all the biases this entails.

Systems such as Dutch-style open list and single transferable vote allow voting for a candidate rather than a party, but do not allow a voter to leverage other people's votes. Under these systems I know where my vote goes—it goes to the candidate I voted for, and if that one is not elected it goes to my next choice (STV) or to the list (Dutch-style open list).[6] However, in the case of Italian-style open-list PR, my vote may leverage the votes of other people who voted for the same party. If I vote for candidate A, I do not know which candidate my vote will be used to support. My vote does not necessarily go to the candidate I voted for; rather, it goes to the candidate who *happens* to be most popular among those in the party that the candidate I voted for *happened* to belong to. In the case of Brazil, this candidate may not even be in same party as the candidate I voted for, but may be in another party that my candidate's party has an agreement with! I would suggest that this is extremely problematic from the point of view of democratic choice—far more problematic than being asked to choose a closed list. We should certainly reject the simplistic conclusion that open-list systems are necessarily more democratic than closed-list systems because they offer voters more choice. The details of how the open-list operates matter, as does the ease with which voters can create new lists in closed-list systems.

Leveraging produces an interesting dilemma in countries that lack a reliable central system of electoral administration and where the possibility of fraud varies by region. A national electoral system with large districts reduces leveraging and thus the incentive for fraud, vote-buying, and intimidation. A vote anywhere in the country counts the same, and therefore no votes are especially worth buying. However, a regional system may serve to isolate the effects of fraud within one region. Suppose that in one region with 25 percent of the population, ballot stuffing is easy. With a national system, this could infect the entire national result, whereas with a regional system there are limits to how many seats can be stolen.

Indirect Effects

In addition to their intrinsic fairness, there is a considerable literature on the effect of electoral institutions on broader political outcomes, especially political economy and governance. Reaching firm conclusions on these issues, however, is difficult for two reasons. First, the effect of electoral institutions will depend on the broader institutional context. For example, Rose-Ackerman and Kunicova (2005) consider the effect of electoral systems on corruption. However, it turns out that PR combined with parliamentary government is associated with extremely low corruption, while PR presidential systems may be extremely corrupt. (This may have something to do with the fact that the PR parliamentary democracies are mostly established northern European democracies, while PR presidential regimes are mainly found in recently democratized countries in Latin America and central Asia.) Second, there are a fairly small number of cases and severe multicollinearity. For example, the PR parliamentary democracies are mostly small, open economies with a history of corporatism, and are mostly European. Separating out what causes what is extremely difficult.

A large number of relationships between electoral systems and outcomes that are commonly stated in both the political science literature and ordinary political discourse turn out to be unsupported by the evidence. For example, it is commonly argued that PR provides more representation, while a winner-take-all system provides more "stability," "accountability," "decisiveness," and so on. There is very little evidence that any of this is so, although often it is a matter of how you define terms like stability (see Farrell 2001; Lijphart 1999; McGann 2006). Neither is there any evidence that electoral systems affect economic growth or inflation. The argument that PR leads to disproportionate influence by small parties has also been discredited (McGann, Ensch, and Moran 2009).

There is, however, robust evidence that PR is associated with certain outcomes. Notably, countries with PR appear to be more egalitarian, more redistributive and have larger welfare states (Lijphart 1999; Crepaz 2001; Iversen and Soskice 2006). Of course, this does not demonstrate the PR *causes* these outcomes. PR also appears to be associated with higher electoral turnout and female parliamentary representation. Lijphart (1999) sums this up by claiming that PR, as one component of "consensus democracy," leads to "kinder, gentler democracies," although I would note that in recent years, PR democracies have been extremely effective in reducing welfare-state spending (McGann and Latner 2006, 2013).

Conclusion

When we attempt systematically to address questions of fairness and bias in electoral systems, the first obvious question is, "bias compared to what?" Fortunately we have an obvious standard for unbiasedness: a situation where all *individual voters* are treated equally. However, it can be shown that individual political equality logically implies the property of proportionality—seats allocated to a party or slate are proportional to its vote share. Therefore we can use deviation from proportionality as an indicator of bias. (Note that this does not require an additional normative assumption that proportionality or proportional-representation elections are intrinsically fair, unbiased, or just; the value of proportionality is logically implied by treating individual voters equally.) We can use this standard to evaluate the bias of various electoral mechanisms that claim to provide "proportional representation." We can also use it as a standard to compare the bias of different districting schemes for plurality elections.

Given the standard of political equality/proportionality, we can go through the various deviations from proportionality, what mechanism has produced this bias, and who benefits from it. It is well known that single-member-district systems (and low-district-magnitude systems in general) have a bias toward large parties, and in particular toward the largest party (provided the district magnitude is odd). However, this bias toward certain parties is possible only because these electoral systems are biased toward certain voters and against others. Some voters live in marginal districts where their votes have impact, while others are packed into safe seats where their votes are essentially irrelevant. Members of geographically concentrated groups get representation, while members of dispersed groups do not. A great deal of the literature has focused on fairness to political parties. What is not always recognized is that there is a direct logical link between this and the equal treatment of voters.

A form of bias that deserves more attention is the bias in favor of existing parties and against new parties. Some electoral systems limit the choice of parties voters have (and the voters' ability to create new parties) far more than others. This is the quality which really distinguishes high-district-magnitude PR (which is quite rare) from the far more common low-and medium-magnitude PR. Whereas going from moderate to high district magnitude leads only to moderate changes in the number of parties and the size of the largest party, it makes it far easier for new parties (or ad hoc citizen lists) to enter parliament. This is crucial from a democratic point of view. If citizens are dissatisfied with the existing parties, they can easily form their own, and have a realistic chance of winning representation. The existing parties do not have the monopoly power that they would have in a system with higher barriers to entry. It also allows the political establishment to be held accountable collectively—if established parties persist (as they do in countries with national PR, in spite of the challenges), they need to address the concerns of the emerging parties. Of course, this logic is unlikely to be very popular among the political establishment and established parties of many countries, which may explain why national PR is very rare.

The "small print" of PR systems also makes a difference. One notable example is where electoral districts are of different sizes, which is actually very common. We know that small-district-magnitude PR can lead to outcomes very much like those of plurality elections (where district magnitude is odd, as in Greece), or virtually guarantee a dead heat (where magnitude is even, as in Chile). However, if district magnitude varies across the country, this gives disproportionate influence to districts that are small and odd. Given that these are disproportionately rural, this creates a form of backdoor malapportionment. As a result of this effect, it seems that the Spanish electoral system produces results much like a plurality system (single-party government or, more often, a large plurality party governing with a few regional parties), despite an average district magnitude of 7. Varying district magnitude actually produces a strong bias in many countries, including some that have been pointed to as exemplary cases of PR, such as Belgium and Switzerland.

It is also important to consider the concept of "leveraging"—the fact that winning a small number of votes in the right place can effectively capture or negate a far larger number of votes. This creates an incentive for fraud, vote buying, and turnout suppression. District systems facilitate leveraging, but so do some open-list PR systems. Here the conventional distinction between open-list and closed-list PR is inadequate. Indeed, Italian-style open list (where preference votes leverage party votes) should probably be considered a completely different system from other forms of PR such as closed-list, Dutch-style open-list, and single transferable vote.

Of course, unbiasedness and fairness are not the only qualities that we care about when considering election systems. There are many other qualities—efficiency, accountability, and governability, to name a few. There may be a tradeoff between these values and fairness—*or there may not*. Too often it is simply assumed that there must a tradeoff between fairness and these other values. In particular, the cliché that PR provides greater fairness, but single-member-district elections provide more accountability, is repeated in the literature with very little scrutiny. While PR and higher district magnitudes certainly produce a few more parties and coalition governments, it is far from obvious that this produces less accountability. Indeed to argue that a system that makes existing parties effective duopolists or oligopolists provides more accountability than one in which new parties can freely enter, seems to me downright perverse. There may turn out to be a tradeoff between fairness in electoral systems and other values such as accountability, but this needs to be proved, not assumed.

References

Carey, John M., and Simon Hix. 2011. "The Electoral Sweet Spot: Low-Magnitude Proportional Electoral Systems." *American Journal of Political Science* 55 (2): 383–97.

Carey, John, and Matthew Shugart. 1995. "Incentives to Cultivate a Personal Vote: A Rank Ordering of Electoral Formulas." *Electoral Studies* 14 (4): 417–39.

Crepaz, Markus. 2001. "Veto Players, Globalization and the Redistributive Capacity of the State: A Panel Study of 15 OCED Countries." *Journal of Public Policy* 21 (1): 1–22.

Duverger, Maurice. 1954. *Political Parties: Their Organization and Activity in the Modern State.* New York: Methuen.

Farrell, David. 2001. *Electoral Systems: A Comparative Introduction.* Basingstoke: Palgrave.

Grofman, Bernard, and Gary King. 2007. "The Future of Partisan Symmetry as a Judicial Test for Partisan Gerrymandering After *Lulac v. Perry.*" *Election Law Journal* 6 (1): 2–35.

Hout, Eliora van der, and Anthony J. McGann. 2009a. "Liberal Political Equality Implies Proportional Representation." *Social Choice and Welfare* 33 (4): 617–20.

———. 2009b. "Proportional Representation Within the Limits of Liberalism Alone." *British Journal of Political Science* 39: 735–54.

Iversen, Torben, and David Soskice. 2006. "Electoral Institutions and the Politics of Coalitions: Why Some Democracies Redistribute More Than Others." *American Political Science Review* 100 (2): 165–81.

Katz, Richard. 1997. *Democracy and Elections.* Oxford: Oxford University Press.

Lijphart, Arend. 1994. *Electoral Systems and Party Systems: A Study of Twenty-Seven Democracies, 1945–1990.* Oxford: Oxford University Press.

———. 1999a. "First-Past-the-Post, PR and the Empirical Evidence." *Representation* 36 (2): 133–36.

———. 1999b. *Patterns of Democracy: Government Forms and Performance in Thirty-Six Countries.* New Haven, Conn.: Yale University Press.

Mayer, Nonna. 1998. "The French National Front." In *The New Politics of the Right: Neo-Populist Parties and Movements in Established Democracies*, ed. Hans-Georg Betz and Stefan Immerfall. New York: St. Martin's. 11–26.

McGann, Anthony. 2006. *The Logic of Democracy: Reconciling Equality, Deliberation and Minority Protection*. Ann Arbor: University of Michigan Press.

———. 2012. "Does Partisan Gerrymandering Violate Individual Rights? Social Science and *Vieth v. Jubilirer*." UCI Center for the Study of Democracy Working Paper Series, Irvine, California.

McGann, Anthony, John Ensch, and Teresa Moran. 2009. "The Myth of the Disproportionate Influence of Small Parties Under Proportional Representation." Presented at Annual Meeting of the American Political Science Association, Toronto.

McGann, Anthony, and Michael Latner. 2006. "Consensus Without Veto-Players: Testing Theories of Consensual Democracy." UCI Center for the Study of Democracy Working Paper Series, Irvine, California.

———. 2013. "The Calculus of Consensual Democracy: Rethinking Patterns of Democracy Without Veto Players." *Comparative Political Studies* 46 (7).

McLean, Iain. 1991. "Forms of Representation and Voting Systems." In *Political Theory Today*, ed. David Held. Palo Alto, Calif.: Stanford University Press. 172–96.

Minkenberg, M. 2001. "The Radical Right in Public Office." *West European Politics* 24 (4): 1–21.

Monroe, Burt, and Amanda Rose. 2002. "Electoral Systems and Unimagined Consequences: Partisan Effects of Districted Proportional Representation." *American Journal of Political Science* 46 (1): 67–89.

Nagel, Jack. 2012. "Evaluating Democracy in New Zealand Under MMP." *Policy Quarterly* 8 (2): 3–11.

Rae, Douglas. 1967. *The Political Consequences of Electoral Laws*. New Haven, Conn.: Yale University Press.

Rose-Ackerman, Susan, and Jana Kunicova. 2005. "Electoral Rules and Constraints on Corruption." *British Journal of Political Science* 35 (4): 573–606.

Samuels, David, and Richard Snyder. 2001. "The Value of a Vote: Malapportionment in Comparative Perspective." *British Journal of Political Science* 31 (4): 651–71.

Sartori, Giovanni. 1997. *Comparative Constitutional Engineering: An Inquiry into Structures, Incentives, and Outcomes*. 2nd ed. New York: New York University Press.

Taagepera, Rein. 2009. *Predicting Party Sizes: The Logic of Simple Electoral Systems*. Oxford: Oxford University Press.

Taagepera, Rein, and Matthew Shugart. 1989. *Seats and Votes: The Effects and Determinants of Electoral Systems*. New Haven, Conn.: Yale University Press.

CHAPTER 6

Political Party Organizations, Civic Representation, and Participation

Georgia Kernell

Parliamentary elections were held in a number of long-standing democracies in 2011, including Canada, Denmark, Finland, Ireland, New Zealand, Portugal, and Spain. With the exception of Ireland, turnout was significantly lower than the historical average in every country. In Portugal, turnout was the lowest in history (58 percent), and in New Zealand a smaller share of the eligible voting population (68 percent) went to the polls than in any election since the 1880s.

With low voter turnout comes a decline in partisanship and campaign activity (Dalton 2000; Dalton, McAllister, and Wattenberg 2000). Advances in education, mass media, and communications technology have led voters to depend less on parties for political information or social networking (Dalton 2000). Today's voters focus more on the qualities of individual candidates than on the positions of their parties when making decisions at the polls. Some split their ticket; others support Independents; and many more opt out of the election process altogether.[1]

Parties are also experiencing a dramatic decrease in membership, and with that an important source of funding (van Biezen 2004). Over the past thirty years, the number of party members has declined by over 200,000 in Finland, Germany, Norway, and Sweden, by over a million in the UK, and by almost 1.5 million in Italy (van Biezen, Mair, and Poguntke 2012). On average, party membership today is half what it was in 1980 (ibid.). As a result, parties not only compete for the support of swing voters, but they must increasingly mobilize their base—to campaign, donate money, and vote. To marshal core supporters, parties provide material incentives for enlisting, and they increase the length of electoral campaigns. Parties seek to expand their membership with more lenient rules and fewer restrictions on joining the party. Many have adopted leadership or candidate quotas to broaden their appeal to a variety of voting blocs. And in many cases, party elites have relinquished control to allow members to participate in candidate and leader selection (Carty 2004; Bille 2001; Hopkin 2001; Pennings and Hazan 2001; Scarrow, Webb, and Farrell 2000).

Research about the effects of these organizational and structural changes is generally limited to single-party or country case studies over a short period of time (e.g., Saglie and Heidar 2004; Hopkin 2001; Rahat and Hazan 2001). While these studies agree that parties purposely adapt their rules to encourage greater participation, they also find that such changes may be "more formal than real" (Hopkin 2001), or that increasing member control over party decisions could actually depress support. Without systematic cross-national studies, many questions are left unanswered. For example, are voters more likely to support parties that institute quotas for female, youth, or minority candidates and leaders? Are they more likely to join a party if it relaxes its rules for membership? And do voters participate more in campaigns and elections when they can directly choose the party leader or the candidates on the party ticket? More generally, are these reforms effective at mobilizing the electorate to vote, to become loyal partisans, and to campaign for the party?

This chapter addresses such questions by examining how party organization shapes citizen engagement and participation. The next section formally measures and describes three internal procedures and institutions that parties may manipulate to attract and energize voters: quotas, membership rules, and candidate selection. Drawing on an original data set of party institutions in twenty parliamentary democracies, I find that key organizational features vary significantly both across and within countries. The second half of the chapter compares three forms of civic engagement and participation across parties: voting, partisanship, and campaign participation. Cross-national election surveys reveal significant variation in participation rates. In some parties, voters are also partisans and campaign activists. In others, voters do little beyond supporting their party at election time. Using primarily bivariate analyses, I then investigate whether parties that mandate representation for specific social groups, or that decentralize key decisions, also enjoy greater participation rates. The results, I find, are mixed. Although quotas in the party leadership are associated with greater civic engagement, allowing members to select candidates appears to depress participation.

Party Institutions in Comparative Perspective

There are a variety of ways to compare political parties. Previous research has typically distinguished among parties by comparing their ideological positions or party families (e.g., Labour, Christian Democratic, Greens) or by separating mass-based or "catch-all" organizations from issue-oriented niche parties. Distinguishing parties on the basis of their institutional rules is less common. Yet institutional rules may be as important as party families, because they structure individual and group control over important party decisions, such as writing the party's manifesto and selecting its parliamentary candidates.

The dearth of cross-national research on party organizations is in part due to the lack of readily available information. While party families are fairly easy to identify, internal rules are typically not made public. And party organizations can vary dramatically within a country. Without national laws in place to limit party practices, a thorough investigation requires a comprehensive data collection. Two previous studies—one by Janda in 1980, and the other by Katz and Mair in 1992—compiled data of this sort. Unfortunately, neither of these impressive studies overlaps with cross-national election surveys such as those in the Comparative Study of Electoral Systems (CSES), which are employed later in the analysis.

The investigation in this chapter draws on a more recent large-scale effort to collect cross-national data on party practices. I examined party statutes for 2001–2008 for sixty parties in twenty long-standing parliamentary democracies to obtain information about how political parties function behind the scenes. (For a list of parties included in the study, please see the Appendix to this chapter.) Most parties in fully consolidated democracies have statutes or constitutions that prescribe their formal procedures. Though these rules cannot typically be enforced in civil courts, there are specialized organizations within most parties that mediate or adjudicate disputes and interpret the statutes. Party statutes generally describe the makeup and function of the national organs of the party. Beyond that, the rules vary a great deal in scope, size, and availability. For example, Japan's Liberal Democratic Party's constitution does not mention one of its most important functions: selecting parliamentary candidates. Conversely, Iceland's Progressive Party describes in great detail the party's decentralized candidate selection procedures, but unlike other party constitutions, it does not discuss membership fees and responsibilities. When information about party rules was not available in the statutes, I followed up with in-person or telephone interviews with party representatives. The three sections below describe how parties vary with respect to quotas, membership rules, and candidate selection.

Quotas

Perhaps the most effective way for a political party to woo the support of a particular group of voters is to adopt policies that members of that group support. Beyond changing their policy appeals, parties employ various institutional measures to gain supporters and promote diversity within their organizations. At the individual level, they organize specialized recruitment campaigns or provide discounted memberships to underrepresented groups within the party. At the elite level, the most common practice is for parties to institute quotas guaranteeing that a given percentage of the leadership positions will go to individuals from a specific group, such as women, men, youth, and union members, or ethnic, linguistic, or religious minorities.[2] Quotas may apply to the leadership in the party's headquarters, the candidates the party fields in elections, or both. For example, the German Christian Democratic Union mandates that at least one-third of the party's executive board and one-third of the candidates on the party's electoral lists be female. In contrast, the Finnish Social Democratic Party exercises a quota of 40 percent for women in the party leadership, but it has no rules governing the number of women on candidate lists.

Quotas are increasingly common among parties in advanced industrialized democracies. Although Socialist and Social Democratic parties in Europe were among the first to institute quotas for women in the early 1970s, moderate and conservative European parties, as well as parties in other regions of the world, have begun to set quotas as well (Krook 2009). Most competitive parties in advanced parliamentary democracies institute some type of quota for an underrepresented group. Table 6.1 displays the distribution

Table 6.1. Percent (Number) of Parties with Quotas for
Parliamentary Candidates or Executive Leaders

Quota	Candidates		Leadership	
Women	28%	(17)	70%	(42)
Men	18%	(11)	23%	(14)
Youth	3%	(2)	73%	(44)
Minorities	0		15%	(9)
Union members	0		20%	(12)
Seniors	0		12%	(7)
Media members	0		3%	(2)
Any quota	28%	(17)	92%	(55)

of party quotas for the parties included in this analysis. I only consider a party as having a quota if the statute language explicitly states it must meet this quota.[3] Of the 60 parties examined in this chapter, 17 mandate a quota for candidate lists and 55 institute quotas for members of national party leadership.

Parliamentary candidate quotas exist for women, men, and youth. About one-quarter of the parties examined here institute a quota in the party constitution for female candidates. Most of these parties also set a quota for men, or specify that there must be gender parity on the ballot. For example, in Denmark's Social Democratic Party the rules state that "the ballot papers of the party shall be drawn up in such a way that there is an even distribution according to gender" (Socialdemokraterne 2008). Two parties—Belgium's Socialist Party (in Flanders) and Luxembourg's center-right Christian Social People's Party—also institute candidate quotas for young people.

Many more parties institute quotas for members of the party leadership. Just over two-thirds reserve positions on the national leadership council for women, and almost three-quarters of the parties reserve positions for younger members of the party. Nine parties also require seats for ethnic, linguistic, or racial minorities. For example, New Zealand's Labour Party reserves three of the 19 seats in their National Council for Maori people. Canada's Liberal and New Democratic parties both reserve positions for representatives from the Aboriginal population.

A number of parties also hold seats for representatives of workers' unions. These include traditional labor parties in Austria, Britain, Ireland, and New Zealand, but also center-left parties in Greece, Iceland, and Portugal. Several parties reserve positions in the national leadership for senior citizens, and in two cases parties require that members of the media be incorporated into the party leadership.

Membership Rules

A second way parties seek to increase engagement and participation is by making membership more appealing and accessible. A sizable assembly of rank and file members is invaluable for a party's success. Members are dependable voters; they provide important funding through fees and donations; they volunteer to work on campaigns or in party offices; they recruit their friends and families to show up at the polls; and they supply the party with a pool of potential candidates (Scarrow 1994). A party's membership size may also signal its success and credibility to voters.

Over the past thirty years, parties in long-standing parliamentary systems have witnessed a dramatic decline in their membership rolls. Voters no longer rely on parties to learn about political news. Modern media are cheap and accessible, allowing individuals to obtain information in a nonpartisan way. Parties today are less rooted in civic society and more closely linked with the state bureaucracy (van Biezen 2004).

To adapt to changes in media and communications technology, parties have changed their activities and recruitment methods. Many provide material incentives for individuals to become "passive" members by handing out glossy magazines, throwing parties, and supplying sympathizers with mugs covered in party logos. Parties have also lowered the barriers to entry by allowing individuals to apply online or through the mail, and by reducing membership fees. In the past, parties typically required that interested individuals apply in person at the local party headquarters. In some cases, membership in the party was contingent on nomination and support from current party members. However, as the benefits of membership for voters have declined, many parties have made the process of joining the party much easier.[4]

Parties today often choose to waive traditional waiting periods that required members to be active for six months or a year before receiving full rights to vote in the party. They have also created different tiers of membership to make joining the party more attractive to a broader segment of the public. Many parties, including those that allow membership by donation only, give a reduced membership status to those who agree with the party position but would rather not become full-fledged members. These affiliates, or "sympathizers," typically hold no voting rights, but they are invited to party fund-raising events and are kept apprised of campaign events. Parties may also give group memberships to organizations, such as labor unions or corporations. In these cases, members of the union or company are automatically given free membership in the party. In some cases they must opt in to become active (but pay no fee); in others they must opt out if they prefer to not be associated with the party.

My interviews confirmed that members of the party elite manipulate the rules for membership, and the rights of members, primarily to attract more core supporters. For example, one top-level party bureaucrat stated: "The last big change of the statutes about ten years ago was necessary because we wanted to make the party's structure more open for people that were not so interested [in] the traditional positions of the party, for people that wanted to go a piece of the way with the [party], but not the whole way. So we had to find structures to integrate this kind of people, who will not get a membership badge, for example."

Table 6.2 displays the variation in membership rules across parties. (Note that data are not available for all 60 parties in each category.) About one-fifth of the parties discount membership fees for different groups. For example, the British Labour Party's fee is reduced from £36 to £12 for students or members eighteen and younger. The Christian Democratic Appeal in the Netherlands allows first-time supporters to purchase a "test" membership for less than half the price of a normal annual membership. About 40 percent of parties require that members apply in person or in writing; in the rest of the parties, applicants may use the Internet. Half the parties require that members be active in the party for a set period of time before re-

Table 6.2. Percent (number) of Parties with
Practices Designed to Make Membership Easier

Membership rules	Parties	
Discounted fees	21%	(12/57)
Internet applications	59%	(35/59)
No wait until vote	51%	(30/59)
Nonvoting memberships	33%	(19/58)
Group memberships	31%	(13/42)

ceiving full voting rights. This waiting period ranges from one week (Iceland's Progressive Party) to a full year (Australia's Labor Party, New Zealand's Labour Party, and Portugal's Socialist Party). But in the other half of the parties examined here, members receive full voting rights and privileges immediately after joining. One-third of parties have reduced memberships, where individuals can join (typically for a discounted fee), and simply attend party functions without having any influence over important party decisions. And a sizable share of the parties (31 percent) allow for group memberships. Although many parties specify that different types of groups can join the party, every case of group membership during this time period involves workers' unions. Almost every labor party in the data allows unions to join.

Perhaps the most important barrier to entry is the fee required to join a party. I collected data for each party on the cost of a standard membership (with full voting rights) for a thirty-five-year-old employed male. Annual subscriptions range from 5 Euros in Sweden's Liberal People's Party to 108 Euros in the People's Party for Freedom and Democracy (VVD) in the Netherlands.[5] The median fee is 21 Euros. The data are displayed in Figure 6.1.

In some countries there is little variation across parties. For example, all of the Swedish parties charge less than 12 Euros. In other countries the discrepancies across parties are much more significant. In Germany, for example, members of Die Linke (The Left) pay 47 Euros per year, whereas

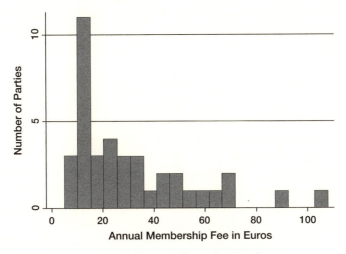

Figure 6.1. Distribution of parties by annual membership fee.

center-right Christian Democratic Union members pay only 14. This example is not atypical; in general I find that fiscally conservative parties are no more likely to charge a high membership fee than those parties favoring a greater social welfare state.

Members' Rights over Candidate Selection

A third way parties woo supporters is by sharing control over internal decision making. In particular, the leadership may grant party members control over selecting parliamentary candidates. This is not a power to be taken lightly. Candidate selection is arguably a party's most important job; it is "the crucial process" (Schattschneider 1942) that shapes the faces and voices of a party, its members of parliament, and ultimately a country's leadership.

Where candidate selection is decentralized, party members at the subnational level play a decisive role in recruiting and selecting candidates within their own districts. In thoroughly decentralized parties, local nominees are not subject to a veto from national party officers or conferences, or from other subnational parties. Members within a district either vote directly for candidates or choose delegates to a local committee assigned to select their party's candidates. Thus, highly decentralized parties are distinguished by autonomous and mutually exclusive local selectorates that are wholly made up of local party members or their elected representatives.

Britain's Liberal Democrats exemplify highly decentralized candidate selection. Local area councils select parliamentary candidates, and the national party has no formal influence over these nominations. Party members in the district choose representatives to the local councils, which are authorized to select candidates who may run in their district. For comparison, both U.S. parties are also extremely decentralized. Primary elections are open to registered voters, not simply party members. This may be one reason that party membership has never taken off in the United States.

At the other end of the spectrum, centralized parties authorize a single party officer or committee to select parliamentary candidates. Such committees are often composed of delegates representing the party's subnational units, but they may also, or instead, include their public officeholders or a group of party officials (e.g., elected leaders or the head of their youth organization). In their most extreme form, centralized parties rely on a single leader to hand-pick all parliamentary candidates, as was the case in Italy's National Alliance Party.[6] In many parties, local and national party organizations share candidate selection duties. In the Dutch Labor Party, for example, subnational party actors choose a pool of potential candidates, and the national party leaders select nominees from this group.

Of the 60 parties examined here, 22 are decentralized. In the remaining parties, the national level of the party controls all or part of the nomination process. Decentralized parties tend to be more common in Scandinavian countries, while centralized organizations are more common in southern Europe, as well as in Ireland. But there is significant variation within, as well as across, countries.

In summary, there are various ways in which parties may adjust their rules to encourage greater voter or member participation. Parties differ markedly in their choice of leadership and candidate quotas, in the rules they employ to attract and enlist members, and the rights they afford these members over a key decision within the party—parliamentary candidate selection. Now that we have established several systematic ways to compare party organizations, let us return to asking how these internal rules may affect civic engagement. Do quotas lead some groups to identify more with parties? Are lenient rules or enhanced responsibilities effective at recruiting and maintaining more active members? The next section begins to answer these questions by examining how party organization relates to voter participation, partisanship, and campaign activity.

Civic Engagement and Participation

To investigate cross-national participation rates, I draw on survey data from the Comparative Study of Electoral Systems (CSES) from 2001 to 2006. The CSES surveys—funded primarily by the National Science Foundation, and administered by a consortium of universities around the world—are designed to explain election-related outcomes. All were conducted within eleven months of the country's parliamentary elections. The surveys were conducted in 17 of the 20 countries for which I collected data on party organizations. They do not yet exist for Austria, Greece, or Luxembourg, so parties in those countries are excluded in the following analyses. The number of survey respondents varies across countries from 860 (in the UK) to 3,023 (in Germany).

I examine four indicators of civic engagement and participation: voting, partisanship, campaign activity, and persuasion. The first two variables measure the share of the voting-eligible population that voted for, or identified with, a particular party. During this period, the percent of votes received by a party in the data ranges from 8 percent (Germany's Green Party) to 45 percent (Portugal's Socialist Party).[7] Partisanship also varies widely. The share of respondents who identify with a party ranges from less than 1 percent in Germany's Free Democratic Party to 42 percent in Australia's Liberal Party.[8]

Two questions in the CSES gauge active political participation. The first, which I refer to as *campaign*, asks if the respondent "showed support for a particular party or candidate by, for example, attending a meeting, putting up a poster, or in some other way." The second, which I label *persuade*, asks the respondent if he or she "talked to other people to persuade them to vote for a particular party or candidate." Both actions gauge electoral participation, but campaigning is significantly more active than persuading. To measure active participation, I limit the analysis to those individuals who reported voting for and identifying with the same party. I only examine these "consistent" voters and partisans because *campaign* and *persuade* do not indicate which party a person supported; they simply ask if the respondent participated in a campaign or persuasive discussion. Limiting the sample to consistent supporters increases the probability that a person involved in a campaign or conversation is in fact doing so to support the party or candidate for whom he or she voted. Thus, I examine how a party's organization affects campaign behavior among its consistent supporters.

The degree to which people campaign or try to persuade someone to vote for their preferred party or candidate varies widely. Only 2 percent of consistent supporters for the Swedish Liberal People's Party reported having campaigned for the party, whereas 22 percent of voters and identifiers for the newly formed New Komeito Party (NKP) in Japan reported campaigning. Figure 6.2 displays the percent of consistent supporters who reported campaigning and persuading, by party. As we can see, the share of respondents who tried to persuade someone to support their preferred party was higher in almost every party than the share that actively campaigned. Persuasion ranges from 6 percent in the Dutch People's Party for Freedom and Democracy to 42 percent—again, in Japan's NKP.

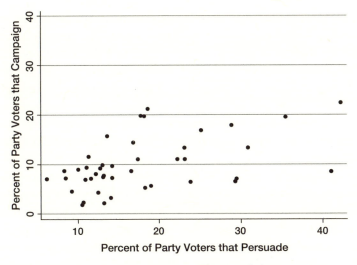

Figure 6.2. Percent of voters who campaign and persuade by party.

Party Organization and Participation

To investigate how party organization shapes civic engagement, I start by examining the bivariate relationships between a party's quotas or candidate selection mechanism and its mean level of partisanship or participation, as well as the relationship between membership rules and campaign activity.[9] Table 6.3 reports the significant ($p < 0.05$) results of bivariate regressions for each of the four dependent variables with country fixed-effects. If a variable was not associated with greater participation or partisanship, it is not included in Table 6.3. (For example, quotas for seniors were not associated with any measure of engagement.) The number in parentheses indicates the change in the percent of respondents who voted, identified with a party, campaigned, or persuaded someone else to vote for their preferred party. A positive sign (+) means that the party organizational variable is associated with greater partisanship or participation, and a negative sign (−) indicates that the organizational variable is associated with less engagement. For example, parties with quotas for female leaders receive 12 percent more of the votes cast than parties without such quotas.

As we can see, party organizational variables are more closely connected to voting and partisanship than to more active forms of participation.

Table 6.3. Bivariate Relationships Between Civic Engagement and Party Rules

Attitude or behavior	Party organizational variable
Voting	Quota for female leaders (+ 12)
	Quota for minority leaders (+ 20)
	Quota for male candidates (+ 13)
	Decentralized candidate selection (− 16)
Partisanship	Quota for female leaders (+ 5)
	Quota for minority leaders (+ 8)
	Quota for male candidates (+ 5)
	Decentralized candidate selection (− 5)
Campaigning	Group memberships (+ 6)
Persuading	Group memberships (+ 9)
	Nonvoting memberships (− 6)
	Membership fee (− 0.7)

Because the results, as well as the population of respondents, differ between the models examining vote choice and partisanship and the models examining campaigning and persuading, I split these into separate sections for the analysis. In the following section I focus only on voting and party identification. I then return to the results for more active forms of civic engagement.

Voting and Party Identification

Quotas. As we can see in Table 6.3, party leadership quotas are associated with equal or greater levels of engagement and participation. On average, parties with quotas for female leaders receive 35 percent of the vote, whereas those without such quotas receive only 23 percent of the vote. Similarly, partisanship is approximately 5 percent higher in parties with female leadership quotas than in those without such rules. Leadership quotas for minority members are also associated with a substantial difference in vote share (20 percent) and partisanship (8 percent). Five of the eight parties with reserved leadership posts for ethnic or linguistic minorities received more than 35 percent of the vote in their respective countries.[10] Leadership quotas for men, youth, union members, and seniors are positively associated with voting and participation as well, but these relationships are not statistically significant.

Parties with candidate quotas for men also receive greater electoral support. On average, they receive 39 percent of the vote, whereas parties without such quotas receive only 30 percent of the vote. Because every party with a candidate quota for men also has an identical quota for women, it is unclear if the increases in vote share and partisanship are due to support for male candidates or gender parity. Quotas for female candidates are also positively associated with both vote share and partisanship, although the relationship is not as significant ($0.10 < p < 0.15$ in both cases).

Parties with leadership or candidate quotas may experience greater turnout and partisanship for a number of reasons. First, quotas ensure a minimum level of descriptive representation for different groups in society. Although these data do not measure the composition of a party's parliamentary delegation or leadership committee directly, parties with quotas for a specific group generally have more representatives from that group than parties without such quotas. For example, 39 percent of a party's parliamentary delegation is female, on average, in parties with quotas for female candidates, whereas only 31 percent of a party's delegations is female, on average, in parties without such quotas. Second, a party that adopts formal rules for representation of specific groups in society may also be more sympathetic to the issues that are important to that group. A party instituting quotas for young voters, for example, may also adopt positions that are similar to those of young voters, regardless of the age composition of its representatives. Third, there may be an increase in the supply of viable candidates from a given group in parties that well represent that segment of the population.

To examine whether or not quotas have varying effects for different populations, I split the sample into three subgroups. The first includes female respondents only, the second includes male respondents only, and the third includes all respondents age 30 and under. I then ran bivariate regressions for voting and partisanship against quotas for members of those specific subpopulations. The results are presented in Table 6.4. (Unfortunately, questions about minority status—race, ethnicity, and native language—were asked in only six of the 17 countries' election studies. The associations between quotas for minorities and vote share or partisanship are significant for minorities and non-minorities when we limit the analysis to the six countries with a significant minority population.)

Table 6.4. Bivariate Relationships Between Civic Engagement and Party Rules for Females, Males, and Youth

Population	Voting	Partisanship
Females	Quota for female leaders (+ 13)	Quota for female leaders (+ 5)
	Quota for female candidates (+ 12)	Quota for female candidates (+ 5)
	Quota for male candidates (+ 16)	Quota for male candidates (+ 6)
Males	Quota for female leaders (+ 12)	Quota for female leaders (+ 5)
Youth (age ≤30)	No significant relationship	No significant relationship

Separating the analysis by gender makes it apparent that men and women are equally likely to vote for and identify with parties that institute leadership quotas for women. Female respondents are also more likely to support parties with candidate quotas for women. (For male respondents, this relationship is positive, but not significant.) Moreover, the increase in support for parties with male candidates found in Table 6.3 appears to be driven primarily by the preferences of female respondents. When the analysis is separated by gender, females are more likely to support parties with candidate quotas for men, but male voters are not. This suggests that support for parties with quotas for male candidates reflects preferences for gender parity more than simply for having more male candidates. Usually, parties with candidate quotas for men have more female candidates than those without. I find that respondents age thirty and under are no more likely to support a party with quotas for young members than one without such quotas.

Membership rights: candidate selection. Returning to the results in Table 6.3, we notice that decentralized (i.e., more inclusive) candidate selection is negatively associated with electoral and partisan support. Individuals are less likely to vote for parties when party members, rather than the central leadership, select candidates. On the whole, decentralized parties receive an average of 26 percent of the vote, whereas fully centralized parties receive an average of 38 percent. Partisanship is also lower among decentralized parties. Nine percent of individuals identify with decentralized parties, whereas 15 percent identify with semi-centralized or centralized parties.

Decentralization may depress citizen engagement for a number of reasons. First, members may select less competitive candidates than party leaders. Members typically join parties for ideological or social reasons. When choosing candidates to run on the party ticket, they may vote according to their sincere preferences, even when those preferences are not representative of the general public. In contrast, party leaders are motivated by the opportunity to win, and their jobs hinge on their party's electoral success (Ware 1996; Scarrow 1994; Clark and Wilson 1961). Leaders are also more likely to invest time and money into determining optimal candidate positions by polling the electorate or educating themselves about aspiring candidates' positions and competing parties' platforms. Leaders can also draw from a larger pool of potential candidates. And they may feel less obliged than local members to support a noncompetitive, yet faithful, party delegate who has moved up in the organizational ranks over time.

Another factor could have to do with the decision-making process itself. Because party members are more familiar and involved with internal party functions when parties are decentralized than when they are centralized, they may also be more familiar with internal factions within the party. If cleavages among vying candidates become salient to general members, members on the losing side may find their party enthusiasm waning in the general election. This argument follows the logic in the "divisive primary" literature in American politics (Atkeson 1998; Hacker 1965), which finds that the percent of the vote a candidate receives in the general election is positively associated with his or her margin of victory in the primary election. When voters are more educated about internal party divisions, they may be less likely to identify with a party's platform or to show up at the polls. (Moreover, highly decentralized primary elections could be one factor driving comparatively low voter turnout in the U.S.)

To test the robustness of these results, I ran two multivariate regression models that include the four party organizational variables found to have a significant association with voting and partisanship. I also include a fifth variable, *deviation,* which indicates the distance between a party and the median voter in the electorate.[11] *Deviation* ranges from 0.003 (Canada's Liberal Party) to 3.6 (Sweden's Moderaterna). If those parties that are closer to the median voter in the electorate are also more popular at the polls, *deviation* should have a negative coefficient.

The first column in Table 6.5 displays the relationships between the party-level organizational variables and a party's vote share. (Standard errors are in parentheses.) As we can see, all the findings from Table 6.3 persist: quotas for female and minority candidates are associated with greater support, as are quotas for male candidates. Decentralized candidate selection remains negatively associated with electoral success. In contrast, a party's

Table 6.5. Multivariate Relationships Between Civic Engagement and Party
Rules

	Voting	Partisanship
Quota female leaders	8.31* (4.57)	2.14 (2.12)
Quota minority leaders	10.00* (5.62)	5.22* (2.73)
Quota male candidates	11.64* (6.01)	3.51 (2.70)
Decentralized candidate selection	−13.10*** (4.10)	−6.86*** (2.42)
Deviation	−1.51 (2.53)	−0.34 (1.17)
Constant	27.10*** (4.10)	15.10*** (5.70)
Number of parties	48	48
Number of countries	16	16

* $p<0.10$, ** $p<0.05$, *** $p<0.01$.

deviation from the median voter appears to be unrelated to its vote share. Although the coefficient is negative, it is not statistically significant.[12]

The results for partisanship, shown in the second column of Table 6.5, are not as robust. While quotas for minority leaders and centralized selection continue to be positively associated with partisanship, quotas for female leaders and male candidates are not. Gender quotas are strong predictors of electoral success, but they may be less closely related to an individual's likelihood of identifying with a party. A party's deviation from the median voter is not a significant indicator of partisanship.[13]

Campaigning and Persuading

This section changes the focus from voting and partisanship to examine more active participation in electoral campaigns.

Quotas. Table 6.3 demonstrates that there is no relationship between party quotas and campaign activity or persuasion. Taken with the results in the previous section, this finding suggests that an individual's choice about which party to support electorally may be very different from his or her decision to go out and actively campaign. These choices may differ if individuals associate one form of participation (e.g., voting) with parties and the other activity (e.g., campaigning) with candidates. For example, voters in multimember parliamentary democracies typically compare party platforms rather than candidate positions when they go to the polls. But campaigning or persuading may reflect an individual's tie to a particular candidate. If parties that institute quotas lead voters to be less connected with candidates (because, for example, the national level of the party interferes with candidate selection to ensure that the quota is met), voters may be less likely to become active in the party.

Membership rules. The results in Table 6.3 indicate that consistent supporters are more likely to campaign or engage in persuasion when parties allow for group memberships. The group memberships in this analysis are made up exclusively of workers' unions, but they are not only found in labor parties. For example, the Conservatives in both Britain and Canada allow unions to join their party. Thus, the positive association between group memberships and activity may reflect unions' ability to mobilize and rally supporters.

Nonvoting memberships are found to be negatively associated with persuasion, but to be unrelated to campaigning. This lends no support to the hypothesis that parties include these memberships to entice their supporters to join and become active in the party. If anything, the opposite is true. In contrast, membership fees are negatively associated with persuasion. People are less likely to try to convince a friend or neighbor to vote for their preferred party if that party charges a steep fee for membership. A one-Euro increase in membership fees is associated with a 0.7 point decrease in the share of consistent voters who are active in party persuasion. Membership fees are also associated with lower levels of campaign activity, but these results are not statistically significant ($0.15 < p < 0.20$).

With the exception of group memberships and the size of the fee, those parties with more lenient rules are no more likely than their counterparts with stricter policies to maintain active party membership. Of course, this does not imply that relaxing membership barriers has no effect on activity. Party rules are not randomly assigned, and it could be the case that introducing nonvoting memberships increased support for those parties that chose to do so. Future research may include a longitudinal study of membership rules and party activity.

Membership rights: candidate selection. While decentralized candidate selection has a robust, negative relationship with voting and partisanship, it appears to be unrelated to levels of campaign activity and persuasion. Once individuals decide to vote for and identify with a party, that party's method for selecting candidates may not affect their political activity. Future research may examine how individual-level determinants of participation—such as education and political sophistication—interact with party institutions to shape participation.

Conclusion

Civic engagement and political participation are essential ingredients in a thriving democracy. When the public closely monitors politics, representatives must remain accountable to their constituents in order to secure reelection. As a result, public policies are better aligned with citizens' preferences. Voters and partisans also exhibit greater trust in government than do nonvoters and nonpartisans. They are more likely to discuss politics, stay informed, and be satisfied with the democratic process.

Yet, while previous research finds that inclusive electoral and governmental institutions encourage greater participation, democracy within parties is not well studied. This chapter asks a simple question: do more inclusive parties encourage greater civic participation?

The results are mixed. Leadership quotas are generally associated with equal or greater electoral success and partisanship. In particular, parties with quotas for female leaders, minority leaders, or male candidates are much more likely to enjoy voter support. Yet, quotas are found to have no effect on campaign activity or persuasion. Once an individual chooses to vote for and identify with a party, the decision to campaign for that party appears unaffected by rules that ensure participation for different social or demographic groups. With the exception of group memberships and membership fees, the results also find no relationship between barriers to entry and civic engagement. Membership subscriptions appear to depress persuasion, and group—specifically, union—memberships are associated with higher levels of both campaign activity and persuasion. Although parties institute varying mechanisms to encourage individuals to enlist in the party, what works in one party may not work in another. Finally, more inclusive candidate selection mechanisms have a negative association with electoral success and partisanship. Greater discretion over party decisions may lead to less, not more, support for the party.

Although the results are highly suggestive, it is important to remember that these associations cannot be interpreted as causal relationships. Future research should investigate the causal effect of leadership and candidate quotas on decision-making within parties by examining participation before and after the implementation of a quota. This research could also use multi-level analyses to examine how individual, as well as party, factors shape participation. Such research would allow us to better control for possible confounders that may influence the results. Similarly, future studies could examine how membership rights shape engagement by asking if candidate positions vary systematically with centralization. Are candidates selected by party members less in touch with the minds of the electorate than those selected by national leaders? Finally, further research should examine how party rules and institutions interact with one another. For example, membership rules may only affect participation when members have sufficient rights over candidate selection. And quotas may lead to greater representation only in those parties where members have less control over candidate selection. While there is still much work to be done, this chapter begins to address an important and growing field of research that examines the role that party institutions play in shaping civic engagement and political behavior.

Appendix: Parties in the Analysis

Parties Included in the Analysis

Country	Election year	Party
Australia	2004	Liberal Party
		Labor Party
Austria	2002	People's Party
		Freedom Party
		Social Democratic Party
		Green Party
Belgium	2003	Flemish Liberals and Democrats
		Flemish Democratic Party
		Christian Democratic and Flemish
Canada	2006	Conservative Party
		Liberal Party
		New Democratic Party
		Quebec Bloc
Denmark	2005	Liberal Party
		Social Democrats
		Danish People's Party
		Conservative People's Party

(continued)

Country	Election year	Party
Finland	2003	Agrarian Centrist Party Social Democratic Party National Coalition Party Left Alliance
Germany	2005	Social Democratic Party Christian Democratic Union Free Democratic Party The Left The Greens
Greece	2004	New Democracy Panhellenic Socialist Movement
Iceland	2003	Independence Party Social Democratic Alliance Progressive Party
Ireland	2002	Soldiers of Destiny Family of the Irish Labour Party
Italy	2001	Forward Italy National Alliance
Japan	2005	Liberal Democratic Party Democratic Party New Komeito Party
Luxembourg	2004	Christian Social People's Party Socialist Workers' Party Democratic Party The Greens
Netherlands	2003	Christian Democratic Appeal Labor Party People's Party for Freedom and Democracy
New Zealand	2005	Labour Party National Party
Norway	2005	Labor Party Progress Party Conservatives
Portugal	2005	Socialist Party Social Democratic Party
Spain	2004	Socialist Workers' Party People's Party

Country	Election year	Party
Sweden	2002	Social Democratic Party
		Moderate Party
		Liberal People's Party
United Kingdom	2005	Labour Party
		Conservative Party
		Liberal Democrats

References

Atkeson, Lonna Rae. 1998. "Divisive Primaries and General Election Outcomes: Another Look at Presidential Campaigns." *American Journal of Political Science* 42 (1): 256–71.

Bille, Lars. 2001. "Democratizing a Democratic Procedure: Myth or Reality?: Candidate Selection in Western European Parties, 1960–1990." *Party Politics* 7 (3): 363–80.

Carty, R. Kenneth. 2004. "Parties as Franchise Systems: The Stratarchical Organizational Imperative." *Party Politics* 10 (1): 5–24.

Clark, Peter B., and James Q. Wilson. 1961. "Incentive Systems: A Theory of Organizations." *Administrative Science Quarterly* 6 (2): 129–66.

Comparative Study of Electoral Systems (CSES), www.cses.org, last accessed 2011.

Dalton, Russell J. 2000. "The Decline of Party Identifications." In *Parties Without Partisans: Political Change in Advanced Industrialized Democracies*, ed. Russell J. Dalton and Martin P. Wattenberg. Oxford: Oxford University Press. 19–36.

Dalton, Russell J., Ian McAllister and Martin P. Wattenberg. 2000. "The Consequences of Partisan Dealignment." In *Parties Without Partisans: Political Change in Advanced Industrialized Democracies*, ed. Russell J. Dalton and Martin P. Wattenberg. Oxford: Oxford University Press. 37–63.

Hacker, Andrew. 1965. "Does a 'Divisive' Primary Harm a Candidate's Election Chances?" *American Political Science Review* 59 (1): 105–10.

Hopkin, Jonathan. 2001. "Bringing the Members Back In? Democratizing Candidate Selection in Britain and Spain." *Party Politics* 7 (3): 343–61.

Janda, Kenneth. 1980. *Political Parties: A Cross-National Survey*. New York: Free Press.

Katz, Richard S., and Peter Mair, eds. 1992. *Party Organizations: A Data Handbook on Party Organizations in Western Democracies, 1960–90*. London: Sage.

Krook, Mona Lena. 2010. *Quotas for Women in Politics: Gender and Candidate Selection Reform Worldwide*. Oxford: Oxford University Press.

Pennings, Paul, and Reuven Y. Hazan. 2001. "Democratizing Candidate Selection: Causes and Consequences." *Party Politics* 7 (3): 267–75.

Rahat, Gideon, and Reuven Y. Hazan. 2001. "Candidate Selection Methods: An Analytical Framework." *Party Politics* 7 (3): 297–322.

Saglie, Jo, and Knut Heidar. 2004. "Democracy Within Norwegian Political Parties: Complacency or Pressure for Change?" *Party Politics* 10 (4): 385–405.

Scarrow, Susan E. 1994. "The 'Paradox of Enrollment': Assessing the Costs and Benefits of Party Memberships." *European Journal of Political Research* 25 (1): 41–60.

Scarrow, Susan E., Paul Webb, and David Farrell. 2000. "From Social Integration to Electoral Contestation: The Changing Distribution of Power Within Political Parties." In *Parties Without Partisans: Political Change in Advanced Industrial Democracies*, ed. Russell J. Dalton and Martin P. Wattenberg. Oxford: Oxford University Press. 129–55.

Schattschneider, E. E. 1942. *Party Government*. New York: Farrar and Rinehart.

Socialdemokraterne "Love." 2005–2008. Statutes of the Danish Social Democratic Party. Official document received by e-mail correspondence with party officials.

van Biezen, Ingrid. 2004. "Political Parties as Public Utilities." *Party Politics* 10 (6): 701–22.

van Biezen, Ingrid, Peter M. Mair, and Thomas Poguntke. 2012. "Going, Going, . . . Gone? The Decline of Party Membership in Contemporary Europe." *European Journal of Political Research* 51: 24–56.

Ware, Alan. 1996. *Political Parties and Party Systems*. Oxford: Oxford University Press.

PART II

Representation Beyond Elections

CHAPTER 7

The Paradox of Voting—for Republicans: Economic Inequality, Political Organization, and the American Voter

Jacob S. Hacker and Paul Pierson

Over the last generation, Americans at the top of the economic ladder have pulled sharply away from everyone else. The share of pretax income earned by the richest 1 percent of households more than doubled, from 9 percent in 1970 to over 23 percent on the eve of the 2008 financial crisis (Piketty and Saez 2003; Saez 2012). Gains higher up the ladder have been more spectacular still, even as earnings growth for most Americans has slowed (Hacker and Pierson 2010a). At the same time, the Republican Party has become more conservative on economic issues. According to a widely used left-right index based on congressional roll-call votes, Republicans in the House of Representatives have become dramatically more conservative, on average, since the 1970s, while Republicans in the Senate have become substantially more conservative. The average Democrat in Congress, by contrast, has moved only modestly to the left (calculated from Poole and Rosenthal 2012).

A long line of democratic theorists, as well as most political science models of redistribution, would predict that under these circumstances, non-rich voters would shift to the Democrats in support of greater government efforts to tackle inequality (e.g., Tocqueville 2000 [1835]; Meltzer and Richard 1981). With the GOP moving right as less affluent voters moved left, the Republican Party would lose ground to the Democratic Party. Yet the GOP has not only gained ground over this period, shifting to essential parity with Democrats in the electoral arena, but also picked up support from a crucial downscale component of the Democrats' coalition, the white working class. Why? Why has there not been a broader electoral backlash against the more conservative party in an era of rising inequality?

Most commentators on this question have focused on voters and values. Thomas Frank, in his bestselling 2004 book, *What's the Matter with Kansas?*— a bible among despairing Democrats after George W. Bush's reelection— argued that Republicans had skillfully used cultural wedge issues to attract working-class support in an era in which the working class had fallen farther and farther behind the well off. From the other side of the political spectrum, *New York Times* columnist David Brooks (2001) countered that working-class voters had turned against a Democratic Party increasingly beholden to wealthy liberal elites. Popular commentary has portrayed an enduring divide in which values trump class: a less affluent Red America filled with NASCAR-loving, gun-toting GOP traditionalists who oppose gay marriage versus a richer Blue America filled with sushi-loving, *New Yorker*-reading Democratic cosmopolitans. In this conventional view, voters are the prime movers, and it is their failure to rise up and demand action that is taken as evidence of either their lack of real interest (Brooks) or GOP manipulation of their conservative social values (Frank).

In this chapter, we present a quite different view—one focused on political organizations as well as voters, and on perceptions (and misperceptions) of inequality and government policy as well as voter ideology. We show that while voters are key players, the American political game has been dominated by political elites, in part because the organizations that once gave voters information and clout have eroded. As a result, growing elite polarization and class stratification have, ironically, occurred alongside a profound demobilization of American voters around issues of inequality. Contrary to the conventional view, the source of this demobilization is organizational far more than it is attitudinal. That is, it is rooted in structural shifts in the nature of American politics—from the rise in business lobbying to the decline of organized labor and large-scale voluntary associations— more than it is based on changes in the fundamental beliefs of voters. These organizational changes, however, have helped spark shifts in voters' views that have reinforced the tilt of American politics away from less affluent voters.

This argument has crucial implications for how we understand what elections can and should do. Over the last generation, students of American politics have almost single-mindedly built their investigations around a view that we call "politics as electoral spectacle," in which public opinion and elections are seen as the driving force behind politicians' positions and, ultimately, public policy. This perspective has enhanced our understanding of elections, opinion, and votes in Congress. But it is gravely deficient for understanding the paradox of less affluent voters' support for the GOP in an era of runaway inequality. In place of this standard narrative, we sketch out an alternative perspective—"politics as organized combat"—that emphasizes the role of organized interests in mediating the ability of voters to become aware of and respond to rising inequality (Hacker and Pierson 2010b).

Elections matter, of course. But without organizations bringing Americans into politics and informing them about their interests and issues that affect them, free and fair elections are no guarantee that the voices of citizens will be heard. It is the organizational transformation of American politics, rather than changes in voter attitudes or partisan attachments, that must be the starting point for any convincing analysis of voters' response to rising inequality, as well as any effective prescription for political reform.

Voting Against Self Interest?

Discussion of the changing voting patterns of less affluent voters has emphasized the shifting allegiances of the "white working class." This is a restrictive focus in some respects, as the white working class has declined as a share of the electorate in tandem with rising levels of education and professionalization. But it has a number of advantages as well. Perhaps most important for us here, long-term change in the white working class's voting allegiances is very difficult to explain with short-term fluctuations in the performance of the economy, such as those that lie at the heart of many political-business cycle models that focus on the effects of fiscal and monetary policy in election years.

Another crucial advantage of examining the voting patterns of the white working class is that they are the subject of a large and growing body of research in political science and sociology that has addressed critical difficulties of measurement and definition (e.g., Kenworthy et al. 2007; Abramowitz and Teixeira 2008; Bartels 2008). Much of the debate over whether the white working class has abandoned the Democratic Party revolves around defining the white working class itself. The basic issue is whether working-class status is principally defined by family income or whether it reflects some alternative or additional characteristics (such as self-identification as "working class" or one's level of educational achievement). Even if income is taken as the marker, there remains the question of how well off someone has to be to be considered "working class." Larry Bartels (2008), for instance, has argued that the popular concern over the Democrats' loss of working-class support is misplaced. Defining the "white working class" as white voters in the lowest third of the national income distribution (below $35,000 in family income in 2004), Bartels argues that there has indeed been a shift away from the Democratic Party toward the Republican Party, but that it is *"entirely* attributable to the demise of the Solid South as a bastion of Democratic allegiance"; outside the South, low-income whites have not moved toward the Republican Party at all (Bartels 2008: 75).

Bartels's argument is a useful reminder that we must take account of the suppression of partisan competition in the South prior to the civil rights revolution. Some decline in Democratic identification was inevitable as the South became electorally competitive and conservative voters moved into the Republican camp. Nonetheless, Bartels's interpretation of his findings and definition of the white working class are both open to serious challenge.

For starters, given how sharp the rise in economic inequality has been, the expectation from models of self-interested voting has to be that lower-income voters would have moved *into* the Democratic fold, especially given the sharp move to the right of the GOP over this period. Over the last generation, we have seen a massive increase in inequality. The typical American voter has fallen farther and farther behind the rich. If people care about their relative economic standing in the way standard political-economic models suggest they should (e.g., Romer 1975; Meltzer and Richard 1981; Roberts 1977), working-class voters should have shifted decidedly to the left. The implications of this would depend, of course, on the position of the two parties—but with the GOP becoming much more conservative on economic issues and the Democrats only modestly more liberal, the expected outcome would be a shift toward the Democratic Party. Indeed, given how sharply skewed income growth has been, the shift should have occurred among the middle (and even upper-middle) class as well as the working class.

Furthermore, Bartels's definition of the white working class is far too narrow. By his standard of $35,000 in family income, any family with at least one full-time worker with an hourly wage greater than about $17 would not be considered working class, nor would a family with two full-time workers earning in excess of about $8.50 an hour. By comparison, the average unionized blue-collar job paid more than $22 an hour in 2003 (Abramowitz and Teixeira 2008: 13). Because Bartels uses national income distribution rather than distribution among whites, moreover, he classifies only about 23 percent of white voters (rather than a full third) as "working class."

In the rest of this chapter, we follow political sociologist Lane Kenworthy in defining the white working class as whites who tell pollsters that they belong to the working class (so-called self identification)—a group that comprised around four in ten whites (Kenworthy et al. 2007). Analyses that use educational level (for example, less than college degree) or occupation (blue collar or manual worker) end up with similar results. All these definitions hone in on a set of voters for whom the paradox of siding with Republicans in an era of rising inequality is particularly acute. Once the backbone of the Democratic Party, white working-class voters have clearly been on the losing end of the dramatic rise in economic inequality. Their shifting allegiances thus provide a revealing window into the forces behind the lack of broad voter backlash against the GOP in the era of winner-take-all inequality.

Compared with defining the white working class, it might seem easy to define "support for Democrats." Just look at how people vote, particularly in presidential elections. Yet votes in any given election rest heavily on the personality and positions of the particular candidate on the ballot, as well as whether that candidate is an incumbent. For these reasons, the partisan identification of voters is a stronger measure of support for a party and its ideology, if, admittedly, one more divorced from actual choices at the ballot box. Party ID represents a relatively stable characteristic of voters that powerfully shapes not just how people vote—for lower-level offices as well as President—but also how they view the world.

Various definitions of party ID are available, but, thankfully again, the definition does not affect the long-term trend: working-class white voters are less likely to support the Democrats and more likely to support Republicans than they were a generation ago. Figure 1, based on the work of Kenworthy and his colleagues (2007), shows the basic story: in the 1970s, roughly 60 percent of whites who identified as working class said they were Democrats (strong partisans, weak partisans, and independents leaning Democratic). By the 1990s, the share was down to around 40 percent. Using these data, Kenworthy runs through and dismisses a number of common

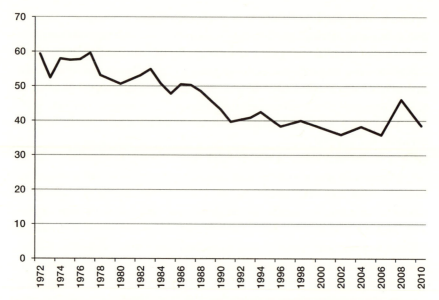

Figure 7.1. Share of white working class identifying with the Democratic Party.
Kenworthy et al. 2007 analysis of General Social Survey, updated by authors.

explanations for the decline. The decline did not just occur in the South, but
was broad-based. Nor was it just a product of general party disaffiliation, as
Republican identification increased. There has been "a genuine decline of
substantial magnitude in Democratic identification among working-class
whites since the mid 1970s" (Kenworthy et al. 2007: 9). Although the white
working class shifted back to the Democrats in 2008, after Kenworthy's paper appeared, by 2010 their support for Democrats had returned to pre-
recession levels.

Class Dismissed?

Whenever a model of the world and reality diverge, it is worth reexamining
the model—not least because doing so makes clear exactly which links in
the chain of logic are weakest. The standard view that less affluent voters
will vote for greater redistribution when inequality increases requires that
voters conceive of their economic interests in a specific way; that they put
their economic interests above other concerns (for example, their social val-

ues); and that they do not have trouble translating their economic interests into policy and partisan preferences. Each link in this chain could break.

To many observers of American politics, the first link in the chain—how voters conceive of their interests—is most vulnerable. Americans do not harbor egalitarian sentiments, skeptics say. Or they insist that all Americans believe they will be rich someday and thus do not believe in redistribution (for the general argument about redistribution and upward mobility, see Benabou and Ok 2001).

Compared with citizens of other rich democracies, Americans do stand out as generally less supportive of government efforts to redistribute income, though the differences are often small. Yet the main message of comparative opinion research is that the United States is *not* a clear outlier with regard to many attitudes regarding inequality (Osberg and Smeeding 2006). Americans are broadly concerned about inequality of income, wealth, and opportunity, and surprisingly (given how much we hear about their *in*egalitarianism), generally supportive of concrete measures to address inequality, insecurity, and hardship (Page and Jacobs 2009).

The key question, in any case, is not whether Americans have distinctive beliefs about redistribution, but whether those beliefs have substantially changed during the era of rising inequality. The evidence is strong they have not. Whether the questions concern basic attitudes toward economic equality or beliefs in upward mobility, the story of the last generation is far more one of stability than of change (Hacker and Pierson 2005).

And to the extent that it is a story of change, the change has probably been toward *greater* concern about inequality, not less. Indeed, according to data from the International Social Survey Programme (ISSP), administered by the General Social Survey in the United States and similar national survey institutions in countries across the globe, Americans grew *more* concerned about inequality in the United States between 1987 and 1999 (Kenworthy and McCall 2007).

While Americans do believe strongly that upward mobility is possible in the United States, they are also more realistic than they are often given credit for about their own prospects. The poll results in Table 7.1 suggest that Americans have not become notably more likely to believe they will climb the income ladder, nor do these numbers suggest that most Americans have a huge amount of faith in the possibility of becoming rich.

Even if Americans are concerned about growing economic gaps and other economic strains, it could be that they do not prioritize these concerns

Table 7.1. Americans' Personal Expectations of Becoming Rich (percent)

"How likely is it that you will ever be rich: very likely, fairly likely, not too likely or not likely at all?"

	1990	1996	2003	2012
Very likely	9	10	10	7
Fairly likely	23	24	21	21

Source: Gallup 2012.

over other issues. Even before *What's the Matter with Kansas?* turned the thesis into conventional wisdom, observers of American politics have argued that many downscale voters put their generally conservative positions on issues of social values, such as abortion and gay marriage, ahead of economic concerns. This thesis is not implausible, particularly when framed around the rise of Christian conservative voters as the cornerstone of the GOP's electoral coalition—a topic we take up later. As a general argument about shifting voter priorities, it falters on several dimensions.

For starters, the idea that economic issues have been eclipsed by values debates in American political debate is directly contradicted by a large and growing body of survey and historical evidence. Mark Smith (2007), for example, has shown that voters have become *more* likely since the 1970s to name the economy as the most important problem facing the nation. Moreover, party platforms (of both parties) are much more focused on economic issues than they were a generation ago. Similarly, Bartels (2008) and Andrew Gelman (2008) both find that economic issues continue to dominate the vote choices of less affluent voters, and indeed that if any segment of the electorate has become more concerned about values debates, it is higher-income voters. And Kenworthy and his colleagues (2007) find that at least until very recently white working-class voters with conservative positions on social issues have been no more likely to defect from the Democrats than white working-class voters with moderate or liberal positions.

By far the biggest oversight of the "values matter most" claim is the clear evidence that the partisan allegiances of Americans have grown more polarized by income since the 1950s and 1960s. This is true whether we look at voting for presidential candidates or identification with one of the two major parties. Republicans now draw their support more consistently from the top of the income distribution, while Democrats draw their support more consistently from the bottom. It is also true of congressional districts. The income gap between districts represented by Republicans and those represented by Democrats has grown (McCarty, Poole, and Rosenthal 2006). The gap is large—voters in the top fifth of the income distribution were about twice as likely to identify with the Republican Party in 2000 as voters in the bottom fifth—and it is larger than the income gap in support for conservative parties than in most other nations for which we have good evidence (Gelman 2008).

Still, this does not resolve the paradox of less affluent voters' support for the GOP. While partisan differences based on income have increased, it remains the case that a substantial—and surprisingly stable—share of less affluent voters are allied with the GOP. Much of the increased relationship between income and party ID is driven by growing GOP allegiance among the well off. This is especially clear when we look at the voting patterns of white Americans. Since the 1960s, African Americans have overwhelmingly voted for the Democratic Party, and this is true among higher-income and lower-income blacks alike. (Hispanics are predominantly but less solidly Democratic, and class is more important in explaining their partisan allegiance, but they were not a large presence in the electorate in the 1960s, a fact that makes long-term analysis more difficult.) Among whites, however, the parties have remained in much closer parity, and there is a substantial and growing gap in support for Democrats between lower- and higher-income voters. Despite that growing gap, whites in the bottom third of the national income distribution have actually shifted toward the Republican Party—they have simply shifted less than whites in the top third of the income distribution.

We can safely dismiss the claim that Americans do not care about economic issues or have no qualms about inequality (or at least care less or have fewer qualms than thirty years ago). A harder-headed view shows a great deal of discontent, yet also a great deal of confusion and a surprising lack of knowledge. This provides an important clue, as we shall see.

An Organizational Policy Perspective

If the problem with the simple median-voter account is not that people are unconcerned with inequality or inherently opposed to redistribution, or that they prioritize other issues at the voting booth, what is left? The set of arguments we focus on are more organizational and informational than attitudinal. They say that, yes, people care about inequality and are relatively egalitarian (or at least no less egalitarian than in the past), but this doesn't translate into consistent votes for the more egalitarian party—that is, the Democrats.

This could be because voters

1. do not understand where they are in distribution of income or how the distribution has changed,
2. do not understand the connection between their position in the distribution and policy or partisan choices,
3. do not believe government and its leaders can or will address their interests, or
4. do not have, or believe they have, the capacity to make their leaders change course.

All four of these sources of disconnect are deeply organizational; they rest on the degree to which voters have the institutional means for understanding and leverage. And all four, we will argue, have been undermined by the transformation of the organizational landscape of American politics over the last generation.

In making our case, we owe much to a famous argument about voters and parties made over two decades ago by Adam Przeworski and John Sprague (1986). Przeworski and Sprague's question was simple: Why do working-class voters sometimes overwhelmingly support left parties and why do they sometimes not? But in contrast with the reigning explanations of their day (and ours), they centered attention on what *parties* did, rather than what voters thought. "Our central thesis," Przeworksi and Sprague (9) argued, "is that the voting behavior of individuals is an effect of the activities of political parties. More precisely, the relative salience of class as a determinant of individual voting behavior is a cumulative consequence of the strategies pursued by political parties of the left." In other words, voters were not naturally aware of some set of objective economic interests. Rather, parties had to bring voters to that awareness and link it concretely to what parties were offering. Rather than focusing on individual attributes of voters, focus on the organizations that bring them into politics—namely, parties.

Przeworski and Sprague stopped their observation at parties, seeing the central problem for parties as balancing the need to mobilize truly working-class voters on the basis of their class interest while also attracting more af-fluent voters to gain a majority. A broader organizational perspective shows that parties are not the only organizations that shape voters' perceived inter-ests. More important, parties do not merely seek votes; they also seek to cultivate—indeed, embody—a coalition of organized interests that may well pull parties away from the demands of voters when interest group and voter priorities or demands diverge (Bawn et al. 2012; Cohen et al. 2008). These broader organizational factors—the groups that bring voters into politics and shape their interests (including but not limited to parties) and the interest-group coalitions that make up parties—are the focus of our account.

That interest groups seek to influence policy through the parties has two important implications for the study of political economy. First, parties often seek to be responsive to the concerns of policy-demanding interest groups even when these threaten to conflict with the preferences of the me-dian voter. To be successful, politicians cultivate the support of organized interests who are capable of providing financial and other valued political resources. The imperative for policymakers is to minimize the tradeoffs when the desires of groups and the desires of voters collide. Second, major shifts in the overall balance of organized interests are likely to exert effects on *both* major parties, although often in different ways. If the balance of power among interests shifts, politicians are likely to adjust their supportive coalitions. For instance, important elements of the Democratic Party have responded to the transformed balance of organized power by repositioning themselves on a number of critical issues, including taxation and deregula-tion, in ways that have undercut the party's ability to present a clear alterna-tive to voters on key economic issues.

In sum, parties are coalitions of policy-seeking organized interests as well as of vote-seeking politicians, and their behavior cannot simply be reduced to the demands of voters. The demands of voters and supportive interests are often in acute tension within a party's orbit. This tension mat-ters, in part, because parties play a crucial role informing voters of their interests and shaping their understanding of the link between those inter-ests and what parties and government do—voters have to be organized into the political economy. And parties are not the only groups that do such or-ganizing. Social networks, voluntary organizations, the media—all these organizations form the crucible within which voters come to see the connections, or not, between the changes in their economic lives and what is happening, or not, in D.C. These organizations have left lower- and middle-income voters unmoored in a way they were not a generation ago.

The Organizational Rise of American Business

The growth of inequality over the last generation coincided with two widely recognized political shifts: the rise of a more powerful and conservative Republican Party (Pierson and Skocpol 2007) and, related, the dramatic increase in political polarization (McCarty, Poole, and Rosenthal 2006; Fiorina, Abrams, and Pope 2004). Another transformation has received far less attention: the balance of organized economic interests has shifted decisively in favor of employers and the affluent. Based on the preceding discussion, it is this profound organizational shift that may be of greatest significance for voters' incentives and abilities to hold politicians to account for rising inequality.

Although signs of steeply rising inequality are visible in many aspects of American life, one of the clearest manifestations has been the sharp shift in organizational power from workers to employers. The critical decade of the 1970s, which signaled the move from a broad-based postwar settlement to a politics of winner-take-all, was marked by a remarkable expansion of business power. The basic story of this expansion has been ably told (Vogel 1989). Always a big part of American political life, employers faced a series of surprising setbacks in the 1960s and early 1970s—particularly the dramatic expansion of regulatory power in Washington on issues from the environment to occupational safety to consumer protection (Melnick 2005). As David Vogel (1989: 59) summarizes, between 1969 and 1972 "virtually the entire American business community experienced a series of political setbacks without parallel in the post-war period." By 1971, future Supreme Court justice Lewis Powell felt compelled to assert, in a memo that helped galvanize business circles, that the "American economic system is under broad attack."

The organizational counteroffensive was swift. The number of corporations with public affairs offices in Washington grew from 100 in 1968 to over 500 in 1978. In 1971, only 175 firms had registered lobbyists in Washington, but by 1982, 2,445 did. The number of corporate PACs increased from under 300 in 1976 to over 1,200 by mid-1980. Of greater political significance was the expansion of the collective capacities of employers, allowing them to mobilize more proactively and on a much broader front.[1]

When he penned his influential memo, Powell was chair of the Education Committee of the Chamber of Commerce, one of a number of business groups that responded to the emerging challenge by becoming much more organized (Vogel 1989). It doubled in membership between 1974 and 1980; its budget tripled. The National Federation of Independent Business doubled its membership between 1970 and 1979. The Business Roundtable, designed to mobilize high-level CEOs for advancement of shared interests, was formed in 1972.

The role of the business community not only grew but expanded. Employers and wealthy families poured vast new resources into efforts designed not just to lobby on particular bills but also to shape the broader political climate. Especially prominent in this effort were wealthy sunbelt activists who were staunch economic conservatives and fiercely critical of the basic contours of the post-World War II domestic settlement between labor and industry. They nurtured an interlocking system of new foundations and think tanks—organizations that saw their role as shaping the political agenda and shifting public opinion and public policy in a conservative direction.[2]

Recognizing that lawmaking in Washington had become more open and dynamic, business groups remade themselves to fit the times. Ironically, the expanding network of business groups hoisted the public interest groups on their own petards. Using rapidly emerging tools of marketing and communications, they developed capacities to generate mass campaigns. Building networks of employees, shareholders, local companies, and firms with shared interests (e.g., retailers and suppliers), they soon could flood Washington with letters and phone calls. Within a few years, these classically top-down organizations thrived at generating "bottom-up" style campaigns that not only matched the efforts of their rivals but surpassed them.

These emerging "outside" strategies were married to "inside" ones. Business organizations developed lists of prominent executives capable of making personal contacts with key legislative figures. In private meetings organized by the Conference Board, CEOs compared notes and discussed how to learn from and outmaneuver organized labor. In the words of one executive, "If you don't know your senators on a first-name basis, you are not doing an adequate job for your stockholders."

As its organizational clout grew, business also massively increased its political giving. Moreover, it did so at precisely the time when the cost of campaigns began to skyrocket (in part because of the ascendance of television). The insatiable need for cash gave politicians good reason to be attentive to those with deep pockets. Business had by far the deepest pockets, and was happy to contribute to members of both parties.

Business did so generously from the mid-1970s to the mid-1980s. But, as Thomas Edsall (1984) has observed, this should not be treated as an indication of nonpartisanship. Rough parity in spending at the level of candidates masked the fact that business was actually treating the two parties very differently. What money business gave to Democrats went almost exclusively to incumbents, especially moderate to conservative ones. Republicans, by contrast, got money for open seats, for challengers, and for party-building efforts. Individual Democratic incumbents could finance their reelection bids, but the difference in the financial resources—and hence the organizational capacities—of the parties became massive in this period.

The targets of business largesse in the two parties differed because the donations served different purposes. Financing the GOP was an investment. Business money nurtured a cadre of elected officials committed to a deregulatory and tax-cutting agenda. It also increased the capacity of the Republican Party to gain power and make the case for the religion of free markets. Corporations and wealthy individuals bankrolled a party infrastructure committed to advancing a business agenda, refining messages for public consumption, and marketing them energetically.

Money to Democrats played a very different but no less important role. It was a form of insurance. The money went largely to individuals rather than to the party as an organization. It was destined for the powerful and "moderates." As prominent business lobbyist Charles Walker (quoted in Blumenthal 1988: 81) put it, corporate PACs were "very important in affecting ideological balance in Congress. Members now have alternative places to look for campaign contributions."

The main goal of channeling money to influential or swing Democrats was to minimize any prospect of distasteful legislation. Carefully targeted contributions could effectively exploit the multiple channels American political institutions make available for diversion, dilution, or delay. Even grudging or quiet support from a handful of Democrats—particularly well-placed ones—could make a huge difference. Such allies could help keep issues off the agenda, substitute symbolic initiatives for real ones, add critical loopholes, or instigate unnecessary compromises with the GOP. Willing Democrats could also provide valuable bipartisan cover for business-friendly Republican initiatives.

In short, the newly mobilized business groups understood that Democrats and Republicans could play distinct but complementary roles in a new politics that fostered rising inequality. Clifton Garvin, chairman of both Exxon and the Business Roundtable in the early 1980s, summarized the attitude toward partisanship this way: "The Roundtable tries to work with whichever political party is in power. We may each individually have our own political alliances, but as a group the Roundtable works with every administration to the degree they let us."

The extraordinary increase in the political capacities of business organizations was the central story in Washington in the mid- to late 1970s. In a few short years, business had gone from a state of panic to unquestioned preeminence. This reversal in governance occurred during the late 1970s, at a time when Democrats held the White House and had large majorities in both houses of Congress. The period prior to Reagan's victory was marked by a series of legislative triumphs: defeat of health care and labor law reform and of efforts to establish a consumer protection agency; the beginnings of the deregulation revolution; and, most dramatically, a major tax bill anchored by steep cuts in the capital gains tax. The broad advance of this business agenda at a time of unified Democratic control provides telling evidence that much of governance is a matter of organized combat rather than electoral spectacle.

The Decline of Middle-Class Organization on Economic Issues

The shifting contours of organized combat were not exclusively a matter of increasing corporate mobilization. While the new clout of business represented the biggest development, it was just one of a number of transformations within the universe of organizations contesting for political influence. These developments were diverse, and flowed from a variety of forces in American society. They included everything from the continuing growth of public interest groups in areas like the environment, feminism, and civil rights to the rise of Christian conservatism. Yet there was a common theme linking these disparate trends: all of them worked to diminish the presence of organized voices addressing the *economic* concerns of ordinary Americans in Washington.[3]

We focus here on three primary causes of this transformation: the decline of labor, the shift away from mass-membership, locally rooted political organizations and toward centralized mailing-list D.C.-based groups (with the notable but revealing exception of Christian conservatism), and the increasing importance of money in political life.

(1) Labor's fall. Second only in importance to the ascent of business was the continuing decline of organized labor. Of course, by international standards the United States has long been distinguished by weak unions. Even from a relatively modest starting point, however, the scale of its decline over the past few decades remains astonishing, and far more severe than what has transpired in most market economies. In the decade after World War II, more than a third of wage and salary workers in the United States were in unions. By 2004 the share had dropped to 12 percent, with just 7.4 percent in the private sector (BLS 2007).

Economists often focus on unions' contribution to greater equality through their bargaining over wages. This is a mistake. It is the *political* role of organized labor on issues of economic and social policy that matters most. The political consequences of union strength are difficult to exaggerate. Social scientists have consistently shown that the strength of organized labor has a very large impact on development of social policies across nations. Strong labor unions are closely associated with low levels of inequality and more generous social programs (Huber and Stephens 2001). In the American context, unions represent by far the most significant organized interest with a sustained stake in the material circumstances of those with modest means. The decline of organized labor has greatly diminished pressure on policy-makers to sustain or refurbish commitments to social provision made in the mid-twentieth century.

(2) Atrophying of mass-membership organizations. The impact of business's rise at the expense of labor—a shift that receives remarkably limited discussion among students of American politics—has been reinforced by other developments in the organizational universe. Union decline has been just one component (although probably the most important one) of what Theda Skocpol has demonstrated to be a broader transformation of political organizations since the 1960s: a shift from "membership to management" (Skocpol 2004).

With one major exception we will discuss in a moment, mass-membership organizations with true grassroots presence have atrophied. In their place have arisen Washington-based advocacy groups with professional management teams and mailing-list memberships. Some of these are "Astroturf" organizations, purporting to be broad-based but in actuality run by industry lobbyists. Others may have memberships in the hundreds of thousands, but the participation of these members is limited to writing a check in response to expertly designed solicitations from headquarters. Organizations that once carried the economic concerns of ordinary citizens to Washington— not just unions, but fraternal societies, broad civic organizations, and, in America's cities, strong local party operations—have largely lost their role in national politics.

To be sure, the shift from membership to management has not pushed politics consistently in one ideological direction. New "public-interest" organizations, organized around the environment, civil rights and liberties, and other single-issue causes associated with the left of the political spectrum, have proliferated (Berry 2000). But it is not just an issue of "left" vs. "right." Rather, it is an issue of the capacity of working- and middle-class citizens to find *organized* expression of their economic interests. The shifts on both left and right have worked to mute that expression.

On the left, the ascendant organized groups in the liberal coalition have become a critical base of support for the Democratic Party. For instance, Emily's List, which supports women candidates for elective office, has become one of the largest sources of financial support for Democratic candidates. Yet with respect to governance, these groups have almost *never* focused on the economic issues that most powerfully affect the working and middle classes. Their concerns, such as environmentalism, women's rights, and civil liberties, are largely those of the most affluent members of the Democratic Party. Even where the potential for a strong focus on economic disadvantage seems evident, as with groups advancing the concerns of minorities and women, D.C. organizations have tended to give such matters low priority (Berry 2000).

The one exception to the trend away from grassroots organization with a solid footing in the working and middle classes is a very big one: the rise of Christian conservatism. Yet far from countering the broad organizational shift in American society away from middle-class economic concerns, this development reinforced it. It did so by aligning a large group of moderate- income voters with a political party highly attuned to the economic concerns of the wealthy.

Of course, the impact of this development can be exaggerated. As Bartels (2008) and others (e.g., Gelman 2008) have convincingly argued, the rise of a more conservative American political establishment does not seem to reflect an eclipse of economic concerns by "moral issues." Yet it is still the case that evangelical voters "tip" to the Republican column at a much lower income level than similar voters who do not identify as evangelicals. They do so, in part, because the groups that help mobilize Christian conservative voters do so explicitly around moral issues rather than economic ones. The leaders of the Christian right have formed an alliance, through the Republican Party, with powerful interests deeply committed to advancing a more unequal economy—another example of how the group basis of the parties profoundly matters for the choices of voters (Hacker and Pierson 2010a: 201–4). In this sense, it is hard to deny that the organizational development of Christian conservatism has provided an important support for a low-tax, pro-business, upwardly redistributive policy agenda.

(3) *Growing importance of political money.* One final shift in the organizational terrain has also been critical. It is not just that business became much more organized, and the reach of traditional mass-membership groups and unions declined. More broadly, the organizational routines of American politics have been monetized. Campaigns, for example, have become more focused on media and advertising, and thus more preoccupied with the huge sums needed to make such efforts. In response, politicians have turned to affluent donors and organized interests as never before to finance these spiraling costs. Moreover, this has happened at exactly the same time as American society has grown much more unequal. The parties, for example, now contact between a quarter (Democratic Party) and a third (Republican Party) of the wealthiest of Americans directly during campaign seasons, up from less than 15 percent of these high-income voters in the 1950s (Campbell 2007).

Thanks to rising gains at the top, moreover, wealthy Americans are vastly richer than they used to be. As donors to campaigns and causes and as political activists in their own right, they simply cannot be ignored. And while they can be found at all points on the political spectrum, they have distinctive policy preferences on economic issues. Though few surveys reach enough truly rich Americans to form reliable inferences about the political preferences of the extremely well off, what evidence there is suggests that the rich are more conservative economically—less supportive of economic re-distribution and measures to provide economic security—and, on average, better informed about policy than ordinary Americans (Gilens 2009). One survey regarding the 2003 tax cuts, for example, found that the wealthiest were both more supportive of and more informed about the dividend and capital gains tax cuts than less affluent voters (Hacker and Pierson 2005).

The growing influence of money in politics has generally been helpful to Republicans. The money chase reinforces the GOP's low-tax, limited-government message. For the Democrats, on the other hand, it introduces major cross-pressures, giving them a strong incentive to reduce their focus on issues of redistribution and economic security in order to appeal to afflu-ent voters and moneyed groups as sources of campaign cash.

On balance, these changes in the organizational universe over the past generation have weakened the political voice of ordinary citizens on eco-nomic issues. As we show in the next section, they have also had a substan-tial impact on the capacities and perceptions of American voters. We continue our earlier focus on the white working class—perhaps the most puzzling case of what Bartels (2008) has evocatively called "self-interest, poorly understood" (a play on Tocqueville's "self-interest, properly under-stood"). Yet we begin our story where Bartels ends off, showing how lack of understanding goes hand in hand with lack of organizational leverage and lack of confidence in government, and how both have deep roots in the or-ganizational changes discussed in the last section.

The Unmoored American Voter

The organizational transformation just explored has had at least three pro-found effects on the ability of working- and middle-class voters to understand the links between their own situation, rising inequality more generally, and what is going on in Washington. First, it has weakened the organizational leverage of these voters; second, it has undermined their confidence in gov-ernment and politicians; and third, it has made it harder for them to grasp the extent of rising inequality, how it specifically affects them, and what, in terms of partisan and policy choices, might be done about it.

(1) Lack of leverage. In the last section, we charted the precipitous decline in the organizational involvement of American voters, driven by the fall of labor and mass-based voluntary membership organizations. All these trends

have been particularly acute for the white working class. In 1974, according to the General Social Survey, more than 70 percent of white working-class voters claimed to be members of at least one organization or club. By 2004, the number was barely over 51 percent. Among white voters who described themselves as "middle class" or "upper class," the decline was substantially more modest—from nearly 81 percent to just over 73 percent. Of course, organization is most crucial for less affluent voters, who are less likely to participate overall (and in particular less capable of donating money to political campaigns and causes), and more reliant on group membership for cues and leverage. Yet the transformation of the American organizational landscape hit the white working class harder than perhaps any other group.

  (2) Lack of confidence. In tandem with a decline in leverage, white working-class voters—indeed, middle- and working-class voters in general—lost confidence in the ability of government to protect their economic standing and security. Among the white working class, voters today are much less confident in Congress, much less likely to say they trust government, and much more likely to say that what government does is controlled by special interests. In 1968, for example, less than half of white working-class voters said they believed government was "run by a few big interests," according to the American National Election Studies (ANES). In the early 1990s, the share was more than 80 percent. Thus, the increased influence of business has both reduced the sway of working-class voters *and* fostered greater pessimism about the capacity of government to respond effectively to their interests.[4]

  (3) Lack of understanding. Finally, the organizational transformations just charted have reduced the degree to which less affluent voters receive strong cues and actionable information—whether from membership organizations such as labor or from political officials and parties. Most Americans simply do not know all that much about economic inequality or the contours of economic policy, and understanding is weakest among those on the short end of the economic stick. This is certainly not new; the weakness of public understanding of basic facts of politics and policy is perhaps the best documented finding of survey research (Hacker and Pierson 2010a). Yet this longstanding feature of American public opinion is much more consequential in an era in which rising economic inequality and dwindling political capacity are both buffeting less affluent voters.

  Perhaps the most arresting illustration is provided by surveys on perceived inequality. In these polls—which, helpfully, have been done across a large number of nations—people are first asked what salaries workers in different occupations earn. Then, survey respondents are asked what people in these different jobs *should* earn. The size of the gap between the two sets of answers—between perceived and desired earnings—provides a rough measure of how much people want to reduce inequality.

According to these surveys, Americans *appear* to be relatively tolerant of inequality, compared with citizens of other nations. The gap between what they think people should earn and what they think they do earn is smaller than the norm. But the reason Americans are tolerant is not because they support greater differences in what people should earn. Rather, it is mostly because they think there is less inequality in what people do earn—even though the United States has far and away the highest level of actual inequality among rich democracies. In other words, Americans are no less egalitarian when it comes to their vision of an ideal world. But they are much less accurate when it comes to their vision of the real world (Osberg and Smeeding 2006).

Revealingly, the greatest misperceptions concern the earnings of those at the top. Americans seem relatively good at figuring out what people in "normal" jobs earn. But when they try to estimate the earnings of wealthier workers, they substantially undershoot the mark. Asked in 2007 what a CEO of a national company earned, the average response was a half a million dollars, at a time when the average CEO of a large national corporation earned over $14 million (Page and Jacobs 2009: 43). Although Americans are not alone in underestimating earnings at the top—people in all countries do—they underestimate earnings at the top much more than do citizens of other nations (Osberg and Smeeding 2006).

Does this misperception matter? A wording variation in the ANES suggests it does. The ANES occasionally includes a question asking whether "it is the responsibility of the government to reduce the differences in income between people with high incomes and those with low incomes." Typically, around one in five Americans agree. In 2008, however, the survey laid out how much people in the top and bottom portions of the income distribution actually earned. After this, the same proposition was read again. This time, *57 percent* favored reducing income inequality.[5]

Of course, artificial interventions like these might not resemble what happens in the real world of politics, in which advocates are waging constant— if often highly lopsided—rhetorical battle. But in a world of declining citizen organization, in which political elites invest huge amounts of time and money to shape how Americans think about issues in ways that favor those elites' agendas, most Americans find it very hard to link their broad economic concerns to the contours of specific policies.

Consider the political struggles over the estate tax that culminated in its phased elimination in 2001 (Graetz and Shapiro 2005). The 2001 tax cuts reflected a fierce battle among organizations and elites. Public opinion simply was not decisive. As late as January 2000—just over a year before the estate tax was repealed—more than half of Americans said "they did not know enough to say" whether the estate tax was too high or too low. In 2003 (*after* repeal passed), two-thirds of Americans either thought the estate tax affected most Americans (49 percent) or had no idea (18 percent), and a large majority of those who supported repeal did so because the estate tax affected "too many people." Support for repeal fell from around 60 percent to just under half when respondents were asked to consider an estate tax with an exemption of at least $1 million (the level that was scheduled to kick in under prior law), and to just over a third when asked to consider an estate tax with an exemption of at least $5 million (a proposed compromise that was rejected) (Birney, Graetz, and Shapiro 2006).

Of course, many voters said they were favorable toward tax cuts in the abstract, just as many voters say they want to spend more on virtually everything government does in the abstract. But poll after poll showed that this support crumbled when voters were asked to rank tax cuts relative to other priorities, or to judge the specific distribution (tilted toward the top) and size (very large) of the Bush tax cuts. Indeed, an internal memo from the Treasury Department communications office cautioned against any mention of tradeoffs, because voters considered tax cuts less important than sustaining financing for education, Social Security, or other social programs (Hacker and Pierson 2005: 52). Perhaps most important, these superficially favorable attitudes toward tax cuts were deeply influenced by public skepticism toward government and its capacity to effectively carry out positive courses of action with public dollars.

We have focused here on tax policy precisely because it is simple compared with other policies—it is comparatively easy to figure out who pays more or less due to tax policy changes. Other government policies, such as health insurance programs and subsidized loans—have much less direct and easily traced effects. As Suzanne Mettler (2011) has convincingly argued, policies today are arguably more complicated than ever, because government is relying more on private contractors and other nongovernmental entities, while doing more through tax breaks like the child- care tax credit that was one of Bill Clinton's signature policies for the middle class. Against the backdrop of this "submerged state," as Mettler calls it, it is all the more important for ordinary voters to have reliable signals and the leverage to translate those signals into pressure on politicians—all the more important, but not all the more likely.

Conclusion

Electoral politics is clearly of great significance. The American electoral structure, with its relatively low voter participation and geographically bounded majoritarian elections that have become less and less competitive, does reduce the voice of less privileged Americans in national politics.

Nonetheless, the hyper-concentrated nature of recent economic gains is exceedingly difficult to reconcile with any simple median-voter account of voters' interests, even one that takes these electoral biases seriously.[6] Instead, the reality of soaring inequality combined with declining government efforts to deal with it calls out for explanations that consider a key element of the political landscape besides voters and legislators: the shifting balance and activities of organized interests. When we take this broader view, it becomes clear that the balance of organized interests—the political actors with the greatest incentive and means to influence complex policy outcomes over long periods of time—has shifted sharply towards employers and the affluent and away from those of low and moderate means.

To be sure, voters wield real power through the ballot box, but their attention to what government actually does is limited and typically brief. In our fragmented polity, victories without enduring organization are fleeting. Struggles over policy—over what the government actually *does* for and to its citizens—are usually long, hard slogs. These are struggles that involve drawn-out conflicts in multiple arenas, extremely complicated issues where only full-time, well-trained participants are likely to be effective, and stakes that can easily reach hundreds of billions of dollars. Inevitably, organized groups are crucial actors, usually *the* crucial actors, in these struggles. And while such groups care deeply about elections, they also are shrewd enough, and experienced enough, to place competition for votes in proper perspective. This helps to explain why only perhaps a tenth of the billions that corporations spend on politics is directly connected to electoral contests—the rest goes to efforts to shape mass and elite opinion and to lobbying, a field where spending has doubled in just a decade (Drutman 2010). For powerful groups, the action is in Washington, not the swing states.

This perspective casts in a very different light the much-examined puzzle of why working-class white voters often support Republicans. As we have seen, there is little question that the identification of working-class white voters with the Democratic Party has declined, and that this decline is not just a result of the partisan realignment of the South (Kenworthy et al. 2007; Abramowitz and Teixeira 2008; cf. Bartels 2008). But this decline, we have argued, should be seen as organizational at least as much as attitudinal. Working-class whites have also experienced a steep decline in their affiliation with associations, such as unions, that once brought them into politics. At the same time, the Democratic Party, in the search for campaign funds and the votes of more affluent social liberals, has lessened its emphasis on the populist elements of its agenda with the most appeal to these voters. And, of course, the GOP has heavily recruited these voters by stressing the individual gains from lower taxes and more limited government. These appeals have had particular resonance at a time when these voters' trust in government has plummeted and other organizational voices have retreated.

Especially important in this perspective is changing public trust in government, driven not just by political rhetoric but also by perceived changes in what government does (and on whose behalf it does it). Notably, GOP electoral inroads among less affluent voters have occurred alongside declining public confidence in government and a growing perception that politicians are excessively responsive to "special interests." In this context, calls for limited government and self-reliance receive greater hearing, especially when there are few contrary organizational signals pushing voters the other way.

Our argument, in short, is that the failure of American political elites to respond effectively to rising inequality—and, indeed, the strong evidence that they have abetted this inequality (Hacker and Pierson 2010a)—can only be explained if we situate the role of voters in a larger organizational context. Elections matter greatly, but their effectiveness in creating responsiveness to voters' economic interests is deeply circumscribed and shaped by the organizational context within which voters' perceptions of their interests and policy understandings are formed. It would be comforting to think that better framing of issues or more effective get-out-the-vote drives on election day would address these larger structural factors. But for those concerned about the declining responsiveness of American political elites to less affluent voters, there is no substitute for the hard work of addressing the broader decline of the organizational foundations of middle-class democracy in the United States.

References

Abramowitz, Alan, and Ruy A. Teixeira. 2008. "The Decline of the White Working Class and the Rise of a Mass Upper Middle Class." In *Red, Blue, and Purple America: The Future of Election Demographics*, ed. Ruy A. Teixeira. Washington, D.C.: Brookings Institution Press. 104–46.

Bartels, Larry. 2008. *Unequal Democracy: The Political Economy of the Gilded Age.* Princeton, N.J.: Princeton University Press.

Bawn, Kathleen, Martin Cohen, David Karol, Seth Masket, Hans Noel, and John Zaller. 2012. "A Theory of Political Parties: Groups, Policy Demands and Nominations in American Politics." Manuscript. http://masket.net/Theory_of_Parties .pdf.

Benabou, Roland, and Efe A. Ok. 2001. "Social Mobility and the Demand for Redistribution: The POUM Hypothesis." *Quarterly Journal of Economics* 116: 447–87.

Berry, Jeffrey. 2000. *The New Liberalism: The Rising Power of Citizen Groups.* Washington, D.C.: Brookings Institution.

Birney, Mayling, Michael Graetz, and Ian Shapiro. 2006. "Public Opinion and the Push to Repeal the Estate Tax." *National Tax Journal* 59 (3): 439–61.

Blumenthal, Sidney. 1988. *The Rise of the Counter-Establishment.* New York: Harper and Row.

Brooks, David. 2001. "One Nation, Slightly Divisible." *Atlantic Monthly*, December.

Bureau of Labor Statistics, U.S. Department of Commerce. 2007. *Union Members Summary.* www.bls.gov/news.release/union2.nr0htm.

Campbell, Andrea Louise. 2007. "Parties, Electoral Participation, and Shifting Voting Blocs." In *The Transformation of American Politics,* ed. Paul Pierson and Theda Skocpol. Princeton, N.J.: Princeton University Press. 68–101.

Cohen, Marty, David Karol, Hans Noel, and John Zaller. 2008. *The Party Decides: Presidential Nominations Before and After Reform.* Chicago: University of Chicago Press.

Drutman, Lee. 2010. "The Business of America Is Lobbying." Ph.D. dissertation. University of California, Berkeley.

Edsall, Thomas. 1984. *The New Politics of Inequality.* New York: Norton.

Fiorina, Morris P., Samuel J. Abrams, and Jeremy Pope. 2004. *Culture War? The Myth of a Polarized America.* New York: Longmans.

Frank, Thomas. 2004. *What's the Matter with Kansas?* New York: Metropolitan Books.

Gallup. 2012. "Views of the Rich." www.gallup.com/file/poll/154622/Views_of_the_ Rich_120511.pdf.

Gelman, Andrew. 2008. *Red State, Blue State, Rich State, Poor State: Why Americans Vote the Way They Do*. Princeton, N.J.: Princeton University Press.

Gilens, Martin. 2009. "Preference Gaps and Inequality in Representation," *PS: Political Science and Politics* 42 (2): 335–41.

Graetz, Michael J., and Ian Shapiro. 2005. *Death by a Thousand Cuts: The Fight over Taxing Inherited Wealth*. Princeton, N.J.: Princeton University Press.

Hacker, Jacob S., and Paul Pierson. 2005. *Off Center: The Republican Revolution and the Erosion of American Democracy*. New Haven, Conn.: Yale University Press.

———. 2010a. *Winner-Take-All Politics: How Washington Made the Rich Richer—and Turned Its Back on the Middle Class*. New York: Simon and Schuster.

———. 2010b. "Winner-Take-All-Politics." *Politics and Society* 38 (June): 152–204.

Huber, Evelyne, and John Stephens. 2001. *Development and Crisis of the Welfare State: Parties and Politics in Global Markets*. Chicago: University of Chicago Press.

Kenworthy, Lane, Sondra Barringer, Daniel Duerr, and Garrett Andrew Schneider. 2007. "The Democrats and Working-Class Whites." Working paper, University of Arizona. http://www.u.arizona.edu/~lkenwor/thedemocratsandworking classwhites.pdf.

Kenworthy, Lane, and Leslie McCall. 2007. "Inequality, Public Opinion and Redistribution." *Socio-Economic Review* 6 (1): 35–68.

Leighley, Jan, and Jonathan Nagler. 2006. "Class Bias in the U.S. Electorate, 1972–2004." Paper presented at Annual Meeting of the American Political Science Association, August 31–September 3, Philadelphia.

McCarty, Nolan, Keith Poole, and Howard Rosenthal. 2006. *Polarized America: The Dance of Ideology and Unequal Riches*. Cambridge, Mass.: MIT Press.

Melnick, R. Shep. 2005. "From Tax-and-Spend to Mandate-and-Sue: Liberalism After the Great Society." In *The Great Society and the High Tide of Liberalism*, ed. Sidney M. Milkis. Amherst: University of Massachusetts Press. 387–410.

Meltzer, Allan, and Scott F. Richard. 1981. "A Rational Theory of the Size of Government." *Journal of Political Economy* 89 (5): 914–27.

Mettler, Suzanne. 2011. *The Submerged State: How Invisible Government Policies Undermine American Democracy*. Chicago: University of Chicago Press.

Osberg, Lars, and Timothy Smeeding. 2006. "'Fair' Inequality? Attitudes Toward Pay Differentials: The United States in Comparative Perspective." *American Sociological Review* 71 (3): 450–73.

Page, Benjamin, and Lawrence Jacobs. 2009. *Class War? What Americans Really Think about Economic Inequality*. Chicago: University of Chicago Press.

Pierson, Paul, and Theda Skocpol, eds. 2007. *The Transformation of American Politics*. Princeton, N.J.: Princeton University Press.

Piketty, Thomas, and Emmanual Saez. 2003. "Income Inequality in the United States, 1913–1998." *Quarterly Journal of Economics* 118 (1): 1–39.

Poole, Keith, and Howard Rosenthal. 2012. Vote View. http://voteview.com/about.asp

Przeworski, Adam, and John D. Sprague. 1986. *Paper Stones: A History of Electoral Socialism*. Chicago: University of Chicago Press.

Rich, Andrew. 2005. "War of Ideas: Why Mainstream and Liberal Foundations and the Think Tanks They Support Are Losing in the War of Ideas in American Politics." *Stanford Social Innovation Review* (Spring).

Roberts, Kevin W. S. 1977. "Voting over Income Tax Schedules." *Journal of Public Economics* 8 (3): 329–40.

Romer, Thomas. 1975. "Individual Welfare, Majority Voting and the Properties of a Linear Income Tax." *Journal of Public Economics* 4 (4): 163–85.

Saez, Emmanuel. 2012. *Striking It Richer: The Evolution of Top Incomes in the United States*. http://elsa.berkeley.edu/~saez/saez-UStopincomes-2010.pdf.

Skocpol, Theda. 2004. *Diminished Democracy: From Membership to Management in American Civic Life*. Norman: University of Oklahoma Press.

Smith, Mark A. 2007. *The Right Talk: How Conservatives Transformed the Great Society into the Economic Society*. Princeton, N.J.: Princeton University Press.

Tocqueville, Alexis de. 2000 [1835]. *Democracy in America*. Trans. and ed. Harvey C. Mansfield and Delba Winthrop. Chicago: University of Chicago Press.

Vogel, David. 1989. *Fluctuating Fortunes: The Political Power of Business in America*. New York: Basic Books.

CHAPTER 8

A Democratic Balance: Bureaucracy, Political Parties, and Political Representation

Pradeep Chhibber and Susan L. Ostermann

Political representation is experiencing an intellectual renaissance. A spate of new work (Manin 1997; Mansbridge 2003; Rehfeld 2006; Urbinati 2000, 2006; Urbinati and Warren 2008; Warren 2008; Williams 1998) has generated renewed interest in political representation—an idea that had been virtually silenced after Pitkin's (1967) masterful treatment of the subject in *The Concept of Representation*. In this paper we focus on political representation in electoral democracies and make one claim—that political representation may not be possible in the absence of a well-functioning and well-disciplined bureaucracy.[1]

We argue that a voter is represented by her elected representative when there is an *institutionalized* policy relationship between the state and the voter—or, a bureaucracy that fairly implements the political decisions authorized by voters. In states where the bureaucracy is corrupt, politicized, or virtually nonexistent, effective representation of voters' interests is unlikely. Political representation, therefore, requires not only a mechanism for electing representatives, but also parties whose organizations have mechanisms for advocacy of voters' interests, and a government that can successfully institutionalize voter interests once they are turned into laws or policies.

Why are we focusing our attention only on political representation in representative democracies?[2] We stress this particular relationship since free and fair elections are equated with representative democracy.[3] If the claims in this chapter hold up, we may be faced with a distinctly uncomfortable theoretical possibility—that electoral democracy need not be representative.[4]

The first part of the paper isolates authorization, sympathy (either as advocacy and/or stand-in representation), and accountability as the three main features that define political representation. Formally (and consistent with the claims of polyarchy), voting is supposed to ensure such representation, especially authorization and accountability. If, however, we ask why a voter votes the way she does, we need to articulate what constitutes a sympathetic relationship between a voter and her representative. Such an articulation leads to the conclusion that minimal notions of democracy are not truly representative and, hence, devoid of any real political content. The development of this sympathetic relationship between the voter and her representative, we argue, is only possible when the interests of the represented to the representative are (effectively) institutionalized *within* the state.

The second part of the chapter discusses the social cleavage theory of party systems. Only those social groups whose interests are institutionalized *within* a state can successfully be represented by a party system. In the third section we introduce, with thanks to Ahuja and Chhibber (2012), the notion of a capricious state—a state in which ad hoc and arbitrary policy implementation is the norm. A capricious state undermines political representation. We claim that in capricious states the norm is not political representation but *selective* political representation—a form of representation that results in a voter seeing the political process as representing someone else's interests, not hers. A capricious state severs the self-interested tie of a voter to her representative.

The fourth section provides evidence from India where—despite fifty years of elections—a capricious state has undermined political representation. We provide evidence for the capricious state and show that these conditions lead citizens to see the state as selectively representative. Consequently, the links between social divisions and the party system are weak and fragile. We then provide evidence that where the bureaucracy is doing its job and parties are not the tools of individual politicians, political representation is possible. We also suggest a mechanism which may be responsible for the failure of many Indian politicians to discipline the bureaucracy and ensure the type of representation their voters demand. Finally, we conclude with some implications and caveats.

The Vote, Political Representation, and Minimal Theories of Democracy

Without prejudice to the various claims and counter-claims about whether political representation is a coherent concept, a consensus exists that political representation in a democracy (an institutional arrangement in which some group of voters elects a representative) entails authorization; a sympathetic relationship between voters and their representatives (either as advocacy and/or as stand-in representation); and accountability (Urbinati and Warren 2008; Rehfeld 2006). Urbinati (2000) states this succinctly when she observes that, for political representation to exist, "a constituency must authorize a person (party) to represent them; that person (party) must act in some way to pursue her constituents' interests; and finally, the constituency must have some ability to hold that representative accountable for what she did." The values associated with each of these terms could, however, vary widely, and this fact is what gives representation its multifaceted slipperiness (Pitkin 1967). Despite this elusiveness, there is consensus among contemporary theorists of representation that the three terms—authorization, "substantive" or "sympathetic" acting for, and accountability, are necessary for any relationship to be properly classed as "representative."

Formally, the very act of voting for someone—either a candidate or a party that has sought a voter's vote—can yield "authorization" and "accountability." In an electoral democracy, where a candidate and/or party is elected by a group of people according to well-established rules (that are understood by all), the candidate and/or party who gets particular voters' votes is authorized to act as their representative. Formal accountability is ensured as long as this representative can be removed from office when the candidate and/or party actively seek votes for reelection. Formal accountability is also preserved so long as a representative can be removed from office by a previously agreed upon legal process or procedure for any illegal actions that representative takes.

This formal understanding of authorization and accountability is consistent with the minimalist theories of democracy in which democracy is almost exclusively dependent upon elections. There are numerous versions of these theories. Dahl's polyarchy (1971: 33–36) requires that control over government decisions about policy be constitutionally vested in elected officials; elected officials must be chosen in frequent and fairly conducted elections in which coercion is comparatively uncommon; practically all adults must have the right to vote in the election of officials and have the right to run for elective offices in the government; citizens must have an effectively enforceable right to express themselves on political matters broadly defined, without danger of severe punishment; and they must also have effective rights to seek out alternative sources of information and to form relatively independent associations or organizations, including independent political parties and interest groups. Yet, like the popular renditions of Dahl's polyarchy, which require only formal authorization, Huntington (1991:7) saw democracy simply as a system in which the "most powerful collective decision-makers are selected through fair, honest, and periodic elections in which candidates freely compete for votes."

Indeed, since the almost universal adoption of this minimal definition of democracy in the policy world and in quantitative democracy research, free and fair elections have become synonymous with democracy, while political representation has largely been brushed aside. This is somewhat ironic, since Dahl (1994) presented polyarchy as central to "representative democracy"—an institutional arrangement he saw as a central characteristic of the national-state. For Dahl, it was the representative nature of contemporary democracy that differentiated it from direct democracy.

Moreover, while elections can indeed bestow formal authorization, this simple relationship can seem sufficient for political representation only if we do not ask why a representative draws votes in an election. The moment we focus on this more difficult question, we assume there must be a sympathetic relationship between the voter and her representative.[5] Accountability poses the same dilemma. Indeed, while a candidate and/or party that is standing for reelection can be removed from office, the formal requirement does not assess the reasons why a voter seeks to reinstate or replace her representative. If we ask why a voter no longer votes for someone whom she had voted for earlier, we are posing a question similar to the one we asked when trying to ascertain the reasons for why a voter voted for a particular candidate or party in the first place. Answers to these questions depend on the extent to which a representative's actions are tied to the interests of those he or she represents. As long as we focus on formal authorization and accountability without asking why one is authorizing someone and what one is holding that person accountable for, we do not need the notion of a sympathetic relationship. However, once we ask these questions, we are placing sympathy at the heart of the relationship between the representative and the represented.[6] Minimal notions of democracy are by definition therefore not consistent with the idea of representative democracy. And, modern democracy is—at least in aspiration—representative democracy. It is this representativeness that distinguishes it from direct democracy, so minimal notions of democracy should, perhaps, no longer be the focus of attention.

Political Parties and Political Representation

Theories of political representation have focused on establishing a direct relationship between the voter and her representative by first asking whether the representative has a sympathetic relationship with the voter and then identifying the conditions that lead to such a relationship. Political parties, as Urbinati and Warren (2008) note, are often absent from this conversation. This is surprising, since political parties are omnipresent and, in modern electoral representative democracies, lie at the very center of the relationship between a voter and her representative. It is also surprising because there are very few independent representatives anywhere in the world, and, as long as there are legislative bodies, representatives form collective organizations (political parties) to make policy. Moreover, they are both representative and accountable institutions, insofar as the mechanisms authorizing them to legislate and govern, such as electoral rules, are in place,[7] and so long as parties seek to return to power through periodic elections. Thus, it seems appropriate to reintroduce political parties to the representation discussion by asking when and how they substantively "act for" the voters.[8]

The classic case of parties acting on behalf of their constituents is the social cleavage theory of party systems. According to Lipset and Rokkan (1967), modern European party systems were stable because of the presence of strong social cleavages that gave rise to thriving and stable electoral preferences. The growth of parties that mobilized these cleavages, and the institutionalization of these cleavage-based parties through repeated electoral competition, ensured a stable party system. Bartolini and Mair (1990) call this "cleavage closure" and argue that strong party-cleavage linkages stabilize party politics by making cross-party alliances less likely and providing fewer viable alternatives to voters. But how was the continuity of this system of representation ensured?

We argue that for a party to represent a social group successfully, a bureaucracy that will reliably implement the policies adopted by politicians becomes essential. If a bureaucracy acts capriciously—and thus distorts the state's authorized projects—a party can no longer remain representative. Why? In most modern states, as Mainwaring (2006) observes, it is bureaucrats who, as the face of the state, implement the policies adopted by political parties. Thus, it is these same bureaucrats who need to "forgo the selfish and capricious satisfaction of their subjective ends" (Hegel 1967: 191) if representation is to be achieved. This is important because "the conduct and culture of officials is the sphere where the laws and government decisions come into contact with individuals and are actually made good. Hence it is on the conduct of officials that depends not only the contentment of citizens and their confidence in the government, but also the execution—or alternatively the distortion and frustration—of state projects" (Hegel 1967: 192).

Indeed, if the conduct of government officials does not conform to the laws and policies put in place by political parties and/or representatives, what Hegel termed "state projects" become distorted. Ahuja and Chhibber (2009) term a state subject to such distortion a capricious state. In a capricious state, all citizens do not share equally in the services provided by a state. Some need the state's services, but do not have access to them, and are consistently (over a long period of time) excluded from the public goods provided by the state. More important, even when public services are provided, the access of the citizens to these public services is not *institutionalized* but is instead sporadic and ad hoc. Policies are made, but they are not properly implemented. In such a situation, when citizens come in contact with state officials, they are treated disrespectfully and often dismissed. If the state's projects are distorted, or the state acts capriciously, the sympathetic relationship between a voter and her representative is weakened.[9] Mainwaring (2006) echoes these sentiments, calling corruption "the state deficiency that probably has the most *direct* effect on citizen confidence in parties and legislatures." In the next section we argue that the stability of party systems under social cleavage theory is due, in large part, to the institutionalization of the policy interests of voters in the instruments of the state.

Representation and the Social Cleavage Theory of Party Systems

The social cleavage theory of party systems provides a clear instance of the representativeness inherent in an institutionalized relationship between voters and their representatives. According to this theory, political parties each represent a particular group in society. Each group is aware of which party represents it. The social cleavage argument—including its various renditions—has tremendous resonance in comparative and party politics and has been invoked to explain the formation of new parties (parties represent groups which care about new issue areas), vote-switching from one party to another (realignment), and situations in which voters lose faith in a party system altogether (dealignment).

Most versions of the social cleavage theory of party systems leave the mechanism by which social cleavages are represented by political parties unclear. That said, one common way in which social divisions are linked to particular political parties is by assuming that voters' social and/or economic interests are ontologically prior to the positions adopted by political parties. Once we know these voter preferences, we can construct (either through quantitative technique or qualitative/textual analysis) how these claims are represented in the party system.

This line of reasoning has one obvious shortcoming. It is nearly impossible to isolate social and/or economic interests that are ontologically prior to a given set of political institutions. Practically speaking, this means that that we cannot construct the manner in which the representation of particular interests is achieved within the party system by starting with prepolitical interests. In the next section we will show that, instead, the extent to which social interests are aligned with a party system is dependent upon whether the relationship between the voter and her representative is institutionalized within the state.

Bureaucracy and Representation in the Social-Cleavage Theory of Party Systems

In the classic version of the social-cleavage theory of party systems—as advocated by Lipset and Rokkan (1967)—the link between parties and social divisions required three institutional arrangements: first, a state in and through which political parties could represent their constituents; second, the institutionalization of voters' policy interests within the state to ensure the representativeness of the party—an assumed institutional arrangement that went unstated; and, third, political parties that were organized to respond to their voters. In Lipset and Rokkan's interpretation, political parties were representative only when there was a state upon which they could make claims on behalf of their supporters. What Lipset and Rokkan assume, but leave unstated, is that once a policy is adopted by a state, it will be implemented reliably for all voters who belong to groups that would benefit from the policy, and the state will refraining from providing those same benefits in situations that are not authorized by law. Only under such circumstances would the voters who constitute that group continue to support the particular party that enacted the policies in question. Examples abound. In Spain, socialist politicians who instituted policies that represented the interests of their voters created class cleavages. These politicians did indeed represent the policy interests of their constituents—labor and pensioners—but, for the class cleavage to have contemporary resonance in Spanish politics, these policies needed to be institutionalized within the state and implemented relatively fairly. Similarly, in Israel, the electoral dominance of the Labour Party was due not only to its tight relationship with *Histradut*, but also to the state's consistent implementation of policies that were pro-labor.

This type of representative relationship need not always be the case. Often, despite the favorable policies a political party adopts for a group, state implementation of these policies is so ad hoc that the group that should benefit from them does so only some of the time. In such instances, the representative relationship between the group and the parties can break down markedly. Voters who belong to a group for whom a set of policies was adopted may not draw any benefit from these policies. It follows, then, that the sympathetic relationship between the representative and the voter is also severed. But what factors lead a state to act capriciously?

Examples of the distortion of voter-authorized state projects by capricious states abound, but they are particularly associated with patronage politics and vote-buying. In patronage politics—especially in the classic versions of Chicago or Tammany Hall—politicians target individual voters rather than larger groups. As long as the relationship between voters and their representatives is contingent and personalistic, as opposed to regular and either group-based or programmatic, political parties cannot be the representatives of a group. Moreover, if individual candidates essentially buy votes from individual voters, the sympathetic relationship between a group of voters and their representative is cut off. Voting is just a cash transaction, with parties feeling no pressure to develop a sympathetic relationship based on advocacy for their supporters. And, indeed, this is what Kitschelt et al. (2010) find—that in Latin America representation fails to occur when patronage prevails.

State projects can also become distorted by a state that appears to act capriciously when political parties exist solely to support the causes of their leaders. The social cleavage theory of party systems presumes that this kind of party will not exist. And yet, parties do take this form—to the detriment of representative democracy. Machiavelli, for one, observed that feuds among politicians do not injure a republic unless they take the form of factions—i.e., party leaders creating partisans to support their personal interests. A political party or a "representative" who sells out her constituents for her own good would not be "acting for" in any substantive way—even though she is authorized and accountable under electoral rules—and hence, would not be properly considered a political representative. Moreover, her actions in support of her own ends might result in the distortion of state programs and the creation of a capricious state.

But politicians are not the only actors who can make states behave capriciously—state projects of representative democracy can also fall apart, even in the presence of representatives who behave as such, if those representatives are unable to discipline the bureaucracies that carry out their mandates. Indeed, we can imagine a situation in which politicians carry out their part of the representation bargain in a sympathetic manner, enacting laws that are in line with their constituents' interests, and, yet, those constituents continue to face a capricious state in their everyday lives. This is because in modern representative democracies, politicians do not carry out the state's work directly. They create rules by which the state and other actors are supposed to play and then hand the project off to the executive branch. While some politicians can influence at a high level who carries out the laws they have enacted, this influence is often limited by institutional design (separation of powers, etc.), and most politicians have remarkably little to do with the execution of the laws they create. Within this context, representation hinges on the decisions—to faithfully apply the law or not—of individual bureaucrats.[10] As such, in assessing effective representation, we must consider not only the tidy relationship that supposedly exists between a voter and her representative but also the bureaucracy and the bureaucrats within it. They have the power to turn a program on its head if representatives are not able ensure that those bureaucrats execute the laws in a disciplined manner.

Political representation requires that the relationship between politician and voter be institutionalized through an impartial bureaucracy. If we have a capricious state and state projects are distorted by patronage and personalistic relationships between voters and their representatives, by parties that exist solely to support their leaders' causes, or by a poorly disciplined bureaucracy (i.e., not impartial), it becomes extremely difficult for a voter to sustain a sympathetic tie with her representative. In these conditions electoral democracy exists without tangible political representation. While this line of reasoning may suggest that there is no representation in a capricious state, we argue that capricious states provide a different type of political representation—which, for lack of a better phrase, we call selective representation. In the next section we provide evidence from India in support of these claims.

Political Representation in India

The Capricious State

In India, the state has a vast bureaucratic apparatus that implements the policies made by politicians—a bureaucracy that refers to itself as the "steel frame" of the state. In India, as in many other countries, implementation of the policies adopted by the state involves leakage. Indeed, according to the Indian government's own estimates, less than half of all of the resources allocated for the marginalized ever reach them.[11] But this on its own is not entirely problematical for political representation. What is problematical is that fact that a citizen's access to state benefits is almost entirely dependent on the whims of the agents of the state—both bureaucrats and politicians. Tellingly, most of the leakages the Indian government reports occur within the arms of the state itself.[12] This situation is compounded by the fact that when citizens take their concerns to the state for redress, they are often either not heard or dismissed. Indeed, agents of the state—particularly bureaucrats—frequently mistreat the marginalized, rendering them even more marginal, despite overt efforts on the part of their representatives to prevent this outcome. Jan Breman (1996) and Akhil Gupta (1998), who both focus on informal labor, offer a penetrating analysis of the situation faced by marginalized groups in India.[13] They show that for many in India, the state remains an important-yet-capricious actor in their lives.

Focus group results regarding the relationship between Indian citizens and the state are also revealing. Amit Ahuja and Pradeep Chhibber find that many voters say that they seldom "count" or matter, and that the state is not interested in addressing the issues they care about. Moreover, these voters claim that when they do contact the state, that interaction is fraught with hurdles. In the absence of resources, the state appears to have adopted a language of favors. Often on those occasions when resources do flow from the state, providers and beneficiaries both understand that these resources must be shared with the state's functionaries as bribes. Most respondents report that when they interact with the state they are frequently treated disrespectfully and summarily dismissed. They also complain of intimidation and coercion by the state's functionaries.[14] Many citizens of democratic India report that they have no control over the performance of school teachers; that they are openly intimidated in police stations; that they face rampant neglect in health centers; and that their petitions get put on the so-called back burner in district offices. Simply put: the state fails them on many counts.

Individual respondents' statements in Ahuja and Chhibber's focus-group evidence often reveal these failures succinctly. One put it: "No one listens, no one is interested. We stand there for hours on end, give up our daily wage, but get only five minutes of their time, and sometimes not even that. How does one keep doing it?" "Gareeb admi ki kaun parva kartha hai?" Or "Who cares about the poor?"[15] In almost all the neighborhoods and settlements in which Ahuja and Chhibber conducted focus groups, respondents wanted to know if the researchers could relay their petitions to government officials and inquired as to why newspapers did not write about these petitions. In some of the discussions the participants were very forthright in expressing their anger, saying things like: "The government is shameless"; and "We are the forgotten people." This perspective is not limited to the poor and traditionally marginalized; even the middle classes feel the capriciousness of the state. A middle-class respondent remarked, "having a contact or two is important and . . . when you do not have money, you need a godfather, or many godfathers to get things done and *when that is not the case, there is no difference between me, and the person who resides in the slum behind my neighborhood.*"

The state also seems capricious to those who *do* have some access to state services. Many citizens report that they lack the ability to improve the quality of services being delivered to them. One of them observed, "The government does many things for us, but we are not happy with the quality of the services in this area. We go with complaints to the administration, and sometimes things improve, but then some official gets transferred, and things go back to being bad again." Another asserted, "Without money or some contact, who gets a job these days? The Municipal councilors, the members of the legislative assembly (MLA), and the members of national parliament (MP), no one will do much. They only promise us things. If you know them personally, things may be different. [On the other hand, k]nowing government officials is very helpful. They can make things happen. Some of them are even more powerful than the politicians."

These brief vignettes provide some evidence for our claim that the Indian state is capricious, but they leave one wondering: what segments of Indian society does the Indian state represent? We will now turn to citizen perceptions regarding whom Indian political parties represent.

Social Divisions and the Party System in India

Sociological arguments have been extremely popular in the study of Indian politics, and it is commonplace for scholars to say that one social cleavage or another structures the party system. There are, however, few empirical verifications of the link between social cleavages and the party system. We will discuss what evidence there is below.

Heath (2005) provides survey evidence that electoral volatility in India can be explained by the extent to which social cleavages are politicized and polarized by the party system. Heath created a cleavage polarization index to attempt to measure the extent to which different political parties represent social cleavages. To construct this index, Heath (2005: 189) examined "the relationship between caste-community and the cluster voted for, and use[s] an index of dissimilarity to measure the degree to which political competition is polarized along caste-community lines." In other words, he considers those Indian states in which parties generate cross-caste, cross-cleavage support to be less polarized.

Chandra and Wilkinson (2008) construct a measure for whether or not voting in a particular country is ethnically based or not. They first use content analysis to classify political parties as ethnic, multiethnic, or nonethnic, based on the campaigns they run. They then look to the results of the ensuing election to see what percentage of the vote these parties captured. They sum the percentage of the vote received by each of the parties categorized as ethnic and translate this percentage into a scale that ranges from 0 to 100, with 0 being associated with no ethnically based voting and 100 with voting that is completely ethnically based. On this scale, India received a score of 38.9 (1991 election), while Canada received a score of 34.4, suggesting that, despite India's diversity, ethnicity does not dominate the electoral arena.

In a similar but more general effort (i.e., looking beyond just ethnicity), Chhibber, Jensensius, and Suryanarayan (2013) create a measure of the extent to which a party has a clear social base. To do so, they derive an algorithm to determine the extent of a party's dependence on a specific group and then examine survey data from six Indian national elections: 1967, 1971, 1979, 1996, 1999, and 2004. The first three were surveys conducted by the Center for the Study of Developing Societies; the latter three were part of the National Election Studies pioneered by Lokniti, a New Delhi research group dedicated to collecting and analyzing election-related data, in 1996 (Planning Commission of India 2005). For each election, in each of the 15 Indian States studied, they cross-tabulated the party a respondent voted for by various social cleavages, including Hindu caste (upper, scheduled, other backward), religion (Muslims, followers of other religious denominations), tribal status (scheduled), class, and urban/rural residency. Chhibber, Jensenius, and Suryanarayan coded parties as having a clear social base according to the following two criteria:

1. The party gets more than 50 percent of votes from a specific group without any other party getting more than 25 percent of votes from the same group. This criterion ensures that the party under consideration is clearly preferred by a particular social group.
2. The party has a maximum of two support groups, as defined in (1). This criterion ensures that the party is indeed preferred by a few groups and is not the preference of all groups in society, which would make it a catch-all party.

If a party fulfilled both criteria, they classified it as a cleavage-based party. Otherwise it was categorized as a catch-all party. In almost 60 percent of the cases, the party did not have a social base. In 30 percent, one party had a clearly defined social base. In 10 percent, two parties had a clear social base. These data show that for the most part in India political parties are not tied to social groups. This is particularly true because, if we exclude the right-wing Bharatiya Janata Party and the *dalit*-supported Bahujan Samaj Party, the proportion of parties that can reliably depend on a social cleavage drops precipitously.

If Not Social Cleavage-Based Groups, Whose Interests do Political Parties Represent?

In a national survey in 2002 respondents were asked whether the first, second, and third most popular parties in their area represented the interests of some citizens, all citizens, or whether they did not know or could not say. The latter two responses were combined into one category; the logic being that since these respondents could not identify whether a party represented particular interests, they regarded parties as representing no one in particular.[16] Table 8.1 reports the responses to the three questions. Forty-one percent of the respondents indicated that the most popular party in their area represents no one's interests known to them. This number jumps to 50 percent for the second most popular party and 64 percent for the third most popular party. We also combined the responses into a scale designed to report whether respondents felt that political parties more generally represent the interests of all, some or no citizens, or no interests. According to this scale, a third of all respondents believe that all three parties in their area do not represent the interests of anyone they can identify.

Table 8.1. Extent of Perceived Representation by
Political Parties

Party	All	Some	No one
Party 1	34%	25%	41%
Party 2	27%	25%	48%
Party 3	17%	19%	64%

The 2002 national survey also asked respondents whether their Member of Parliament (MP) and Member of the Legislative Assembly (MLA) cared for the interests of some, the interests of all, or whether they did not know or could not say. As with the political party questions, we combined the latter two responses to create an indicator of whether elected politicians cared for no one respondents could identify: 65 percent could not identify whose interests their MP represented, and over 40 percent could not identify whom their MLAs represent. Once again we combined responses for both MPs and MLAs into one scale. This time, almost half (49 percent) of the respondents could not identify whose interests their elected politicians represent.

In short, many Indian citizens, despite a relatively long history of supposedly representative electoral democracy, do not find political parties or their elected politicians to be representative of their interests, or those of anyone they can identify. We consider this to be evidence for an observable implication of the existence of a capricious state in India.

If People Do Not Feel Represented, Why Do They Go to Vote?

The evidence we've presented thus far indicates that there is scant support for the idea that political parties represent social cleavages. It also shows that average Indians do not feel represented by either their parties or their particular politicians. This evidence, however, leaves one wondering: why do Indians go to vote? Interestingly, for many people in India, voting may have very little connection with representation.

This relationship is not entirely unanticipated. Ahuja and Chhibber (2012) observe that the capriciousness of the bureaucracy, police, and politicians (without recourse to any redress) leads voters to use the language of political rights rather than representation to explain why they vote. Their finding mirrors arguments made by Skinner (1997) and Pettit (1997), that voters who face a capricious state are more likely to stress their political rights when they are given the opportunity. Skinner asserts that freedom is properly understood as freedom from the "whims" of the rulers. He states, "our rulers may choose not to exercise these powers, or may exercise them only with the tenderest regard for your individual liberties. So you may in practice continue to enjoy the full range of your civil rights. The very fact, however, that your rulers possess such arbitrary powers means that the continued enjoyment of your civil liberty remains at all times dependent on their goodwill" (70). Pettit broadly agrees with this assertion: "Domination is subjection to an arbitrary power of interference on the part of another—a dominus or master—even another who chooses not actually to exercise that power . . . freedom, I maintained, should be defined as nondomination" (340).[17]

So, how does this play out in the Indian context? In India, though elections are held regularly, they mark a sharp departure from the regular state of affairs. Elections are one of the few occasions when the state does not act whimsically with respect to its duties to its citizens. Indeed, the state takes seriously its obligation to extend a right, the right to vote, to all the citizens. Moreover, in sharp contrast to the usual state of affairs, at the time of elections the state is not absent, and it does not dismiss and ignore the marginalized. It turns up on their doorsteps asking for votes and participation! And, when people find themselves needed by the state (to legitimize its work through voting), they seem keen to exercise their voting rights.[18]

Empirical evidence bears this out. In focus groups Ahuja and Chhibber presented participants with a question: "What if nothing changes over the next two elections in terms of your material conditions, would you still continue to vote?" In a large number of cases, the answer was an unequivocal "yes." As one poor villager in Azamgarh put it, "I am because I vote on Election Day, otherwise, what is my stature in this society?" Another participant said, "Election is the one event which ties us to the government. Politicians, people like you, journalists, everyone comes looking for us. If we did not vote, there will be no elections and we will be left for dead."

Does This Mean That Indian Voters Have Given Up on Representation?

Despite the evidence presented above about the large-scale failure of representation in India and despite the fact that many Indian voters seem to vote simply because it is one of the few rights they have that the state consistently protects and honors, Indian voters do not seem to have given up on representative democracy. Indeed, empirical evidence indicates that, though they face a capricious state and politicians who seek to look after themselves first, Indian voters continue to seek honesty and integrity from their political leaders and bureaucrats, rather than the standard bundle of economic benefits and/or private goods. The 2002 survey asked respondents what they expected from politicians, officials and parties. This was an open-ended question. We recoded the open-ended answers into five broad categories—those asking for public services/goods, private goods, integrity, and other unclassifiable requests, and those who said they did not know. In Figure 8.1, we report the proportion of respondents that sought public goods, private goods, and integrity (after dropping those who could not identify what they

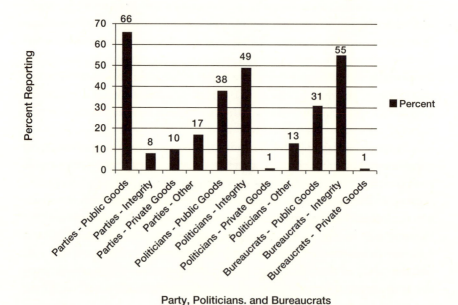

Figure 8.1. What do people expect from parties, politicians, and bureaucrats?

expected of their politicians). What we find is that a large plurality of respondents looked for integrity in their politicians and bureaucrats above all else (Figure 8.1). In other words, more than any specific, personal gains that voters might hope to receive from politicians, officials, and parties, voters still want their elected representatives and bureaucrats to act in a manner that is essential to representative democracy. The implication here is that, since Indian voters want something that they largely do not have, they may use the electoral system to hold their representatives accountable.

Where Does the Bureaucracy Fit into This Picture?

Voters can hold their representatives accountable and vote them out of office, but they cannot vote their bureaucrats out of office. Yet, politicians do not carry out the state's work, bureaucrats do. Thus, as we suggest above, if politicians are to act as true representatives, they must act through the bureaucracy. The implication here is that if politicians fail to discipline the bureaucracy in such a way that it faithfully and consistently carries out the laws and policies they create, the representation project will fail.

To assess whether bureaucratic performance makes a difference in terms of representation, we created a composite index of political representation. In this index we standardized the responses to the three questions regarding the interests represented by political parties and the interests represented by Members of Parliament and Members of the Legislative Assembly, generated z scores, and then added them to create a scaled composite index that goes from low values (for those according to whom the political system represented no one) to high (for those who thought that the political system was representative of all). On this index more generally, positive and higher numbers suggest more political representation, and negative numbers mean less representation. In the 2002 survey, respondents were asked what proportion of bureaucrats—all, some, or none—in their area had the qualities they expected of bureaucrats (most, as Figure 8.1 tells us, want honest bureaucrats). In Figure 8.2, we report the average score on the index of political representation for the various proportions of bureaucrats who had the qualities that respondents desired. We find a dramatic difference. For those respondents according to whom all bureaucrats had the qualities desired in the political system, the political system was far more representative than for those who did not see any bureaucrat as displaying the

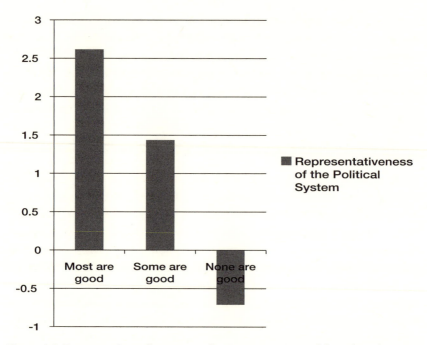

Figure 8.2. Bureaucratic performance and representativeness of the political system.

qualities they desired. In other words, those who wanted honest bureau-crats and encountered honest bureaucrats felt more represented by their representatives.

Caveats and Implications

In this paper we have argued that the administration of the state can have a significant impact on a political representative's development of a sympa-thetic relationship with her voters. In states where there are regular elections, but those elections are accompanied by arbitrary policy implementation, representation dissolves into formal authorization and accountability. If one takes a more substantive view of authorization and accountability by asking why citizens vote they way they do, this descent of electoral democracy into the type of competition among and between the elite described by Schum-peter clearly fails to fulfill all that voters hope and expect that representative democracies will provide. A cynic might argue that this is exactly the type of system that Indian elites want, and politicians, as agents of the elite, ensure that it is in place. It is tempting to take this view. But one has to wonder: are there other, more charitable ways to view Indian politicians and their representativeness?

Stand-In Representation

While advocacy may indeed be difficult without an institutionalized relationship between a voter and her representative, "stand-in" or "descriptive" representation is indeed plausible. Stand-in representation occurs when a voter votes for someone who is like her without regard for the policies the person stands for (Williams 1998). Stand-in representation is common in capricious states, especially if the capriciousness is directed toward a particular group or groups. In such cases, stand-in representation may occur because members of the group discriminated against tend to believe that someone who is like them will understand their plight and be more likely to act as their representative. Importantly, the kind of systematic discrimination that voters react to when choosing stand-in representatives is not really capricious. In such situations there is usually a clear bias in the institutions of the state and in the political process that favors one group over another. The archetypical case of this is the U.S., where African Americans living in the South faced clear discrimination until the latter portion of the twentieth century.[19] Political institutions were in fact structured to ensure that systemic bias was sustained. Representative politics in the South was centered on maintaining white control (Key 1949). Similar types of systemic bias have plagued Indian politics in the past, and there is certainly an argument to be made that such bias continues to this day. Thus, even in the absence of a sympathetic relationship between voters and representatives, some Indian politicians may be engaging in stand-in representation.

A Semi-Random Walk Down Rajpath

Stand-in representation is not, however, the only way to view Indian politicians and/or parties and their representativeness charitably. In contrast to the systemic discrimination theory presented above, it may be the case that the capriciousness of the Indian state is completely random. If the state is capricious "randomly," stand-in representation will rarely seem like a solution. Yet no state undertakes actions that are completely random. What is more common is that elements of systemic bias and random capriciousness coexist. In these situations, a group can elect a stand-in representative or a true policy representative, but this does not change the situation on the ground. Indeed, while voters may attempt to elect representative politicians, and while in some cases social bias may permit the election of a candidate from a group that is discriminated against, representatives, once elected, may find it difficult to persist as advocates for those they represent. When nothing changes for voters on the ground, the representative nature of these relationships eventually collapses.

Selective Representation

Political representation, as it is currently defined, focuses on self-interest (Pitkin 1967; Urbinati 2000; Urbinati and Warren 2008). In contemporary conceptions, political representation requires that *a* voter authorize *a* representative to act on her behalf, as she believes that the representative will be an advocate for her interests. Furthermore, the very same voter can hold this representative accountable for her actions. A central concern of contemporary theorists of political representation, therefore, is the relationship between a voter and the representative and the extent to which they have a sympathetic relationship (either as a stand-in representative or as a policy advocate). In capricious states, another type of political representation may be the norm—selective representation. Under a selectively representative system, politicians and parties may represent their constituents some of the time, but not consistently.

When selective representation is dominant, most voters do not see their representatives as sympathetic to them, but rather as advocates of the interests of voters who have characteristics that they do not happen to have. In other words, according to voters, in a selectively representative system, parties and/or candidates have a sympathetic relationship with someone other than themselves. The result is that the voter does not have a sympathetic relationship with any representative. Therefore, in capricious states derived from selective representation, political representation is representation of the other, not the self.

Bureaucratic Obfuscation of Sincere Efforts at Representation

But voters have few means by which to determine whether selective representation is occurring or whether their politicians are making honest but ineffectual efforts at representation. Indeed, as discussed briefly above, there are situations in which politicians act as representatives, but fail to appear as such because it is the bureaucracy that carries out their mandates and they are unable to get that bureaucracy to conform its behavior to that required by law. This may be what is happening, at least for some politicians, in India.

Indeed, a politician who strives for representation in India faces an uphill battle. Once elected, that politicians must first attempt to pass legislation that furthers her constituents' interests and to prevent passage of legislation that harms them. At both the state and federal levels, this is a difficult task, as that politician is just one of hundreds trying to do the same. Parties, as we might expect, simplify this task. Yet, even if our politician manages to act in a representative manner and succeeds at passing or preventing the passage of legislation accordingly, the Indian bureaucracy, despite being described as the "steel frame of the state," may not carry out this legislation in an impartial manner. The bureaucracy may take bribes, favor individuals from certain groups, and so on. There is little our politician can do about this directly, but she is not without recourse. Indeed, if her party is in power, she might attempt to influence those running the bureaucracy. A party in power can influence appointments to high-level ministry positions and, through those appointments, attempt to discipline the bureaucracy. But high-level ministry officials are not interfacing with the public on a regular basis, so these officials must, in turn, discipline those below them in the hierarchy.

In India, bureaucratic discipline is carried out primarily through transfers—bureaucrats who comply with orders are transferred to favorable locations or positions, while those who do not are transferred to undesirable locations or positions.[20] This system may work, just not quickly enough for electoral imperatives. Indeed, because electoral volatility is relatively high in India,[21] it may be the case that voters are regularly presented with opportunities to hold their representatives accountable before those representatives have had a chance not only to enact representative legislation, but also to ensure that it is carried out by the bureaucracy in an impartial manner. The resulting pattern of behavior—coming from both bureaucrats and politicians—is one that voters are hard-pressed to differentiate from the pattern they might see in a selectively representative system. Thus, the bureaucracy is the key link between voters and politicians/parties in any system aspiring to be a representative democracy. If politicians want to avoid the appearance of selective representation, they must discipline the bureaucracy and ensure that their representative political acts appear as such to voters.

References

Ahuja, Amit and Pradeep Chhibber. 2012. "Why the Poor Vote in India: If I Don't Vote I'm Dead to the State." *Studies in Comparative International Development* 47(4): 365–88.

Ankersmit, Frank R. 2002. *Political Representation.* Stanford, Calif.: Stanford University Press.

Banerjee, Mukulika. 2007. "Sacred Election." *Economic and Political Weekly* (April 28): 1556–62.

Banik, Dan. 2001. "The Transfer Raj: Indian Civil Servants on the Move." *European Journal of Development Research* 13(1) : 106–34.

Bartolini, S. and P. Mair. 1990. *Identity, Competition and Electoral Availability: The Stabilisation of European Electorates, 1885–1995.* Cambridge: Cambridge University Press.

Beteille, Tara. 2009. "Absenteeism, Transfers and Patronage: The Political Economy of Teacher Labor Markets in India." Dissertation on file at Stanford University.

Breman, Jan. 1996. *Footloose Labor: Working in India's Informal Economy.* Cambridge: Cambridge University Press.

Chandra, Kanchan, and Scott Wilkinson. 2008. "Measuring the Effect of Ethnicity." *Comparative Political Studies* 41: 515–63.

Chhibber, Pradeep, Francesca Jensensius and Pavithra Suryanarayan. 2013. "Party Organization and Party Proliferation in India." *Party Politics*, April 13.

Corbridge, Stuart, Glyn Williams, Manoj Srivastava, and René Véron. 2005. *Seeing the State: Governance and Governmentality in India.* Cambridge: Cambridge University Press.

Dahl, Robert A. 1971. *Polyarchy: Participation and Opposition.* New Haven, Conn.: Yale University Press.

———. 1994. "A Democratic Dilemma: System Effectiveness Versus Citizen Participation." *Political Science Quarterly* 109: 23–34.

Goyal, Ashima. 2005. *Making the Politician and the Bureaucrat Deliver: Employment Guarantee in India.* Indira Gandhi Institute of Development Research.

Gupta, Akhil. 1998. *Postcolonial Development: Agriculture in the Making of Modern India.* Durham, N.C.: Duke University Press.

Heath, Oliver. 2005. "Party Systems, Political Cleavages and Electoral Volatility in India: A State-Wise Analysis, 1998–1999." *Electoral Studies* 24 (2): 177–99.

Hegel G. W. F. 1967 (1821). *Philosophy of Right.* Trans. T. M. Knox. Oxford: Oxford University Press.

Hirst, Paul. 2005. "Representative Democracy and Its Limits." *Political Quarterly* 59 (2): 190–205.

Huntington, Samuel P. 1991. *The Third Wave: Democratization in the Late Twentieth Century.* Norman: University of Oklahoma Press, 1991.

Iyer, Lakshmi, and Anandi Mani. 2012. "Traveling Agents: Political Change and Bureaucratic Turnover in India." *Review of Economics and Statistics* 94(3): 723–39.

Key, V. O. 1957. *Southern Politics in State and Nation.* New York: Knopf.

Kitschelt, Herbert, Kirk A. Hawkins, Juan Pablo Luna, Guillermo Rosas, and Elizabeth J. Zechmeister. 2010. *Latin American Party Systems.* Cambridge: Cambridge University Press.

Lipset, Seymour M., and Stein Rokkan. 1967. *Party Systems and Voter Alignments: Cross-National Perspectives* [Contributors Robert R. Alford and Others]. New York: Free Press.

Mainwaring, Scott. 2006. "State Deficiencies, Party Competition, and Confidence in Democratic Representation in the Andes," in *The Crisis of Democratic Representation in the Andes,* ed. Scott Mainwaring, Ana María Bejarano, and Eduardo Pizzaro Leongómez. Stanford, Calif.: Stanford University Press, 295–346. Also editors' introduction, 1–45.

Manin, B. 1997. *The Principles of Representative Government.* Cambridge: Cambridge University Press.

Mansbridge Jane. 1999. "Should Blacks Represent Blacks and Women Represent Women? A Contingent 'Yes.'" *Journal of Politics* 61 (3): 628–57.

———. 2003. "Rethinking Representation." *American Political Science Review* 97: 515–28.

Meier, Kenneth J., and Lawrence J. O'Toole. 2006. *Bureaucracy in a Democratic State: A Governance Perspective.* Baltimore: Johns Hopkins University Press.

Nichter, Simeon. 2008. "Vote Buying or Turnout Buying? Machine Politics and the Secret Ballot," *American Political Science Review* 102: 19–31.

O'Brien, Kevin and Lianjiang, Li. 2006. *Rightful Resistance in Rural China.* Cambridge: Cambridge University Press.

Pettit, Philip. 1997. *Republicanism: A Theory of Freedom and Government.* Oxford: Clarendon.

———. 2001. *A Theory of Freedom: From the Psychology to the Politics of Agency.* New York: Oxford University Press.

Piattoni, Simona, ed. 2001. *Clientelism, Interests, and Democratic Representation: The European Experience in Comparative and Historical Perspective.* Cambridge: Cambridge University Press.

Pitkin, Hanna F. 1967. *The Concept of Representation.* Berkeley: University of California Press.

Planning Commission of India. 2005. "Performance Evaluation of Targeted Public Distribution System (TPDS)." March.

Plotke, David. 1997. "Representation Is Democracy." *Constellations* 4 (1): 19–34.

Powell, G. Bingham, Jr. 2000. *Elections as Instruments of Democracy: Majoritarian and Proportional Visions.* New Haven, Conn: Yale University Press.

———. 2004. "Political Representation in Comparative Politics." *Annual Review of Political Science* 7: 273–96.

Rehfeld, Andrew. 2006. "Towards a General Theory of Political Representation." *Journal of Politics* 68 (1): 1–21.

Rosenblum, Nancy L. 2008. *On the Side of the Angels: An Appreciation of Parties and Partisanship.* Princeton, N.J.: Princeton University Press.

Sartori, Giovanni. 1976. *Parties and Party Systems: A Framework for Analysis.* Cambridge: Cambridge University Press.

Schmitter, Philippe C., and Terry Lynn Karl. 1991. "What Democracy Is . . . and Is Not," *Journal of Democracy* 2 (Summer): 75–88.

Schumpeter, Joseph. 1947. *Capitalism, Socialism, and Democracy.* 2nd ed. New York: Harper.

Scott, James. 1985. *Weapons of the Weak: Everyday Forms of Peasant Resistance.* New Haven, Conn.: Yale University Press.

Shah, Parth, and Naveen Mandava, eds. 2005. *Law, Liberty and Livelihood: Making A Living On The Street.* New Delhi: Dev Publisher.

Skinner, Quentin. 1997. *Liberty Before Liberalism.* Cambridge: Cambridge University Press.

Urbinati, Nadia. 2000. "Representation as Advocacy: A Study of Democratic Deliberation." *Political Theory* 28 (6): 758–86.

———. 2006. *Representative Democracy: Principles and Genealogy.* Chicago: University of Chicago Press.

Urbinati, Nadia, and Mark Warren. 2008. "The Concept of Representation in Contemporary Democratic Theory." *Annual Review of Political Science* 11: 387–412.

Warren, Mark E. 2001. *Democracy and Association.* Princeton, N.J.: Princeton University Press.

———. 2006. "Democracy and Deceit: Regulating Appearances of Corruption. *American Journal of Political Science* 50: 160–74.

———. 2008. "Citizen Representatives." In *Designing Deliberative Democracy: The British Columbia Citizens' Assembly,* ed. Mark E. Warren and Hillary Pearse. Cambridge: Cambridge University Press. 50–69.

Weber. Max. 1969. *Economy and Society.* New York: Bedminster Press.

Williams, Melissa S. 1998. *Voice, Trust, and Memory: Marginalized Groups and the Failings of Liberal Representation.* Princeton, N.J.: Princeton University Press.

Wood, Elisabeth Jean. 2003. *Insurgent Collective Action and Civil War in El Salvador.* Cambridge: Cambridge University Press.

Yadav, Yogendra, and Sanjay Kumar.1999. "Interpreting the Mandate." *Frontline* 16, November 5, 22.

CHAPTER 9

The Closing of the Frontier: Political Blogs, the 2008 Election, and the Online Public Sphere

Matthew Hindman

The Growing Stakes

This essay is about blogs, the online public sphere more broadly, and blogs' role as a platform for political discourse. My central theme is that blogging is not what it used to be. In the years since the 2004 election, blogging has been normalized, professionalized, and institutionalized, and I try to detail what these interrelated changes mean for U.S. politics. I also propose concrete policy remedies to help address blogging's civic failures.

Yet to some degree, discussions of blogging and the online public sphere have been overshadowed by other events. The past few years have seen a series of increasingly ominous setbacks for American newspaper publishers. Industry-wide, print advertising revenues dropped from $46.6 billion in 2006 to $24.8 billion in 2009 (Newspaper Association of America 2010). Nearly all major American newspapers have seen dramatic cutbacks and layoffs, and thousands of reporters have lost their jobs. The *Rocky Mountain News*, *Tucson Citizen*, and *Seattle Post-Intelligencer* ceased publication. The *Chicago Tribune* and *Philadelphia Inquirer* (among others) have undergone bankruptcy reorganization. Even the *New York Times* has struggled to survive, forced to borrow money at loan shark rates and to sell off its headquarters building and other assets (Yu and Bensinger 2009).

I do not want to focus just on the travails of the newspaper industry, a topic that deserves its own fuller treatment. But the deterioration of the newspaper business recasts our assessment of the online public sphere in general, and of political blogs in particular. Though newspapers' current decline is many decades in the making, the speed of the current crisis has surprised even many pessimistic observers. When overall newspaper readership began declining during the 1980s, the problem was partly masked as newspaper revenues continued to rise. In recent decades, only about 1 percent of daily papers have had a direct competitor publishing in the same city (Dertouzos and Trautman 1990: 1; see also Rosse 1980). Newspapers' monopoly status led to a surge of acquisitions and conglomerations, as publishers found that protected businesses with 15- to 40-percent profit margins could win stratospheric valuations as public companies. The wave of newspaper acquisitions continued up to the eve of the crisis, with the result that many publishers had a large amount of debt on their balance sheets (Pérez-Peña 2009). The *Chicago Tribune* is a case in point: while every part of the organization was reportedly profitable, the Tribune Company was forced into bankruptcy because it was unable to service its enormous debt.

Whatever role poor financial decisions played in accelerating the crisis, there is no denying that the fundamental economics of newspaper publishing has changed dramatically for the worse. Circulation and readership declines have accelerated. According to the Pew Center for the People and the Press, in 2008, for the first time, more survey respondents listed the Internet than a print newspaper as one of their two primary news sources (Pew Research Center 2008). Dramatically lower online advertising rates mean that it currently takes 30 online readers to offset the loss of one paid print newspaper subscriber (Project for Excellence in Journalism 2008). And while the drop in display advertising has been dramatic, the loss of classified advertising—which previously accounted for a quarter of the profits at a typical midsized newspaper—has been arguably more damaging. No single Website has hurt the prospects for the American newspaper industry as much as Craigslist.

Newspapers have long employed more local and state political reporters than all other forms of media combined (e.g., Carroll 2006). There have been numerous reports that accountability journalism has been particularly hard hit. Paul Starr (2009), in assessing the impact of these cutbacks, dourly predicts that the decline of local reporting will lead to a new era of public corruption. Making matters worse, the movement of newspaper readers online has benefited large, nationally prominent daily papers far more than smaller outlets. The *New York Times* online market share is 2.5 times its market share in print (Hindman 2009: 98).

It is one thing if blogs serve as a supplement to traditional media sources, filtering political information and public discussion through a different set of biases and concerns. It is quite another if traditional watchdogs have been greatly weakened by the Internet, and if blogs must therefore be expected to shoulder the burden that traditional media outlets have dropped.

Changes in the media environment therefore force us to ask larger, and harder, questions. My aim here is partly to offer an overview and a synthesis of our knowledge of the online public sphere, and to present and defend my own assessment of what blogs do well and what they do badly. While discussion of blogs both in and out of the academy has become less sensational, it is still common to read descriptions of blogging that make it sound like the Wild West. In fact, the 2008 election cycle shows us that the frontier has closed.

Blogging as a format has succeeded far beyond early expectations; and yet the "blogosphere," as conceived by both its defenders and its critics, has been transformed beyond recognition. These changes alter the opportunities for collective action, and they may partially ameliorate concerns about substantive representation online. But in the area where the need is most dire—coverage of state and local politics—it is not at all clear that blogs are up to the task.

Where Does the Public Go Online?

In any discussion of the online public sphere, it is worth emphasizing a point that should be obvious, but that is often overlooked: we should avoid characterizing the Web, or blogging as a whole, on the basis of content that gets only a handful of readers. Studies of the online public sphere should first and foremost consider content that is truly public—content that attracts a large audience. Starting from this premise means that deductive arguments about the abstract "possibilities" or "affordances" of the online public sphere are of little help. What we need is data on what sorts of content citizens see and how the medium is actually used.

Blog traffic was dramatically higher during the 2007–2008 campaign than in previous cycles. Yet blogs' very success made visits to blog content

Table 9.1. The 20 Most-Visited Sites in Hitwise's
"Politics" Category, October 2008

Site	Traffic share (percent
Huffington Post	8.2
Real Clear Politics	5.4
Barack Obama	5.3
The Politico	4.0
CNN Political Ticker	3.9
FoxNews.com Elections	3.6
Daily Kos	3.0
Free Republic	2.9
John McCain 2008	2.7
Townhall.com	1.7
Electoral Vote Predictor	1.5
Human Events Online	1.3
First Read (MSNBC)	1.3
Michelle Malkin	1.3
CatholicVote.com	1.2
Democratic Underground	1.1
Rasmussen Reports	1.1
PalinAsPresident.com	1.0
Annenberg Political Fact Check	0.9
Infowars.com	0.9

harder to measure. In 2004 a majority of the most popular political blogs subscribed to the free SiteMeter tracking service, providing a rough metric of how their traffic compared. Four years later, fewer top blogs used the Site-Meter service, and SiteMeter results were less reliable because of unscrupulous but widespread attempts to inflate traffic numbers. The 2008 election cycle also saw greater adoption of RSS feeds and other blog syndication technologies that are often excluded from traffic logs.

Still, there are a few data sources that can give us a reliable macro-level view of Web traffic. Table 9.1 presents traffic share data from Hitwise, a large Web tracking company. Hitwise partners with Internet service providers to collect aggregate, anonymous data on the surfing behavior of their subscribers. Ten million U.S. households are included in the Hitwise sample. Shown in the table are the top 20 Websites, as of October 2008, in Hitwise's "Politics" category, ranked by the number of visits they receive. (A "visit" is an industry standard metric defined as a request for a page or series of pages from a Website with no more than 30 minutes between clicks.)

One basic test for claims about the online public sphere is this: are they consistent with the broad patterns of Web traffic? Overall, traffic to Hitwise's "Politics" and "News and Media" categories remains a small portion of what citizens seek out online. During the month of October—peak election season—4.7 percent of traffic went to the news and media category, while just 0.50 percent went to the politics category. With the election over, in February 2009, those levels were 4.8 percent and 0.26 percent respectively.

It is not just that the total amount of traffic remains small. In 2008, as in previous years, political traffic remains highly concentrated on top outlets. Hitwise tracked 1,097 political outlets in October 2008, and yet the top 20 sites received 52 percent of all visits. Still, while Web traffic in these areas is highly focused, a wide variety of different kinds of organizations have earned a spot in the category's upper ranks. In these top 20 sites we can see commercial media organizations, candidate Websites, group blogs, opinion aggregators, online discussion forums, nonprofit organizations, parody Websites, and more. Of course, different definitions of what should be included in the "politics" category, and what counts as a " Website," would lead to slightly different conclusions.[1] But it is clear that many different models of political content creation have succeeded in reaching a substantial audience.

A closer look at these numbers also illustrates the difficulties in measuring blog traffic (a topic returned to below). The large majority of these top 20 sites have some form of blog or blog-style content, but Hitwise does not provide more detailed breakdowns of traffic within sections of these sites. We do not know the proportion of BarackObama.com users who visited the official campaign blog, or how many visitors to the upstart news organization Politico visited blogs as opposed to the site's other content.

Moreover, consistent with other research, the volume of political traffic continues to favor progressive- and Democratic-leaning online outlets. Barack Obama's campaign site hosted roughly twice as much traffic in October 2008 as John McCain's site. More broadly, liberal sites continue to outpace conservative sites by roughly the same 2-to-1 margin. This dramatic advantage in left-leaning Web traffic has been a persistent feature of the online political landscape for a decade. Additionally, just as previous studies have found (Adamic and Glance 2005), Hitwise shows that conservative sites are more concentrated than liberal sites, with the top outlets receiving a greater portion of the community's overall traffic. Intriguingly, liberal, conservative, and ostensibly neutral content all became more concentrated as the campaign progressed. As public attention increased during the course of the campaign, the largest sites benefited the most.

Normalized, Professionalized, and Institutionalized

The Normalization of Blogging

Discussions of political blogs naturally raise the question of what, exactly, a blog is. The answer has gotten more complicated since 2004. The minimal definition suggests that blogs are regularly updated online journals, with entries presented in reverse chronological order. Traditionally, blogging has also been presented in a first- person, informal style. During the 2004 cycle most prominent political bloggers saw themselves as engaging in an activity fundamentally distinct from that performed by the "elite media." Political blogging was seen not just as a genre of content, but as the product of a defined community of participants sharing common norms and cultural practices.

By the 2008 election cycle this definition of blogging had become far harder to sustain. Blogs have become the default format for publishing almost any kind of time-sensitive content. Not confined just to politics, blogs have proliferated in countless other areas. A large majority of competitive congressional and statewide campaigns by the 2008 cycle had at least one blog on their Website. Members of Congress and other public officials have tried their hand at blogging (not to mention related technologies such as YouTube and Twitter).

Even more significantly, traditional media outlets have turned to blogging with fervor. The *New York Times, Washington Post,* and *Wall Street Journal* all host dozens of blogs; local and regional papers host hundreds more. Katie Couric, Brian Williams, and Charles Gibson—the three network news anchors as of this writing—all blog, as do many of their high-profile reporters and correspondents (not to mention their competitors at CNN, Fox News, and MSNBC). *Time, Newsweek,* and myriad other magazines publish blogs. When reporters like Jake Tapper and Brian Ross write blogs about politics, along with opinion journalists such as Nicholas Kristof and Paul Krugman, it is difficult to see bloggers as a discrete class engaging in a separate activity.

Perhaps as a consequence, in the 2008 election cycle it seems harder to find news stories that would have been overlooked were it not for the influence of bloggers. Both in popular accounts and in previous scholarship, there has been much emphasis on blogs' ability to uncover and focus attention on stories that otherwise would have been ignored. Several examples in particular have been widely celebrated. Bloggers were credited with a key role in the resignation of Trent Lott as Senate Republican leader in 2002 (e.g., von Sternberg 2004). In 2004, blogs played a key role in what some termed the "Rathergate" scandal, in which CBS reporting was found to have been based on forged documents (Wallsten 2004; Seper 2004). In 2006, in the case with perhaps the clearest electoral consequences, a small online blog set off the Mark Foley scandal (Levey 2006). Survey evidence provides strong, if circumstantial, evidence that the scandal cost Republicans seats in the House of Representatives (Franklin 2006).

Obama's offhand remark that residents of small towns are "bitter" and that they "cling" to guns and religion might qualify as a blog-initiated story. Obama's comments were first publicized by a blogger writing for the *Huffington Post* OffTheBus project (Fowler 2008; more on OffTheBus and the *Huffington Post* below). Still, it is harder to find any blog-sparked story that had as large an impact on the 2008 election as the Foley scandal had in 2006.

Blogs have become less distinct in other ways as well. Many leading blogs have redesigned their Websites, and have begun to present themselves not just as diaries of political commentary but as constantly updated news portals, including links to traditional reporting and wire service stories. Consider the example of *Talking Points Memo* (TPM), a blog started in 2000 by Josh Marshall, then a Ph.D. candidate in early American history at Brown and a Washington reporter for *American Prospect*. The earliest iteration of TPM was a single, unadorned column of text. By 2009, the site had expanded to include half a dozen other reporter-bloggers, added sections such as TPM Muckraker and TPM DC, added a discussion and issues forum called TPM Café, and expanded into video with TPM TV. The front page of the site was transformed to look more like a news site than a traditional blog. As Nicholas Carr (2008) notes, overall blogs' shift in format has meant that blog pages are now larger, with more images, more javascript, and more Flash-based advertising and video.

Blogging, then, is now the most widely read form of opinion journalism. At the same time, much of what previously made blogging distinct is gone. There is also ample evidence that candidates and public officials have begun to court bloggers in the same way they court other opinion journalists. Prominent political bloggers now routinely participate in conference calls with congressional leadership. For example, Obama's preinaugural meetings with opinion journalists invited blogger Andrew Sullivan along with broadcast and print journalists.

Professionalization

Hand-in-hand with the normalization of blogs has been a rapid professionalization in the upper echelons of the blogosphere. Journalists have often criticized bloggers as uncredentialed amateurs—in the widely repeated formulation of CNN president Jonathan Klein, the worry has been that blogs empower "a guy sitting in his living room in his pajamas" (quoted in Colford 2004). Surprisingly, these criticisms have continued to be repeated even as journalists themselves have begun to blog in large numbers. NBC News anchor Brian Williams remarked in 2007 that after spending "all of my life, developing credentials to cover my field of work . . . I'm up against a guy named Vinny in an efficiency apartment in the Bronx who hasn't left the efficiency apartment in two years" (quoted in O'Gorman 2007).

From its inception, however, blogging as a medium has been dominated by educational elites–indeed, by individuals with stronger educational credentials than the typical journalist, or even the elite class of journalists that appear on national television broadcasts and write for the nation's leading opinion pages. At the end of the 2004 election cycle, at least half of blog traffic went to blogs published by a Ph.D., M.D., or J.D. (Hindman 2009).

The new bloggers and blog publishers who rose to prominence between 2004 and 2008 also come from remarkable backgrounds. Consider the case of Arianna Huffington, publisher of the *Huffington Post*, which was founded in 2005 and is of this writing the most widely read political site on the Web (see Table 9.1). Born in Greece, Huffington was educated at Cambridge and became the first immigrant president of the prestigious Cambridge Union debating society. Huffington had a lengthy romantic relationship with British opinion columnist Bernard Levin, one of the UK's most prominent journalists (Huffington 2004). In 1980 Huffington moved to the United States, and from 1986 to 1997 she was married to oil millionaire Michael Huffington, during which he made a run for the Senate. By 2008 the *Huffington Post* had received more than $25 million in venture capital to sustain its operations

(Kaplan 2008). While it is still common to hear claims that blogs are empowering ordinary citizens, it seems unlikely that Huffington herself qualifies for inclusion in that category.

If notions of bloggers as pajama-clad amateurs have always been more fiction than fact, a glance at the top 20 sites listed above shows that blogging has become increasingly professionalized. The *Huffington Post* is of course a for-profit venture, and paid editors determine which content is promoted on the front page of the site. Bloggers on BarackObama.com and Politico are paid professionals. Recent years have also seen journalists move between traditional media organizations and online sites that began as blogs. TPM's Greg Sargent was hired by the *Washington Post*, while journalist Matt Cooper, formerly of *Time*, briefly took a job with TPM. In early 2009, in a portentous shift, the *New York Times* recruited as its new opinion columnist Ross Douthat, previously best known as a blogger at *Atlantic Monthly*.

Institutionalization

The professionalization and commercialization of blogging is closely tied with the institutionalization of the medium. At the end of the 2004 election cycle, the large majority of widely read blogs were still sole proprietorships, started and run by a single blogger. Even bloggers who used common hosting platforms, such as WordPress or Blogspot, rarely had formal relationships with other likeminded bloggers. At the end of the 2008 cycle the landscape looked dramatically different. With a handful of exceptions, the most widely read blogs are now either group publications, components of a larger Website, or part of a panel of blogs hosted by a single organization.

The reasons behind this institutionalization of blogging are not self-evident, and more research on this phenomenon remains to be done. Yet some of the contributing factors are clear. Established bloggers have been enticed to moving their blogs under the umbrella of a larger group or publication by the promise of more money, more exposure, or (most often) both. Research on Web traffic also emphasizes the importance of "stickiness," a site's ability to convert those who stumble across it into regular visitors. A key predictor of stickiness, according to usability research, is the frequency with which content is updated (Nielsen 1999: 382). All else being equal, group blogs offer content that is more frequently updated than that of solo blogs. And even if a blog remains largely the product of a single individual, displaying content alongside other constantly changing blogs and frequently refreshed news stories is likely to increase a blog's stickiness.

Of all the changes in blogging between 2004 and 2008, the institutional-ization of blogging is likely to have the most profound, and profoundly mixed, impacts on the online public sphere. A blogosphere dominated by sole proprietorships is quite different, in both normative and practical terms, from a blogosphere in which most readers go to group blogs or blog-ging consortiums, and where paid bloggers and paid editors play the central role in determining which views get aired.

Social scientists, of course, have long studied institutions for reasons both theoretical and practical. Institutions are a locus for collective action. They shape the incentives of individual actors, and situating bloggers within powerful, durable institutions may change their behavior. Different institu-tional structures may result in the promotion and filtering of different con-tent and different views. Moreover, studies of news organizations have long argued that media institutions often pursue goals quite distinct from the ones reporters or editors would pursue on their own (e.g., Epstein 1973).

In short, the institutionalization of blogging forces us to pay attention not just to blogging about politics, but to the politics of blogging. The ques-tion (as in Harold Lasswell's definition of politics) is who gets what kind of money and attention, and the process by which these are distributed. With so much of the online audience for political content focused on a few top online outlets, the internal politics and political economy of a handful of top blogs now have an outsized effect on the U.S. public sphere.

On many Websites the production of online content mirrors that of tra-ditional media. The vetting and editorial mechanisms that apply to tradi-tional journalists in their online pursuits are similar to those that govern their work in television or in print. Still, some of the largest sources of on-line news and political commentary have adopted models of content pro-duction that are quite different from established patterns.

One important example of this is *Daily Kos*, one of the earliest (and still one of the largest) collaborative blogs, and a site which (as of early 2009) claimed to have 200,000 registered members.[2] *Daily Kos* was originally es-tablished in 2002 as the blog of Markos Moulitsas, a Democratic activist. Beginning in 2003, the site began to select three or four community mem-bers a year to serve as contributing editors. Bloggers granted this position could post directly to the front page, either by writing their own missives, or through the promotion of community members' writings. *Daily Kos* also encouraged site members to recommend diary entries they liked, and employed "Rescue Rangers" to find and promote deserving blog entries to the front page. As of spring 2009 the site had about a dozen contributing editors.

The *Huffington Post*, by contrast, seeks to provide a hybrid between commercial and community-based production. As cofounder Jonah Peretti explains it, the site employs a "mullet strategy": just like the infamous haircut, the *Huffington Post* is "business in the front, party in the back" (quoted in Alterman 2008). Despite the popularity of user-generated content, Peretti argues that "most of it totally sucks," but that is fine:

> [Users can] argue and vent on the secondary pages, but professional editors keep the front page looking sharp. The mullet strategy is here to stay, because the best way for Web companies to increase traffic is to let users have control, but the best way to sell advertising is a slick, pretty front page where corporate sponsors can admire their brands. (Alterman 2008)

Peretti noted that the "News" and "Blog" sections of the *Huffington Post* were kept separate, with the news section produced by a paid reporting staff, and the blog section supported by unpaid writers. Still, many of those who blogged for the *Huffington Post* were highly paid in their profession of choice, and presumably benefited from the exposure that their *Huffington Post* writings gave them. Many of the unpaid bloggers who were not successful professionals in other fields wrote in the hopes of earning a paid position.

Alongside community-based models like *Daily Kos* and hybrid models like the *Huffington Post*, many traditional media organizations have raced to buy up stables of established bloggers. *Time, Atlantic Monthly, Washington Monthly, National Review, Foreign Policy*, and numerous other publications have engaged in this practice. Interest groups and think tanks have also shown a willingness to hire established bloggers. For example, in 2008 the Center for American Progress hired blogger Matthew Yglesias to help raise their online visibility. In these cases, blogs seem to be used as loss leaders; while these professional bloggers rarely generate large amounts of direct revenue for an organization, they *do* generate a disproportionate amount of traffic. Frequently updated blog material is particularly important for print periodicals' Websites, where the non-blog content available may only change once a week or once a month.

Increasingly, established blogs have also provided a high-visibility platform for political elites. During the 2008 cycle many Democratic politicians wrote for sites like *Talking Points Memo, Daily Kos*, and *Huffington Post*. Barack Obama and Hillary Clinton both wrote for the *Huffington Post*; Obama also wrote for *Daily Kos*.

New Models

Large blogs have been institutionalized in another way as well. Both scholarly and popular accounts commonly describe the Web, and especially the blogosphere, as a place in constant flux. But for blogs at least, this is much less true than it used to be.

In previous election cycles, the biennial political process brought a number of new blogs to wide attention. That was the case in 2000, 2002, 2004, and 2006. Among the top hundred sites in Hitwise's October 2008 political Website category, though, only two were genuinely new blogs that had not existed during the 2005–2006 cycle.[3] One was a small, pro-Hillary Clinton Website named *Hillbuzz*; it ranked 89th. The more notable addition was *FiveThirtyEight.com*, ranked 23rd, a blog founded and run by Nate Silver.

The case of *FiveThirtyEight.com* is an instructive one, and suggests that new blogs have come to rely heavily on established sites to make a name for themselves. Silver comes from a different background from that of a traditional opinion journalist, though he is very far from being a typical citizen. The son of a political scientist, Silver earned a degree in economics from the University of Chicago and spent three and a half years working for the accounting firm KPMG. He left the firm to focus on baseball statistics, where he rose to prominence as the inventor of the PECOTA system for forecasting players' performance.

In 2007, Silver began using the pseudonym Poblano to post as a diarist on *Daily Kos*, applying similar sorts of statistical techniques to the prediction of election results. Poblano's posts were widely read and earned him considerable attention within the *Daily Kos* community. In March 2008, Silver founded *FiveThirtyEight.com*, offering even more extensive analysis of the 2008 election cycle. Silver's success in forecasting the primary and general election outcomes won him voluminous coverage in traditional media, including many appearances on television and print feature articles in the *New York Times* and *Time*. Silver has even moved his blog to NYTimes.com, providing a stark example of how blogging has been assimilated by traditional news organizations.

Another important new outlet—and a widely discussed new model for journalism—was the OffTheBus project, a "citizen-powered" campaign news site organized by the *Huffington Post* in partnership with NYU's Carter Journalism Institute. As cofounder Amanda Michel (2009) wrote, the aim was to "let a distributed, diverse crowd of amateur users with lots of different starting points have a go at campaign news and commentary, seeded by a few pros." Through the course of the campaign, OffTheBus managed to convince 12,000 individuals to sign up as contributors, all managed by a staff of about half a dozen. OffTheBus hoped to avoid the horse race reporting that dominates much traditional campaign journalism, and aimed to use its extraordinarily broad organization to cover the campaign at the grass roots. Assessments of the project are mixed, even among those who organized it. Responding to claims that OffTheBus produced stories that were "journalistically uneven," Michel writes that

> I agree. One reason why was simple: good writers are scarce and OTB wasn't a paying gig. Our editorial focus wasn't providing the Big Picture, as outlets like the *Post* and *The New York Times* attempt to do; it was correcting that picture with ground-level details that might be messier but are also closer to an election's beating heart. (Michel 2009)

With the 2008 election over, the OffTheBus organization largely disappeared.

The Wages of Institutionalization

The implications of institutionalization on the online public sphere are far-reaching. The growth of prominent group blogs provides greater opportunities for quality control. Widespread criticism of bloggers for their alleged inaccuracy has been mostly misguided, with readership highly focused on bloggers with backgrounds in the academy, law, journalism, or other fields with strong standards of factual accuracy. But community filtering and hybrid "pro-am" editing models are supposed to benefit especially those *without* such impressive résumés. The hope of some (including those who organized

OffTheBus) was that with enough training, filtering, and editing nontraditional political observers could write stories that lots of other citizens would want to read.

The growth of group and collaborative blogs also provides opportunities for bloggers to work their way up through the ranks. With *Daily Kos*, for example, diarists who earn attention and respect from their contributions can hope, someday, to be selected as contributing editors. Bloggers at the *Huffington Post* can similarly build up a name and reputation, particularly if editors like their work and place it prominently on the site. A lucky few might then parlay their unpaid commentary into a paid position. The number of bloggers at these large sites who will earn wide attention, of course, is small, but the fearsome level of competition ensures that those who succeed will be highly skilled.

The institutionalization of blogging also has significant implications for substantive representation in the online public sphere. Despite initial claims that the blogosphere was radically more inclusive, empirical studies have found that blog readership overwhelmingly accrues to upper-middle-class white men, with female and minority voices dramatically underrepresented (Hindman 2009: chap. 7). Still, as audiences have increasingly focused on group blogs, the nature of the issue has shifted, as have the responses to it. In many ways, online publications have replicated the problems–and the subsequent if partial solutions–that we are familiar with from traditional media.

There have long been concerns about the underrepresentation of women and minorities in opinion journalism. As former *New York Times* columnist Anna Quindlen wrote in 2006, most of the nation's op-ed pages continued to have a "quota of one" for female columnists, even after decades of debate on the issue (Quindlen 2006). With this context in mind, it is worth considering the *Atlantic Monthly*, one of the nation's most venerable magazines. In 2007, the *Atlantic* began investing more heavily in its online presence, and especially in acquiring a number of bloggers to be featured on its Website. By that summer, the "Voices" section featured five bloggers, all Harvard-educated white men.

A high-profile media organization like the *Atlantic* faces a different set of pressures and constraints from those faced by bloggers running sole proprietorships. While the rationale behind the *Atlantic's* subsequent hiring was not publicly disclosed, the *Atlantic* replicated the typical gender and racial makeup of top newspaper op-ed pages. It hired two new bloggers:

Megan McArdle (an established blogger) and Ta-nehisi Coates (a journalist and author who is black).

Other prominent sites have adopted a different approach. One study, focusing on the *Huffington Post*, found that only 23 percent of "Featured Blog Posts" linked from the front page of the site were written by female bloggers (Wakeman 2008). Yet this same study also found that at least one female blogger was always included in these listings, a result unlikely to have occurred by chance. This suggests that *Huffington Post* editors are considering gender in deciding which posts to highlight.

The raw number of prominent female bloggers was certainly higher at the end of the 2008 election cycle than it was in 2004. In addition to opinion-journalist-turned-blogger Michelle Malkin, by 2008 the ranks of prominent women in the blogosphere included Jane Hamsher (of *FireDogLake*), Susan Gardner (of *Daily Kos*), and of course Arianna Huffington. Still, any gains in the portion of readership going to female-authored blog posts have been modest.

Crowdsourcing

The dominance of a few blogs with a large and established readership provides opportunities for new kinds of production, and new forms of collective action. The model here is sometimes referred to as "crowdsourcing," of which Wikipedia is the canonical example. Michel (2009) referred to the OffTheBus project as "crowd-powered" newsgathering. Scholars of similar methods have employed different terms, including Yochai Benkler's focus on "peer production" (Benkler 2007), Steven Weber's discussion of "open source" methods (Weber 2004), and Eric von Hippel's description of "community-centered innovation" (von Hippel 2005).

No matter which terminology we use, all of these theories suggest that when a valuable information resource is viewed by a large number of people, many viewers will be willing to put in a small amount of effort to improve and refine it. This model certainly applies to the *Huffington Post* and *Daily Kos*, where engaged bloggers and diarists debate issues, point out errors, and recommend posts that deserve wider exposure. To a lesser degree this model applies to other bloggers, too. Michelle Malkin or Andrew Sullivan may be the only posters on their blogs on a typical day, but part of the value of their writings comes from the wide net of readers who occasionally send an e-mail that—even more occasionally—shapes coverage, or is excerpted on the site.

Malkin's or Sullivan's sites may not promote the same level of interactivity as the *Huffington Post* and *Daily Kos* do, but the relationship between writer and audience on these sites is still distinct from that of traditional journalism. While the impact of this different relationship is hard to measure in the aggregate, in some instances it has had dramatic real-world consequences. Consider *Talking Points Memo*'s award-winning coverage of the U.S. attorney scandal, in which the Bush administration dismissed federal prosecutors for partisan reasons. As Josh Marshall himself has explained, TPM's ability to break and cover the story depended on tips and updates from its widely distributed network of readers (Cohen 2008). While the firings of U.S. attorneys had been covered piecemeal in local papers, *Talking Points Memo* was able to use the eyes and ears of its readership to put the broader story together. Ultimately, coverage of the U.S. attorney scandal and related issues led to the resignation of attorney general Alberto Gonzales.

This widely recognized success, though, underscores an obvious weakness with crowdsourcing: it requires a crowd. Again, claims about the online public sphere have to be consistent with existing patterns of traffic on the Web. Concentrated traffic means that true crowdsourcing is something that only a small number of blogs and Websites can achieve. How big a site needs to be in order to make the crowdsourcing model work remains a question for future research. Still, the number of political blogs or similar sites that can benefit from a crowdsourcing model is likely to be small—perhaps in the high double digits or the low hundreds. We should not forget that the U.S. public sphere serves a nation of 50 states and 300 million citizens. The concentration in the online public sphere that makes crowdsourcing possible also raises the same questions of scale that have dogged democratic theorists since Plato. Ensuring that citizens' voices are considered equally is easier in the Athenian agora or a New England town meeting than it is in a handful of sites that serve hundreds of thousands of citizens a day.

Crowdsourcing is doubly problematic when we consider the area of the public sphere most at risk. Recent years have seen dramatic cutbacks in coverage of state and local politics. Whatever the civic costs of these cuts, their economic logic is clear: local and state accountability journalism is comparatively expensive, and it generates less reader interest than many other types of newspaper content. But crowdsourcing models, even more than advertising-supported models, depend on high levels of interest from readers.

The content hardest for newspapers to produce is likely to be especially challenging to replicate using a model of community production. Dozens upon dozens of small-scale, local, and state-level sites focused on civic affairs and citizen engagement have been founded over the past decade. Overwhelmingly, these sites have been failures: as Andrew Chadwick (2006: 102) summarizes, "The road to e-democracy is littered with the burnt-out hulks of failed projects." While blogs focusing on state and local politics have done somewhat better than sites that aspired to be online discussion forums, traffic levels have been uniformly dismal. Scholarship has emphasized differences between the commercial media model and the community-centered model, but we should remember the similarities, too: both require an audience to work.

Strengthening the Online Public Sphere

Popular writings about the Web, and indeed many scholarly treatments of the Internet, have been permeated by the assumption that institutions matter little online. Instead, we have heard talk of "disintermediation," of how citizen journalists are going to replace paid professionals, about how with blogging "the universe of permissible opinions will expand, unconstrained by the prejudices, tastes or interests of the old media elite" (Andrew Sullivan, quoted in Last 2002).

As this essay has argued, these assumptions are obsolete. While some uncertainty remains about the future of blogging and the online public sphere as a whole, blogging as a medium is a decade old, and the emergence of a popular new source of political information and commentary is now a rare event. We should not wait for the next *Daily Kos* to come along, any more than we should wait for a new technology startup to displace Google. And as the *Huffington Post*'s example suggests, new entrants must overcome substantial barriers to entry. Few players will be able to raise the tens of millions of dollars necessary to compete effectively with the *Huffington Post*.

But what if we were to take online institutions seriously? What if our default assumption was that online public discussion and commentary would continue to be dominated by a handful of large Websites? What if we were less captivated by notions of engaged citizens doing their own newsgathering, and more focused on helping well-positioned if self-interested elites perform valuable civic tasks?

Such a shift in perspective suggests several ways in which the online public sphere can be strengthened. To begin with, publishers of the top blogs need to take their gatekeeping role seriously. Some already do, but on the whole this group has been highly resistant to claims that they represent a new media elite. Bloggers Hugh Hewitt (2005), Glenn Reynolds (2006), Markos Moulitsas (2008), and the editors of the *Huffington Post* (2008) have each written books espousing the power of the Internet to amplify the voice of ordinary citizens. For bloggers who have lived their own digital Horatio Alger story, who have gone from a handful of readers to hundreds of thousands of hits a day, it may seem as if anyone who is smart and hardworking can replicate their success. There is also an element of self-aggrandizement in this "aw shucks" democratic posturing.

In 2002, perhaps it was possible to start the next *Daily Kos*. But the Internet has demonstrated extraordinarily powerful first-mover advantages, even more so than traditional industries. To pretend that the blogosphere today is open as it was a decade ago is simply silly. Those who direct the most widely read sources of online news and online commentary should recognize that they do in fact hold a privileged position—indeed, they hold a public trust. If they believe certain content is important for the public sphere to provide, they need to take part of the responsibility for providing it. To improve the public sphere, the largest online publishers must first drop the pretense that any teenager with an Internet connection can compete with them.

Making National Sites Carry Local Content

In the same vein, those concerned about making democratic discourse work in practice need to focus on working with the institutions that already exist. If we do not like the content being produced by the local television station or the local newspaper, we do not content ourselves with the thought that, if we just wait, maybe things will get better. Yet the "wait and see" approach, backstopped by faith in the Internet's "democratizing" power, has been the cornerstone of much of our policy toward the Internet.

Consider one example of how taking current institutions seriously, and assuming that they are going to be durable, can change the policies we pursue. As I began by noting, democratic theorists of many stripes are concerned that the shift to the Web has reduced the amount of local news consumed. Local newspaper readers could not avoid exposure to local news.

Now the majority of online news readers eschew local sources for national ones. One solution is to push national news outlets—from Yahoo! News to CNN.com, FoxNews.com to the *Huffington Post*—to present every reader of their sites, by default, with news tailored to each user's state and locality.

As a technical matter, this is eminently possible. Many sites require users to register with a zip code. For those that do not, the user's IP address will usually identify the city and state. A small portion of the screen real estate—say, 5 or 10 percent of the "above the fold" content that users can see without downward scrolling—could be dedicated to local content, enough to include four or five headlines. This content could be provided by local news organizations, by established wire services, or by the site itself. In the case of large blogging sites such as *Huffington Post* or *Daily Kos*, users can be provided with blog posts from others in their local area. This would provide a small amount of revenue for local media outlets—not enough to save local news on its own, certainly, but enough to help. For citizens, this plan would allow them to consume higher quality national news at the most widely read sites, while also ensuring that they receive at least some exposure to local news.

Minimal "must carry" provisions for local and state content might need to be voluntary, but a variety of means could encourage compliance. The carrot of tax credits or direct subsidies could lessen any financial impact. Some Websites, particularly Internet news portals, might even find this approach to be good business. The *Huffington Post* has expressed interest in expanding into local content, though as of this writing the form and scope of this proposed expansion remains unclear. A variety of sticks, from public pressure to regulatory intervention, might be brought to bear on those sites reluctant to participate. Moreover, compliance need not be perfect in order to have a substantial impact. The online market for news and political commentary, again, is extraordinarily concentrated. Convincing just the top ten news sites to include default links to local content would reach 30 percent of the online news market nationwide.

Bringing Back Party Papers

Last, to the extent that we do try to create new institutions, we should abandon the hope that ordinary citizens can consistently produce the content that is most endangered. Citizen journalism or advertisement-supported content are unlikely to work at the state or local level. Readers may in some cases improve and refine online content, but we cannot rely on readers themselves to produce it.

Consider what would be needed to start a small online publication, offering a mix of blog and news content, with a focus on state government. To make such a venture work, a core of skilled writers (though not necessarily journalists) would have to be recruited. Because the venture would likely not be financially self-supporting, these individuals would need other full-time jobs where they enjoy a large deal of autonomy or informal employer support for their blogging. Outside commitments would require that most individual contributions be small, and contributors would have to be strongly motivated to keep contributing content over the long term. As traditional media coverage shrinks, contributors would require strong contacts with those in state government in order to produce original content.

Surprisingly enough, these requirements can be met. And there are models to emulate—noncommercial, or more accurately pre-commercial models—that still remain to be tried. Perhaps most promising is the solution that Madison and Jefferson themselves would recognize: small publications with formal and informal support from a political party.

In 1791, Jefferson and Madison helped establish the *National Gazette*, a new Democratic-Republican paper intended as counterweight to Alexander Hamilton's *Gazette of the United States*, a Federalist organ founded two years earlier. Both papers used the same organizational model (Burns 2006). Government sinecures were provided to the editors, who used their government salary and lack of other responsibilities to focus on newspaper publishing (Starr 2004). Most of the content for the two newspapers was produced by correspondents in the traditional sense: as the professional journalist had yet to be invented, many prominent party members (including Hamilton and Jefferson and Madison themselves) contributed articles to be published pseudonymously.

If we are truly concerned about revitalizing the public sphere, these early newspapers deserve a second look. Every state legislature in the country employs dozens of people whose job description includes writing press releases and handling media. Fewer and fewer members of the press remain to read those releases, to interview members of the legislature, and to report legislators' views and activities to the broader public. In this changing environment there are strong incentives for partisan press professionals to produce their own online content, and the realities of getting that content read point strongly toward the creation of a *Huffington Post*-style publication. A small number of outside contributors—those employed by allied interest groups, longtime party activists, sympathetic lawyers and professors—might also be interested in participating. Little direct financial support would be necessary, and what money would be required could be raised through traditional political fundraising channels.

Such a venture would take advantage of the possibilities for collective action afforded by new technologies, while replicating the ethos of party papers that dominated much of America until the rise of the modern commercial press in the latter half of the 1800s. The story of politics on the Web is, in large part, the story of niche dominance. At least one Democratic-leaning and one Republican-leaning political portal in each state could count on thousands of visits a day—hardly a complete substitute for the coverage that local newspapers are failing to provide, but successful enough that political elites would find these online publications worth pursuing. For normative theorists, highly partisan media come with their own steep costs and tradeoffs. A new partisan press would likely make political polarization worse. But civic-mindedness will not provide the consistent coverage of local and regional politics that a federal system needs. Ambition counteracting ambition, however, might help replace part of what has been lost.

Whatever the merits of bringing back the partisan media, or pushing national outlets to provide local news, it is clear that online discourse is no longer ruled just by rugged individualism. At the close of 2008, the *Huffington Post* venture capital fundraising placed a $115 million value on the company. The era when political comment on the Web was dominated by solo bloggers writing for free is gone. Going forward, the health of the public sphere depends on our ability to shape online institutions—and mostly *already existing* online institutions—in ways that strengthen democratic values. This is not an easy task; but as the number of laid-off reporters continues to grow, it is an increasingly critical one.

References

Adamic, Lada, and Natalie Glance. 2005. "The Political Blogosphere in the 2004 U.S. Election: Divided They Blog." *Proceedings of the Third International Conference on Link Discovery*, 36–43.

Alterman, Eric. 2008. "Out of Print: The Death and Life of the American Newspaper." *New Yorker*, March 31.

Benkler, Yochai. 2007. *The Wealth of Networks*. New Haven, Conn.: Yale University Press.

Burns, Eric. 2006. *Infamous Scribblers*. New York: PublicAffairs.

Carr, Nicholas. 2008. "Who Killed the Blogosphere?" *Rough Type*, November 7. http://www.roughtype.com/archives/2008/11/who_killed_the.php.

Carroll, John S. 2006. "John S. Carroll on Why Newspapers Matter." *Niemann Watchdog*, April 2008. http://www.niemanwatchdog.org/index.cfm?fuseaction=ask_this.view&askthisid=00203

Chadwick, Andrew. 2006. *Internet Politics*. Oxford: Oxford University Press.

Cohen, Noam. 2008. "Blogger, Sans Pajamas, Rakes Muck and a Prize." *New York Times*, February 25.

Colford, Paul D. 2004. "Big Blog Bucks." *New York Daily News*, October 5, 52.

Dertouzos, James N., and William B. Trautman. 1990. "Economic Effects of Media Concentration: Estimates from a Model of the Newspaper Firm." *Journal of Industrial Economics* 39: 1–14.

Editors of the Huffington Post. 2008. *The Huffington Post Complete Guide to Blogging*. New York: Simon and Schuster.

Epstein, Edward Jay. 1973. *News from Nowhere: Television and the News*. New York: Random House.

"The Future of Journalism." 2005. *The Economist*, April 21.

Fowler, Mayhill. 2008. "Obama: No Surprise That Hard-Pressed Pennsylvanians Turn Bitter." *Huffington Post*, April 11.

Franklin, Charles. 2006. "Generic Ballot: Dem Lead Widens Post Foley." *Pollster.com*, October 10. http://www.pollster.com/blogs/generic_ballot_dem_lead_widens.php.

Harris, Paul. 2006. "Hurricane Arianna." *The Observer*, December 10.

Hewitt, Hugh. 2005. *Blog: Understanding the Information Reformation That's Changing Your World*. Nashville, Tenn.: Nelson Books.

Hindman, Matthew. 2009. *The Myth of Digital Democracy*. Princeton, N.J.: Princeton University Press.

Huffington, Arianna. 2004. "The Odd Couple." *Sunday Times* (London), August 15.

Kaplan, David. 2008. "Huffington Post Closes $25 Million Third Round." *paidContent*, December 1. http://www.paidcontent.org/entry/419-huffington-post-closes-25-million-third-round/.

King, Ian. 2008. "Business Big Shot: Arianna Huffington, Online Entrepreneur." *The Times* (London), November 21.

Last, Jonathan V. 2002. "Reading, Writing, and Blogging." *Weekly Standard*, March 14. http://www.weeklystandard.com/Content/Public/Articles/000/000/001/009flofq.asp.

Levey, Noam M. 2006. "Anti-Foley Blogger Speaks Out." *Los Angeles Times*, November 10, A13.

Michel, Amanda. 2009. "Get Off the Bus." *Columbia Journalism Review*, March/April.

Moulitsas Zuniga, Markos. 2008. *Taking on the System: Rules for Radical Change in a Digital Era*. New York: Celebra.

Newspaper Association of America. 2010. "Advertising Expenditures." http://www.naa
.org/Trends-and-Numbers/Advertising-Expenditures/Annual-All-Categories.aspx

Nielsen, Jakob. 1999. *Designing Web Usability: The Practice of Simplicity*. New York:
New Riders Press.

O'Gorman, Kristen. 2007. "Brian Williams Weighs in on New Medium." *We Want
Media*, April 6. http://journalism.nyu.edu//pubzone/wewantmedia/node=487.

Pérez-Peña, Richard. 2009. "As Cities Go from Two Papers to One, Talk of Zero." *New
York Times*, March 11.

Pew Research Center for the People and the Press. 2008. "Internet Overtakes Newspapers as News Outlet." December 28. http://people-press.org/report/479/Internet
-overtakes-newspapers-as-news-source.

Quindlen, Anna. 2006. "The Glass Half Empty." *New York Times*, November 22, A27.

Reynolds, Glenn. 2006. *An Army of Davids: How Markets and Technology Empower
Ordinary People to Beat Big Media, Big Government, and Other Goliaths*. Washington, D.C.: Nelson Current.

Rosse, James N. 1980. "The Decline of Direct Newspaper Competition." *Journal of
Competition* 30: 65–71.

Seper, Chris. 2004. "For Good or Ill, Blogs Make Waves." *Cleveland Plain Dealer*, October 7, A1.

Starr, Paul. 2004. *The Creation of the American Media: The Political Origins of Modern
Communications*. New York: Basic Books.

———. 2009. "Goodbye to the Age of Newspapers (Hello to a New Era of Corruption)."
New Republic, March 4.

Project for Excellence in Journalism. *The State of the News Media 2008*. http://www
.stateofthemedia.org/2008/.

———. *The State of the News Media 2009*. March 16.

von Hippel, Eric. 2005. *Democratizing Innovation*. Cambridge, Mass.: MIT Press.

von Sternberg, Bob. 2004. "From Geek to Chic: Blogs Gain Influence." *Minneapolis
Star-Tribune*, September 22, 1A.

Wakeman, Jessica. 2008. "Huffington Post Mutes Women's Voices." *Fairness and Accuracy in Reporting*, November/December. http://www.fair.org/index.php
?page=3647.

Wallsten, Peter. 2004. "No Disputing It: Blogs Are Major Players." *Los Angeles Times*,
September 12.

Weber, Steven. 2004. *The Success of Open Source*. Cambridge, Mass.: Harvard University Press.

Yu, Hui-yong and Greg Bensinger. 2009. "New York Times Sells Building Stake for
$225 Million." *Bloomberg.com*, February 11.

CHAPTER 10

The Technological Basis of Organizational Membership: Representation of Interests in the New Media Age

David Karpf

American citizens are represented not only through government institutions, but also through civic and political associations. Dating back to Tocqueville's observation that America was a nation of joiners, social scientists have highlighted the important intermediary role that membership associations play in public life. Membership-based civic associations serve as "laboratories of democracy." They impart democratic skills to their participants, foster social capital among their membership, and provide an organizational substrate for social movements. The composition of America's associational universe has changed dramatically over time, however. Membership-based associations—particularly in the political realm—employ a range of different definitions of the roles and responsibilities of the member. These definitions have evolved over time, partly in response to changing technological capacities embedded within the communications environment. As the organization-to-member relationship has changed, the representational role of political associations in public life has changed as well. This chapter explores the structure of these organization-to-member relationships, highlighting the representational benefits and challenges created by competing models. It examines membership from three perspectives—the member's, the organization's, and the technological intermediary's. Drawing on evidence from MoveOn.org, it demonstrates how new media tools simultaneously weaken and enhance membership engagement in political associations.

A Citizen and Her Associations

As a guiding example, imagine the membership affiliations of a present-day college-aged political activist. The student is a member of a few campus groups. Membership in these groups entails attending meetings . . . lots of meetings. Some meetings feature a guest speaker or engaging discussion of important problems at the campus, community, national, or international level. Other meetings feature tiresome bickering over organizational minutiae. These events foster a "culture of commitment" (Han 2009). They impart participatory skills and support the formation of strong social ties between our activist and her peers. A few of the groups are campus chapters of a national federated organization—Young Republicans or Amnesty International. If she becomes particularly involved in these groups, she might attend the organization's nationwide convention. Involvement at the national level may yield internships or career opportunities. All those meetings are also a lot of work, though. As the semester gets busy, the student likely abandons a group or two, redirecting her energies toward higher priorities like finishing the midterm assignment for her political science class. Her membership in these campus activist groups is *thick and participatory*. The groups ask for her time and her physical co-presence.

If this hypothetical college activist has enough disposable income, she may also be a member of national political organizations. Whatever her preferred issue area—women's rights, environmental protection, civil rights, gun rights—there is a longstanding advocacy group representing her interests in Washington. Those groups rely in part upon the small annual dues contributions provided by check-writing members. In return for those contributions, she may receive some largely symbolic incentive—a backpack, a t-shirt, a calendar, or a newsletter. She also gives to the organization for the mental satisfaction of knowing that some professional organization is representing her strongest political positions in Washington. Joining the ranks of the organization means they can make reference to a slightly larger membership list during their lobby visits. She doesn't know whether such claims make a difference (Baumgartner et al. 2009), but she likes to think that they do. Having joined one such organization, she also has been added to the mailing lists of several related organizations. Her campus mailbox is full of membership solicitations. She won't give money to them all (some money needs to be reserved for ramen noodles!), but she'll give to a few. Membership in these national advocacy groups is *thin and financial*. The groups ask for little besides her money. The member gives of her bank account, rather than her time.

Our college activist also spends entirely too much time on the Internet. Some of that time is spent looking at funny cat photos, YouTube videos, and Tumblr sites. Some is spent on Wikipedia, researching topics for her political science midterm assignment. But some of that time also is devoted to participating in politics. The student follows a few of the larger political blogs that match her partisan persuasion (Lawrence, Sides, and Farrell 2010; Hindman 2009). She shares interesting content with her social network through Facebook and Twitter. If our student is a progressive activist, she doubtless has taken some online action with a "netroots" political organization—MoveOn.org, most likely.[1] Having signed an e-petition once, our student now receives three or four messages per week from these new advocacy groups. These messages always begin with the salutation "Dear MoveOn Member." They provide an outlet for her to take action around the national controversies she is reading about on political blogs or watching on partisan news programs. They occasionally ask for a little money, but not as a precursor to membership. Membership in these groups is *thin and participatory*. These netroots groups don't ask for much of her time or money. Her membership ties to them impart few new social ties or democratic skills, but they do leave her feeling a bit more knowledgeable and engaged with national politics.

All the groups in this example are membership associations. Yet membership clearly entails more in the first example than in the other two. Historically, America's associational universe was once populated by national federated organizations (Elks' Club, Lions' Club, Rotary Club). In the 1960s and 1970s, membership in these organizations steeply declined. Theda Skocpol (2003) aptly describes it as a shift "from membership to management." Marshall Ganz (1997) has referred to the wave of interest groups appearing in those decades as "bodyless heads." Today, the thick, participatory membership style is found in campus groups, church organizations, and a few holdover organizations from years past. During the "interest group explosion" of the 1970s (Berry 1999, 1984; Baumgartner and Jones 1993; Walker, McCarthy and Baumgartner 2011), direct mail-based membership became the standard among advocacy organizations. The revenues from direct mail supported an infrastructure of D.C. policy experts and lobbyists, providing representation for post-materialist public interests. The 2000s have seen the rise of a third wave of membership organizations—"netroots" groups with minimal staff infrastructure in D.C. who rely on the Internet to communicate quickly and cheaply with online supporters and mobilize them around the issue of the moment.

These three divergent membership styles represent distinct membership regimes, grounded in historical periods of civic representation, producing a mosaic of member relationships today (Karpf 2012; Bimber, Flanagin and Stohl 2012). The first membership regime is *identity-based*—membership in an organization is tied to an individual's self-identity.[2] A member of the Rotary Club or of the Campus Young Democrats will self-identify as a Rotarian or a Young Dem. The second membership regime is *issue-based*. Dues-paying members of Environmental Defense Fund or Children's International will self-identify as an environmentalist or a humanitarian. They give to those organizations because of the overlap in issue interests, rather than because of thick participatory ties. The third membership regime is *activity-based*. A member of MoveOn.org takes an occasional action with that organization—signing a petition or attending a rally. They may not give money to the organization at all, and often are unaware that they are counted among the membership. Newer entrants into the associational universe tend to adopt the MoveOn-style membership regime (Karpf 2012). Some legacy organizations have done so as well (Bimber, Flanagin, and Stohl 2012).

The progression of these three membership regimes depicts a general "thinning" trend. From the strong ties of identity-based associations, organizations have redefined membership, first to entail check-writing and then to entail nothing more than a mouse click. Membership means less in the newer organizations than it means in their older peers. It asks less of the individual, and imparts fewer civic skills and social ties as a result. Yet a deeper look at these competing membership regimes yields a more complicated understanding. From the member's perspective, less is required of a member. But from the organization's perspective, more feedback can (surprisingly) be heard. While the generational shift among advocacy organizations results in the loss of some types of representation, it also yields a bounty of other types. To understand changes in membership regimes, it is helpful to examine the organization-to-member relationship through three distinct lenses: the member's perspective, the organization's perspective, and the "affordance" (Earl and Kimport 2011) on intermediary communications technologies.

Associational Membership from the Individual's Perspective

From the perspective of our hypothetical college student, these overlapping memberships carry very different meanings. The thick membership experience of her preferred campus group demands substantial time commitments, but also offers social and experiential rewards. The student must choose between the demands of the organization and competing demands on her limited time. Those organizations which best foster a "culture of commitment" and succeed in connecting with her personal convictions will crowd out competing demands on her time (Han 2009). The thin, financial membership experience of legacy organizations requires less, but also provides less. Meanwhile, our student likely does not think of herself as a MoveOn member, but she also takes multiple online actions with them per month.

From the individual's perspective, the most noteworthy feature of these membership regimes is that *both* issue-based and activity-based memberships are vanishingly thin relationships. The thick membership association is a rarity in twenty-first-century America. The associational universe of the bygone era described by Tocqueville and Skocpol (2003) declined long before the creation of the World Wide Web. For the past forty years, membership-based political associations in America have been typified by strong centralized staff operations and weak membership engagement. Skocpol offers several explanations for the decline of federated civic associations and the thick membership model they fostered. Changes in entertainment options—particularly the rise of television—created new competition for citizens' free time. Changes in family roles also played a role, as mothers entered the workforce and faced increased demands on their time. At least as important was the success of rights-based social movements in the 1960s, which yielded a new government opportunity structure that supported the professional turn among new advocacy organizations. Newly founded groups in the 1970s saw more value in hiring policy experts, lobbyists, and litigators than in investing in local amateur supporter groups. The emergence of mainframe computing and cheap databases also made direct mail member communications a more viable alternative for membership associations.

Identity-based membership organizations still exist today, but only under exceptional circumstances. Campus organizations, as indicated in the opening example, are one such exception. Young people sent away from the communities where they grew up have a particularly strong impetus to forge new social ties. Campus political groups provide one suitable outlet. Religious organizations (though not expressly political in character) are another exception. Religion remains a central characteristic of many Americans' identities, and strongly religious Americans often become deeply involved in congregational organizations. Longstanding organizations like the American Legion and the Rotary Club also maintain federated membership structures. Those organizations that have survived to the present day continue to provide a rewarding experience to their engaged membership, though they face a generational challenge as their membership ages.

Alarmed observers such as Gladwell (2010) and Shulman (2009) express concern that the new membership regime reduces social movements and political mobilization to mere "clicktivism." Shulman argues that the ease of online participation creates "perverse incentives in the context of interest group-initiated mass e-mail campaigns about U.S. regulatory policy." Specifically, he worries that waves of online participation will drown out more substantive forms of citizen engagement, furthering citizen apathy and distrust of government. In response, Karpf (2010) argues that the minimal threshold of clicktivism is a replacement for the "armchair activism" of the previous regime, which in turn produced similar concerns. There are many overlaps between the thin issue- and activity-based membership regimes.

The activity-based membership model is particularly common among advocacy organizations founded in the past dozen years.[3] Membership in the direct mail era required the active choice to write an annual check in support of an organization's efforts. Members of Internet-mediated advocacy groups like MoveOn.org make no such active choice to join the organization. While MoveOn is able to boast a membership list of over 7 million individuals (approximately 2.25 percent of the American public), this is a far cry from the Women's Christian Temperance Union in the 1920s, which also boasted over 1 percent of the U.S. population (Skocpol 2003). Members were actively engaged in the work of the organization. They deliberated at meetings, forging cross-class social ties and building participatory skills in the process. The average member of MoveOn, by contrast, occasionally takes part in an online action.

While both newer membership regimes are characteristically thin, they also frequently provide greater depth for those members who choose to become more involved. Membership in the Sierra Club, for instance, is issue-based, and most of its 600,000+ members simply write an annual check and receive a free backpack in return. But tens of thousands also choose to participate in a federated system of local groups and state chapters. These more active members self-identify as "sierrans," and are granted greater voice in the organization's policy deliberations. Likewise, while membership in MoveOn is activity-based, MoveOn also features over 200 local "councils"—groups of at least four volunteers who plan local events and are granted greater support from and voice within the organization. Bimber, Flanagin, and Stohl (2012) note how identity-based associations like the American Legion use new information technology to provide increased participatory opportunities to their members, while the issue-based AARP allows non-members to engage in online actions. Organizations commonly describe these offerings as forming a "ladder of engagement" (Han 2009), in which membership provides the baseline of support, but then there are higher gradients of participatory engagement.

Our hypothetical student activist might thus consider herself a part of the MoveOn community or Amnesty International community if she has taken advantage of online and offline participatory opportunities (Bimber, Flanagin, and Stohl 2012). But this would make her the exception to the rule. Membership in most advocacy groups entails very little from the individual's perspective. Members are asked for limited money or limited participation. Thicker forms of membership participation appear in rare circumstances, thus raising important concerns that political representation through political associations has declined. Why has this transition occurred? To answer this question, we turn to membership from the organization's perspective.

Associational Membership from the Organization's Perspective

Why have groups like MoveOn.org redefined membership? Why, indeed, did an earlier set of organizations move from thick participation to armchair activism? The answer lies in a combination of factors—some related to technology, others related to government opportunity structure. Thinner definitions of membership allow for more expansive member lists. New fundraising practices allow for effective fundraising through those massive lists, while older fundraising practices were cost-effective only when applied to smaller, concentrated lists. Changes in the media system—particularly the emergence of the 24-hour news cycle and online news outlets—advantage more nimble tactical repertoires which, in turn, demand online communications routines. In short, the structure of citizen interest representation through advocacy groups is accomplished through "leveraged affordances" of available information technologies (Earl and Kimport 2011).

Since MoveOn.org has been the pioneer in this area, we will treat it as the model example for this section. For MoveOn's purposes, unlike the purposes of large political advocacy associations that predate it, the thin definition of membership carries substantial advantages. There is virtually no downside to having an expansive list. Matt Bai (2007) makes this distinction, terming it "The Power of the List:" "In a virtual world . . . few things [are] as valuable as a massive list—that is, a database of names and e-mail addresses that could be identified with a single need or interest, and thus could be mobilized with the push of a button." The distinction here lies in the dramatic reduction in transaction costs online. When organizations communicate with their membership through the mail, a large, disorganized list consumes too many resources. The savings through economies of scale are minimal: the postage on 1,000 pieces of mail is 10 times the postage on 100. Online, however, an e-mail to 100 consumes the same resources as an e-mail to 1,000 or 10,000.[4] The marginal cost of e-mail or Web-based communication is nearly zero.[5]

A similar transition occurred during the rise of direct mail-based membership. Skocpol (2003) makes note of the technological underpinnings of that transition. Simply put, armchair activism required cheap database technology to be viable for nonprofit organizations. Organizations prior to the late 1960s *had* to engage in the costly task of developing local federated infrastructure, because mainframe computing was prohibitively costly until that time. The falling cost of information, broadly defined, leads to disruptive changes in membership and fundraising regimes, giving rise to new types of political association. Bimber (2003) discusses this process in greater historical detail, describing the Internet broadly as a new "information regime" that gives rise to "postbureaucratic" advocacy organizations. Previous information regimes gave rise to the party organizations of the 1800s and single-issue organizations of the mid-twentieth century.

MoveOn's membership grows through sedimentary waves of political mobilization. The organization seeks to mobilize public pressure around whatever issue is dominating the current media agenda. It was founded by technology entrepreneurs Joan Blades and Wes Boyd, a married couple who had made their fortune in the mid-90s tech boom when they created, among other things, the highly popular "flying toasters" screen saver. In 1998, during the midst of the Clinton-Lewinsky affair, the two grew tired of scandal politics and started a simple Web site where visitors could sign a petition asking Congress to censure Clinton and "move on." Attention to the Web site diffused virally, and within a week 100,000 people had signed the petition, which eventually attracted 500,000 signers (Zetter 2004). In the aftermath of that issue mobilization, the couple was left with a list of 500,000 motivated partisans that they could contact in the future. MoveOn's membership growth has continued to be based around these sedimentary mobilization efforts. The organization grew to over 3 million members as a result of its efforts in opposition to the Iraq War in 2002–2004. During the 2008 presidential campaign, MoveOn endorsed Barack Obama days before the "Super Tuesday" set of primaries. The organization's membership donated over $88 million to presidential campaign efforts in that cycle, and 933,800 of its members volunteered over 20,841,507 hours to the Obama campaign. Those efforts also ballooned the member list to over 5 million, much of it based on eye-catching viral videos and offers of free Obama/Biden merchandise. In general, the sedimentary character of MoveOn's membership growth leads it to prioritize timely action appeals, optimized to the fast-moving media cycle.

Importantly, MoveOn's redefinition of organizational membership is accompanied by innovation in online fundraising. The advantage of armchair activism over thick, participatory membership was that it provided an expanded pool of small dues payments that could be invested in D.C. office space, policy experts, and lobbying staff. That advantage has begun to erode in the first decade of the twenty-first century, as direct mail fundraising has entered a steep industry-wide decline (Monitor Institute 2011). Fundraising for issue-based organizations has long hinged upon loss-leading "prospecting" efforts, in which mass mailings yield a negative return, but unearth issue-supporters who are likely to provide reliable long-term donations (Klein 1994). MoveOn, by contrast, develops an expansive member list and then makes targeted action appeals to that membership. These targeted appeals are usually tied to a specific result—$10 to put a commercial on the air, for instance. While legacy organizations have also moved into online fundraising, the financial demands presented by existing overhead costs prevent them from fully adopting MoveOn's fundraising strategies. Legacy organizations built their infrastructure while relying on unrestricted direct mail revenue. The specificity of targeted online appeals limits an organization's ability to apply revenues to overhead expenses. Netroots organizations, by comparison, carry much smaller staffing and overhead costs.

Consider the following fundraising e-mails, the first from SaveOurEnvironment.org, the second from MoveOn, both sent out a few days prior to December 31, 2008:

> We have less than 48 hours to reach our goal of raising $10,000 by 11:59PM on December 31—and we're not there yet . . .
>
> There are lots of reasons why you should give to SaveOurEnvironment.org right now:
>
> First, because we're counting on you. . . .
>
> Second, because the year is coming to a close. . . .
>
> And third, because there is no time like the present. The time for excuses is over: America needs strong environmental policies that support a sustainable green economy today. Help us make it happen.

SaveOurEnvironment has, in essence, moved traditional direct mail-based fundraising operations online. They thus take advantage of the reduced costs of the medium, but reach a much smaller audience than MoveOn, and their appeal lacks clear issue salience, suggesting that members should give "because there is no time like the present." Compare this to MoveOn's appeal:

> Dear MoveOn member, You've probably heard about how Wall Street financier Bernard Madoff scammed investors out of at least $50 billion. But you may not have heard that his victims included the foundations that support some really important progressive organizations. Groups that fight for human rights, fair elections and racial justice are getting hit hard—just in time for the holidays. We've worked side-by-side with many of them.
>
> If these groups can't replace the funding that came from investment accounts that Madoff stole, they may be forced to start cutting important projects or, in some cases, even lay off staff. Can you pitch in $25 or $50 for each of the four organizations we're highlighting below? Our friends at Atlantic Philanthropies and the Open Society

Institute will each match every dollar that comes in until January 1! So, for the next three days, your donation of $25 or $50 means $75 or $150 for groups affected by Madoff. If a few thousand of us give together, it can make an enormous difference—and help repair some of the damage Madoff has done. Click here to contribute.

MoveOn goes on to note that the year-end contribution will be 100 percent tax-deductible and provides a brief description of the four organizations it is supporting. In previous research, I have defined the difference between these two strategies as "the MoveOn Effect" (Karpf 2012). While direct mail fundraising uses relatively *generic* issue appeals to solicit small *general funding* donations, netroots organizations like MoveOn use *targeted* e-mail fundraising to make *timely* appeals related to a *specific* fundraising purpose. In a large-scale study of online fundraising appeals by progressive advocacy groups, I found that organizations founded prior to 1996 almost exclusively use e-mail to make generic funding appeals. Organizations founded after 1996 apply a mixture of funding appeals, including generic appeals, targeted appeals, and "passthrough appeals," where they ask their membership to pool donations that will go directly to an electoral candidate (Karpf 2012). Even though all advocacy organizations use the Internet today, newer organizations use technology differently from their legacy peers.

The gap in fundraising practices is tied to path-dependent organizational features. The specificity of MoveOn-style targeted funding requests comes at a cost: legally, organizations must obey "donor intent" in their expenditures. MoveOn-style fundraising appeals ask for a highly targeted form of support — $10 to put a campaign commercial on the air or place a field organizer in a critical state. Targeted appeals have always had a higher rate of success, and they are routinely used by large nonprofits when approaching major donors and foundations. Anyone familiar with university administration is aware of the challenge this presents: donors would prefer to give money toward a particular, specific project or outcome rather than toward the general fund. Many nonprofits divide their fundraising efforts accordingly, with direct mail based in a "Development" office and major gifts coordinated through an "Advancement" office. One longstanding benefit of direct mail fundraising is that the money comes without any restrictions. It can be used to pay for Human Resources departments, staff training, and physical infrastructure, whereas organizations are legally prevented from applying too large a percentage of targeted, project-specific funds to these overhead costs. MoveOn and its netroots peers carry minimal overhead costs—MoveOn employs fewer than forty full-time staff members, and has no physical office space. Older organizations that relied upon issue-based member lists to purchase large office buildings and employ hundreds of policy experts are constrained in their use of online fundraising. For these legacy organizations developed under previous membership regimes, all fundraising dollars are not created equal.

Some legacy organizations have chosen to adopt MoveOn's membership model, turning to alternate funding sources or slashing overhead costs in order to make up for the lost membership dues. But this transition is fraught with institutional challenges—both organizational and legal. At the organizational level, reducing overhead costs is a questionable proposition. Web-native organizations like MoveOn conduct their advocacy work with minimal staff and office space, but there are some key functions that these netroots organizations cannot fill. An Internet-mediated issue generalist like MoveOn is never going to sit across the table from management to negotiate a union contract, for instance. MoveOn employs no policy experts, and few MoveOn staff lobby on Capitol Hill. Netroots organizations fill a specific niche within the interest group ecology of American politics. That niche developed in response to the occupation of other niches by peer organizations with larger staffing and overhead costs. Likewise, legacy organizations are also constrained by their existing bylaws and state laws. The Sierra Club, for instance, is incorporated in California, which offers broad legal rights to members of nonprofits.[6] Redefining membership to adopt MoveOn's activity-based model is thus a far from simple proposition for an established organization like the Sierra Club.

Broadly speaking, membership from the organization's perspective can be understood through what Jennifer Earl and Katrina Kimport (2011) label a "leveraged affordance" perspective. Technological affordances are "the actions and uses that a technology makes qualitatively easier or possible when compared to prior technologies" (32). In the 1970s, a new wave of nonprofits leveraged the affordances of direct mail to redefine membership. They did so because it produced reliable funding sources that, in turn, let them take advantage of a changing government opportunity structure. In the 2000s, this pattern has repeated itself. New advocacy groups have leveraged the affordances of e-mail to raise millions in targeted donations. They have redefined membership in the process, in order to take advantage of the 24-hour online media cycle.

We are left to wonder, however, just what the new membership regime means for citizen representation through political associations. If newly formed nonprofits continue to adopt the activity-based membership model, will that lead to a further hollowing out of civic representation at the organizational layer of American politics? A closer look at the affordances of the intermediary communications technology provides a (perhaps surprising) reason for optimism. Specifically, the abundant data provided through e-mail analytics programs allow for a form of *passive democratic feedback* unavailable in previous eras.

Organizational Membership Through the Intermediary Technology Perspective

Between the individual perspective and the organizational perspective on membership, a set of intermediary communication technologies also shape the nature of organizational representation. In the bygone era of identity-based membership in federated associations, interaction occurred primarily through "personalized political communication" (Nielsen 2012). Large national organizations planned elaborate national conventions where the membership could meet, bond, and discuss governance issues. The emergence of direct mail enabled the redefinition of membership as issue-based, and also led to a decline in these cumbersome and expensive national conventions. Membership became mediated by the mail, and thus membership also became impersonal (Bimber, Flanagin, and Stohl 2012). Like most communications media of that era, these mailings were fundamentally a broadcast outlet. They were effective for organization-to-member communications, but less effective for member-to-organization communication and completely ineffective for member-to-member engagement. Interestingly, as the activity-based model has begun to mediate membership through e-mail, organizations have experimented with new cheap and effective methods for hearing the will of the membership. This passive democratic feedback is often impersonal, but its abundant availability carries substantial promise for improving membership representation. MoveOn.org will again serve as a guiding example.

The infinitesimal marginal costs of e-mail give rise to a "culture of testing" in MoveOn and other netroots organizations. MoveOn is able to engage in elaborate forms of message testing on a day-to-day basis. The organization actively monitors data on "open-rates" (how many recipients open the e-mail), "clickthrough" (how many readers take action), and "removal" (how many recipients ask to be removed from the list). On a daily basis, test messages are sent to subsets of MoveOn's list, often with varying issue frames and political "asks," in a methodology that approximates a randomized field experiment.[7] Only messages that receive acceptably high open and clickthrough rates are distributed to MoveOn's entire list for action.

Such practices, known as "A/B testing" originated with direct mail fundraising, but take on a different texture in the new medium. Traditional organizations have long engaged in limited amounts of testing with their direct mail fundraising programs. The lowered transaction costs, however, mean that MoveOn can conduct several tests in a single day, immediately analyze the results, and incorporate them into messages later that afternoon. Older groups, in contrast, face the barriers of more expensive direct mail and more time-consuming feedback, limiting them to a single test per month rather than several tests per day. Whereas testing a direct mail package takes weeks to yield results, and carries with it significant financial expenditures, testing an e-mail produces results within hours and incurs no incremental expense. Likewise, the low costs of information storage and retrieval allow MoveOn to parse the list in a variety of ways, identifying high-activity and low-activity members, as well as members who display or report interests in specific issue areas. Activity-based organizations are capable of rapidly identifying member sentiment with regard to breaking issues, and they have an incentive to follow this member sentiment because they are so heavily reliant on targeted donations.

The transition toward a "culture of testing" has illustrative parallels in the news industry. In his landmark newsroom study, Herbert Gans (1979) noted his surprise "that [television journalists] had little knowledge about the actual audience and rejected feedback from it. Although they had a vague image of the audience, they paid little attention to it; instead, they filmed and wrote for their superiors and themselves" (1979: 229). Recent research from Joseph Turow (2005), Philip Napoli (2010), and C. W. Anderson (2011a) examines how changes in the "industrial construction of audiences" have affected newsrooms. Anderson describes how the introduction of web metrics (the number of clicks and comments per story) facilitates "management strategies that emphasized the widespread diffusion of audience metrics" (Anderson 2011a: 555). At one online news site, Anderson finds, "It is not an exaggeration to say that website traffic often appeared to be the *pri-*

mary ingredient in news judgment" (561). The introduction of tools that provide a rough quantitative measure of audience interest—the "quantified audience"—can dramatically change work routines for a news organization. Once a measure of audience feedback has been constructed, it takes on meaning within the newsroom.

Consider the parallel among advocacy groups: for traditional federated membership organizations, member input moved slowly up the organizational hierarchy. Annual conventions leave little space for fast-moving governance challenges. For the issue-based, professionalized membership organizations, member input is limited to slow and costly broadcast mailings. Membership surveys among these professional organizations frequently arrived as thinly disguised fundraising appeals, meant to increase supporter response rates through a veneer of grassroots participation.

MoveOn, by contrast, is capable of measuring, nearly in real time, which issue topics, message frames, and action requests are of greatest interest to their online membership. A/B testing, in this sense, serves not only to optimize the efficiency of their action requests, but also to keep them abreast of member interest. This is a particularly important point to consider in light of some of the group's more controversial tactics. MoveOn received a formal Congressional rebuke and outraged national headlines after a 2007 *New York Times* full-page advertisement referring to General David Petraeus as "General Betray-Us." As one staffer noted in an interview, this tactic was overwhelmingly popular with the membership. Not only had thousands of individual small donors "chipped in" for that specific ad; the comparative open and clickthrough rates revealed that this action was more popular than more moderate frames. The supposedly radical action gave voice to the preferences of a massive, participatory membership.

Just as the "quantified audience" is a mixed blessing for newsrooms, awareness of these activist preferences carries some inherent drawbacks. It is a boon to fundraising and engagement practices—MoveOn does not need to guess whether a message frame or action request is too strident for its membership; it can run a test. But, having already attracted a polarized segment of the broader populace, it then selects tactics that appeal to the engaged minority. Much as A/B testing at the *Huffington Post* yields strident headlines even when little controversy is present (Anderson 2011b), A/B testing within activity-based political associations moves them further away from the passive and moderate median American voter. The result, discussed in the following section, is a phenomenon of polarization-through-participation.

Issue-based membership organizations claim to speak for hundreds of thousands of "armchair activists" who support their day-to-day strategic choices through a small annual donation. By contrast, activity-based membership organizations are constantly aware of the *revealed* preferences of their activity-based, online membership. And, importantly, such results can only be obtained if an organization embraces the participatory definition of membership. Issue-based membership associations have also developed large e-mail lists, but they generally maintain a distinction between e-mail "supporters" and dues-paying "members." While doing so offers some of the benefits of the new communications environment, it raises the technical challenge that these constitute two non-overlapping sets of stakeholders.[8]

MoveOn.org also employs a range of active democratic engagement tools. Research and Development Director Daniel Mintz describes the organization's guiding philosophy as "Strong Vision, Big Ears" (Pearce 2008), and this is evidenced in three forms of member input. MoveOn sends out a weekly membership survey to a random segment of its list. Through this active form of input, they seek clear indications of what the organization's affirmative priorities ought to be. Former staffer Matt Ewing noted that input from these surveys guided the organization's decision to endorse Barack Obama on February 1, 2008—before the "Super Tuesday" primaries, when Hillary Clinton still appeared to be a strong frontrunner for the nomination. For weeks, MoveOn had monitored member interest through the weekly surveys. After John Edwards suspended his campaign, member interest in a MoveOn endorsement rose dramatically. Ewing described it as a "very scary moment" when the organization sent out a membership-wide vote, yielding 70 percent support for Obama over Clinton.

In a similar vein, after the Democratic Party retook the congressional majority in 2007, MoveOn began holding a biennial voting process to establish its major priority campaigns. These campaigns help the organization to avoid relying too much on "headline chasing," as members tend to respond most strongly to the issues that dominate the daily headlines. The multi-stage process includes online submissions of suggested priorities, local deliberation at house party events, and worldwide Internet-based voting on priority issues (Bai 2007). Membership votes serve to minimize the downsides of headline chasing. They provide digital members with greater ownership of MoveOn's campaign efforts, while also attracting media attention by signaling the results of a membership vote. A final element of MoveOn's participatory framework is the aforementioned "MoveOn Council" system, which provides member-to-member engagement opportunities similar to those of identity-based membership organizations. The Council system attracts a dedicated minority of MoveOn members, providing them with increased voice within the organization.

MoveOn's 2008 Obama endorsement decision is particularly illustrative. The organization's passive democratic feedback tools created a "quantified audience" of sorts. The "analytics" tools employed by the organization alerted it to changes in member sentiment. These tools in turn informed key decision-makers, influencing their choice in a major electoral strategic moment. And it all occurred within the space of a few days. Personalized political communication, by contrast, moves at a far slower pace. Broadcast political communication not only is slower than online feedback but also offers a coarser signal of member preferences. The passive democratic feedback of netroots political associations does not replace the lost member-to-member social capital present in the older era of identity-based membership associations. But it represents a dramatic improvement in membership representation over the interest group population of America's immediate past. Passive democratic feedback is enabled by the affordances of digital communications technologies. For organizational representation, this constitutes a remarkably positive development.

Hidden Costs of Passive Democratic Feedback: Spatial Voting Problems and Merry Pranksters

The benefit of analytics-based passive democratic feedback is that it allows the organization to track member sentiment, thus injecting a quantified representation of activity-based member sentiment into strategic decision-making. This new form of passive representation through civic associations has two noteworthy drawbacks, however. I term the first the "spatial voting problem" and the second the "merry prankster" problem.

The spatial voting problem is as follows: partisan political organizations like MoveOn.org attract a motivated segment of the American populace. A/B testing of MoveOn messages and political tactics approximates the median policy preference *of a MoveOn member*. By definition, however, the policy preferences of these engaged partisans are to the left of the median American voter. Thus MoveOn is guided toward adopting messages and tactics that are popular with activists but occasionally out of step with the broader public. The "General Betray-Us" *New York Times* advertisement mentioned previously is one such example. This tactic was popular with the membership, but unpopular with broader audiences. Likewise, the spatial voting problem creates an issue for campaign commercials marketed to and funded by MoveOn's membership. Indeed, there is anecdotal evidence that this flaw creates practical issues, as with a 2008 campaign spot titled "Alex." Popular comedian Jon Stewart previewed a clip of the campaign ad on *The Daily Show*, and Stewart followed it with the punchline: "That ad of course brought to you by MoveOn.org—ten years of making even people who agree with you cringe."[9]

The merry prankster problem is particularly challenging for smaller organizations seeking to emulate MoveOn's practices. There are no barriers to entry in a political association that defines membership through online participation. Anyone can join, and through joining, exert an influence on the organization's policy stances and strategies. MoveOn not only tracks clickstream data, but also sends out member surveys and holds membership-wide votes on key decisions such as the 2008 Presidential Primary endorsement. What is to stop motivated conservatives from joining the organization en masse and swaying these decisions? For MoveOn specifically, safety lies in numbers. With over 7 million members, assembling a conservative strategic voting bloc large enough to sway the outcome of such deliberation would represent a major collective action challenge in its own right. Conservatives would not be able to achieve this goal without the effort becoming public, and the staff of MoveOn could then respond by modifying their algorithms or canceling the targeted vote. Yet for smaller organizations seeking to emulate this organizational style, the threat of prankful opponents is a substantial problem. The low transaction costs of online participation have been particularly beneficial for groups seeking "lulz"—online entertainment coming at the expense of others. One reason why conservative organizations have failed to adopt the open participatory styles of MoveOn, Daily Kos, and other netroots political associations is the threat posed by online progressive partisans who occasionally descend upon their comment boards and online voting systems for comedic ends (Karpf 2012: chap. 6). Passive democratic feedback is a representation of quantified member sentiment through analytic tools and algorithms. Like most digital algorithms, these metrics of member sentiment can be gamed—particularly in the case of newly formed organizations whose small size makes statistical inference difficult.

Passive democratic feedback is a new form of citizen representation. Political associations are presently adopting and adapting it to their own ends. While it holds promise for expanding the representative voice of engaged partisans, this promise also comes with the threats of spatial voting and merry pranksters.

Conclusion

Let's return once more to our hypothetical college-aged political activist. Her thick, participatory memberships in campus groups are the most rewarding of her membership ties. Those memberships are also a rarity, however. The great majority of present-day political associations do not expect their membership to participate through face-to-face local meetings. Previous observers have noted this as cause for grave concern (Skocpol 2003)—lacking representation through civic organizations, citizens lose an important venue for engaging with government institutions. Indeed, the trend toward thinner and thinner membership is alarming on its face. What does it mean when an organization's "members" no longer identify with such a title?

Yet when we look at organizational membership from multiple angles, the representational implications of this progression of membership regimes seems less threatening. From the member's perspective, membership has indeed become thinner. From the organization's perspective, this is at least partially because thick membership necessitates slow and expensive communication. And the intermediary communications technologies that make activity-based online membership possible also render new possibilities for organizations to "hear" from their membership. Supporters of MoveOn .org and similar organizations often do not realize that their decisions to open an e-mail or click on the link are treated as democratic participation. These acts exhibit far less intensity than the participatory acts required by previous membership associations. Yet they are also plentiful, and the technology for harvesting and analyzing these actions is becoming increasingly useful to advocacy organizations. Combined with the "ladder of engagement," where organizations encourage their most interested members to assume greater roles and receive increased voice, the new membership style holds surprising promise for representation through the new generation of political associations.

Passive democratic feedback is not without its limitations. Partisan organizations can fall prey to the spatial voting problem, allowing the clickstream decisions of the membership to function as an echo chamber, leaving
the organization farther and farther removed from the broader public. Indeed, there is a more general concern here of polarization *through* participation. To date, the political organizations that have newly flourished in the
twenty-first century have a firmly partisan character. The stronger such organizations become, the less represented the quiet center of the country will be.
Equally concerning is the threat to smaller organizations posed by the merry
prankster problem. Analytics-based political advocacy only yields benefits
to large-scale organizations. For smaller groups representing controversial
perspectives, and for nascent organizations seeking to build their ranks, it
may prove challenging to adopt the tools relied on by large organizations
like MoveOn. In the end, the challenges posed by representation through
organizations vary depending on which perspective we view them through.

References

Anderson, Chris W. 2011a. "Between Creative and Quantified Audiences: Web Met-
    rics and Changing Patterns of Newswork in Local U.S. Newsrooms." *Journalism*
    12 (5): 550–66.
———. 2011b. "What Aggregators Do." Paper Presentation, Workshop on Social Media
    as Politics by Other Means. Rutgers University, April 11.
Bai, Matthew. 2007. *The Argument: Billionaires, Bloggers, and the Battle to Remake
    Democratic Politics*. New York: Penguin.
Baumgartner, Frank, Jeffrey Berry, Marie Hojnacki, David Kimball, and Beth Leech.
    2009. *Lobbying and Policy Change*. Chicago: University of Chicago Press.
Baumgartner, Frank and Bryan Jones. 1993. *Agendas and Instability in American Poli-
    tics*. Chicago: University of Chicago Press.
Berry, Jeffrey. 1984. *The Interest Group Society*. New York: Little, Brown.
———. 1999. *The New Liberalism: The Rising Power of Citizen Groups*. Washington,
    D.C.: Brookings Institution Press.
Bimber, Bruce. 2003. *Information and American Democracy*. Cambridge: Cambridge
    University Press.
Bimber, Bruce, Andrew Flanagin and Cynthia Stohl. 2012. *Collective Action in Orga-
    nizations*. New York: Cambridge University Press.
Earl, Jennifer and Katrina Kimport. 2011. *Digitally Enabled Social Change*. Cam-
    bridge, Mass.: MIT Press.

Gans, Herbert. 1979. *Deciding What's News: A Study of CBS Evening News, NBC Nightly News, Newsweek and Time.* Evanston, Ill.: Northwestern University Press.

Gladwell, Malcolm. 2010. "Small Change: Why the Revolution Will Not Be Tweeted." *New Yorker,* October 4.

Han, Hahrie. 2009. *Moved to Action: Motivation, Participation, and Action in American Politics.* Stanford, Calif.: Stanford University Press.

Hindman, Matthew. 2009. *The Myth of Digital Democracy.* Princeton, N.J.: Princeton University Press.

Karpf, David. 2010. "Online Political Mobilization from the Advocacy Group's Perspective: Looking Beyond Clicktivism." *Policy and Internet* 2 (4): 7–41.

———. 2012. *The MoveOn Effect: The Unexpected Transformation of American Political Advocacy.* New York: Oxford University Press.

Klein, Kim. 1994. *Fundraising for Social Change.* 3rd ed. Berkeley, Calif.: Chardon Press.

Lawrence, Eric, John Sides, and Henry Farrell. 2010. "Self-Segregation or Deliberation? Blog Readership, Participation and Polarization in American Politics." *Perspectives on Politics* 8 (1): 141–57.

Monitor Institute. April 2011. "Disruption: Evolving Models of Engagement and Support: A National Study of Member-Based Advocacy Groups."

Napoli, Philip. 2010. *Audience Evolution: New Technologies and the Transformation of Media Audiences.* New York: Columbia University Press.

Nielsen, Rasmus Kleis. 2012. *Ground Wars: Personally Communication in Political Campaigns.* Princeton, N.J.: Princeton University Press.

Pearce, Seth. 2008. "Daniel Mintz Is Living Liberally." Blog post, http://livingliberally .org/talking-liberally/blog/Daniel-Mintz-Living-Liberally, April 14 2009.

Shulman, Stuart. 2009. "The Case Against Mass E-mails: Perverse Incentives and Low Quality Public Participation in U.S. Federal Rulemaking." *Policy and Internet* 1 (1): 23–53.

Skocpol. Theda. 2003. *Diminished Democracy: From Membership to Management in American Civic Life.* Norman: University of Oklahoma Press.

Tocqueville, Alexis de. 1969. *Democracy in America.* Garden City, N.Y.: Doubleday.

Turow, Joseph. 2005. "Audience Construction and Culture Production: Marketing Surveillance in the Digital Age." *Annals of the American Academy of Political and Social Science* 597 (1): 103–21.

Walker, Edward, John McCarthy, and Frank Baumgartner. 2011. "Replacing Members with Managers? Mutualism Among Membership and Nonmembership Advocacy Associations in the United States." *American Journal of Sociology* 116 (4): 1284–1337.

Weir, Margaret, and Marshall Ganz. 1997. "Reconnecting People and Politics." In *The New Majority: Toward a Popular Progressive Politics,* ed. Stanley B. Greenberg and Theda Skocpol. New Haven, Conn.: Yale University Press. 141–71.

Zetter, Kim. 2004. "MoveOn Moves Up in the World." *Wired,* July 26.

CHAPTER 11

The Principle of Affected Interests:
An Interpretation and Defense

Archon Fung

Many chapters in this book focus on the proper relationship between citizens and their government: problems of inclusion, equality, political opportunity, political expression, representation, and responsiveness. But even if we managed to perfect the processes connecting citizens to their state, democratic ambitions would remain unsatisfied in light of the circumstances of twenty-first-century governance. The actions of many organizations—private corporations, nongovernmental organizations, and other states would still redound on citizens, and those citizens would have little influence over the actions of those organizations. For this reason, democratic theorists should expand their sights beyond the state to encompass those other organizations that affect citizens and the ordering of social life more broadly. This chapter develops the principle of affected interests as a normative democratic foundation to guide that expansion.

The question of inclusion in democratic theory has focused largely upon the relationship of citizens to their state. Theorists have sought to provide an account of the political rights of individuals living under the legitimate authority of a democratic government. These accounts seek to ground the judgment that adult citizens living under such authority should be treated as equals who have, among other liberties, rights to participate in the decisions of that state. Two starting points lead to this end of equal citizenship in a state that is legitimate because it is democratic.

The first is the principle of popular sovereignty. This principle frequently emerges from contractarian and constitutionalist reasoning. Historically and philosophically, a democracy of equal citizens is the answer to the question of how a collection of individuals who expect to live with one another in a society should organize their common affairs. Effective organization requires authority. Authority resides in the territorial state and takes the form of laws that impose obligations of obedience upon citizens. To be acceptable to the citizens whom they obligate, laws must be made democratically: by citizens themselves as political equals. From the principle of popular sovereignty, a legitimate order is a "self-legislating demos, of citizens ruling and being ruled in turn, consisting of all and only those who are full citizens and thus both authors and subjects of the law" (Bohman 2007, emphasis original).[1]

A second starting point begins with the principle of affected interests (see Mill 1991 (1861); Dahl 1989: 93–95, 119–31; Goodin 2007). That principle, perhaps the most basic of democratic intuitions, is that individuals should be able to influence decisions that affect them. Absent such influence, decisions may be taken in ways that do not properly regard the interests of those they affect. Furthermore, exercising such influence is a critical aspect of individual autonomy.

This chapter aims to articulate a plausible formulation of the principle of affected interests that has three main features. First, we should interpret the principle as applying not only to legislatures but also to administrative agencies, private corporations, civic organizations, and governments of other societies. Second, we should interpret the principle in a continuing, regulative way. That is, the principle of affected interests does not establish a boundary of inclusion once and for all. It guides the adjustment of boundaries of inclusion and standing as the effects of the decisions of various organizations ebb and flow. Finally, we should understand the term "influence" in the principle to include not just direct influence of a participatory democratic kind, but also indirect (e.g., delegated) and passive (e.g., structural or cultural) kinds of influence. This formulation addresses some important objections to the principle of affected interests such as incoherence, regress, and impracticality.

Those who begin from each of these different starting points–popular sovereignty and affected interests–have for the most part converged upon the state as their main focus in democratic theory. From the principle of popular sovereignty, individuals have a special relationship to their state because it alone commands them. Citizens come together as equals and rule themselves through their state. Within any territory, the state makes the binding decisions for the territory as a whole that are backed by coercive power. Constitutional democracy is the answer to the question of why citizens should regard such binding decisions as legitimate and authoritative. From the perspective of the principle of affected interest, the actions of states usually have the most potent effects on individuals' most important interests. At the extreme, states send their citizens to war, imprison them, and even execute them. More commonly, government actions and public policies affect the security, prosperity, and overall well-being of individuals. Territorially organized representative government in which citizens are political equals provides the normative ideal that justifies an ongoing structure through which citizens can shape laws to protect their interests.[2]

For all of these reasons, states and their laws have been and will properly remain an important object of political philosophy. However, scholars in many areas of social investigation and practice—in political science, sociology, and public policy—point out that contemporary conditions have constrained the reach and capability of formal state structures (Nye and Keohane 2000; Bohman 2007). Sites of power and influence have proliferated, even as the state's ability to bridle them has diminished. Either the state is less capable today of ordering the affairs of its citizens, or we have expected too much of the state in organizing our complex interdependencies. In either case, the actions and consequences of other states, corporations, nongovernmental organizations, public agencies, and even individual citizens now escape, perhaps inevitably and irrevocably, the regulatory control of democratically directed governments.

A broad ebb of the state as the principal actor in organizing common affairs and accomplishing public objectives is now widely called the shift from government to governance. The term governance denotes activities that, like projects of government, aim to achieve common purposes. However, the new term is meant to mark changes in both who acts to achieve those purposes and how they are achieved. With regard to means, public leaders and policy makers now frequently rely less on state commands and more on efforts to "steer" the behavior of actors in society. They also rely on collaborations that include actors outside of government. With regard to who acts, governance activities are undertaken by entities not only in the state sector but also in the private sector and civil society (Nye and Keohane 2000). In global climate change, economic development, human rights protection, basic education, disaster relief, and many other issues, the most promising strategies consist not of states making binding laws but rather of complex governance activities that involve collaborations between government and nongovernmental actors.

Whether or not this shift from government to governance is truly novel, it suggests that states acting through laws can fulfill neither the aim of popular sovereignty—to direct supreme authority according to the will of the people—nor the aim of the principle of affected interests. Rules of inclusion that provide equal opportunities for the participation of citizens in decisions of their state then become insufficient for either understanding of democracy. From the perspective of popular sovereignty, enfranchisement in state decision-making is insufficient for self-rule, when many important decisions that order the common affairs of citizens are made by non-state actors or at levels above or below that of the nation. For the proponent of the affected-interests principle, individuals should be able to exercise influence over a range of decisions broader than those made by the state when such decisions affect their important interests.

From both perspectives, the shift from government to governance demands an expanded account of democratic inclusion in which individuals influence not just state decisions, but the decisions of other organizations as well. In this chapter, I develop the principle of affected interests to offer an account of inclusion appropriate for the contemporary circumstance of governance. The principle of affected interests strikes me as the most promising for grappling with the challenges of contemporary governance. Popular sovereignty, especially in its common contractarian and constitutional forms, begins by delineating a group of individuals—the demos—who form a persistent political community.[3] But one feature of governance is that different problems encircle quite different groups of individuals. From the perspective of affected interests, very different sets of individuals should exercise influence over decisions concerning global climate change, health care policy, local education, and international labor conditions.

It may in fact be fruitful to think of the principles of affected interests and popular sovereignty as complementary, rather than exclusive and opposed, justifications of democracy. [4] Both have their place in the political culture of democratic societies and the justification of democratic institutions

and practices, our commitments to representative governments of territorial nation-states through which we rule ourselves as free and equal citizens.[5] But increasingly, we face situations that arouse democratic concerns
in which nation-states fail to govern actions that impact citizens' interests.
When we face the local indignities of tyrannical school principals, authoritarian employers, or the harms of powerful global corporations, we have
strong democratic impulses. We feel we ought to have a say and often we
do not. The principle of affected interests accounts for our democratic sen-
sibilities in these increasingly common areas of social life. More important, it can justify the creation of certain democratic controls that elude
the grasp of the account of representative government as popular sovereignty.

The second section of this essay elaborates how and why the principle of
affected interests, not that of popular sovereignty, is best suited to help adjust our understandings of democracy to the realities of modern constrained
states. The third section offers a formulation of the principle holding that
individuals ought to be able to influence the decisions of a large range of
organizations, not just territorial states, whose actions regularly or deeply
affect their interests. The fourth section elaborates two implications of this
formulation of the principle. Unlike the one-to-one relationship of citizen to
state, each individual has the warrant, through this principle, to influence
many different organizations. I call this warrant membership. In this account, each individual has multiple memberships. Furthermore, these circles
of membership change dynamically over time as individuals and organizations evolve. The circumstances of governance indicate that the principle
should apply in medias res, rather than fixing boundaries of inclusion once
and for all.[6] The fifth section develops a broad notion of "influence" in
which individuals ought to affect decisions not just through active and direct means, but also indirectly and passively. The sixth section indicates
how disputes about inclusion and influence might be adjudicated. The sev-
enth and final section illustrates the principle with international and domestic applications.

Beyond and Below the Nation-State

My argument begins not from first principles, but from stylized empirical
developments. If they are accurately rendered, those developments demand

that we adjust our institutions and that we revise underlying principles that justify those institutions.

Contemporary Governance

If there once was a time when the laws of a nation-state could adequately protect the fundamental interests of its citizens, many argue that time is past. Consider briefly five stylized facts that support this conclusion.

First, globalization makes citizens of one state more vulnerable to financial, environmental, security, and even sociocultural decisions that originate outside that state. It may be that the extent to which global forces constrain sovereignty has increased, or that global factors have limited state power for centuries.[7] What matters for this portion of the argument is that global forces render the state less capable of social ordering than citizens would like. Second, privatization both increases citizens' dependence upon corporations—especially financial institutions and multinational corporations—and reduces states' capacities to control them.[8] Third, decentralization and contracting-out of activities that were previously executed by national governments—on issues such as social services, security and policing, education and training, regulation, economic development, and health care—in many states reduces the scope of national laws and policies. Fourth, the rise of the administrative state effaces democratic representation.[9] For at least a century, the complexity of modern conditions has dictated that state action occur largely through policies formulated through administrative agencies rather than only, or even principally, through laws passed by elected representatives. Scholars have long noted the challenges to democracy posed by administrative delegation.

A fifth development that may well have diminished the role of national laws in ordering social affairs has been, as noted, a shift from government to governance. Governance signals the power of actors other than the nation-state—such as local and regional governments, private firms, voluntary associations, and transnational organizations—and the use of non-binding means—soft power, voluntary standards and protocols,[10] collaboration, and negotiation. Joseph Nye and Robert Keohane (Nye and Keohane 2000: 12–13) write that governance is created by

the processes and institutions that guide and constrain the collective activities of a group. Government is the subset that acts with authority and creates formal obligations . . . . Private firms, associations of firms, non-governmental organizations (NGOs), and associations of NGOs all engage in [these processes and institutions], often in association with governmental bodies, to create governance; sometimes without governmental authority . . . . [M]ore governance activities will occur outside the box represented by national capitals of nation states.

This shift away from the national state in public ordering and public action has resulted from practical necessity rather than merely a political ideology of state retrenchment. Circumstances in the world have made states less capable of protecting the interests of their citizens through binding laws.

In response, individuals increasingly organize their common affairs not just through their state and its laws but also through a host of other organizations and measures. For example, nongovernmental organizations such as charitable foundations and advocacy groups increasingly provide financial resources, expertise, and staff to address problems such as health and education. This phenomenon is most visible in the large-scale activities of organizations such as the Bill and Melinda Gates Foundation in developing countries, but it is also common in the U.S. and other developed nations.[11] Responding in part to the limitations of governmental standard setting, efforts to protect the environment increasingly involve joint efforts between government agencies, nonprofit organizations, and private sector firms.[12] Actions to address concerns that cross national boundaries, such as transnational migration, trade, security, human rights, natural resource exploitation, and global labor standards, frequently involve not just a single national government but multiple states, as well as international organizations, private sector groups, and nongovernmental organizations whose activities occur inside state boundaries as well as across them (Nye and Keohane 2000).

This essay supposes that the account of these stylized developments is largely true. If it is not, then I offer no reason for those who now accept the popular sovereignty justification of representative democracy organized through nation-states to revise their view. Those who accept these developments as true enough might nevertheless attempt to defend limiting the focus of democratic theory to cover just the binding laws of the nation-state. Consider two such defenses.

FREEDOM IS THE ONLY CRITICAL INTEREST (NECESSITY)

The first reason for limiting democracy to nation-states begins with the notion that claims to inclusion in decision-making are warranted only when important interests are at stake. Binding decisions—those that are backed by the coercive, potentially violent, force of the state—affect individuals' critical interest in freedom. The binding decisions of governments are the most obvious—and perhaps most important—way individuals' choices can be deliberately constrained. Unless an individual can influence such decisions, these restrictions are objectionably arbitrary. The individual becomes merely a subject and not a citizen, ruled without in turn ruling. Thus, many democratic theorists have addressed the question of how the coercive authority of the state can be legitimate. In a strongly limiting formulation of the scope of democracy, citizens have rights to political participation in collective decision-making only if those decisions determine binding laws that are backed by the coercive authority of the state.

But the arbitrary binding decisions of government are only one source of interference with individual choice. Nonbinding decisions made by nongovernmental actors—the power of employers over workers—may threaten an individual's freedom just as much.[13] This understanding of freedom thus seems to support inclusion in other decisions—those that do not involve coercive power and those made by non-nation state actors—as well.

BINDING LAWS CAN SECURE ALL IMPORTANT INTERESTS (SUFFICIENCY)

A quite different reason for limiting democracy to a state's binding decisions supposes that such decisions can secure all of the important interests of that state's citizens. Binding workplace standards and discrimination laws might, for example, protect workers from the arbitrary power of employers. In this way, individuals' influence over binding state decisions might be sufficient to protect all of their important interests from a broad range of threats from all other quarters.

The claim that state action through binding laws and policies is sufficient to protect important interests seems obvious to many. If not the state, then who? Yet there are many reasons to doubt that states have the reach—despite their authority, monopoly on violence, financial resources, and bureaucratic capacities—adequately to protect individuals' interests in this era of globalization and "wicked" social problems.[14] The question of whether individuals' important interests can better be secured by extending their influence to other organizations such as workplaces and nonprofit enterprises, and to decisions other than binding laws, is an empirical one. The reasons to answer this question affirmatively are contained in the five stylized developments above.

Those who see these developments as comprising an inevitable and perhaps even desirable shift away from national governments as the paramount agents of social ordering must also reject the claim that the binding laws of states are sufficient to protect the important interests of individuals. Governance means that many social decisions—some that do not involve binding laws and some that are made by organizations outside of the state—affect individuals' interests.

WHEN THE SOCIAL CONTRACT RUNS OUT

This reasoning—admittedly dependent on plausible but controversial empirical claims—opens the door to normative arguments for expanding the scope of citizen participation and influence beyond national governments to a much wider range of organizations. The principle of affected interests is a more promising point of departure for those arguments. Contractarian justifications begin by (i) delineating a fixed group—the parties to a social contract— and then (ii) identifying the first-order terms of their sociopolitical order (the "basic structure" in John Rawls's formulation). The democratic components of contractarian justifications usually involve the translation of citizen's moral equality into political equality in determining the laws of a central state.

Consider first domestic governance. Suppose a contractarian democrat agrees that the modern developments discussed above reduce the ability of citizens to regulate their affairs adequately and protect their interests through national laws even against decisions and actions that occur within a country's borders. That democrat might acknowledge that contemporary democracy requires that individuals be able to participate in many other kinds of decision-making—administrative rule-making, choices of service bureaucracies and planning agencies, in local governments and authorities, in civic associations, and even in the management of economic enterprises.[15] Such measures would certainly be consistent with democracy understood as a social contract among moral equals. There is no inconsistency between contractarian justifications of democracy and these extensions of democracy beyond the nation-state.

Yet it seems difficult to wring more specific normative guidance from the bare idea of a social contract, because that idea is focused on the basic, enduring features of government, and because its moral emphasis is on the equal political status of citizens. Participation in the countless decisions that occur throughout any complex society requires a more highly differentiated and dynamic account than is natural for contractarian reasoning. We do not think, for example, of each state or province within a nation, much less each public school or workplace, as having its own social contract embedded within the larger national one.

To justify extensions of democracy, a contractarian might rely upon other principles that parties to the social contract could endorse. The principle of subsidiarity and the principle of affected interests come to mind as likely candidates for such an account. However, the success of that justification would then depend upon a compelling articulation of those principles. I aim to do part of that work by developing a plausible interpretation of the principle of affected interest.

The contractarian approach seems even more limited for threats to self-government that stem from decisions and actions occurring outside territorial borders, such as pollution, trade, multinational corporate decisions, and transnational advocacy. Contractarians have two natural responses. The first is to insist upon a global, cosmopolitan democratic social contract that creates participation rights in a world government.[16] Although there is much that is appealing in such a proposal, it would also lose some of what makes contractarian justifications attractive—realism and compatibility with many traditions and political cultures.

The second route is to insist that the constitution of nation-states should remain the principal subject of the democratic social contract, and that efforts to regulate actions emanating from outside territorial boundaries should occur through international bodies in which citizens are represented by their national governments. This path leaves too much on the table, democratically speaking. In many urgent areas such as disease and public health, labor conditions, environment, economic development, and food and product safety, individuals can potentially regulate actions affecting their lives through routes of participation and influence that bypass national states. Individuals from one country can connect directly with foreign governments, transnational organizations, or firms. Many of these forms of engagement have been regularized and institutionalized. They are valuable for democracy, but they find little justification from nation-state-oriented social contract traditions.

The Principle of Affected Interests—Formulation

The principle of affected interests may offer a more promising point of departure. Though it captures an enduring impulse in democratic thought, it has not received as much sustained attention in political theory.[17] Several of those who have considered the principle have rejected it as undesirable (Nozick 1975), incoherent, or impractical.[18] This section addresses some of these difficulties by offering a specific formulation and interpretation of the principle.

Rudimentary Formulation

The most common statement of the principle of affected interests runs like this:

(1) Individuals should be able to influence decisions that affect their interests.

This rudimentary formulation is underspecified in at least three ways. What kinds of decisions and decision-making entities are regulated by the principle? What kinds of interests grant individuals a warrant for influence? And, what sort of influence does the principle require?

Robert Nozick, for example, raises the following example as a *reductio* against the principle:

> If four men propose marriage to a woman, her decision about whom . . . to marry importantly affects each of the lives of those four persons, her own life, and the lives of any other person wishing to marry one of these four men, and so on. Would anyone propose, even limiting the group to include only the primary parties, that all five persons vote to decide whom she shall marry? (1975: 268–71)

Of course not. Nozick's example illustrates how formulation (1) of the principle is underspecified on the first dimension of domain.[19] Most of those who have written about the principle have considered its application not to the decisions of individuals, but rather to the territorial states, the only entities that make binding and coercively backed law:

(2) Individuals should be able to be able to exercise voice [voting] to influence decisions that affect their interests through binding and coercively backed law.

Drawing on the discussion of the limits of nation-states above, this specification is unduly restrictive in at least four ways. Entities other than legislatures make decisions that affect individuals (underinclusion of entities).

Individuals' important interests are affected by many kinds of decisions, not just binding laws backed by coercive power (underinclusion of decisions and interests). Legislatures make decisions that affect those who do not live within their territorial boundaries (underinclusion of individuals). Finally, voice through voting is just one way to influence a decision. Sometimes, both more direct and less direct modes of influence are appropriate (underinclusion of modes of influence).

I will defend a third formulation of the principle that is more specific but also more expansive:

(3) An individual should be able to influence an organization if and only if that organization makes decisions that regularly or deeply affect that individual's important interests.[20]

Regularly or Deeply Affected Interests

In his illuminating essay on affected interests, Robert Goodin (2007) holds fixed both kind of entity and mode of influence. He presumes that the principle governs public legislative bodies and, at least implicitly, that individuals will exercise influence through voting and representation. He focuses upon the question of whose interests ought to be included. In particular, should those whose interests are *possibly* affected by a decision exercise influence, or only those whose interests are *actually* affected? He rejects the "actually affected" formulation on grounds of incoherence:

> Notice first that whose interests are "affected" by any actual decision depends upon what the decision actually turns out to be. Notice second that what the decision actually turns out to be depends, in turn, upon who actually makes the decision. Hence the "all actually affected interests" principle suffers the same incoherence as discussed at the outset: it is unable to tell us who is entitled to vote on a decision until after that very decision has been decided. (Goodin 2007: 52, emphasis mine)[21]

There are two related but distinct potential difficulties here: endogeneity and indeterminacy. The "actually affected" formulation has the endogenous characteristic that the delineation of who is entitled to influence a decision depends on the substance of the choice itself. That formulation is also subject to indeterminacy in that a different substantive choice might be made if a different set of people had been entitled to influence that decision. These technical observations are interesting, but the conclusion of incoherence is too quick. Goodin is correct that the "actually affected" formulation cannot uniquely determine the set of individuals who ought to be included. But neither endogeneity nor indeterminacy provide compelling reasons for rejecting a political arrangement as incoherent.

To see why, suppose that two towns, A and B, have a common boundary. Only the residents of each town make decisions for that town, and they are made in a democratic way. Over a certain period of time, the residents of each town make decisions that have no spillover consequences onto the other town and produce no injustice between them. It is certainly true that if the border between A and B were to shift by a few blocks and some residents of B became new residents of the expanded town A', we would expect the decisions of A' to affect a slightly wider set of individuals, and the choices made would be different from the choices made by A. But those observations by themselves do not provide a reason to reject A's boundaries. Indeed, both political arrangements—A/B and A'/B'—satisfy the principle of including all and only actually (not possibly) affected interests.

Suppose now that residents of B are possibly affected by the decisions of A. Residents of A could decide to build power plants that emit toxins into B or to construct buildings that are an eyesore to B's townsfolk. If the people of A begin to make such decisions, then the people of B have a claim to be included in influencing A's decisions under the principle of affected interests, and the circle of inclusion should change.

Goodin's formulation of possibly affected interests is motivated by his desire for the principle to yield the delineation of a single demos that persists through time.[22] In order to ensure against decisions that are impermissible because they affect the unincluded, such as B's residents in A's toxin-emitting period, the circle of inclusion in decision-making must be very wide indeed. But the principle of affected interests can also be understood in a way that makes this tradeoff more tractable by making it more fluid. It can be understood as a regulative principle for continuously adjusting the boundaries of inclusion. A/B, A'/B', and a metro government of A+B might all be justified by the principle of affected interests under various circumstances. If the capacities of these towns, the problems they face, and the priorities of residents are such that the decisions made in A do not affect those in B, then residents might well prefer separate towns to a metropolitan

government that fuses A and B, in order to be able to exercise more meaningful influence over the harms or goods that might affect them. If however,
environmental, economic, or other conditions create substantial interdependencies between A and B, then the importance of influencing decisions that
address those encompassing concerns weighs in favor of larger political units.

Organizations as Decision-Makers and Objects of Democratization

Formulation (3) above also specifies that the domain over which the principle operates consists of organizations such as governments, international
organizations, administrative agencies, private corporations, and civic organizations. This specification is broader than a domain that includes just
nation-states, but far narrower than formulation (1), which could be interpreted to include individuals making intimate decisions about their lives.
Formulation (3) directs us to look to the organizational entities that make
decisions. This shift is necessary to make sense of the term "regularly,"
which describes not a single decision but rather multiple related decisions. It
is natural to understand those decisions as being made by organizations,
because organizations are entities of sufficient coherence to enfranchise or
exclude individuals. This shift also renders the principle in a way that fits
with the sociological reality of organizations and the everyday ways in
which the notion of affected interests is used.[23]

I define organizations as entities that collectively control resources, advance purposes, and make decisions whose effects are moderately consistent
over time. To a first approximation, it is usually sensible to say whether or
not the interests of a particular individual are "regularly affected" by the
decisions of a particular organization. The decisions of a territorial state
regularly affect all those living within its boundaries and often those living
outside it. The decisions of a multinational corporation regularly affect its
managers, workers, shareholders, customers, and some of the residents of
communities where it, its subsidiaries, and its suppliers operate. The decisions of a school board in Sacramento, California, do not regularly affect
residents of Massachusetts.

Such organizations are sufficiently coherent that they typically possess
durable procedures of decision-making that specify boundaries of inclusion
and exclusion. Democratic states have rules of citizenship, suffrage, parties

and elections, administrative and executive consultations, judicial and administrative standing. Public corporations have directors, shareholders, and sometimes works councils and stakeholder boards. Organizations—rather than free-floating decisions—are typically the object of demands for inclusion. Those demands frequently arise from the claim that the organization acts in ways that affect individuals who have no influence on them ("no taxation without representation"). Demands for inclusion can be rejected or satisfied by modifying the existing decision-making procedures of the target organization.

Consider a real example. Today most nongovernmental international development organizations may be operating in acknowledged noncompliance with the principle of affected interests. In a fascinating study, Hans Peter Schmitz, Paloma Raggo, and Tosca M. Bruno-van Vijfeljken (2011) at Syracuse University asked leaders of international NGOs two questions. First, to whom ought their organizations be accountable? Second, to whom are their organizations actually accountable? Responses to the first question were consistent with the principle of affected interests. NGO leaders felt that they should be accountable to donors, board members, program beneficiaries, host governments, staff, and then the general public. When asked whom they were actually accountable to, however, these NGO leaders responded that they were primarily accountable to donors and board members through mechanisms such as financial audits and program evaluations, but that they were largely unaccountable to the other entities—especially beneficiaries— affected by their activities. Some of the NGOs, however, are developing mechanisms such as consultations and expanded representation to bring their accountability practices in line with their aspirations for democratic governance.

Finally, the set of individuals whose interests are regularly affected by any organization's decisions typically changes over time. Corporations abandon some communities and move into others. Individuals leave and join firms, local communities, and even national states. The environmental consequences of production and regulation expand, contract, and shift over land and sea. Societies engage and disengage from various trading and security relationships. Organizations take on new priorities and missions even as they shed and gain capacities (the United States engages in a War on Terror; General Electric shifts from industrial production to financial services). These shifts favor a dynamic understanding of the principle of affected interests, in which the definition of those who ought be included in influencing any particular organization's decisions changes over time as the consequences of that organization's actions fall on different individuals.

Multiple Membership and Dynamic Inclusion

This interpretation of the principle of affected interests entails a much more complicated structure of political "membership" than an account of democratic inclusion that maps individuals onto states in many-to-one way. This view envisions many overlapping circles of inclusion. Associated with every organization—government or other—is a set of individuals whose important interests are regularly (or deeply) touched by the decisions of that organization. Under the principle of affected interests, all individuals in that set should have some capacity to influence the decisions of that organization. Each individual is a member of many such sets, because he or she is touched by the decisions of many organizations. Furthermore, these circles of inclusion around organizations and individuals must change over time as those organizations and individuals evolve.

Frederick Whelan has raised this dynamic feature as an objection to the principle of affected interests:

> An obvious practical difficulty with the all-affected principle is that it would require a different constituency of voters or participants for every decision: the status of fellow citizens would not be permanent, as is the case in territorial states with which we ordinarily associate the concept of citizenship, but would shift in relation to the issue proposed. (1983: 19)

Guilty as charged.

There are two responses to this objection from impracticality. First, the proposal is not altogether impractical, because many organizations and individuals are already accustomed to operating in a world with many circles of inclusion and membership. Multinational corporations, international governance organizations, administrative agencies, social service groups, and local governments all regularly sponsor various forms of stakeholder and public engagement. Many individuals are accustomed to exercising influence in ways that include not just voting in national elections but also participating in school councils, labor unions, employee groups, local authorities and boards, and so on. The principle of affected interests provides a way of justifying the circles of inclusion and participation in such venues.

The next section addresses concerns about the excessive demands of multiple membership by developing a more capacious understanding of "influence" that economizes on the cognitive capacities and time that individuals spend influencing organizational decisions. Although existing circles of inclusion are far from satisfying the principle of affected interest, the basic organizational and individual practices of multiple membership are neither novel nor alien. Indeed, it is Whelan's political philosophic ideal of one person, one state, one vote that lies at some remove from contemporary reality.

Second, the two obvious alternatives to this account of multiple memberships are unappealing. The discussion above explains why the account of individual influence operating through single membership in the nation-state unduly constrains the scope of popular control. Consider now why an account of single membership in a world government is less appealing than the multiple membership account favored here.

Problems with World Government

One way to work out the principle of affected interests is to derive its implications for durable boundaries of citizenship. How big (or small) should a *demos* be? Decades ago, Robert Dahl began to address this question in his reflections on the question of scale and democracy:

> That larger political systems often possess relatively greater capacity to accomplish tasks beyond the capacity of smaller systems leads sometimes to a paradox. In very small political systems a citizen may be able to participate extensively in decisions that do not matter much but cannot participate much in decisions that matter a great deal; whereas very large systems may be able to cope with problems that matter more to a citizen, the opportunities for the citizen to participate in and greatly influence decisions are vastly reduced.[24]

Concern for the scope of influence—assuring that one can influence the maximal number of decisions that might affect one's interests—weighs in favor of larger political units. Conversely, concern for depth of influence—assuring that one's voice will be meaningfully considered—weighs in favor of smaller political units.

A similar concern for scope leads Goodin to favor an interpretation of the affected-interests principle in which all who could "possibly" be affected by a decision are included in influencing it. Since it is conceivable that just about any government could make decisions that would affect just about anyone in the world, this expansive formulation leads to the conclusion that only a government that is global in scale conforms to the principle of affected interests. Any smaller unit is unstable with respect to the principle of affected interests, because the individuals in that smaller unit might make decisions that affect individuals outside of it.[25] Properly understood, the principle of (all possibly) affected interests requires "giving virtually everyone everywhere a vote on virtually everything decided anywhere" (Goodin 2007: 68)

Above, I argued that institutions of world government do not necessarily follow from accepting the principle of affected interests. The "regularly or deeply affected interests" formulation of the principle is compatible with institutions of multiple memberships. Compared with multiple memberships, a world government is unattractive for two reasons. First, its institutions would sacrifice almost completely the value of meaningful influence for the sake of expanding the scope of influence over many decisions that have minor or only potential effects on an individual's interests (Dahl 1967). The tradeoff between a very large *demos* that includes all possibly affected interests and smaller ones that afford more consequential individual influence is intractable if, as both Goodin and Robert Dahl before him supposed, the aim of an account of inclusion is to delineate the boundaries of a demos permanently. The multiple, dynamic membership account solves that problem by discarding the premise that the delineation of inclusion must be permanent. Second, the possibility of constructing political institutions on such a global scale seems remote.

Dynamic Adjustment, Not Durable Citizenship

The multiple membership account accepts that organizations' decisions, the interests they affect, and the individuals who influence those decisions will all shift over time. Goodin's proposal accommodates those shifts by positing a world government whose jurisdiction is large enough to encompass all such possible shifts. The multiple membership model seeks to accommodate these shifts by adjusting the boundaries of membership over time.

In this way, the principle of affected interests becomes a critical and regulative principle. At any particular moment, organizations may make decisions affecting individuals who have little influence on those organizations. At such moments, it is democratically imperative to expand inclusion of decision-making in those organizations in order to satisfy the principle of affected interests. If such democratic reform efforts were successful, they would usher in moments in which the principle of affected interests in its third formulation was fully satisfied. Every individual would be able to influence in some way any organization whose decisions regularly affected that individual's interests.

The approach is also necessarily dynamic. It does not imagine that all organizations will be fully compliant at every point in time. In reality, many, if not all, organizations would make some decisions affecting individuals who had no influence over those decisions. Organizations change in their relation to their contexts. Firms seek new markets, states embark on new adventures, civic organizations drop old agendas in favor of new ones. Periods of noncompliance or lesser compliance will emerge. During such periods, the principle of affected interests again demands institutional reform efforts that alter the boundaries of organization to include those who are affected but lack influence.[26]

If noncompliant periods of adjustment were sufficiently brief, the realization of this dynamic account of the principle of affected interests would be more appealing than the realization of a full-compliance account that requires a world demos. The multiple, dynamic approach envisions many overlapping circles of inclusion, one per organization. Because each circle is determined by the regular impacts of decisions made by a particular organization, the size of each circle (the number of individuals in it) strikes a more sensible balance between the scope of influence and its meaningfulness than a circle that includes the whole world. Furthermore, the individuals in any particular circle are all connected by the fact that they are all commonly affected by an organization's actions. While that consequential tie may be less thick than the ties of a community united by blood-and-soil or avowed membership, it is more substantial than ephemeral bonds between individuals in far corners of the earth who might possibly be affected by the decisions of a global political entity.

Varieties of Influence

One immediate objection to this understanding of the principle of affected interests is that it would place excessive demands on individuals, overloading their cognitive and political capacities. Every individual is affected by the decisions of countless organizations. Few people could even list all of the organizations that make decisions affecting them, much less muster the capacity to try to influence decisions that they all make. The limits of attention and understanding seem more manageable if citizens need only worry about influencing the decisions of a single organization, their state.

It is common to think of exercising political "influence" in a participatory democratic way—as individuals exercising influence deliberately and directly. But this understanding of the notion of "influence" is too narrow.[27] Drawing upon standard discussions of power, we say that individuals influence a decision made by an organization when their avowed interests or preferences have some causal effect on that organization's decision.

Even when the target of individual influence is the state, much of this influence occurs indirectly. In their use of the affected-interests principle to justify representative government, authors such as Robert Dahl and Robert Goodin understandably think of individuals exercising "influence" by casting a vote for a politician or party, rather than directly deciding upon policies through referenda or other directly democratic mechanisms. Political representation is a familiar method of deliberate and active influence–but it is indirect, in the sense that citizens' influence is mediated through their political agents. Politicians, however, are just the first level of indirection. Influence over the actions of the state also flows through the bewildering network of committees, agencies, and authorities that constitutes the administrative state.

Individuals can *actively* influence—in the sense that they deliberately seek to press their avowed preference—in both direct and indirect ways: ranging from casting a ballot to campaigning to making an argument in the public sphere. But individuals can also exert *passive* influence over organizations' decisions. In passive forms of influence, individuals need not act at all to sway organizational decisions in ways that favor their interests. For example, investors in many capitalist countries benefit from laws and norms of fiduciary responsibility, backed by a regulatory apparatus, that induces executives in those firms to make decisions that advance "shareholder interests," even when those shareholders do not voice their preferences.[28]

In his 2010 State of the Union address, President Obama justified the U.S. bank bailout by saying, "It was not easy to do. And if there's one thing that has unified Democrats and Republicans, and everybody in between, it's that we all hated the bank bailout. I hated it. [applause] I hated it. You hated it. It was about as popular as a root canal." If it is true that the bank bailout was liked by bankers but disliked by just about everyone else—by most Americans and by Democrats and Republicans alike, how did it become policy? One cause of the U.S. Government's decision to aid the financial industry in the way that it did in 2008 and 2009 may be what some political scientists and social theorists have called "structural power." On this theory, politicians and policy-makers have incentives to act according to the preferences of those who control capital above other interests in society (such as those of consumers or workers). As Charles Lindblom put it, investors and businessmen must be enticed by policy-makers to create the conditions upon which the rest of society depends ("invest, hire workers, curb industrial pollution"). Whereas other actors in society must organize to assert their interests, those who control capital (while they certainly organize as well) can exert this additional form of political influence simply by virtue of their position in the structure of a market society.[29]

Structural power is one kind of influence over an organization that is exercised passively but directly, in the sense that those who make decisions in an organization (such as politicians and policymakers) respond without intermediation to the interests of particular affected individuals (in this case capitalists). The general notion of this kind of passive direct influence applies to many other instances, such as the power that husbands exert over wives in marriage in societies where divorced women face highly diminished life chances. Concepts of structural power have been used to explain how dominant interests exert influence that subordinates the interests of the weak. But this basic insight might also be used to explain and indeed design institutional mechanisms that create more egalitarian opportunities for influence over significant decisions. In a society with generous social welfare provisions, including a basic income (van Parijs 1991) and other protections, employers are less likely to exploit and degrade their employees, because the well-being and self-respect of the employees is less dependent on labor market success. While such measures would certainly enhance the bargaining position of employees, they would also enable employees to protect their interests through passive direct structural influence over workplace decisions.

Finally, individuals can also influence the decisions of organizations in ways that are passive and indirect. Those who make decisions in organizations are subject to countless norms of appropriateness, moral standards, cultural perspectives, and habits of thought that we acquire through numerous channels of socialization. These forces affect how they assess choices before them and ultimately act. Very different scholars have explored how

Table 11.1. Modes of Influence, Applied to Firm Wage Decisions

	Active	Passive
Direct	I Worker bargains with employer.	III Worker less hostage to labor market due to social welfare provisions.
Indirect (mediated)	II Worker votes for politician who enacts minimum wage laws.	IV Worker lives in community with potent pro-labor norms.

such forces systematically influence decisions in favor of some interests against others: the American pragmatists with their accounts of habit (e.g., William James (1887: 446–47); Antonio Gramsci with hegemony; and the related "third face of power" explored by Steven Lukes, John Gaventa, and other power theorists.[30]

Table 11.1 shows the four modes of influence discussed above and their application to the issue of employee wages. In formulation (3) above, the principle of affected interests requires workers at a firm to have influence over its wage policies. The principle of affected interests requires some sort of workplace democracy, as workers are deeply affected by workplace decisions (I in Table 11.1). The participatory democratic approach of giving workers active and direct influence is one way to satisfy the principle, but not the only one. Workers might also vote for political representatives who legislate minimum wage laws (II, active and indirect). Workers might live in communities that offer generous social welfare safety nets and perhaps even a basic income. These de-commodification measures give them structural power in their interactions with employers by decoupling their prospects from labor market success (III, passive and direct). Or, workers might work for employers who are subject to broader social norms of solidarity, care, and respect for producers (passive and indirect).

It may seem odd to count what I have called the passive modes as influence at all. Our use of the term usually refers to agents who are deliberate in the ways that they seek to advance their interests. Those who are drawn to the principle of affected interests primarily from the values of autonomy and self-mastery may resist this broader formulation of influence, and any institutional account of the principle of affected interests must make substantial room for active modes of influence. But there are ample reasons to include passive modes of influence as well.

First, it is much more plausible to see how the principle of affected interests could be satisfied when one understands that decisions are affected by factors that include not just formal provisions for voice, but also indirect laws and regulatory mechanisms, social structures of power, and the collective creation and reproduction of culture and habit. Second, this enlarged view of influence has practical implications. For any particular organization, there are many routes through which to satisfy the principle of affected interests. If one particular route of influence is blocked by force or circumstance, politicians, activists, and other reformers might seek others.

Third, this broader understanding offers a more social, less individualistic conception of influence, one in which organizations can be embedded in webs of incentive and control that pressure their decisions to protect individual interests. The most obvious include the mediated influences of representative government and regulatory systems, but there are many others. The long-term construction and maintenance of such webs of influence is not less important for democratic social control or protection of individual interests than establishing routes through which individuals can participate directly and deliberately in collective decision-making.

Finally, this broader notion of influence is congruent with contemporary psychological understandings of decision-making. Even at the individual level, the psychology of decisions tells us that we accomplish most of our ends through a-rational, non-deliberate processes. Many psychologists distinguish between "central" and "peripheral" routes of cognition.[31] In the central route, individuals employ the tools of deliberate choice in full consciousness, weighing the costs and benefits, gauging the likelihood of various scenarios, and the like. In the peripheral route, decisions result from habits or affective factors that do not rely upon deliberate appraisal of options. Think of the many decisions that enabled you to get yourself from your home to work this morning, or those that culminated in the last box of breakfast cereal you purchased. Most decisions employ the peripheral rather than the central route of cognition. Passive routes of influence at the level of democratic society are analogous to peripheral routes of cognition at the level of individual decision-making. They can both operate to advance our interests, and they are both necessary because of our limited time and cognitive capacity.

The principle of affected interests may be satisfied through any of these modes of influence. Popular control over any particular organization will usually depend on a mix of all four. For a society, the principle requires that every individual be able to influence all of the organizations that make decisions regularly or deeply affecting his important interests through at least one of the modes shown in Table 11.1. A corollary is that the principle also requires that every organization offer at least one mode of influence to every individual whose interests are regularly or deeply affected by its decisions.[32] It is far more plausible that the principle could be satisfied with this broader notion of influence than through just active (or worse, active and direct) modes of influence.

Working out the factors that determine the optimal mix of different kinds of influence lies beyond the scope of this chapter. Any such effort must include at least two important factors: the extent to which the mix of modes allows individuals to protect their important interests and the extent to which such modes allow individuals to economize on the attention and energy that they devote to influencing organizational decisions. A fuller theory incorporating the principle of affected interests would specify how to assess the degree to which various governance procedures and social practices satisfy the principle and whether the principle requires alternative arrangements. How, for example, ought the balance between protecting important interests and economizing on time and attention be struck? Short of offering such an account, the next section illustrates how the principle of affected interests guides the evaluation of democratic control mechanisms.

Two Illustrative Applications

Decisions with International Effects

Perhaps more than ever, states make decisions that affect those who live outside their borders and have no formal voice in the decision-making processes of those states. Many people from all over the world follow U.S. presidential elections closely as much from self-interest as from voyeuristic fascination. Powerful nations make decisions about security, economy, environment, property, and technology, among other issues, that touch the interests of billions outside their borders. Decades ago, Robert Dahl mused that the principle of affected interests may require people in Latin America to be able to vote in U.S. elections, for no one doubts that U.S. decisions have profound consequences for them. He cautions us not to dismiss this thought as absurd, for "the real absurdity is the absence of any system of government in which that joint interest is effectively represented" (1990: 51). He writes that if a first transformation gave birth to the democratic city-state, and the second was the shift from local to nation-state democracy, we now face a third transformation in which "the boundaries of a country, even a large country such as the United States, are now much smaller than the boundaries of decisions that significantly affect the fundamental interests of its citizens . . . the governments of countries are becoming local governments" (319).

As discussed above, Robert Goodin suggests that the principle of affected interests requires a world government to address this challenge to democracy. But, as Steven Macedo (2008) points out, there are many other ways to satisfy the principle of affected interests in the face of decisions with trans-boundary effects. Suppose state A makes decisions that affect individuals living in the territory of state B. If both A and B are members of multilateral institutions such as the WTO, EU, and UN, those institutions sometimes allow those in B to have more influence on A's decisions than they would otherwise have. The mode of this influence is active when individuals vote for political officials in B and is mediated through those officials, multilateral institutions, and the response of State A.

For some kinds of decisions, influence might be exercised directly as well as actively. When decisions made by a corporation of State A affect those living in B, those in B sometimes circumvent the mediation of state organizations in favor of negotiating directly with that corporation to secure decisions that will protect their interests.[33] Influence over transnational decisions can also operate in passive ways. The advocacy of Bono Vox may be said to give Africans who suffer from AIDS some influence (perhaps only a little, but more than they would otherwise have) over the decisions about foreign aid of national governments, transnational international property rights regimes, and global pharmaceutical corporations.[34] Similarly, efforts of nongovernmental organizations such as Oxfam and Care can be said to give the world's poor some influence over the formulation of the rules of international trade. There is in political theory a lively discussion about whether such organizations "represent" the poor or Africans suffering from AIDS. But it is easier to see how these international advocates afford their intended beneficiaries some influence over international decisions. Whether or not they can be said properly to represent, one of the central aims of these advocacy groups is to shift the decisions of powerful organizations in ways that protect the interests of highly disadvantaged individuals like the poor or AIDS suffers in Africa. If those disadvantaged individuals did not exist, or if they had interests very different from what they presently are, those advocacy groups would likely embrace very different goals.[35]

None of this is to say that the operations of multilateral institutions, stakeholder negotiations, or international norms currently confer actual influence over transnational decisions, much less that they confer sufficient influence to satisfy a democratically demanding interpretation of the principle of affected interests. Rather, this discussion simply lays out a number of alternative institutionalizations through which that principle could be satisfied.

Second-Generation Gender and Race Discrimination

A claim of the fact of governance is not just that states lack reach over decisions that originate outside their borders, but that they also lack the capacity to protect the important interests of individuals even for decisions inside their territory. To illustrate the plausibility of this claim, consider the problem of racial and gender discrimination at workplaces in the United States.

Susan Sturm describes the difference between what she calls first- and second-generation discrimination. First-generation employment discrimination is intentional and explicit: "workplace segregation was maintained through overt exclusion, segregation of job opportunity, and conscious stereotyping. Dominant individuals and groups deliberately excluded or subordinated woman and people of color" (2001: 465). During the civil-rights movement and afterward, legislators and advocates passed laws that made this form of discrimination illegal by prohibiting the use of race or gender as a factor in hiring decisions, requiring the same standards and processes for recruitment, hiring, training, promotion, and so on (467).

Though this first generation of discrimination persists, Sturm shows that it is now compounded by a second generation of discrimination that is more subtle and complex. Second-generation discrimination consists of patterns of exclusion that result from personal interactions over time that may not involve intentional exclusion or bias. Second-generation harassment may, for example, "consist of undermining women's perceived competence, freezing them out of crucial social interactions." The "glass ceiling" that blocks the advancement of women and people of color remains "largely because of patterns of interaction, informal norms, networking, training, mentoring, and evaluation" (2001: 469). These more subtle patterns of discrimination have proven resistant to the antidiscrimination laws that successfully addressed much first-generation discrimination, because practices that produce second-generation discrimination vary across workplaces and frequently elude explicit understanding by either perpetrators or victims of discrimination. The force of binding law is insufficient to secure equality of economic opportunity against the challenges of second-generation discrimination.

But these problems have been addressed successfully in many workplaces. Successful strategies often result from groups of employees and managers who engage in workplace problem-solving to identify the behavioral patterns, norms, and policies that constitute second-generation discrimination. To mitigate discrimination, these findings must then be incorporated in the human resource practices and culture of the organization (Sturm 2001: 479). Firms who engage in this sort of introspection and internal reform are frequently prodded, and then assisted, by external groups who advocate on behalf of female or minority professionals.

Women and people of color have an important interest in nondiscrimination. During the civil rights and women's movements, many of them actively exercised influence over employment decisions through the power of antidiscrimination laws to protect these interests. These tools of active/indirect influence have shown themselves to be much less effective against a second generation of workplace discrimination. But other forms of influence, in particular the active-direct mode of employee participation (I in Table 11.1) in the formation of human resource and promotion policies, have proven more effective. These efforts may in the medium term help to alter norms and habits of organizational management in ways that promote equal opportunity (IV in Table 11.1). When representative government does not enable individuals to influence decisions affecting their important interests, the principle of affected interests demands other avenues of influence be created.

Conflicts of Authority and Membership

In a world of multiple and dynamic memberships, conflicts over who ought to have influence, how much they should have, and over which organizations are bound to arise.[36] Adjudicating these conflicts requires both appropriate principles and adequate institutions. Adjudication principles would specify what kinds of interests are sufficient to warrant participation in an organization's decisions, the priority of different interests, and the kinds of influence that ought to be conferred. In a conflict between, for example, the "affected interest" of a homosexual couple who would benefit from laws permitting same-sex marriage and a third party who is offended by the notion of same-sex marriage, one might argue that the interest in successful long-term partnership is more fundamental than the interest in non-offense.

Principles of adjudication would also specify how influence should be distributed. A natural interpretation of the principle of affected interests would be to distribute influence in proportion to the degree that interests are affected, rather than affording all who are affected an equal opportunity to influence a decision.[37] Working out these principles of adjudication must, however, be left for another occasion.

As an institutional matter, who would apply these principles of adjudication to assure that organizational enfranchisement satisfies the principle of affected interests? A complex world requires complex institutions to protect participation rights. Despite many flaws, the nexus of laws, courts, and administrative practices such as notice-and-comment, administrative hearings, and regulatory negotiation in the United States offers some insight into how participation rights might be adjudicated. That experience covers only administrative agencies in a single country, and the principle of affected interests would regulate a much larger array of organizations in many other areas. In a future imagined to be more democratic than the present, there might be many juridical bodies (perhaps both courts and citizens' juries) charged with enforcing the principle of affected interests and its associated rights to participation in different territories (Kenya, the U.S., New York State), across sectors (different courts for businesses, administrative agencies, civil society, and government), or issue areas (environment, education, infrastructure projects funded by international development assistance). If the principle of affected interests were widely accepted, it is not difficult to imagine how institutions would enforce it.[38]

As a practical reality, however, a full-fledged structure of juridical institutions that enforces the principle of affected interests is as fanciful as a cosmopolitan democratic government. Today, the principle of affected interests is vindicated incrementally and haphazardly through the court of public opinion. When obviously important interests—human rights, health, economic livelihood, children's education, and so on—are adversely affected by the decisions of governments, international financial and trade organizations, corporations, and even nongovernmental organizations, those who are affected sometimes rise up to demand influence. When investors and community residents demand more voice in the decisions of corporations, neighborhood groups ask for participatory planning, and governments of developing countries want greater say in UN Security Council or world trade decisions, they appeal to the principle of affected interests. Because organizations and their constituencies are not immune from the appeal of this norm and the pressures that it generates, targeted organizations sometimes enfranchise their critics. Such spontaneous compulsion, however, enforces the principle in a highly uneven way. Perhaps in the fullness of time, this democratic norm will spread from the world of impulsive political movement to institutionalized law and regulation.

Conclusion

The principle of affected interests remains one of the most firm and widespread democratic intuitions. The sensibility that people should be able to influence decisions that affect them grounds not only commitments to representative government, but complaints about the democratic deficits of organizations like the European Union, World Trade Organization, and Royal Dutch Shell corporation. It drives demands for participation not just upward from the nation-state, but also outward—into corporations and nongovernmental organizations—as well as downward—into local governments, administrative agencies, communities, and neighborhoods. In the pages above, I have tried to formulate that principle in a way that is plausible and attractive.

This discussion is incomplete. I have not specified which individual interests are sufficiently important to warrant having influence. I have not specified the values—economy of time and attention, extent of influence, deliberateness of control—that guide choices among alternative ways to satisfy the principle of affected interests. Furthermore, individual influence is not the same thing as democratic control. Influence must be rise above a threshold and be distributed fairly to count as democratic. Authoritarian leaders know that they can go so far that they will be overthrown, and so avoid that precipice. Though these countries are far from democratic, people in them have some weak influence over their political leaders.

Nevertheless, I have tried to develop the principle of affected interests in several ways that render it coherent, feasible, compatible with the complexity of contemporary governance, and yet still responsive to these radical democratic intuitions in two main ways. First, this conception urges citizens to focus their democratic ambitions beyond the state. Standing at the beginning of the twenty-first century, we need a democratic theory that accounts for the bewildering range of nonstate actors that profoundly affect our fundamental interests and the ordering of our collective lives together. What range of decisions and actions of those "private" actors should be subject to democratic control? Who has warrant to exercise that control? The principle of affected interests provides answers to both these questions.

Second, my rendering of the principle of affected interests sketches four pathways to influence. Private, civic, or extraterritorial power may be brought to heel, democratically speaking, not just through the regulatory machinery of states (active, indirect control), but through mechanisms of direct, citizen to non-state actor, influence (e.g., governing board representation or consultation), as well through passive mechanisms. This more capacious conception of democratic influence provides a normative lens to make sense of the plethora of consultative and representative mechanisms created by nonstate actors such as international organizations, NGOs, and even private corporations. The principle of affected interests articulates a standard for judging the democratic sufficiency of such mechanisms. Finally, it provides a justification for mechanisms that control forms of private power that elude the modern state's grasp.

According to the principle of affected interests, an individual should have influence over many different organizations because many affect his or her important interests. If we imagine every organization as having a circle of inclusion around it with all of those in the circle having some influence, every individual would be a member of many circles—some above the level of the nation-state and many below it. In some of those circles, individuals might exercise their influence directly through committee democracy, and in others indirectly through votes for representatives. In many, perhaps most, circles, however, individuals would exercise a passive influence that causes organizations to make decisions that are responsive to their interests and preferences through structural inducements, norms, or regulatory provisions. As the effects of organizations shifted, constricted, or expanded, political leaders, citizens, and advocates would press them to adjust their boundaries of inclusion according to a broadly accepted principle of affected interests. Such a world would better realize the democratic ambition to subject fate and arbitrary power to popular control.

References

Archibugi, Daniele, and David Held. 1995. *Cosmopolitan Democracy: An Agenda for a New World Order*. London: Polity Press.

Arrhenius, Gustaf. 2005. "The Boundary Problem in Democratic Theory." In *Democracy Unbound: Basic Explorations*, ed. F. Tersman. Stockholm Studies in Democratic Theory 1. Stockholm: Stockholm University. 14–29.

Beitz, Charles. 1989. *Political Equality: An Essay in Democratic Theory*. Princeton, N.J.: Princeton University Press.

Benkler, Yochai. 2006. *The Wealth of Networks: How Social Production Transforms Markets and Freedom*. New Haven, Conn.: Yale University Press.

Blake, Michael. 2001. "Distributive Justice, State Coercion, and Autonomy." *Philosophy and Public Affairs* 30 (3): 257–96.

Block, Fred. 1977. "The Ruling Class Does Not Rule: Notes on the Marxist Theory of the State." Reprinted in Fred Block, *Revising State Theory: Essay in Politics and Postindustrialism*. Philadelphia: Temple University Press, 1987.

Bohman, James. 2007. *Democracy Across Borders: From Dêmos to Dêmoi*. Studies in Contemporary German Social Thought. Cambridge, Mass.: MIT Press.

Cohen, Joshua. 1997. "Deliberation and Democratic Legitimacy." In *Deliberative Democracy: Essays on Reason and Politics*, ed. James Bohman and William Rehg. Cambridge, Mass.: MIT Press. 67–92.

Cohen, Joshua, and Joel Rogers. *On Democracy*. New York: Penguin, 1983.

Dahl, Robert. 1967. "The City in the Future of Democracy." *American Political Science Review* 61 (4): 953–70.

———. *Democracy and Its Critics*. 1990. New Haven, Conn.: Yale University Press, 1989.

———. *After the Revolution?: Authority in a Good Society*. Rev. ed. Yale Fastback Series. New Haven, Conn.: Yale University Press.

———. 1994. "A Democratic Dilemma: System Effectiveness Versus Citizen Participation." *Political Science Quarterly* 109 (1): 23–34.

Dahl, Robert A., and Edward R. Tufte. 1973. *Size and Democracy*. Stanford, Calif.: Stanford University Press.

Dewey, John. 1927. *The Public and Its Problems*. Athens: Ohio University Press.

Fair Labor Association. 2002. "First Public Report: Towards Improving Workers' Lives." Washington, D.C., July 31, 2002.

Goodin, Robert. 2007. "Enfranchising All Affected Interests, and Its Alternatives." *Philosophy and Public Affairs* 35 (1): 40–68.

Grewal, David Singh. 2009. *Network Power: The Social Dynamics of Globalization.* New Haven, Conn.: Yale University Press.

James, William. 1887. "The Laws of Habit." *Popular Science Monthly* 30 (February): 433–51.

Kahneman, Daniel. 2011. *Thinking, Fast and Slow.* New York: Farrar, Straus and Giroux.

Lessig, Lawrence. 2006. *Code: And Other Laws of Cyberspace*, Version 2.0. New York: Basic Books.

Lindblom, Charles E. 1977. *Politics and Markets.* New York: Basic Books.

———. 1982. "The Market as Prison." *Journal of Politics* 44 (2): 324–36.

Lukes, Steven. 2005. *Power: A Radical View.* 2nd ed. London: Palgrave Macmillan.

Macedo, Steven. 2008. "Representation-Reinforcing Multilateralism: How International Institutions Can Promote Fairer Representation and (Non-Electoral) Democracy." Presented at Representation Workshop, University Center for Human Values, Princeton University, December 5–6.

Mansbridge, Jane. 2003. "Rethinking Representation." *American Political Science Review* 97 (4): 515–28.

———. 2008. "The Place of Self-Interest in Deliberative Democracy." Manuscript.

Mansbridge, Jane, James Bohman, Simone Chambers, David Estlund, Andreas Føllesdal, Archon Fung, Cristina Lafont, Bernard Manin, and José luis Martí 2010. "The Place of Self-Interest and the Role of Power in Deliberative Democracy." *Journal of Political Philosophy* 18 (1): 64–100.

Mill, John Stuart. 1991 (1861). *Considerations on Representative Government.* New York: Prometheus.

Montenaro, Laura. 2008. "Self-Authorized Representation." Presented at Representation Workshop, University Center for Human Values, Princeton University, December 5–6.

Nozick, Robert. 1974. *Anarchy, State and Utopia.* New York: Basic Books.

Nye, Joseph and Robert Keohane. 2000. "Introduction." In *Governance in a Globalizing World*, ed. Joseph Nye and John D. Donahue. Washington, D.C.: Brookings Institution Press. 12–13.

Obama, Barack. 2010. Address before a joint session of the Congress on the state of the union, January 27. http://www.whitehouse.gov/the-press-office/remarks-president-state-union-address

Ogden, Timothy. 2011. "How Much Difference Is It Making (Living with the Gates Foundation)." *Alliance Magazine.*

Parijs, Philippe van. 1991. "Why Surfers Should be Fed: The Liberal Case for an Unconditional Basic Income." *Philosophy and Public Affairs* 20 (2): 101–31.

Pettit, Philip. 2000. *Republicanism: A Theory of Freedom and Government.* Oxford Political Theory. New York: Oxford University Press.

Pratkanis, Anthony and Eliot Aronson. 2001. *Age of Propaganda: The Everyday Use and Abuse of Persuasion.* Rev. ed. New York: Owl Books.

Rawls, John. 1971. *A Theory of Justice.* Cambridge, Mass.: Harvard University Press.

Reich, Rob. 2012. "A Failure of Philanthropy: American Charity Shortchanges the Poor, and Public Policy Is Partly to Blame." *Voices in Urban Education* 32: 42–48.

Rittel, Horst, and Melvin Webber. 1973. "Dilemmas in a General Theory of Planning." *Policy Sciences* 4: 155–69.

Rubenstein, Jennifer. 2007. "Accountability in an Unequal World." *Journal of Politics* 69 (3): 616–32.

Saward, Michael. 2008. "Citizens in the Grey Zone: Democratic Credibility and Non-elective Representation." Presented at Representation Workshop, University Center for Human Values, Princeton University, December 5–6.

Schmitz, Hans Peter, Paloma Raggo, and Tosca Bruno-van Vijfeijken. 2011. "Accountability of Transnational NGOs: Aspirations vs. Practice." *Non-Profit and Voluntary Sector Quarterly* 20 (10): 1–20.

Sen, Amartya. 2009. *The Idea of Justice*. Cambridge, Mass.: Belknap Press of Harvard University Press.

Smith, Mark A. 1999. "Public Opinion, Elections, and Representation Within a Market Economy: Does the Structural Power of Business Undermine Popular Sovereignty?" *American Journal of Political Science* 43 (3): 842–63.

Stewart, Richard B. 1975. "The Reform of American Administrative Law." *Harvard Law Review* 88 (8): 1667–813.

Sturm, Susan. 2001. 2001. "Second Generation Employment Discrimination: A Structural Approach." *Columbia Law Review* 101 (458): 1–121.

Sunstein, Cass. 1990. *After the Rights Revolution: Reconceiving the Regulatory State*. Cambridge, Mass.: Harvard University Press.

Weber, Edward P. 2003. *Bringing Society Back In: Grassroots Ecosystem Management, Accountability, and Sustainable Communities*. American and Comparative Environmental Policy. Cambridge, Mass.: MIT Press.

Whelan, Frederick G. 1983. "Prologue: Democratic Theory and the Boundary Problem." In *Liberal Democracy*, ed. J. Roland Pennock, and John W. Chapman. Nomos 25. New York: New York University Press, 13–47.

CHAPTER 12

Citizen Representatives

Mark E. Warren

Democratic theorists commonly distinguish between *direct* democracy and *representative* democracy. In a direct democracy, citizens rule themselves, while in a representative democracy they elect representatives to rule on their behalf. Today's democracies are all representative in structure—a form dictated by scale and complexity—with some direct elements such as initiatives and referendums, as well as some forms of citizen engagement. The concept of *participatory democracy* usually refers to these latter two elements: direct decision-making as well as citizen involvement in decision-making within representative structures. If, however, we consider these two forms of participation from the perspective of representation, the first involves citizen participation in government or other formalized decision-making, on the assumption that citizens *represent themselves* within these processes. The second involves citizens themselves serving in *representative capacities*: lay citizens represent other citizens. I shall refer to these roles as *citizen representatives*—a form of representation that is increasingly common in practice, but almost untheorized in democratic theory.[1]

To be sure, the idea that citizens are best represented by other lay citizens serving as representatives is an old democratic ideal. It justified early notions that elected representatives should be salaried so as to enable ordinary citizens—not just the rich—to serve in public office, as well as the more recent idea that term limits will prevent elected representatives from becoming professional political elites. These and other devices are based on the presumption that when citizens represent other citizens, the representative relationship is secured through common experience. The presumption is not a good one, however. Common experience usually gives way to the realities of running for and holding office, which subject lay citizens and professional politicians alike to the same constraints of campaigning, brokering, and responding to interest group pressures, and lead to very similar behaviors (Fisher and Herrick 2003). Moreover, as Max Weber noted almost a century ago, governing complex societies provides little room for amateurs and dilettantes, who are at best ineffective and at worst more easily manipulated by interest groups and bureaucrats than are professional politicians.

Over the last few decades, however, new forms of citizen representation have been rapidly evolving (Fiorino 1990; Rowe and Frewer 2000; Warren 2003; Brown 2006). These forms involve nonprofessionals who are selected or self-selected, rather than elected, for representative purposes. The oldest form of citizen representative is the legal jury, which represents the considered judgment of peers within courtroom proceedings (Dzur 2012). We can now add to this limited form more recent experiments with citizen juries and panels, advisory councils, stakeholder meetings, lay members of professional review boards, representations at public hearings, public submissions, citizen surveys, deliberative polling, deliberative forums, focus groups, and advocacy group representations (Fung 2006b; Fiorino 1990; Rowe and Frewer 2000). Citizen representatives typically function not as alternatives but rather as supplements to elected representative bodies or administrative bodies in areas of weakness, usually having to do with limitations of communication, deliberation, legitimacy, governability, or attentiveness to public norms and common goods (Brown 2006; Warren 2009).

Although it has been common to refer these forms of political activity under the category of "participatory democracy" or (more recently) "participatory governance," the term fails to identify what is perhaps their most important feature: each involves a form of representation that depends upon the *active participation of a relatively few citizens who function as representatives of other citizens*. Thus, whereas the notion of *participatory* democracy suggests that most citizens participate in self-rule—a worthy ideal—what is most important about these new forms is their *representative* qualities. Accordingly, they should not be measured by *how many* citizens are enabled to participate through these forms (although this remains a valid measure of democracy), but rather by the *nature and quality of democratic representation* achieved through these forms. Theories of participatory democracy are not equipped to guide these judgments (Urbinati 2006).

This theoretical deficit is highlighted by the case of the British Columbia Citizens' Assembly on Electoral Reform (CA), a remarkable political experience convened in British Columbia, Canada, in 2004, precisely because it was constructed as a body of nonprofessional citizens who would represent other citizens in the fundamental constitutional matter of assessing and designing an electoral system. In this chapter, I address this theoretical gap first by highlighting deficits in democratic representation through elected legislative bodies. Second, I suggest that strategies for increasing citizen participation often frame the democratic deficit problem in ways that are unlikely to be successful. At the same time, the lens of participatory democracy tends to obscure the increasingly important concept of representative relationships among citizens—usually, between the active few and the passive many. Third, if we approach citizen-based political venues through the framework of representation, we can ask about how well emerging forms of citizen participation measure up as *citizen representatives*: who authorizes citizen representatives? How egalitarian are their effects? How are they held accountable? Using these criteria, I assess the CA model as a *citizen representative body*. Considered as a representative body, the CA shows strengths in areas where both elected legislatures and other kinds of citizen representative bodies tend to be weak. Finally, I conclude that, owing to certain weaknesses of CA-style citizen representative bodies—particularly with respect to accountability to constituencies—they should be viewed as supplements to, rather than replacements for, other forms of representation (Lang and Warren 2012).

Representation Deficits

Most conceptions of democratic electoral representation share certain formal features, which in turn indicate criteria in terms of which the quality of representation might be judged (Pitkin 1967; Mansbridge 2003; Warren and Castiglione 2004). The most recognized of these features is the role of elections in *authorizing* representatives to represent those who inhabit geographical constituencies. Electoral representation is held to be *egalitarian and inclusive*, owing to the universal franchise. Every member of an electoral unit, excluding those unfit or not yet fit to exercise the responsibilities of citizenship, is entitled to one vote. Subsequent elections function to hold representatives *accountable* for their performance while in office.

As is well known, democratic linkages between citizens and representatives can and do break down in numerous ways (see, e.g., Fung 2006a). Citizens may have unstable preferences that are neither adequately formed by the electoral process, nor communicated by the blunt instrument of the vote. Voting may not serve as a sufficiently strong incentive to hold representatives accountable, especially when voters are inattentive, information is incomplete, and other forms of power permeate the system, including actors that can provide or withhold economic resources, or administrative officials who have knowledge representatives cannot match. Electoral mechanisms such as single member plurality systems may function to disadvantage or exclude minorities. Where there are descriptive differences between representatives and constituents, distinctive group experiences and disadvantages may not be represented at all. And because pressure groups tend to represent those who have the resources to organize and who care intensely about a single issue, constituency communication may systematically disadvantage public will formation around common goods. Finally, citizens may demand contradictory things from government, such as first-rate health care and schools combined with low taxes. All these possibilities are, of course, common in the developed democracies.

The concept of an *institutional* representation deficit is poorly developed in theories of electoral democracy, in part because the very notion of representative institutions serving as collective representatives of the people is poorly developed, with the exception of those theories that focus on the democratic functions of political parties. However, people tend to expect legislatures to do their work—deliver decisions—in ways that are responsive, competent, and fair. And there is a sense in which the kind of accountability that attaches to these expectations is quite different from the expectations leveled at individual representatives. Voters are quite willing, as the 2006 mid-term elections in the United States demonstrated, to use their votes for individual representatives to hold the institution to account *as an institution*.

Theoretically, there are at least two distinct senses of accountability at the institutional level. The first is, simply, whether the institution can "do its job"—delivering legislation. And its capacity for accountability in this sense will depend upon its institutional capacity to handle conflict by avoiding stalemate, as well as its capacity to handle the high levels of complexity that come with many legislative decisions. The second sense of accountability has to do with whether the institution can provide *public justifications* for its decisions. No doubt there are tradeoffs between these dimensions of institutional accountability: the ability of a legislative body to broker complex agreements, for example, may mean that its capacity to justify its decisions *as a body* to the public may be quite low.

Certainly citizens are increasingly likely to *believe* that representative linkages are not working well. Nor, to judge by the American case, do they believe that legislative institutions are doing a good job of representing the public interest. Approval of Congress, for example, rarely ranges above 50 percent, is typically in the 30–40 percent range (National Election Studies 2007), and more recently has fallen close to the single digits. As Dalton (2004), Norris (1999), and others have argued, the developed democracies now contain a new group of "critical citizens," who tend to be well educated; they have "postmaterial" values, some of which are expressed in high democratic expectations. These citizens appear to be on the leading edge of political disengagement and distrust, and are more likely to view the gap between politicians, government, and citizens as wider than ever. Citizens' expectations are increasingly difficult to meet, it appears, the more complex and politicized the governing environment. In Dalton's view, "contemporary democracies do not suffer from a surfeit of interest articulation, but from a lack of institutions and processes that can aggregate and balance divergent interests into a coherent policy program that participants can accept" (2004: 205; see also Norris 2011).

Even if the U.S. is a limiting case, the broader picture is that the traditional and recognizable forms of democratic representation—elected officials convened in representative assemblies such as legislatures, parliaments, and councils—are no longer sufficient to carry out the functions of democratic representation, at least not as stand-alone institutions. Many of the problems are probably intrinsic to the *electoral* form of representative democracy under contemporary conditions, and include the following:

- Owing to the electoral context, representative institutions respond better to intense and well-organized special interests than to latent interests, unorganized interests, and public goods.
- Because representatives function within a context that combines public visibility and adversarial relations, they must weigh the strategic and symbolic impact of speech. Thus, representative institutions have limited capacities for deliberation, which requires a suspension of the strategic impact of communication in favour of persuasion and argument.

- Because of electoral cycles, representative institutions have limited capacity to develop and improve public policies over a long period of time.
- Because representatives must attend to vested interests, representative institutions are have limited capacities for innovation and experimentation.

The nature of the electoral system will affect the degree to which each of these limits holds. Indeed, this is what the CA was charged with investigating. Its recommended Single Transferable Vote electoral system (a form of proportional representation that the CA proposed to replace British Columbia's Single Member Plurality electoral system) might very well lead to improvements in the first three of these areas. However, even the best electoral institutions will remain limited by the electoral form of accountability—which, even when it serves accountability, produces a structural bias toward aggregative accountability at the expense of deliberative accountability. I hasten to add two points. First, it is not the initial authorization, but the subsequent electoral form of accountability—the *serial* nature of elections—that produces these tendencies. Second, for key aspects of democratic government, there are no good alternatives to elected representation. The questions are, therefore,

- How might we reform the electoral systems to provide for better representation? This was the mandate for the CA, but not the topic of this chapter.
- How might we supplement the electoral form of representation with other forms of representation so as to produce a system in which institutions complement one another according to their strengths and weaknesses? This is the question I am addressing here.

Democratic Deficits in the Participation Response

These observations are not new. What is new is that decision-makers have increasingly identified "democratic deficits" as an issue in all of the consolidated democracies. We have thus seen a number of initiatives aimed at increasing governability—initiatives that aim, varyingly, at more trust in government, more legitimacy, more efficiency, and less political gridlock. These initiatives often include increasing "citizen participation," "citizen involvement," and/or "citizen engagement" as ways of closing the gap between what citizens want and what government provides. It is surely interesting that the initiatives have come mostly from the administrative/policy arenas rather than from representative institutions—with the CA a notable exception.[2] Perhaps the administrative sources of these initiatives are to be expected: the first concern of elected representatives is to be reelected—not to govern. Those who do govern—administrators—must square legislated goals with resource constraints, personnel, and organizational structures, and then fit these with citizen expectations and, often, the resistance of organized interests (Warren 2009).

So it is also not surprising that, as governance strategies, citizen "participation" and "engagement" tend *not* to be understood as *political* processes of representation and decision-making (the exceptions, perhaps, being democratic corporatism based on functional constituencies in Sweden, Norway, Austria, and Germany). In most democracies, "politics" has been understood as a legislative matter, with legislative results turned over to administrators to execute. Administrators typically understand "participation" as a strategy for gaining advice, co-opting pressures, and improving services, in this way seeking to increase the legitimacy of their policies (Brown 2006). They are looking for citizen "engagement" and "involvement"— not citizen decision-making. There is, no doubt, often much professionalism and little ill-will toward citizens. But the frameworks remain administrative rather than political, and citizen participation is viewed as a matter of advice-giving rather than empowered participation.

But because the new experiments *are* political, it is not surprising that the conceptions of "participation," "involvement," and "engagement" prove insufficient, so much so that we can now see a number of democratic deficits in what was thought to be the most democratic of activities. At the system level, expanding opportunities for participation can actually exacerbate deficits in democratic representation. Many kinds of new opportunities, for example, are based on self-selection, and therefore tend to favor those who are better educated and wealthier. On a system-wide level, more participation may increase the overrepresentation of those who are already well represented, generating the paradox that increasing citizen opportunities for participation may increase political inequality and reduce democracy (Cain, Dalton, and Scarrow, 2003; Warren 2009).

At the institutional level, unmediated participation tends to suffer from a number of defects. Because participants often self-select, the most intense interests and loudest voices often dominate, leading to underrepresentation of those who are less organized, less educated, and have fewer resources (Mansbridge 1980). Participatory venues can increase the neglect of public goods or increase the unjust distribution of their burdens by empowering local resistance by well-organized groups. Forms of participation that merely aggregate existing opinion (e.g., public submissions and hearings) contribute little to the deliberative formation of preferences and policy. And participation without power can lead to more disaffection, as citizens go through the exercise of engaging, only to have decisions taken elsewhere and for other reasons (Abelson and Eyles 2002: 8ff, 16; Irvin and Stansbury 2004: 58–60).

Citizen Representatives

Owing in large part to the lens of participatory democracy, it has largely escaped notice that *with respect to most citizens* the functions of these participatory institutions are less *participatory* than they are *representative* (cf. Stephan 2004; Brown 2006). Most participatory institutions are, in fact, designed in such a way that some citizens represent others, either as segments of the population, or as considered public opinion, or as common goods that would not otherwise be represented (Hanley et al. 2001; Lenaghan 1999; Parkinson 2003; Smith and Wales 2000; Ward et al. 2003; Fishkin 1995). Because most citizens do not participate through these institutions—subject, as they are, to the same constraints of scale and complexity as other institutions—we should be conceiving of them as *citizen representatives*.

The defining criterion of a "citizen representative body" is that members are *selected or self-selected, or authorized through initial election alone*—rather than functioning as professional elected representatives. In this way, members are freed, as it were, from the imperatives of the election cycle that produce representative deficits. At the same time, *precisely because of this freedom from electoral accountability*, the kinds of questions that apply to elected representative bodies are more urgent, especially if citizen representatives have influence or power. It follows that we should apply criteria of democratic representation to citizen representatives, looking for the functional equivalents of the representative functions of legislative bodies with respect to authorization, egalitarian inclusiveness, and accountability.

The example I use to develop this approach is the British Columbia Citizens' Assembly on Electoral Reform (CA). The CA was a response to two provincial elections in British Columbia that produced results that were difficult to justify on the basis of any theory of democratic representation. The Single Member Plurality system had allocated a majority of seats to the New Democratic Party in 1996, despite the fact that the Liberals won a majority of the popular vote. In 2000, under the same system, a majority popular vote awarded the Liberals 77 out of 79 seats in the Legislative Assembly, leaving parliament without an opposition. Shortly after their election in 2000, the BC Liberal Government made good on an election promise to reconsider the province's electoral system. Here is where the story becomes interesting for democratic theory and practice: rather than appoint an expert commission, the government devised a highly novel method for turning the decision over to ordinary citizens. They legislated into existence what they called the British Columbia Citizens' Assembly for Electoral Reform, provided it with a budget of $5 million, a staff, and timeline of about a year. They charged the CA with the task of assessing the province's electoral system, and proposing another if the assembly felt that it was lacking. And, remarkably, the Government precommitted to putting the Assembly's recommendation to a popular vote in the form of a referendum.

The Assembly was constituted by means of a near random process, with one man and one women from each of the 79 ridings in BC. The staff of the CA then compared the resulting body to BC demographics, and found that there was insufficient Aboriginal representation; they went back to the pool and drew names until they had added two more Aboriginal members, for an assembly of 160 individuals. Those with vested interests in the political system—elected officials, party officials, and others with potentially conflicted interests—were barred from serving, much as with jury service. Advocates could and did, however, present their cases and written materials to the Assembly—again, in much the same way as advocates present arguments and evidence before a jury. Once constituted, the Assembly met every other weekend. Their work was divided into three phases: they spent three months learning about electoral systems, three months conducting public hearings, and three months deliberating. At the conclusion of the deliberation period, the CA delivered their recommendation that the province adopt a modified version of a Single Transferable Vote system, and was legally dissolved. As promised, the Government put the recommendation to the voters during the May 2005 election, subject to a supermajority threshold of 60 percent, and 50 percent in 60 percent of the ridings. The proposal passed in 77 out of 79 ridings, but polled 57.4 percent, just short of the 60 percent threshold (for a complete account and analysis of the CA, see Warren and Pearse 2008, Fournier et al. 2011).

The question I address here is this: what kind of democratic representation did this *citizen representative* body provide for the citizens of British Columbia? To address this question, I develop the case with respect to each of several criteria that, together, comprise democratic representation.

Authorization

Elected representatives and bodies benefit from clear authorization. In contrast, the initial authorization of citizen representatives is often ambiguous. For most nongovernmental (civil society) associations and forums, there are no authorization procedures beyond self-selection. Groups initially *claim* to represent (in the sense of "speak for") citizens or issues, and these claims are "authorized" only retrospectively, usually as a consequence of a representative claim attracting a following (Montanaro 2012; Saward 2010). Formal advisory processes are explicitly authorized, often with a representative mandate to include, for example, "community representation" or similar terms that lack content or direction. In part because such terms are vague, in practice authorization can be quite arbitrary.

In contrast, the CA was a body legislated into existence by an elected government. Authorization was explicit, coming in the form of enabling legislation that specified the manner in which CA members would be chosen, the task, and the timetable for completion. With respect to formal authorization, the CA is more comparable to citizen juries than to other kinds of citizen representatives.

It is another question as to whether the citizens of BC perceived the Legislative Assembly's formal authorization of the CA as representative authorization. In the CA case, the level of trust—a key indication of authorization—expressed by citizens far exceeded the level of trust they typically place in politicians and legislative bodies. Theoretically, trust in the CA might be based on (a) perceptions of convergent interests, and/or (b) descriptive similarities between the body and the citizenry. Survey findings (Cutler et al. 2008) suggest that most citizens viewed the CA and its members as "ordinary citizens" who had the public interest in view in their deliberations and decision-making. Two mechanisms seem important to this result. First, the near-random selection in fact produced a large number of "ordinary citizens" with no apparent vested interests. And the screen against organized political interests and professional politicians assured that the body would not incorporate those with immediate stakes in the outcomes. While cases of designed democratic corporatism in Europe suggest that a screen against politicians and organized interests is not generally necessary for legitimacy, the case of electoral reform is distinct, since politicians and closely identified interests would be in a clear conflict of interest (Thompson 2008). The CA experience suggests that near-random selection performs at least as well as elections to authorize representatives, and in some ways better, since a body constituted in this way can claim both to be "of the people" and to have the legitimacy of impartiality (Rosanvallon 2011, part II).

Egalitarian inclusiveness

If a representative body is "democratic," then it will include ways and means of representing all affected interests. One way of including affected interests is through descriptive representation—and this was the key mechanism of inclusion in the CA (Gibson 2002). The egalitarian inclusiveness of citizen representatives is often suspect, since most are constituted through self-selection, thus favoring the intensely interested and those with political resources—particularly education, but also time, experience, and income (Verba, Schlozman, and Brady 1995). In the case of some public hearings, public submissions, and single-issue advocacy groups, self-selection combines with the natural exclusions that follow from the issue. In most cases, egalitarian inclusiveness is not even an aim of representatives: their interests are in other citizens with similar or convergent interests. This *aggregative* pattern of citizen representation achieves egalitarian inclusion only when the range of representatives in the public domain is sufficient to include the interests of every citizen. In practice, these conditions are rarely if ever met.

But it is possible for citizen representative bodies to be constituted in such a way that they are egalitarian and inclusive of all affected interests, either through random selection or initial stratification of the sample from which selections are made. These techniques are used to constitute legal juries, citizens' juries, and deliberative polls. The CA used both: geography and sex were used in such a way that each riding was represented by a man and a woman. Other descriptive categories such as race and ethnicity, religion, income, education, and age, were left to the process of random selection, though the Chair was empowered to add members of groups underrepresented in the sample—a power he exercised in adding two Aboriginal members who had agreed to serve, but were not among the final 158 who were drawn at random.

Several features of the process introduced some bias. First, the voter rolls were used to as the basis for random invitations to serve. Second, those who received letters had to respond affirmatively if they were interested in serving. Third, fluency in English was a requirement of service. These features no doubt produced the overrepresentation of people with more education, more income, and more time (e.g., retired people), and an under-representation of less educated, lower income, younger, and recently arrived citizens, which in turn produced an under-representation of visible minorities. These likely biases were known and justified in advance: Gibson argued that they were necessary to produce a group of capable people sufficiently committed to the process (Gibson 2002: 12–13). The direct effects of income inequality, however, were mitigated with modest pay for service and reimbursement for expenses.

While the CA might have been more inclusive and egalitarian (James 2008), when compared to two other alternatives, it looks very inclusive indeed. Elected representation tends to produce bodies with highly biased demographic characteristics, while forms of citizen representation that rely on self-selection magnify biases of education, income, time, and ethnicity.

Accountability

Taken at face value, the democratic accountability of the CA appears to be problematic. On the one hand, the CA lacked the formal accountability mechanisms of reelection or removal from office. On the other hand, these forms of accountability would seem to be *more* important in the case of the CA than with other citizen bodies, for two reasons. First, the CA was *involuntary* from the perspective of the citizens it represented. Thus, the market-like accountability mechanisms at work in the case of advocacy group representation—members "vote with their feet" by exiting if they feel they are misrepresented—could not function in this case. Citizens of BC could opt out of being represented by the CA only by moving from the province. Second, with the exception of legal juries, the CA was unique among citizen representative bodies in being *empowered* to set the agenda for electoral reform. To be sure, the CA's recommendation went to a referendum (and did so again in 2009), allowing citizens to exercise a check over the CA's power. But the CA was empowered to set the agenda, which is a nice bit of power indeed. Under democratic expectations, when representation is involuntary and empowered (as with states), the normative requirements for democratic accountability increase—and this is what makes the lack of formal accountability mechanisms apparently troubling.

At the same time, what it means for a representative or representative institution to be "accountable" is multifaceted. It is a peculiar strength of the CA model that it includes forms of democratic accountability that do not depend on election of representatives, and would be undermined by electoral accountability. To see this, we need look no farther than the conflicting features of accountability within elected legislatures, which will both identify the senses in which the CA was accountable, and identify the ways in which the CA model might complement electoral accountability.

Elected representatives are accountable not only to the constituents who elected them, but also to the public purposes of the legislative bodies in which they serve—a complexity that has been covered, inadequately, by the distinction between the delegate and trustee roles of representatives (Pitkin 1967; Mansbridge 2003). In addition, there is an accountability that attaches to the institutions themselves: people expect legislatures to do their work with effectiveness and fairness. They will use their votes for individual representatives against the institution if they perceive that it is not performing, or is performing in ways that are unfair or corrupt.

To develop these dimensions of accountability sufficiently to assess the CA, I shall combine a distinction borrowed from theories of deliberative democracy between the *aggregation* and *deliberation* of interests and values (e.g., Habermas 1994), with the observation that the *individual representatives* and the *legislative institution* each define distinct loci of accountability. Although this is not commonly discussed in theories of electoral democracy, individuals should be able to have their interests, values, and positions not only formulated and represented by members of representative bodies, but also formed into decisions by those same bodies, in a way that citizens can recognize the outputs as representing either their aggregated and negotiated interests and

Table 12.1. Forms of Accountability

	Aggregative	Deliberative
Member (input) accountability	A1: Accountability for interest and value represen- tation	A2: Discursive account- ability to constituents
Institutional (output) accountability	A3: Accountability for decision-making (institu- tional capacity to deal with conflict and complexity)	A4: Public accountability (institutional capacity to justify decisions)

values, or a public will (Urbinati 2006). So, for their part, legislative bodies may be accountable for *brokering agreements* among the interests represented by representatives, or for forming *public wills* through deliberation. From the point of view of process, the distinction between the accountability of representatives and the accountability of institutions is roughly parallel to a distinction now common in discussions of the European Union between "input legitimacy" based on democratic inputs and "output legitimacy" based on institutional performance, so we might also speak of "input accountabil- ity" through representatives, and "output accountability" of the institution. Combining these distinctions, we can speak of four kinds of accountability, two of which are attached to individual representatives, and two of which attach to representative institutions, as summarized in Table 12.1.

Thus, (A1) *accountability for interest and value representation* identifies the relationship between the representative and her constituents' interests and values. In this role, the representative articulates her constituents' interests as she best understands them, and votes accordingly. (A2) *Discursive account- ability to constituents* identifies the representative's role in representing po- sitions and arguments both within legislatures, and before constituents. In this role, the representative engages in persuasion, serving as a pivot between the public arguments and positions of constituents, and the processes of ar- gumentative persuasion within legislatures. (A3) *Accountability for decision- making* names the institutional responsibility for aggregating interests sufficiently to produce compromises and brokered agreements, based on inputs of constituents' interests and values as articulated by representatives. This responsibility depends on institutional capacities to not only to manage conflict, but also to manage complex decisions. (A4) *Public accountability* identifies an institutional responsibility as a public forum, for producing agreements that reflect considered public opinion refined through processes of debate. Ideally, all four modes of accountability are present and empowered in democratic institutions, varying, of course, by the nature of the issue, levels of interest definition, mobilization, polarization, and citizen interest and involvement.

So how does the CA measure up in each of these four modes of accountability?

- *A1. Member accountability: accountability for interest and value representation*

Precisely because of the lack of constituency-based electoral accountability, we should expect accountability to the values and interests of defined constituencies to be minimal. But it was not absent: although no *member* of the CA was subject to electoral recall or removal from office, the *product* of the CA was subject to the stricture that it had to be approved not just by a 60 percent super-majority of voters, but also by a majority in 60 percent of the ridings, thus introducing an element of accountability to interests of geographically defined constituencies—evidenced, for example, in the emergence of "the North" as an interest group within the CA (Pearse 2008). Still, the CA was designed in large part to sever these ties: not only were there no formal constituent accountability mechanisms, but ties to specific constituencies were weakened by the exclusion of organized interests and politicians. These exclusions, together with the demographic inclusiveness of the assembly, the internal deliberative structure, and the explicit and narrowly defined mandate from the Legislative Assembly, were all factors that limited members' accountability to specific constituencies, while focusing their attention on the CA and its task.

Member accountability for representing the interests and values of constituents is best achieved by other means of representation. Electoral representation, for example, is responsive to constituencies with the power to elect or remove from office. And for issue-specific representation, civil society groups are likely to be superior, unconstrained as they are by mandates or timetables, and under no particular pressure to deliberate or otherwise compromise the full range of interests and values within society. At the same time, from a normative perspective we should not be too worried about low accountability to specific constituencies, in part because this kind of accountability often trades off against *public* accountability. If one of the aims of the CA design was to avoid the weaknesses of legislative bodies in this respect, then weak accountability to specific constituencies was both necessary and appropriate.

- *A2. Member accountability: discursive accountability*

In the dimension of discursive accountability, the CA fares better. In contrast to representation that reflects the values and interests of specific constituencies, the CA structure provided incentives for members to develop and represent discursive arguments and positions. This particular representative role was not explicitly defined for members. But it was, as it were, "discovered" as members sought to make sense of their tasks and responsibilities (Pearse 2008). During the first stage, members learned about electoral systems. There were no distinct accountability issues in this stage, simply because it was unclear to most members what the impacts of their potential decisions would be. In the second stage, members engaged in public hearings in their ridings, and the CA office collected public submissions. During this stage, members were faced with the question of what, exactly, their representative roles required (Pearse 2008). Some simply saw their task as one of learning from others and then making informed decisions as individuals—much as would a professional public official who holds a "public trust" and acts as a trustee. Others saw their tasks in more complex, "political" ways: they actively organized public hearings and created, as it were, constituencies for electoral reform that they would later represent within Assembly deliberations. In such cases, representation was about discovering the common good through learning and deliberation. Finally—and perhaps most interesting—in the deliberation phase members were careful to create an atmosphere of deliberation. Most chose not to commit to positions, presumably so they would not contribute to the formation of interest blocs within the Assembly. Importantly, the effect was to maintain a representative relationship between the CA and the public considered as a whole rather than as an aggregate of constituencies. The only apparent compromise with a partial constituency involved the rural areas of BC—"the North"—for whom the STV recommendation was altered to provide for closer geographical proximity of elected members of the legislative assembly.

- *A3. Institutional accountability: delivering the decision*

In what ways was the CA accountable as an *institution* responsible for delivering a specific outcome? From a legal perspective, this dimension of accountability is quite clear. The legislation that created the CA provided it with a specific performance mandate: to return to the people of BC a judgment about the suitability of the current electoral system, and, if necessary, a proposal for change. Had the CA not met this mandate, presumably its accountability to the legislature would have been breached. In this sense, the CA *as a body* was accountable to the Legislative Assembly for a specific performance, within a specific period of time. Behind this form of accountability, however, is the question of institutional capacity to deliver on a formal mandate. Of particular relevance to representative political institutions are their capacities to handle *conflict* and *complexity*, which are necessary conditions of accountability.

With respect to *conflict*, voluntary organizations tend to externalize conflict through exit. In contrast, involuntary organizations must develop ways and means of handling the conflict that cannot be externalized (Warren 2001: 96–109). The CA falls on the "involuntary" side of the spectrum, in the sense that although members chose to serve, they did not choose to be grouped with others who were chosen, and those others represented a broad range of interests and values in the province. For this reason, as its first agenda item the CA developed rules of conflict management, which included norms of civility and rules of discourse. No doubt possible and legitimate conflicts were dampened by these rules (Lang 2008). Nonetheless, the CA managed conflict sufficiently to produce a near-consensus decision on schedule.

With respect to complexity, the CA's mandate was not as complex as, say, most areas of health care policy. But neither was it simple, as the design of electoral systems has aspects that are relatively technical. The fact that the CA was structured with a learning period was crucial to its ability to render a decision, and, indeed, the decision was a learned and sophisticated one. Most members transformed themselves from lay citizens with little knowledge of electoral systems into experts over a period of several months, a process assisted by the generous staffing of the CA office (Pearse 2008; Blais et al. 2008).

That the CA was designed to have high capacities to handle conflict and complexity was no doubt essential to the fact that it was able to deliver its product—a referendum item—on time and within budget, replete with reports and other materials to showcase the process and back up its reasoning. It is not clear that these capacities would translate into other issue areas: the CA benefited from the fact that few members had specific preferences about electoral reform prior to serving in the CA. No doubt matters would have been different with a higher-profile, more volatile issue such as health care. At the same time, experiments with citizens' juries and deliberative polling suggest that citizen representatives might be constituted in ways that may be successful in these kinds of arenas as well (Fishkin 1995; Smith and Wales 2000).

- *A4. Institutional accountability: forming the public will*

Perhaps the highest threshold for accountability is "public" in nature: does the output of the representative body represent a formation of the public will? Was the CA able to *give a public account* of its reasoning and decisions? Did it seek to motivate the public by providing reasons and justifications?

From one perspective, the CA was, perhaps, not successful in forming a public will: by the time of the referendum, only slightly more than half of the BC electorate was aware of the CA and its work, leading to an important gap between the mini-public of the CA, and the public at large (Cutler et al. 2008). From the perspective of institutional design, however, the CA seemed optimally structured for public accountability. Its mandate was to provide an assessment and proposal in the interests of "the people of BC," as was certainly appropriate for a fundamental issue of constitutional change. And the members sought to represent the justifications for the collective decision of the CA to the people of BC. The motivations, capacities, and incentives for public accountability were part of the CA design. With respect to motivations, two design factors were especially important: organized interests were screened out, while self-selection into the pool of potential CA members biased the assembly toward public-spirited individuals (Warren and Pearse 2008: Introduction). These factors created a strong likelihood that members of the assembly would understand themselves as accountable to the people of BC as a whole rather than to particular constituencies.

From the perspective of the CA's capacities for public accountability, broad inclusions of interests and values combined with a deliberative structure provided necessary material and opportunity for discerning the public interest. In addition, the CA sought several forms of public input, including public hearings and Internet submissions. These circumstances meant that members of the CA had to create representative roles for themselves that would bridge, as it were, input from particular constituencies with the common good. But because of the lack of any particular constituency-based accountability mechanisms, the members were free to translate particular representations into a common position. Viewed in this way, the lack of formal, constituency-based accountability may be a condition of public accountability (see, e.g., Mansbridge 2004).

A further design factor provided a powerful incentive for the public orientation of the CA: the body did not have power over the *outcome*, but rather over the *agenda*. As a body, the CA naturally developed a strategic interest in their (close to consensus) recommendation. But because the CA did not have power over the outcome, its sole means of influence was to explain and justify its proposal to the public—that is, engage in discursive public will-formation. In this way, the design of the process introduced a relationship of accountability between the CA and the public, based on public argumentation and justification. This relationship between the mini-public of the CA and the BC public was not well supported in the period before the referendum. It is precisely this relationship that the province funded in the period before the second referendum in 2009. But the government decided to support public education about the referendum by funding "yes" and "no" campaigns. The result, however, was a highly adversarial public debate that produced little in the way of new public knowledge. Instead, the campaigns used their budgets to mostly to increase distrust of the other side. The CA itself had no presence in the debates—it had been dissolved in 2004. Few remembered its role, and so it would be hard to judge that it played any representative function at all in this referendum, a fact that may have figured in the fall of the "yes" vote from over 57 percent in 2005 to 39 percent this time around (Carty et al. 2009).

But if we limit our assessment to the CA itself and referendum that followed right after it was dissolved, we can say that with respect to democratic accountability, the combination of initial constitution, deliberative structure, and mission produced a kind of citizen representative with weak accountability of members to individual constituents, but strong discursive accountability of members to the public, as well as strong

institutional accountability for forming and delivering a publicly justifi-
able decision.

Assessing the CA Model in the Ecology
of Representative Institutions

The theoretical frame of *citizen representative*, I am arguing, highlights the
novelty of the CA, which was designed at the outset as a new kind of *representative* institution focused on electoral reform, much as if it was a special
single-issue legislature constituted by lay citizens. Considered as a representative institution, should it be put to other uses? This question is, in part,
now answered: the CA model can carry out some kinds of democratic representation, and it may even carry these out better than other kinds of institutions. Yet because the CA model is a nonelected, purpose-built institution, it
cannot cover all the representative requirements of a democratic system. But
then neither can any other institution. So we should think about the CA as a
supplementary form of representation, perhaps aimed a particular kinds of
intractable public problems, or problems for which electoral institutions and
other kinds of citizen venues do not generate legitimacy sufficient to solutions (Lang and Warren 2012). This claim, however, depends on a more systematic comparison of the CA model to other representative venues, in terms
of which we could identify its niche role in democratic systems.

While a full comparison is beyond the scope of this chapter, Table 12.2 is
indicative of what a comparison might look like. The table combines a set of
structural and functional distinctions across the top, with normative criteria of representation in the left-hand column. The theoretical claim is that
the structural and functional distinctions across the top have an impact on
the kind of representative functions a venue might serve within a democratic system. The cells represent the expectations, with a summary reason
for the expectation.

The most obvious distinction is between bodies that are elected and regularized, and bodies and venues that serve as citizen representatives. Within
the class of citizen representatives, we can distinguish between formal and
informal venues. *Formal* representatives are constituted by governments,
and serve as complements or supplements to the formal political, administrative, and judicial systems. *Informal* representatives are nongovernment,
including NGOs, associations, and devices such as deliberative polls. The

importance of this distinction is that, on average, formal venues will be more successful at integrating public interests and opinion into policy, just because they are designed for particular kinds of governmental purposes. But informal venues will be more sensitive to emerging issues and existing exclusions and injustices, just because they do not need to reflect government agendas or institutional constraints.

In addition, we should distinguish between *empowered* and *non-empowered* venues. Empowered venues, such as legal juries and the CA, are more immediately consequential, and for this reason must be more carefully designed to ensure democratic authorization and inclusion. Venues that are not empowered—and this includes most citizen representative bodies and venues—are freer to reflect particular interests, as well as to engage in broader public deliberation and debate, because they are less constrained by the constraints of agendas, timetables, and processes.

Finally, it is important to distinguish *deliberative* from *aggregative* venues. Aggregative venues such as public hearings and surveys collect existing preferences. Deliberative venues, such as juries and deliberative polls, form, inform and solidify preferences, a condition for producing stable and legitimate collective decisions.

We can then ask about the representative capacities of each kind of venue, using the dimensions of accountability applied to the CA in the discussion above, and make some rough judgments as to what we might expect of each kind. The judgments in the table are only indicative—their purpose is only to suggest that we understand the CA as a potential part of the ecology of democratic institutions, and then judge its contributions to democratic representation in terms of its relative strengths and weakness. Nonetheless, by combining a number of expectations about representative functions into a single table, it is easy to see that the CA model ranks higher on most dimensions than other forms of representation, while ranking much lower in one dimension. The CA form is particularly weak in constituency accountability, which implies that it should be externally constituted by bodies that are inherently responsive to emerging issues—legislatures under pressure from civil society groups, for example. But importantly, once constituted, the CA form is likely to have representative strengths where legislatures, advisory groups, and civil society groups are weak—or so the expectations represented in Table 12.2 would suggest.

In sum, if the judgments in Table 12.2 are credible, then we should see the CA is a uniquely powerful form of democratic representation. But we

Table 12.2. Assessing Citizens' Assembly Model in Ecology of Representative Institutions

Criteria of democratic representation	Forms of representation					
		Citizen representatives				
	Elected representative bodies	Formal empowered	Formal advisory		Informal (nongovernmental bodies)	
	Deliberative	Deliberative	Deliberative	Aggregative	Deliberative	Aggregative
	Elected legislatures, councils, boards	Citizens' Assembly, legal juries	Citizen juries, advisory councils, stakeholder meetings	Public hearings, public submissions, citizen surveys	Deliberative polling, deliberative forums	Single issue advocacy, interest group brokering
Authorization	High (voting)	High (explicit authorization procedures)	Mixed (explicit authorization; often vague directives for representation)	Low (no authorization procedures)	Mixed to Low (ambiguous or "market" authorization)	Low ("market-style" authorization)
Egalitarian inclusiveness	Mixed to Low (universal franchise limited by SMP majoritarianism and responsiveness to organized interests)	High (selection often random, subject to screens)	Mixed to Low (selection by elites and self-selection does not assure inclusiveness)	Mixed (low where self-selection produces exclusion, high for random sampling)	High (selection often random, subject to screens)	Low (self-selection produces exclusion)

Member accountability (interests)	Mixed (responsive to organized interests)	Low (externally-fixed agendas)	Mixed to Low (externally-fixed agendas)	High (low institutional threshold for voice)	Mixed (lay sensitivities limited by elite agendas)	High (low institutional threshold for voice)
Member accountability (discursive)	Mixed (responsiveness to organized interest competes with public justifications)	High (deliberative influences dominate decision processes)	High (deliberative influences dominate decision processes)	Low (expressions of revealed preferences rather than reasons)	High (deliberative influences dominate process)	Mixed (advocacy stimulates public debate)
Institutional accountability (capacity to deliver decision)	High (specialized for conflict; handles complexity though internal divisions of labour)	Mixed to High (rules for interaction limit conflict; high capacity to deal with complexity though learning)	Mixed to High (rules for interaction limit conflict; high capacity to deal with complexity though learning)	Low (no mechanisms for deliberating conflicting positions; no context or incentives for learning)	Mixed to High (rules for interaction limit conflict; high capacity to deal with complexity though learning)	Low (conflict leads to exit; no context or incentives for learning or deliberation)
Institutional accountability (public will-formation)	Mixed (deliberative structure limited by responsive to organized interests and electoral exigencies)	High (deliberative structure without organized interests)	High (deliberative structure)	Low (expression of segmented and partial preferences)	High (deliberative structures responsive to common goods)	Mixed (advocacy stimulates public debate)

should also understand the CA model as a potential supplement to, rather than replacement for, other democratic institutions and practices within a broader ecology of democratic institutions and practices.

References

Abelson, Julia and John Eyles. 2002. "Public Participation and Citizen Governance in the Canadian Health System." Commission on the Future of Health Care in Canada, Discussion Paper 7.

American National Election Studies. 2007. *The ANES Guide to Public Opinion and Electoral Behavior*. Ann Arbor: University of Michigan Center for Political Studies. www.electionstudies.org. Accessed February 7, 2007.

Blais, Andre, R. Kenneth Carty, and Patrick Fournier. 2008. "Do Citizens' Assemblies Make Reasoned Choices?" In *Designing Deliberative Democracy: The British Columbia Citizens' Assembly*, ed. Mark E. Warren and Hilary Pearse. Cambridge: Cambridge University Press. 127–44.

Brown, Mark B. 2006. "Citizen Panels and the Concept of Representation." *Journal of Political Philosophy*, 14 (2): 203–29.

Cain, Bruce, Russell Dalton, and Susan Scarrow. 2003. "Democratic Publics and Democratic Institutions." In *Democracy Transformed? Expanding Political Opportunities in Advanced Industrial Democracies*, ed. Bruce Cain, Russell Dalton, and Susan Scarrow. Oxford: Oxford University Press. 251–75.

Carty, R. Kenneth, Fred Cutler, and Patrick Fournier. 2009. "Who Killed BC-STV?" *The Tyee*, July 8.

Cutler, Fred, Richard Johnston, R. Kenneth Carty, Andre Blais, and Patrick Fournier. 2008. "Deliberation, Information, and Trust: the British Columbia Citizens' Assembly as Agenda Setter." In *Designing Deliberative Democracy: The British Columbia Citizens' Assembly*, ed. Mark E. Warren and Hilary Pearse. Cambridge: Cambridge University Press. 166–91.

Dalton, Russell. 2004. *Democratic Challenges, Democratic Choices: The Erosion of Political Support in the Advanced Industrial Democracies*. Oxford: Oxford University Press.

Dzur, Albert. 2012. *Punishment, Participatory Democracy, and the Jury*. Oxford: Oxford University Press.

Fiorino, Daniel J. 1990. "Citizen Participation and Environmental Risk: A Survey of Institutional Mechanisms." *Science, Technology, and Human Values* 15: 226–43.

Fisher, Samuel and Rebekah Herrick. 2003. "Citizen Legislators in the Modern U.S. House of Representatives." Presented at Midwest Political Science Association, Chicago, April 2–6.

Fishkin, James. 1995. *The Voice of the People: Public Opinion and Democracy*. New Haven, Conn.: Yale University Press.

Fournier, Patrick, Henk van der Kolk, R. Kenneth Carty, Andre Blais, and Jonathan Rose. 2011. *When Citizens Decide: Lessons from Citizen Assemblies on Electoral Reform*. Oxford: Oxford University Press.

Fung, Archon 2006a. "Democratizing the Policy Process." In *Oxford Handbook of Public Policy*, ed. Robert Goodin, Michael Moran, and Martin Rein. Oxford: Oxford University Press. 669–85.

———. 2006b. "Varieties of Participation in Complex Governance." *Public Administration Review* 66 (1): 66–75.

Gibson, Gordon. 2002. *Report on the Constitution of the Citizens' Assembly on Electoral Reform*. Submitted to Hon. P. Geoffrey Plant, Attorney General of British Columbia, December 23, 2002.

Habermas, Jürgen. 1994. "Three Normative Models of Democracy." *Constellations*: 1: 1–10.

Hanley, Nick, Wendy Kenyon, and Ceara Nevin. 2001. "Citizens' Juries: An Aid to Environmental Valuation?" *Environmental Planning C: Government and Policy* 19: 557–66.

Irvin, Renee, and John Stansbury, 2004. "Citizen Participation in Decision Making: Is It Worth the Effort?" *Public Administration Review* 64 (1): 55–65.

James, Michael Rabinder. 2008. "Descriptive Representation in the British Columbia Citizens' Assembly." In. *Designing Deliberative Democracy: The British Columbia Citizens' Assembly*, ed. Mark E. Warren and Hilary Pearse. Cambridge: Cambridge University Press. 106–26.

Lang, Amy. 2008. "Agenda Setting in Deliberative Forums: Expert Influence and Citizen Autonomy in the British Columbia Citizens' Assembly." In *Designing Deliberative Democracy: The British Columbia Citizens' Assembly*, ed. Mark E. Warren and Hilary Pearse. Cambridge: Cambridge University Press. 85–105.

Lang, Amy, and Mark E. Warren. 2012. "Supplementary Democracy? Democratic Deficits and Citizens' Assemblies." In *Imperfect Democracies*, ed. Patti Lenard and Richard Simeon. Vancouver: University of British Columbia Press. 291–314.

Lenaghan, Jo. 1999. "Involving the Public in Rationing Decisions. The Experience of Citizens Juries." *Health Policy* 49: 45–61.

Mansbridge, Jane. 1980. *Beyond Adversary Democracy*. Chicago: University of Chicago Press.

———. 2003. "Rethinking Representation." *American Political Science Review* 97 (4): 515–28

———. 2004. "Representation Revisited: An Introduction to the Case Against Electoral Accountability." *Democracy and Society* 2 (1): 1, 12–13.

Montanaro, Laura. 2012. "The Democratic Legitimacy of Self-Appointed Representatives." *Journal of Politics* 74 (4): 1094–1107.

Norris, Pippa, ed. 1999. *Critical Citizens: Global Support for Democratic Government*. Oxford: Oxford University Press.

——. 2011. *Democratic Deficit: Critical Citizens Revisited*. Cambridge: Cambridge University Press.

Parkinson, John. 2003. "Hearing Voices: Negotiating Representation Claims in Public Deliberation." European Consortium for Political Research: Edinburgh Joint Sessions.

Pearse, Hilary. 2008. "Institutional Design and Citizen Deliberation." In *Designing Deliberative Democracy: The British Columbia Citizens' Assembly*, ed. Mark E. Warren and Hilary Pearse. Cambridge: Cambridge University Press. 70–84.

Pitkin, Hanna. 1967. *The Concept of Representation*. Berkeley: University of California Press.

Rehfeld, Andrew. 2005. *The Concept of Constituency*. Cambridge: Cambridge University Press.

Rosanvallon, Pierre. 2011. *Democratic Legitimacy: Impartiality, Reflexivity, Proximity*. Trans. Arthur Goldhammer. Princeton, N.J.: Princeton University Press.

Rowe, Gene, and Lynn J. Frewer. 2000. "Public Participation Methods: A Framework for Evaluation." *Science, Technology, and Human Values* 25: 3–29.

Saward, Michael. 2010. *The Representative Claim*. Oxford: Oxford University Press.

Smith, Graham and Corinne Wales. 2000. "Citizens' Juries and Deliberative Democracy." *Political Studies* 48: 51–65.

Stephan, Mark. 2004. "Citizens as Representatives: Bridging the Democratic Theory Divides." *Politics and Policy* 32 (1): 118–35.

Thompson, Dennis F. 2008. "Who Should Govern Who Governs? The Role of Citizens in Reforming the Electoral System." In *Designing Deliberative Democracy: The British Columbia Citizens' Assembly*, ed. Mark E. Warren and Hilary Pearse. Cambridge: Cambridge University Press. 20–49.

Urbinati, Nadia. 2006. *Representative Democracy: Principles and Genealogy*. Chicago: University of Chicago Press.

Verba, Sidney, Kay Schlozman, and Henry Brady. 1995. *Voice and Equality: Civic Volunteerism in American Politics*. Cambridge, Mass.: Harvard University Press.

Ward, Hugh, Aletta Norval, Todd Landman, and Jules Pretty. 2003. "Open Citizens' Juries and the Politics of Sustainability." *Political Studies* 51: 282–99.

Warren, Mark E. 2001. *Democracy and Association*. Princeton, N.J.: Princeton University Press.

——. 2003. "A Second Transformation of Democracy?" In *New Forms of Democracy? The Reform and Transformation of Democratic Institutions*, ed. Bruce Cain, Russell Dalton, and Susan Scarrow. Oxford: Oxford University Press, 2004. 223–49.

——. 2009. "Governance-Driven Democratization." *Critical Policy Analysis* 3 (1): 3–13.

Warren, Mark E., and Dario Castliglione. 2004. "The Transformation of Democratic Representation." *Democracy and Society* 2 (1): 5, 20–22.

Warren, Mark E., and Hilary Pearse, eds. 2008. *Designing Deliberative Democracy: The British Columbia Citizens' Assembly*. Cambridge: Cambridge University Press.

NOTES

Chapter 1. Evaluating U.S. Electoral Institutions in Comparative Perspective

I thank Carol Galais for her research assistance and Jack Nagel and Rogers Smith for extremely useful comments.

1. I focus here entirely on *electoral* institutions and leave aside the choice of a presidential rather than a parliamentary system. The predominant view among political scientists is that parliamentary democracies are "superior" (see Linz 1990).

2. This is clearly not the only reason. As important is the great difficulty of amending the Constitution and overcoming multiple veto points in the decision-making process.

Chapter 2. Are American Elections Sufficiently Democratic?

1. This is the question posed to the speakers at the public forum at the National Constitution Center in September 2008 as part of the Penn Program on Democracy, Citizenship, and Constitutionalism. To their credit, none of the participants took the question as an opportunity to call for more or fewer *Democratic* elections. I am grateful for the helpful comments and criticisms raised at the forum and for the suggestions later provided by the reviewers of the manuscript.

Chapter 3. Barriers to Voting in the Twenty-First Century

This chapter draws extensively on Chapter 9, "The Story Unfinished," in Alexander Keyssar, *The Right to Vote: The Contested History of Democracy in the United States*, rev. ed. (New York: Basic Books, 2009), 258–94; reprinted by permission.

1. *Boston Globe*, 2 August 1997; *Boston Herald*, August 3, 1997.

2. *Boston Herald*, 3 August 1997; *Boston Globe*, August 13, 1997, July 30, 1998, June 29, October 29, 2000; *Durham (N.C.) Herald-Sun*, September 10, 2000; Secretary of the Commonwealth of Massachusetts, "Massachusetts Statewide Ballot Measures: 1919–2004," 53. http://www.sec.state.ma.us/ELE/elebalm/balmidx.htm.

3. An estimated 960,000 Floridians were barred from voting in the 2004 election (Sentencing Project 2011).

4. In 2009, for example, the State of Washington eliminated the requirement that all fines and fees be paid before voting rights are restored.

5. Ibid.

6. Manza and Uggen 2006: 286–87; Sentencing Project 2008"; news release, June 20, 2008, http://www.sentencingproject.org/NewsDetails.aspx?Ne; *Sarasota Herald-Tribune*, April 6, 2007; *Baltimore Sun*, April 25, 2007; *St. Petersburg Times*, September 27, 2007; Ray Henry, *Associated Press* (Providence, R.I.), November 8, 2006; *Lexington Herald-Leader*, February 6, March 4, 2008; see also the compilation by the ACLU 2007; ACLU, "Tennessee Legislature Simplifies Voting Restoration for Ex-Felons," press release, May 17, 2006. For the most complete account of legal changes in the states through 2006, see King 2006. The ACLU of Florida has also published and posted detailed accounts of developments in that state.

7. Manza and Uggen 2006: 287; *Hattiesburg American*, March 4, 2008; Wood 2009: 5, 14–15; *New York Times*, July 22, 2004; *USA Today*, 1 June 2006; Sentencing Project, "Disenfranchisement News," January 3, 2008; *Wall Street Journal*, March 31, 2008.

8. Manza and Uggen, 2006: 14; *Sarasota Herald-Tribune*, April 6, 2007; *Chattanooga Times Free Press*, October 2, 2006; Sentencing Project, News Update, April 18, 2008; *Washington Times*, February 15, 2006; *New York Times*, July 11, 2004.

9. On September 26, 2008, Senator Russ Feingold and Representative John Conyers introduced the Democracy Restoration Act of 2008 (S.3640, H.R. 7136), to restore the franchise to those released from prison. *Charleston Gazette*, May 27, 2008. Regarding legal challenges, particularly those claiming that felon disfranchisement violated the Voting Rights Act, see Manza and Uggen 2006: 225–27. In the state of Washington, a suit was filed challenging the requirement that ex-felons remain disfranchised until they had paid off all their legal financial obligations. The claim was rebuffed by the Washington Supreme Court. *Madison v. Washington*, 78598-8 (Washington Supreme Court 2007).

10. Wood 2009: 3; as the map on page 3 makes clear, the states with the most exclusionary provisions tended to be in the South. Data regarding European practices are presented on p. 5. In April 2008, the House of Representatives of Kentucky (one of the two states that retained lifetime disfranchisement) voted to restore the rights of some ex-felons. *Louisville Courier-Journal*, April 21, 2008. In California, people in jail awaiting trial are permitted to vote. *San Jose Mercury-News*, February 4, 2008, online edition.

11. Pew Center on the States 2008: 5–9; *New York Times*, February 29, April 23, 2008; *Washington Post*, June 12, 2008; UN Committee on the Elimination of Racial Discrimination, 72nd sess., Geneva, February 18–March 7, 2008, http://www2.ohchr .org/english/bodies/cerd/docs/co/CERD-C-USA-CO-6.pdf. Wood 2009: 5 indicates that the UN Human Rights Committee in 2006 had taken a similar step. The 5.3 mil-

lion figure, now widely cited, is an estimate for 2006 developed by Manza and Uggen 2006: 94. According to the Sentencing Project (December 27, 2007), roughly 630,000 persons had regained their voting rights as a result of the legal changes in 16 states over the preceding ten years.

12. *New York Times*, July 10, 2004; Wood 2009: 13–14.

13. *New York Times*, June 10, August 16, 20, September 30, October 7, 2004, October 27, 2006; National Commission on the Voting Rights Act 2006: 11, 12, 44–50; Overton 2006: 149–50, 160; *Louisville Courier-Journal*, July 30, 2004; *Detroit Free Press*, July 16, 2004; *Associated Press*, June 10, July 21, 2004; *Washington Post*, August 26, 2004 (See also McDonald 2002; Miller 2008). Regarding Native American voting issues in general during this period, see McCool, Olson, and Robinson 2007.

14. *New York Times*, April 28, June 13, 2008; *Washington Post*, October 6, 2004; *Los Angeles Times*, March 29, 2007. Florida's 2006 law was prompted by widely circulated reports that the community organization ACORN had engaged in multiple acts of fraud while conducting a registration drive in the state, including failure to turn in registration forms filled out by Republicans. Subsequent litigation suggested that these acts of fraud had not occurred. Minnite, "The Politics of Voter Fraud," 24.

15. Conyers 2005: 3–4, 17–34, 37–43; Kennedy 2006; Hitchens 2005: 214. These investigations also recount details of irregularities with the state's voting machines and with its preliminary recount (the latter of which led to jail sentences for two officials). Most studies of the irregularities in Ohio, however, concluded that they were not on a scale large enough to have affected the outcome of the election (Brady et al. 2004; Alvarez et al. 2005).

16. An extensive list of Republican charges regarding Democratic voter suppression is contained in a report from the American Center for Voting Rights Legislative Fund, ACVR 2005: see both the letter of introduction and the section "Charges of Voter Intimidation and Suppression Made Against Democratic Supporters." The ACVR, as noted below, was the creation of Republican activists. Both the organization and its website were dismantled in 2007. The archival address for this report is http://www.foxnews.com/projects/pdf/Vote_Fraud_Intimidation_Suppression_2004_Pres_Election_v2.pdf. More information about ACVR can be found on the website of one of its adversaries, Brad Friedman; see http://www.bradblog.com/?page_id=4418.

17. Fund 2008: 41–110; Hearne 2005; *New York Times*, April 11, 2007. The outcome of the Miami election had been reversed, months after the election, when it was determined that numerous absentee ballots were fraudulent. The issues in Missouri included fraudulent registrations, felon voting, and the necessity of keeping the polls open beyond normal hours.

18. See, for examples: Fund 2008; Overton 2006; ACVR 2005; and a study sponsored by Demos, Minnite and Callahan 2003. In March 2007, Minnite published a follow-up study with *Project Vote* as "The Politics of Voter Fraud," and in December 2007 she then further updated her 2003 report for *Demos* under a new title "An Analysis of Voter Fraud in the U.S."

19. *New York Times*, April 11, 2007; Lester 2006; "Election Assistance Commission's Voter Fraud Report," *USFed News*, December 13, 2006; *Washington Post*, June 22, 2007; Wang 2007; U.S. EAC2006; Murray 2007a, b; "Statement by Commissioner Gracia Hillman U.S. EAC Regarding Release of Voter Fraud Consultant Report," *States News Service*, April 16, 2007; a detailed critique of the EAC report can be found in Neas 2006. Serebrov, in an email to an EAC staff member in October 2006, claimed that he and Wang had "worked hard to produce a correct, accurate, and truthful report. . . . Neither one of us was willing to conform results for political expediency." *New York Times*, April 11, 2007. See also Hebert 2008.

20. Wang 2007 wrote that there was no "smoking gun showing political motives in the handling of the draft." The inspector general's report was prompted both by news articles and by expressions of concern by congressional committees. Submitted in March 2008, the text of the report contained confusing, potentially contradictory statements. It concluded that there was "no evidence to support allegations that the changes were made to the report due to improper reasons or political motivations." At the same time, it cited interviews with commissioners and staffers suggesting that political pressure was applied to keep the draft report from being released. U.S. EAC, Office of Inspector General 2008. 1, 13–16.

21. *New York Times*, April 11, 2007; Minnite, "Analysis of Voter Fraud," 9.

22. Hearne 2005; ACVR 2005: 1. Another key figure in the ACVR was Jim Dyke, who had worked for the Republican National Committee and later was employed by Vice President Cheney. Brian Lunde, a board member of the ACVR, was officially a Democrat and had co-chaired Democrats for Bush in 2004. *The Brad Blog*, March 15, 2007, http://www.bradblog.com/?p=1708.

23. National Public Radio, *Morning Edition*, June 6, 2007; "ACVR Praises Carter-Baker Commission Report," ACVR, Press Release, September 22, 2005; Thor Hearne to John Tanner, Chief, Voting Rights Section, Department of Justice, April 20, 2006; Hasen 2007; Fitrakis 2007; *Pittsburgh Tribune-Review*, August 8, 2005. For numerous articles regarding the ACVR, penned by Brad Friedman, a blogger Hearne later blamed for the demise of the organization, see *The Brad Blog*, http://www.bradblog.com/?page _id=4418. Refutations of some of the ACVR's fraud allegations can be found in Minnite, "The Politics of Voter Fraud," 17, 20, 23.

24. *New York Times*, March 14, 16, 18, 29, April 12, 20 , 2007; *Washington Post*, March 13, 26, 30, March, April 19, May 11, 14, 2007; Rich 2007; *Boston Globe*, May 6, 2007; Isikoff 2007; Tumulty and Calabresi 2007; *Seattle Times*, May 17, 2007; *Baltimore Chronicle and Sentinel*, March 10, 2008. Seven of the federal prosecutors were fired on December 7, 2006; Graves had resigned, under pressure, in March 2006. In all the cases mentioned, it is known that the White House—and particularly Rove's office—communicated its displeasure to the Justice Department. One of the other targeted prosecutors was Tom Heffelfinger of Minnesota who happened to resign before the firings were put into effect: he had resisted efforts to prohibit Native Americans from using tribal ID documents to vote when they were not on reservations. See

Los Angeles Times, May 31, 2007 and *Houston Chronicle*, June 3, 2007. Evidence that Native American voting issues were involved in several of the firings is presented in Lee 2007.

25. Leopold 2008a; Gordon 2007b; Palazzolo 2007; *Washington Post*, August 28, 2007; *New York Times*, March 30, August 27, 28 , 2007; Leopold 2008b. Gonzales may have committed perjury, in testimony to Congress, as he attempted to conceal his own role and the role of the White House in the firings; his own chief of staff, D. Kyle Sampson, testified (after resigning) that Gonzales' testimony had been inaccurate.

26. *New York Times*, April 12, 2007; *Christian Science Monitor*, April 5, 2007; Toobin 2004.

27. Gordon 2007b; Minnite, "The Politics of Voter Fraud," 3–4, 8–9, 12–13, 17–36. As Minnite observes, there are no reliable state or national statistics on vote fraud. See also Minnite and Callahan 2003: 39–49.

28. Fund, 2008: 136–38; ACVR 2006; Epps 2008. Mark Hearne argued: "photo ID is the kind of confidence-building measure that is warranted in light of past fraud." *Washington Post*, November 3, 2006. The official name of the Commission was the Carter-Baker Commission on Federal Election Reform. Several members of the commission dissented vigorously from this recommendation. Carter-Bacon Commission 2005: 18–21, 80, 88–90.

29. Fund 2008: 138; Overton 2006: 155; Epps 2007; Hasen 2007; Suillinger 2008; cf. *Lawrence (Massachusetts) Eagle-Tribune*, June 5, 2008; according to senator Dianne Feinstein, "no federal cases of impersonation voter fraud" had been successfully prosecuted between 2002 and spring 2008. "Opening Remarks of Senator Feinstein," Senate Rules and Administration Committee Hearing, March 12, 2008.

30. Overton 2006: 152–55; "Could a Photo ID Law Hurt Representation at Polls?" National Public Radio, September 20, 2006, 9 A.M.; *New York Times*, September 24, 2007; Wang 2005. Disabled voters constituted another group that would be disproportionately affected by ID laws.

31. For a summary of such laws, see National Conference of State Legislatures 2007, 2008. "Requirements for Voter Identification" is updated periodically, here based on February 1, 2007, and January 9, 2008. An increasing number of states requested photo ID but permitted other forms of identification. All states offered the possibility of casting provisional ballots for those without ID, but Indiana and Georgia required voters to return within a few days and present photo IDs to officials if their provisional ballots were to be counted. For a summary of state laws and initiatives as of January 2008, see Testimony of Wendy R. Weiser before the Senate Special Subcommittee on Aging, "Older Voters: Opportunities and Challenges for the 2008 Election," 110th Cong., 2nd Sess., January 31, 2008 (available also from Brennan Center for Justice at NYU), 2–3.

32. National Conference of State Legislatures 2008: 1–2; *USA Today*, January 24, 2007; *Los Angeles Times*, September 12, 2006; *Albuquerque Journal*, October 5, 28, 2005; February 14, 2007; *Washington Post*, October 21, 2006; *Arizona Capital Times*,

August 31, 2007; Gordon 2007a; Epps 2007: 2–3. Regarding Georgia's law, see *New York Times*, July 20, 2005, January 25, July 8, 2006; *Washington Post*, October 28, 2005, September 20, 2006; ACLU Press Release, "Voting Rights Advocates Challenge Georgia Photo ID Law," September 19, 2005; McCaffrey 2007; Haines 2007; *Jacksonville Florida Times Union*, September 7, 2007; *Atlanta Constitution*, September 7, 2007. According to the *Washington Post*, November 17, 2005, 4 of 5 career officials in the Justice Department recommended against preclearing the Georgia law, but they were overruled by political appointees. Revealing elements of the history of Georgia's law can be found in Wang 2006.

33. *New York Times*, September 26, 27, 2007, January 7, 2008; Toobin 2008: 28.

34. *Crawford v. Marion County Election Bd.*, 553 U.S. (2008), Stevens Opinion 11, 12, 15, 17, 18; Souter Dissent 3, 7, 30. Justice Stephen Breyer wrote a separate dissent. Antonin Scalia, Clarence Thomas, and Samuel A. Alito, Jr., concurred with the decision while maintaining that there was no reason for the court to even assess the impact of the law on any individual voters because it was "a generally applicable, nondiscriminatory voting regulation." *New York Times*, *Washington Post*, *Los Angeles Times*, all April 29, 2008.

35. By spring 2012, 30 states had voter ID requirements in place. Half these laws demanded photo ID. For details and current information, see National Conferences of Legislatures 2012: May 28.

36. *Chicago Tribune*, April 28, 2008; *New York Times*, April 29, May 12, 13, 17, 2008; *KTAR.com*, "Arizona to Seek Dismissal of Challenge to Voter ID Law," May 27, 2008; "New Lawsuit Filed Challenging Voter ID Law," *Indianapolis Associated Press State and Local Wire*, June 20, 2008; *Clarionledger.com* (Mississippi),"Court Overturns Voter ID Ruling," May 29, 2008; *Atlanta Journal Constitution*; "Republicans Plan to Push for New Voter ID Law in Alabama," *Associated Press State and Local Wire*; *San Jose (California) Mercury News*; *St. Louis Post-Dispatch*; *Albuquerque Journal*; *Houston Chronicle*, all April 29, 2008. In 2006, Republicans in Congress had also sponsored the Federal Election Integrity Act of 2006, which would have imposed a national requirement for photo ID as well as proof of citizenship to register to vote. Efforts to pass such a law were stalled by the election of Democratic majorities in November 2006. *Deseret Morning News* (Salt Lake City), September 20, 2006; U.S. House, Federal Election Integrity Act of 2006 (H.R. 4844), 109th Cong., 2nd sess. A website tracking state bills requiring proof of citizenship to register is maintained by the Brennan Center for Justice at NYU; http://www.brennancenter.org/content/resource /proof_of_citizenship_requirements_chart_of_state_legislation/.

37. National Conferences of State Legislatures, "Voter Identification Requirements" (2012).

38. The findings of the early rounds of scholarship regarding the impact of ID requirements are not uniform, but most do find some impact on turnout, particularly the turnout of the less educated and less well off (and particularly with stricter ID requirements). A valuable summary of the literature (as well as a good listing of research

studies) is contained in Alvarez, Bailey, and Katz 2008. See also Logan and Darrah 2008 and Mulhausen and Sikich 2007. Regarding the nuns in Indiana, see *South Bend (Indiana) Tribune*, May 7, 2008.

Chapter 4. Uneven Democracy: Turnout, Minority Interests, and Local Government Spending

1. Cross-national comparisons have, however, found that turnout can significantly affect the prospects of left-leaning or workers' parties (Pacek and Radcliff 1995). It is also clear that at times in American history, the disenfranchisement of groups like African Americans has led to highly discriminatory policies (Parker 1990).

2. These results have not gone undisputed. Other research has found either that class bias in turnout at the state level has no effect on policy or that increases in minority voter turnout actually lead to white backlash and less spending on minority-preferred outcomes (Radcliff and Saiz 1995).

3. Several urban scholars do, however, note the importance of group mobilization for political incorporation (Dahl 1961; Browning, Marshall, and Tabb 1984). This is a central theme in accounts of the civil rights movement (Parker 1990).

4. The notion that business interests and other privileged groups regularly seek greater developmental spending is widely supported in the urban politics literature (Logan and Molotch 1987).

5. What is less clear in this pluralist model is whether governmental actors need to respond to the preferences of all residents or can safely listen only to voters. Dahl (1961) and others argue that because of the threat of voting, all interests, whether active or not, are likely to be considered in the decision-making process. However, one could certainly argue, as we have done, that governments can often safely ignore residents who are not actively involved in local politics. If this latter perspective is correct, then the preferences of the median voter rather than the median resident will be primary.

6. Many of those who cite the role of intergovernmental structure believe, in fact, that cities have very little control over their own spending or policy. However, this conclusion belies the fact that there is considerable variation in local government spending over time within the same city as well as across cities. For example, analysis of Census of Government spending between 1986 and 2006 reveals that across the nation, the average change in city spending on redistributive functions over a five-year period was a large as mean spending on redistribution.

7. Using the entire series of the Voter News Service exit polls, Census data on the racial makeup of each state and published state-level voter turnout figures (McDonald 2008), we supplemented existing work by analyzing the relationship between aggregate state turnout and racial bias in turnout. Our tests indicate that higher state level

turnout is associated with marked decreases in the overrepresentation of white voters ($r = -.20$) and marked increases in the representation of Latino ($r = .35$) and Asian American ($r = .31$) voters.

8. Representation here is measured as the proportion of the group in the voting population (as measured by exit polls) minus the proportion of the group in the adult population of the city (from the Census). The pattern is the same if we use a representation ratio (the proportion of the group voting divided by the proportion in the city population) or a logged representation ratio. The same pattern was evident for class. Higher turnout meant residents with limited educations represented a much larger share of the electorate.

9. Analysis comparing the socioeconomic status and racial demographics of ICMA cities with the population of all U.S. cities indicates that the ICMA is representative of the nation as a whole Similar analysis comparing cities that responded to the survey with cities that did not indicates that there is no obvious response bias. (Aghion, Alesina, and Trebbi 2005).

10. City clerk turnout reports have been validated elsewhere (Hajnal et al. 2002). When we compared city clerk turnout figures to actual election returns reported by the board of elections for a sample of elections, we also found that the city clerk reports were quite accurate.

11. Since different jurisdictions have used a range of registration requirements to exclude or include different segments of the population (Parker 1990), one might want to focus exclusively on the turnout of eligible voters. The problem is that city clerks have to estimate the eligible population. There is no data source that provides yearly data on local eligible populations. Since cities and counties (often city clerks themselves) must compile and record data on total voter turnout and voter registration for every election, reports of registered voter turnout are more accurate. In the end, it does not matter which measure we use. Turnout of registered and turnout of eligible voters are closely correlated ($r = .87$). Also, when we repeat the analysis with the percent of eligible voters, we get similar results.

12. In alternate tests, we also measured redistributive, developmental, and allocational spending as a proportion of all spending that went to these three areas (rather than as a proportion of total expenditures across all areas). The results were effectively identical.

13. Our primary focus is not on these smaller subcategories of spending because we believe there is too much noise in these more specific categories. Variability in functional responsibility across cities means that many cities are not responsible for many of the specific subcategories. Many cities, for example, have no airport spending, and others do not control education. By aggregating to the three larger spending areas, we average out at least some of this noise.

14. Another factor that might affect spending is the partisan leaning of the city council. However, since 76 percent of the localities we examine hold nonpartisan elections, it is impossible to get the partisan makeup of the council.

15. Since county boundaries do not always conform well to city geographic boundaries, we performed additional analysis that suggests that the county presidential vote provides a reasonable approximation of city preferences. Specifically, we compared the city and county level presidential vote for the largest 100 cities and for all California cities. The county and city vote were correlated at .84 at the national level.

16. Since it is possible that the proportion of spending going to each area is related to the proportion of spending going to the other two areas, we utilize seemingly unrelated regressions for all the regressions in this chapter.

17. We reach the same conclusion if we measure spending as per capita spending rather than as a proportion of government spending.

18. When we re-ran the analysis using subcategories of spending, we found that areas of spending most closely associated with poor, minority interests were most affected by turnout. Specifically, in terms of allocational spending, the only area where changes in turnout were significantly and substantially linked to changes in spending was waste management—an area that is a higher priority for middle-class communities (Trounstine 2008). Spending on parks and recreation and police services, two areas that may be similarly important for middle- and lower-class interests, were not as clearly related to turnout. Most subcategories of redistributive spending were related to turnout. In particular, we found that increased turnout led to substantial increases in both welfare spending and educational spending. Perhaps most interestingly, the only subcategory of developmental spending where we found a significant relationship with turnout was airport spending. Higher turnout meant less developmental spending on airports. Since airport spending is the area of developmental spending that could be the least popular among poor, minority populations who rarely fly, we might have expected to find the strongest negative relationship here. Given that most cities do not have any fiscal responsibility for airports, this last result may be more suggestive than conclusive.

19. All other independent variables are held constant at their mean value.

20. To help ensure that the results in Table 4.1 do measure the underlying relationship between turnout and spending, we undertook a series of additional tests. First, we re-ran the analysis using turnout of the eligible population rather than turnout of registered voters. This alternate measure led to the same basic conclusion. Second, to ensure that the results were not due to the fact that different cities have different spending mandates imposed from above, we tested a range of measures of fiscal responsibility or functional assignments (Stein 1990). Third, we repeated the analysis using a series of alternate measures of fiscal capacity including total debt, current bond ratings, the current tax rate, and available cash and securities. Across all these tests, the basic pattern of results did not change.

21. Table 4.2 does, however, reveal some more anomalous findings. Specifically, a more Democratic or liberal population is associated with less rather than more debt. We suspect that this is because Democrats (as evidenced by Table 4.2) are more willing

to pay for higher taxes, an outcome that leads to less fiscal strain and ultimately less need for debt.

22. This incumbent reelection measure comes from responses to the ICMA survey and refers to the incumbents running in the most recent council election.

23. Ideally, we would like to have a measure of change in racial/ethnic representation. There is, unfortunately, no complete data set that has racial representation on city councils by year. The data on council racial/ethnic makeup come from the 1986 ICMA survey.

24. Table 4.2 also indicates that spending is not significantly related to the proportion of nonwhites on the city council. This implies that descriptive representation on city councils has little effect on redistributive spending net the effects of turnout and public preferences.

25. Of the 474 California cities in existence at the time of the survey, 397 clerks returned surveys with at least some of the necessary responses. Our sample of cities is generally representative of all cities in the state of California. A random sample of questionnaire responses was validated using municipal web pages and published newspaper accounts.

26. One disadvantage is that the effects of nonpartisanship cannot be evaluated in California because all cities in the state are required to hold nonpartisan elections. Similarly, since the vast majority (97 percent) of California's cities in our sample are council-manager cities, any assessment of the effect of the council-manager form of government on turnout would have to be viewed with extreme caution.

27. To further address this concern, we repeated the national analysis with cities clustered by state in one case and with state-fixed effects in another. The basic results did not change substantially.

28. The relationship between turnout and per capita taxes was only significant for larger cities in the state.

29. We also looked to see whether turnout effects were dependent on the racial and ethnic makeup of the city council but once again found racial and ethnic representation on the city council is not necessary for turnout to affect local government spending priorities. Again, this suggests that both white and non-white elected officials are responding to changes in who turns out to vote.

Chapter 5. Fairness and Bias in Electoral Systems

1. For example, Lijphart (1994: 10) argues that for advocates of proportional representation, proportionality is often taken as a goal in itself, "virtually synonymous with political justice."

2. U.S. Supreme Court, *Richard Vieth et al. v. Robert C. Jubelirer, President of the Pennsylvania Senate, et al.* 541 US 267 (2004).

3. Justice Kennedy joined with Justices Scalia, Rehnquist, O'Connor and Thomas in affirming the decision of the District Court, but wrote a concurring opinion arguing that although no standard for determining political gerrymandering was currently available, one may be found, and therefore judicial relief should not be foreclosed.

4. Effective number of parties = $1/\Sigma s_i^2$, where s_i is the seat share of party i. The intuition behind the concept is that there is a big difference between five equally sized parties and a situation where two parties have 95 percent of the seats and three parties the remaining 5 percent. In the first case the effective number of parties would be 5, whereas in the second it would be barely above 2.

5. This probably depends on voter behavior. In most two-tier systems, voters get only one vote. If a system is quite clientelist, voters may be most concerned to get the district candidate of their choice, who can then deliver local benefits. In this case, voters would shun parties with no chance of winning a district seat. Voting for a party whose support is dispersed would result in that party winning a compensation seat, but a remote nationally elected candidate is less useful than a local champion in these political cultures. This may approximate the case of countries such as Austria. On the other hand, this does not seem to fit the Scandinavian cases, which also have two-tier systems. Here voters seem to vote on the basis of national politics and are willing to vote for parties with dispersed support.

6. Since 1998 the Dutch electoral system allows a limited amount of leveraging, in that a candidate who receives half a quota of votes directly is promoted up the list order. However, given that the number of votes required is considerable, the effect is limited.

Chapter 6. Political Party Organizations, Civic Representation, and Participation

1. These changes are not limited to parliamentary systems. The U.S., for example, saw a steady decrease in partisanship, campaign activity, and political interest from 1960 to 2000 (Dalton 2000; Dalton, McAllister, and Wattenberg 2000). Since then partisanship and participation have become relatively stable.

2. Although these groups are the most likely to have quotas, some parties also institute quotas for students, disabled persons, seniors, journalists, media members, or citizens who live abroad.

3. For example, most party statutes state that greater female representation in parliament is an important goal. But only 17 of the parties specify an exact percent of elected representatives who must be women.

4. In some cases, this has backfired when would-be candidates have personally registered and paid for hundreds of new members to show up and vote for them at the

local nomination meeting. These new members are otherwise disinterested in party politics and relinquish their membership (and sometimes electoral support) after the nominations. Experiences like this have often escalated from intraparty disputes to public controversies, causing some parties to strengthen the restrictions on enrollment.

5. These fees are standardized across countries to be in Euros.

6. The National Alliance is no longer an official party in Italy. It first ran candidates with Forward Italy under the name The People of Freedom (PdL) in the 2008 parliamentary elections, and officially merged with the PdL in 2009.

7. For purposes of feasibility and comparability, parties are only included if they received at least 8 percent of the vote in the parliamentary election.

8. Party identifiers are those respondents who answer "yes" to the question, "Do you usually think of yourself as close to any particular political party?" and then name a valid party in response to the follow-up question, "What party is that?"

9. Lenient rules for joining a party may encourage people who already support that party to join, but they are unlikely to have a direct effect on increasing a party's electoral appeal or its number of partisans in the first place. Thus, I only examine the effect of membership rules on campaigning and persuading—not on vote choice and partisanship.

10. This relationship is still significant if we limit the analysis to the six countries in which there is a significant minority population: Australia, Canada, Finland, New Zealand, Portugal, and UK.

11. CSES respondents were asked to place themselves as well as the political parties in their country on a left-right scale from zero to ten. To calculate each party's position, I take the mean of the respondents' placements of that party. The results in Table 6.5 do not change significantly if party positions are measured using experts' placement or the average placement by the most educated CSES respondents.

12. I have also included a measure of a party's left-right position with and without *deviation*, and this variable is also not significant.

13. Deviation may be more likely to have a negative association with vote share or partisanship if parties with less than 8 percent of the vote were included in the analysis. Right-wing nationalist parties, for example, tend to be far from the median voter and also to receive a lower vote share.

Chapter 7. The Paradox of Voting—for Republicans: Economic Inequality, Political Organization, and the American Voter

1. The story of business's political rise is told in greater depth in Hacker and Pierson 2010a, from which much of this section is drawn. Full citations are available there.

2. In 2004, for example, the establishment Brookings Institution spent 3 percent of its budget on communications. The Heritage Foundation spent 20 percent of its

budget on "public and government affairs" in 2002, the last year for which information is available (Rich 2005).

3. This section draws heavily on Hacker and Pierson 2010b.

4. The figures in this section were calculated from the General Social Survey and American National Election Studies, with "working class whites" defined as white voters who self-identify as working class. We thank Jason Anastasopoulos for his assistance with these analyses.

5. The question was asked in two ways: one told respondents how much households in the top 5 percent earned relative to those in the bottom 5 percent; the other about earnings in the top and bottom 20 percent.

6. A 2006 analysis by Jan Leighley and Jonathan Nagler finds a rise in class bias in voting over the last generation. But this increase seems to be driven by the stagnation of voting rates in the bottom quintile. Trends in voting rates for the middle three quintiles—which are most crucial for the median-voter approach—appear to track the top quintiles closely.

Chapter 8. A Democratic Balance: Bureaucracy, Political Parties, and Political Representation

1. Political representation is not unique to any particular institutional arrangement and can be found in almost any kind of political regime—democratic and nondemocratic.

2. Urbinati (2000) justifies a focus on the act of voting when she claims that "Representation—and the electoral trial that is a necessary part of democratic representation—projects citizens into a future-oriented perspective, and thus confers on politics an ideological dimension. In this sense, it gives ideas full residence in the house of politics. Representation is a comprehensive filtering, refining, and mediating process of political will formation and expression. It shapes the object, style, and procedures of political competition. Finally, it helps to depersonalize claims and opinions, and in this way makes them a vehicle for the mingling and associating of citizens." She goes on to say that Hegel captured extremely well the idealizing function of representation when he pointed out its power of unifying the "fluctuating" "atomic units" of civil society.

3. Electoral democracy has been a vibrant research area for almost half a century, with multiple intellectual currents examining the various aspects of elections and electoral democracy: how it comes about, how is it sustained and whether there are economic or social preconditions that are likely to generate it.

4. The general claim that political representation is tied to the nature of the administrative state is not entirely new. Ankersmit in *Political Representation* (2002) attributes the withering of political representation to excessive bureaucratization of the

modern nation-state. This paper questions that claim by asserting exactly the opposite—that, in nation-states where there is either no bureaucracy or a weak and ineffectual bureaucracy political representation is a direct casualty. And more recently, Mainwaring 2006 argues that both poor state performance and widely held citizen perceptions that a particular state is performing poorly are correlated with what he calls a "crisis of representation."

5. Mansbridge 2003 discusses four types of representation—promissory, anticipatory, gyroscopic, and surrogacy. Each of these is a way a sympathetic relationship can develop between a voter and her representative.

6. Plotke 1997 notes that, while accountability and authorization are useful concepts to distinguish democratic and authoritarian governments, they are less helpful when we ask what a representative should be doing.

7. Electoral rules do not allow all voices to be represented, as electoral systems give some voices more prominence than others (though proportional representation with low thresholds allows a very diverse set of voices access to the legislature).

8. Critics of political parties as democratic institutions have often pointed to two dangers associated with parties. First, political parties become associated with particular segments of society, and this particularization of parties tends to undermine either the representation of a national interest or, in the extreme situation, may make for a less democratic polity. The second danger is that parties become insular and vehicles for the advancement of the individual interests of those holding positions of power in these parties. When political parties are associated with individual interests rather than group interests they fail as representative institutions. The first criticism of parties is misplaced, since political parties are by definition supposed to represent only a part (for a robust defense of the partisan nature of parties, see Sartori 1976 and Rosenblum 2006). The second criticism is spot on.

9. There is some empirical support for these claims. Work done on the U.S. shows that an autonomous bureaucracy can ensure the representative nature of the state. Where it is totally dominated by a political system that need not follow (Meier and O'Toole 2006).

10. Leaving aside for the moment the issues that arise if representatives have enacted laws that are contradictory, confusing, or difficult to apply in a way that does not appear capricious.

11. Why is this important? Weber noted that while the direct democracy is a type of rule, representative democracy is actually a form of legitimation of that rule (Weber 1969, 3: 941).

12. The reports of the Planning Commission provide ample evidence. Planning Commission of India 2005.

13. See for example Shah and Mandava 2005. They document the daily struggles of street hawkers and pavement dwellers in Delhi, who despite regularly bribing the police and municipality officials live in fear of these functionaries.

14. For the urban poor, unlike in rural areas where the state is absent or intermittent, the state is present. Yet the marginalized in urban areas observed that bureaucrats and elected representatives discriminated between citizens on the basis of socioeconomic status. This discrimination manifested itself in how the officials interacted with them (made them wait for long hours) and often did not give due attention to their petitions. Ahuja and Chhibber 2012.

15. Corbridge et al. 2005 confirm this finding when they state that the poor see the state when the state wants to see them.

16. This is not a simple "I do not know"—for, in a democracy where elections have been held for many years, citizens should know whose interests parties and elected representatives stand for. That Ahuja and Chhibber's respondents do not know is probably a reflection of the fact that neither parties nor MP/MLAs care for the poor and otherwise marginalized. Among the educated and the middle classes, the reaction to parties and politicians is generally negative, but that does not mean that they do not know that politicians and parties represent particular interests—it is just that parties do not represent the interests they would like.

17. Research on the poor across the world has generated evidence to suggest that resource shortage and domination may constrain but do not rule out political assertion. The poor exert agency against the dominant classes as well as against the state. In *Weapons of the Weak*, Scott (1985) shows that the poor and marginalized in Malaysian villages do not give in to subjugation. In the absence of opportunity, they resort to passive or hidden forms of resistance against the dominant classes. Indeed, they hold the dominant classes accountable for their behavior, subscribing to a framework for action grounded in ideas of religion and traditional norms of reciprocity. O' Brien and Li 2006 point out that poor citizens in China try to hold the state accountable by using the rhetoric of the state, terming this behavior rightful resistance. Moreover, in her work in El Salvador, Elizabeth Wood finds that close to one third of poor peasants who admit to supporting the insurgency do not cite material gains to explain their actions. They view their participation as rooted in their desire to defy the violent state, exert their historical agency in the remaking of class relations and participate in building God's kingdom.

18. Ethnographic research provides a different explanation for why people go to vote in India. Banerjee 2007 sees the vote as "sacred" largely because it possesses "both symbolic power, in expressing people's self-respect and self-worth, and instrumental power, in helping to ward off potential attacks by the state upon that self-worth" (1561). We agree that the poor do indeed vote to express self-worth and that the vote does offer the poor some protection against the state. But our research does not find that all social groups in India have similar motivations to vote.

19. There are also reasonable arguments that this systemic bias is ongoing.

20. Iyer and Mani 2012; Beteille 2009; Goyal 2005; Banik 2001.

21. Yadav and Kumar 1999; Heath 2005.

Chapter 9. The Closing of the Frontier: Political Blogs, the 2008 Election, and the Online Public Sphere

1. It should be noted that Hitwise makes qualitative assessments of what counts as a Website, instead of relying just on URL structure. For example, yahoo.com and mail.yahoo.com are two different Websites in the Hitwise data.

2. The claim of 200,000 members should be treated cautiously, as it is based on the number of registered user names, not on estimates of the number of active users. In that sense, this is an estimate of the cumulative number of users who have *ever* been active, including duplicate memberships and one-time guests.

3. In this regard, I am counting as "blogs" sites that featured blog content on their front page. Larger sites that might have had blogs hosted elsewhere on the site were not included.

Chapter 10. The Technological Basis of Organizational Membership: Representation of Interests in the New Media Age

1. Conservative activists have repeatedly tried and failed to build their own parallel to MoveOn.org (see Karpf 2012). If our student is a conservative activist, she likely is a member of a range of conservative listservs and has attended an in-person training with the Leadership Institute.

2. It bears noting that "identity-based membership" is distinct from "identity politics" as usually discussed in America. Skocpol (2003) describes these civic memberships as leaving a lasting impression on their participants. We can see traces today across tombstones and memorabilia from earlier generations. Participating in civic associations formed a part of an individual's identity, whereas the membership-by-mail that replaced it created far less attachment.

3. The Membership Communications Project (Karpf 2010, 2012) gathered six months of e-mail from 70 prominent progressive advocacy organizations. Tellingly, all organizations founded post-1998 (the year MoveOn was founded) adopt the activity-based membership regime pioneered by MoveOn. Several legacy organizations have likewise expanded their membership programs to include nonfinancial participants. Due to path-dependent bureaucratic structures, significant differences appear in *how* legacy organizations and Internet-native organizations use information and communication technologies like e-mail.

4. Within limits. Organizations must avoid mailing so broadly that they become classified as spam and have their messages rejected. These limits are well known to list managers, however.

5. Specifically, the marginal cost of additional communications, once a new member has been acquired, is approximately zero. Database software, customer relations management software, and staff support can be quite costly for advocacy organiza-

tions. But the cost of sending an e-mail to 10,001 members is virtually identical to the cost of sending an e-mail to 10,000 members.

6. In particular, a California nonprofit's membership is entitled to vote for its Board of Directors. In 2004, a contentious internal election produced a legal challenge that reached the California Supreme Court—*Club Members for an Honest Election v. Sierra Club*. (The author was elected to the Sierra Club Board that year, and thus personally learned of this constraint as a defendant in the lawsuit!)

7. The Analyst Institute, a Democratic think tank founded by former students of Donald Green and Alan Gerber's Center for the Study of American Politics has worked with MoveOn in the past and actively promotes this "culture of testing" to legacy organizations.

8. The simple solution theoretically would be to obtain e-mail addresses for all dues-paying members. In practice, the combination of "spam" prevention systems and individual reluctance to offer an e-mail address to organizations that have for years widely sold mailing address lists renders this solution impracticable.

9. Jon Stewart, *Daily Show*, June 24, 2008.

Chapter 11. The Principle of Affected Interests: An Interpretation and Defense

I thank Arthur Applbaum, Robert Goodin, Jane Mansbridge, Jack Nagel, David Owen, Claus Offe, Rogers Smith, Annie Stilz, Dennis Thompson, and participants of the Yale Legal Theory Workshop for guidance on prior drafts of this paper.

1. Compare Rawls's (1971) formulation of his goal as identifying principles of justice to regulate a society, where "a society is a more or less self-sufficient association of persons" and Cohen's (1997: 67) formulation of a deliberative democracy as "an association whose affairs are governed by the public deliberation of its members."

2. Although any particular law might affect some individuals more than others (e.g., laws governing Medicare in the United States are especially consequential for the elderly), one might nevertheless say that representative government with political equality is consistent with the principle of affected interests, because that government determines an inextricably connected package of laws and policies, each interlinked with the others (e.g., tax regime + general health care + Medicare). When citizens are considered through their whole lives across the many dimensions touched by laws and policies, they are affected equally to a first approximation and should thus exercise equal influence.

3. For very different delineations, see Dahl 1967; Dahl and Tufte 1973; and Goodin 2007.

4. I thank Jane Mansbridge and Dennis Thompson for the approach suggested in this paragraph.

5. See, for example, Beitz 1989.

6. Contrast this domain of application to Goodin 2007 and Dahl 1989, who are concerned with applying the principle of affected interests to address questions of constitutional structure.

7. For a particularly lucid discussion of the character of power in this global age, see Grewal 2009.

8. This is not a particularly new phenomenon, and state provision of social protection through the welfare state is far more recent than democracy in human history. Nevertheless, limitations of the state in this regard are limitations of the scope of democracy. See Lindblom 1982.

9. Stewart (1975); Sunstein 1990.

10. See Lessig (2006) and Benkler 2006.

11. See, for example, Ogden 2011; Reich 2012.

12. See, for example, Weber 2003.

13. This example comes from Philip Pettit's (2000: 85–86) discussion.

14. A "wicked" problem—common in social policy and planning—is one that has many complex causes and so lacks the determinate, definitive, or elegant solutions found in fields such as mathematics or chess. See Rittel and Webber 1967.

15. See Dahl 1986.

16. See Archibugi and Held 1995.

17. For exceptions, see Whelan 1983; Goodin 2007; Dahl 1989; Arrhenius 2005.

18. See Arrhenius 2005 for discussion.

19. Arrhenius responds to Nozick's example in a different way. He notes that voting is not the only mode of influence, and that suitors may properly seek to influence the woman's decision by making their case through courtship. He also notes correctly that it is incumbent upon the defender of the principle of affected interests to provide an account of the relationship between the kind of influence and the importance of the interest. In the case of marriage, he writes, one reasonably thinks that the interest of the woman gives her a veto over the matter.

20. I do not discuss the "only if" portion of this principle in this essay.

21. Whelan (1983: 19) articulates the same problem as infinite regress: "The deeper problem is that before a democratic decision could be made on a particular issue (by those affected), a prior decision would have to be made, in each case, as to who is affected and therefore entitled to vote on the substantive issue—a decision, that is, on the proper bounds of the relevant constituency. And how is this decision, which will be determinative of the ensuing substantive decision, to be made? It too should be made democratically, by those affected—but now we encounter a regression from which no procedural escape is possible."

22. He can be forgiven for this ambition toward what Sen has criticized as "transcendental institutionalism," for the ambition is shared by many political philosophers, at least since Rawls. The approach of this chapter embraces Sen's call (see 2009)

to develop principles that can better guide the incremental quest to reach more desirable states of the world that are within reach.

23. But organizations need not be the subject of the principle of affected interests. One might work out a version of the principle in which each decision has its own circle of affected interest and so its own included decision-makers (suggested to me by Bob Goodin). Alternatively, the unit of regulation might be a problem—such as water disputes, ecosystems, service catchment areas. On this problem-based account, the circle of inclusion might encompass all those who inhabit the problem-shed (suggested to me by Larry Suskind).

24. Dahl (1994: 23–34); discussed earlier in Dahl and Tufte 1973. What Dahl calls effectiveness in this discussion, I call depth of influence, and what he calls capacity I call scope of influence.

25. Goodin (2007: 63). Goodin writes, "Notice, however, that on the expansive analysis of what interests might be 'possibly affected,' any given decision is highly likely to affect a great many interests, at least some of which are likely not to be included in any relatively restricted demos. On this "decisional power" reading of the 'all affected interests' principle, any restricted demos would be debarred from making those sorts of decisions, which, empirically, seems to be most decisions." It isn't clear why this is the case. Although it is true that many bodies could make decisions that affect anyone in the world, most bodies most of the time make decisions that affect a much more delineated set of interests and individuals.

26. This recursive account of political institutions, in which the scale and shape of governance institutions is reciprocally determined by the consequences of the decisions emanating from those institutions, echoes John Dewey's account in *The Public and Its Problems* (1927). Put in another way, the multiple-membership approach embraces what some critics have seen as problematic about the principle of affected interests: its potential for radical pluralism and regress. Those two features are problems if one seeks a durable delineation of a single polity. The dynamic aspect of the approach suggested here embraces the regress, as it were, rather than trying to find a way to halt it.

27. The work of Pettit (on responsive and indicative representation) and Mansbridge (2003) (on gyroscopic representation) informs the discussion in this section on varieties of influence.

28. See the discussion of Mansbridge et al. (2010), drawing on Jack Nagel. We understand "causal effect" in the probabilistic sense. It is the probabilistic expected outcome of that decision, not the decision itself, that must be different from what it would have been be if the causing individual had different avowed interests or preference.

29. See Lindblom 1982, 1977; Block 1977; Cohen and Rogers 1983. For an empirical argument against this position, see Smith, 1999.

30. See Lukes (2005)

31. Pratkanis et al. 2003; Kahneman 2011.

32. Note that the existence of these channels of influence is a necessary, but not sufficient, condition. In order to be fully satisfied, the principle of affected interests would also require that the extent of these influences be significant. This essay does not investigate the levels of influence that the principle requires.

33. See Fair Labor Association 2002.

34. See Laura Montenaro 2008; Michael Saward 2008; and Jennifer Rubenstein (2007).

35. Of course, the advocacy efforts of NGOs do not perfectly track the avowed interests or preferences of individuals on whose behalf they advocate. If there is no correlation between (i) advocacy efforts on one hand and (ii) individuals' interests and preferences on the other, then these NGOs confer no influence. The closer the tracking, the more influence is conferred to otherwise powerless individuals.

36. I thank Anna Stilz for emphasizing this problem in the account of multiple memberships. Unfortunately, I am only able to suggest here some directions for a solution rather than the solution itself.

37. As Blake 2001 has noted in another context, moral equality does not imply political equality. That noncorrespondence illuminates how the principle of affected interests can violate intuitively appealing formulas such as one-person, one-vote, yet still treat people as moral equals.

38. One immediate objection is to this institutional suggestion is that it is so ambitious that, at the limit, it proposes what I criticized earlier: Robert Goodin's world democratic government. There are two key differences, however. First, the adjudicative bodies suggested here have a narrow focus on what are in the U.S. called "due process" concerns—they are not all-purpose governments. Second, as the paragraph describes, I imagine a wide network of adjudicatory bodies that is perhaps similar to the structure of criminal courts. There is an International Criminal Court, but it operates in complement with national and local courts everywhere.

Chapter 12. Citizen Representatives

I am indebted to Lisa Disch, David Laycock, Hilary Pearse, Dennis Thompson, and members of the British Columbia Citizens' Assembly Workshops at the University of British Columbia for their comments and criticisms. I am grateful to Menaka Philips and Hilary Pearse for research assistance. An earlier version of this chapter appeared in *Designing Deliberative Democracy: The British Columbia Citizens' Assembly*, ed. Mark Warren and Hilary Pearse (Cambridge: Cambridge University Press, 2008), 50–69. Copyright © 2008 Cambridge University Press, reprinted by permission.

1. The two exceptions are Stephan 2004 and Brown 2006.

2. The 1989 Oregon Health Reform Plan is another exception.

CONTRIBUTORS

André Blais holds a Canada Research Chair in Electoral Studies and is Professor of Political Science at the University of Montreal. He is a fellow of the Royal Society of Canada and past president of the Canadian Political Science Association.

Pradeep Chhibber is Professor of Political Science at the University of California, Berkeley, where he also directs the Institute of International Studies and holds the Indo-American Endowed Chair and the Bedford Chair.

Archon Fung is Ford Foundation Professor of Democracy and Citizenship in the Kennedy School of Government at Harvard University. He is author of numerous books and articles on governance, participation, and transparency.

Jacob Hacker is Stanley Resor Professor of Political Science at Yale University, where he also directs the Institution for Social and Policy Studies. His most recent book is *Winner-Take-All Politics*, co-authored with Paul Pierson.

Zoltan Hajnal is Professor of Political Science at the University of California, San Diego. He is author of *America's Uneven Democracy* (winner of the award for Best Book in Urban Politics of the American Political Science Association) and *Why Americans Don't Join the Party*.

Matthew Hindman is Associate Professor in the School of Media and Public Affairs at George Washington University. He is author of an award-winning book, *The Myth of Digital Democracy*.

David Karpf teaches in the School of Media and Public Affairs, George Washington University. He served for six years as a member of the national board of directors of the Sierra Club. He is author of *The Move-On Effect*.

Georgia Kernell teaches Political Science at Northwestern University. A former postdoctoral fellow in the Penn Program on Democracy, Citizenship, and Constitutionalism, she is working on a book examining how party organization affects electoral success in parliamentary systems.

Alexander Keyssar is Matthew W. Stirling Jr. Professor of History and Social Policy at Harvard's Kennedy School of Government. The first edition of his book *The Right to Vote* was named best book in American history by the American Historical Association. In 2004–5, Keyssar chaired the Social Science Research Council National Research Commission on Voting and Elections.

Anthony McGann is Associate Professor of Political Science at the University of California, Irvine. He is author of *The Logic of Democracy*.

Jack Nagel is Professor Emeritus of Political Science at the University of Pennsylvania. Prior to his retirement in 2012, he served as Penn's Associate Dean for the Social Sciences. His recent research focuses on electoral systems and electoral reforms.

Susan Ostermann is a Ph.D. student in political science at the University of California, Berkeley. Her research concerns state capacity in the developing world, with a focus on India and Nepal.

Paul Pierson is John Gross Professor of Political Science at the University of California, Berkeley, where he chaired the political science department in 2007–10. He is author of numerous books on American politics, including most recently *Winner-Take-All Politics*, co-authored with Jacob Hacker.

Rogers M. Smith is Christopher H. Browne Distinguished Professor of Political Science at the University of Pennsylvania and Director of the Penn Program on Democracy, Citizenship, and Constitutionalism. His most recent book is *Still a House Divided: Race and Politics in Obama's America*, co-authored with Desmond King.

Dennis Thompson is Alfred North Whitehead Professor of Political Philosophy at Harvard University. His most recent book is *The Spirit of Compromise*, co-authored with Amy Gutmann.

Jessica Trounstine is Associate Professor of Political Science at the University of California, Merced. She is author of *Political Monopolies in American Cities*, which won the prize for Best Book in Urban Politics from the American Political Science Association.

Mark Warren holds the Harold and Dorrie Merilees Chair for the Study of Democracy in the Department of Political Science of the University of British Columbia, where he formerly directed the Centre for the Study of Democratic Institutions. He is author of the prize-winning book, *Democracy and Associations*.

INDEX

Note: An italicized *f* or *t* following a page number indicates a figure or table.

AARP, 221

Aboriginal populations (Canada), 118, 277, 280

A/B testing, 228, 229, 231

access to representatives, 30

accountability: aggregative versus deliberative, 274, 281–83, 282*t*; British Columbia Citizens Assembly on Electoral Reform (CA) and, 276, 280–89; for decision-making, 282; discursive, 284, 287, 291*t*; district magnitude/PR and, 104, 112; elections and, 168–69, 274; engagement and participation and, 132, 301n5; forms of, 282–88; India and, 182; institutional, 272–73, 282, 284–88, 291*t*; journalism and, 193; majoritarian systems and, 30; NGOs and, 250; political parties and, 100–103, 111; proportionality and, 100–101; public, 282–84, 286–87; representation and, 167, 186–88, 271–72, 308n6; single-member districts and, 112; sympathy and, 169–70; two-party systems and, 31; winner-take-all systems and, 109

ACORN, 297n14

active influence, 257*t*, 260, 262, 265

activity-based membership, 218, 220, 221, 227–30, 310n3

ACVR. *See* American Center for Voting Rights

administrative agencies. *See* bureaucracies and administrative agencies

advertising: blogs and, 202, 210–11; crowd-sourcing versus, 207; Internet and, 109, 193, 202; political campaigns and, 156; print revenues, 192, 193; state and local level voter turnout and spending and, 210

affected interests, principle of: applications, 259–64; authority/membership and, 262–64; conclusion, 264–66; defined, 237; equality and, 311n2, 314n37; formulation, 245–51; freedom and, 242–44; infinite regress of constituencies and, 312n21; influence and, 314n32; multiple membership and, 251–59, 313n26; nation-state and, 237–39; nonstate actors and, 10–11, 239–42; organizations and, 313n23

affluence. *See* elites and elitism

affordances, 219, 222, 226, 231

Africa, 105, 260, 261

African Americans: city councils and, 78–79; Democratic Party and, 147; disenfranchisement of, 301n1; election fraud and, 55; felon disenfranchisement and, 42; framers and, 27; incarceration rates, 40–41, 43; local spending and, 64, 77*t*, 78–79; need and, 68; photo identification and, 52; population statistics, 61; U.S. South and, 185; voter suppression and, 44, 45. *See also* ethnicity and race; minorities

aggregation of interests, 281–83, 282*t*

aggregative/deliberative venues, 289, 290*t*–91*t*

Ahuja, Amit, 167, 171, 180–81

airports, 67, 303n18

Alabama, 42

Alito, Jr., Samuel A., 300n34

allocational spending, 63–64, 67, 79, 80–83, 81*t*, 82*t*, 84

Alozie, Nicholas O., 63–64

alternative vote (AV), 16

ACKNOWLEDGMENTS

This volume originated in papers written for a Faculty Workshop Series organized by the University of Pennsylvania's Democracy, Citizenship, and Constitutionalism (DCC) Program. The Andrew W. Mellon Foundation and the Mary and David Boies Family Graduate Fund provided generous support.

The editors are grateful to the members of the DCC Program Planning Committee for the Workshop Series, Richard Beeman, Sarah Igo, Richard Johnston, Diana Mutz, Vincent Price, and Joel Waldfogel; to DCC graduate student assistants Elspeth Wilson, Chloé Bakalar, Chelsea Schafer, and David Karpf (who also became a contributor to this volume); and to all the series attendees, whose comments greatly benefited the authors and editors. At the University of Pennsylvania Press, Editor-in-Chief Peter Agree has provided superb support for this as for all volumes in the Press's Democracy, Citizenship, and Constitutionalism Series. We are indebted as well to the excellent contributions that Penn Press staffers Alison Anderson, Kate McGuire, Julia Rose Roberts, and Rachel Taube made in getting the manuscript to completion, and to Nancy Gerth for her usual masterful work on its index.